1984

GEORGE ORWELL

1984

THE GRAPHIC NOVEL

ILLUSTRATED BY
FIDO NESTI

HOUGHTON MIFFLIN HARCOURT
BOSTON NEW YORK
2021

First U.S. edition 2021

Copyright © 2021 by The Estate of Sonia Brownell Orwell and
Frederico Carvalhaes Nesti

1984 copyright © 1949 by Harcourt, Inc. and renewed 1977 by Sonia Brownell Orwell

For information about permission to reproduce selections from this book, write to
trade.permissions@hmhco.com or to Permissions, Houghton Mifflin Harcourt Publishing
Company, 3 Park Avenue, 19th Floor, New York, New York 10016.

First published in Brazil as *1984* in 2020.

First published in Great Britain by Penguin Classics as *Nineteen Eighty-Four:
The Graphic Novel* in 2021.

hmhbooks.com

Library of Congress Cataloging-in-Publication data is available.

ISBN 978-0-358-35992-0

Printed in China

SCP 10 9 8 7 6 5 4 3 2 1

PART 1

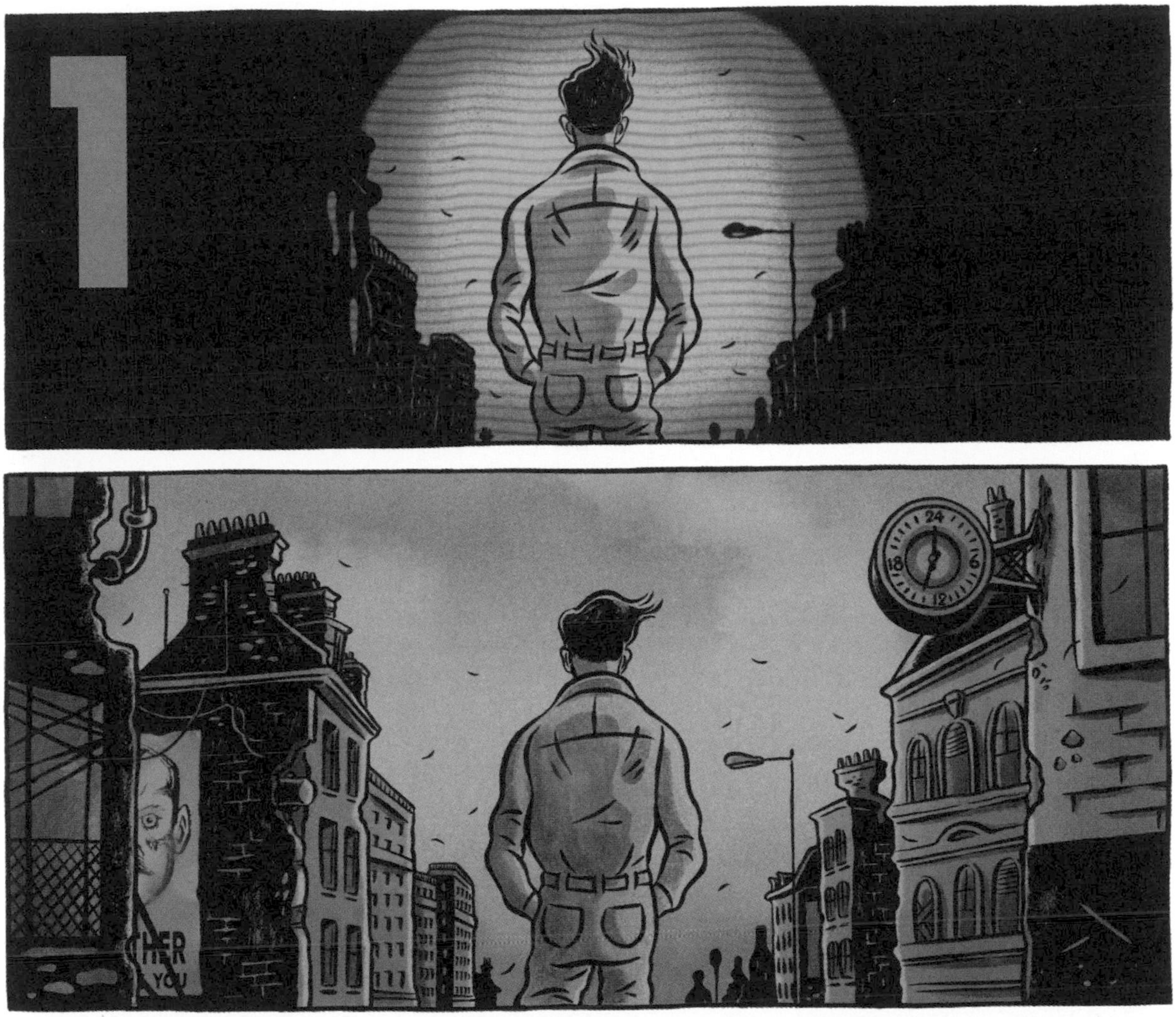
1

IT WAS A BRIGHT COLD DAY IN APRIL, AND THE CLOCKS WERE STRIKING THIRTEEN. WINSTON SMITH, HIS CHIN NUZZLED INTO HIS BREAST IN AN EFFORT TO ESCAPE THE VILE WIND, SLIPPED QUICKLY THROUGH THE GLASS DOORS OF **VICTORY MANSIONS**, THOUGH NOT QUICKLY ENOUGH TO PREVENT A SWIRL OF GRITTY DUST FROM ENTERING ALONG WITH HIM.

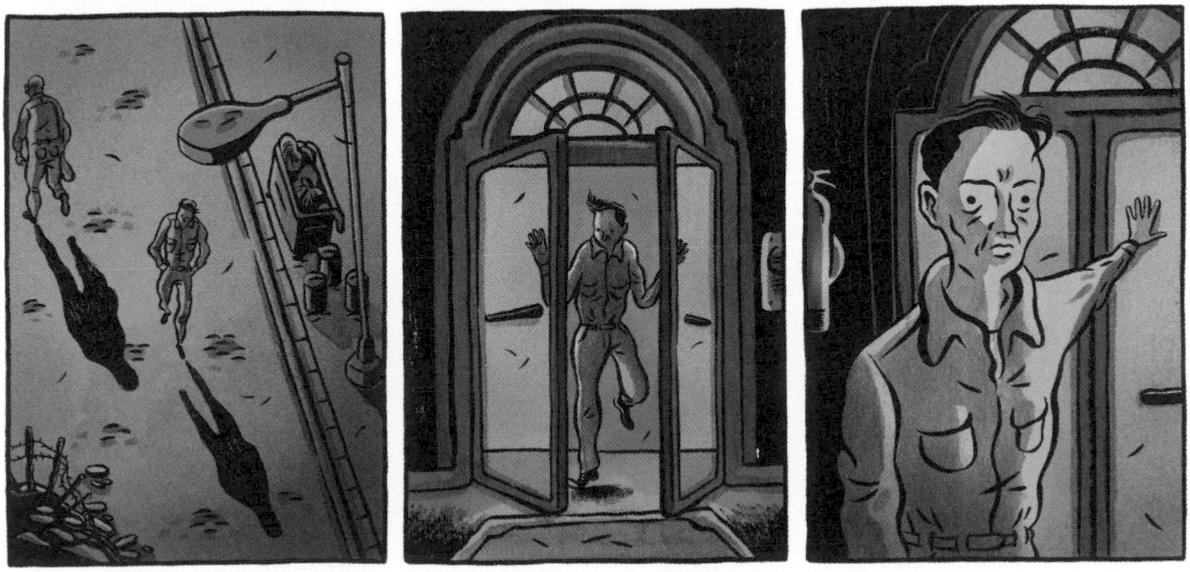

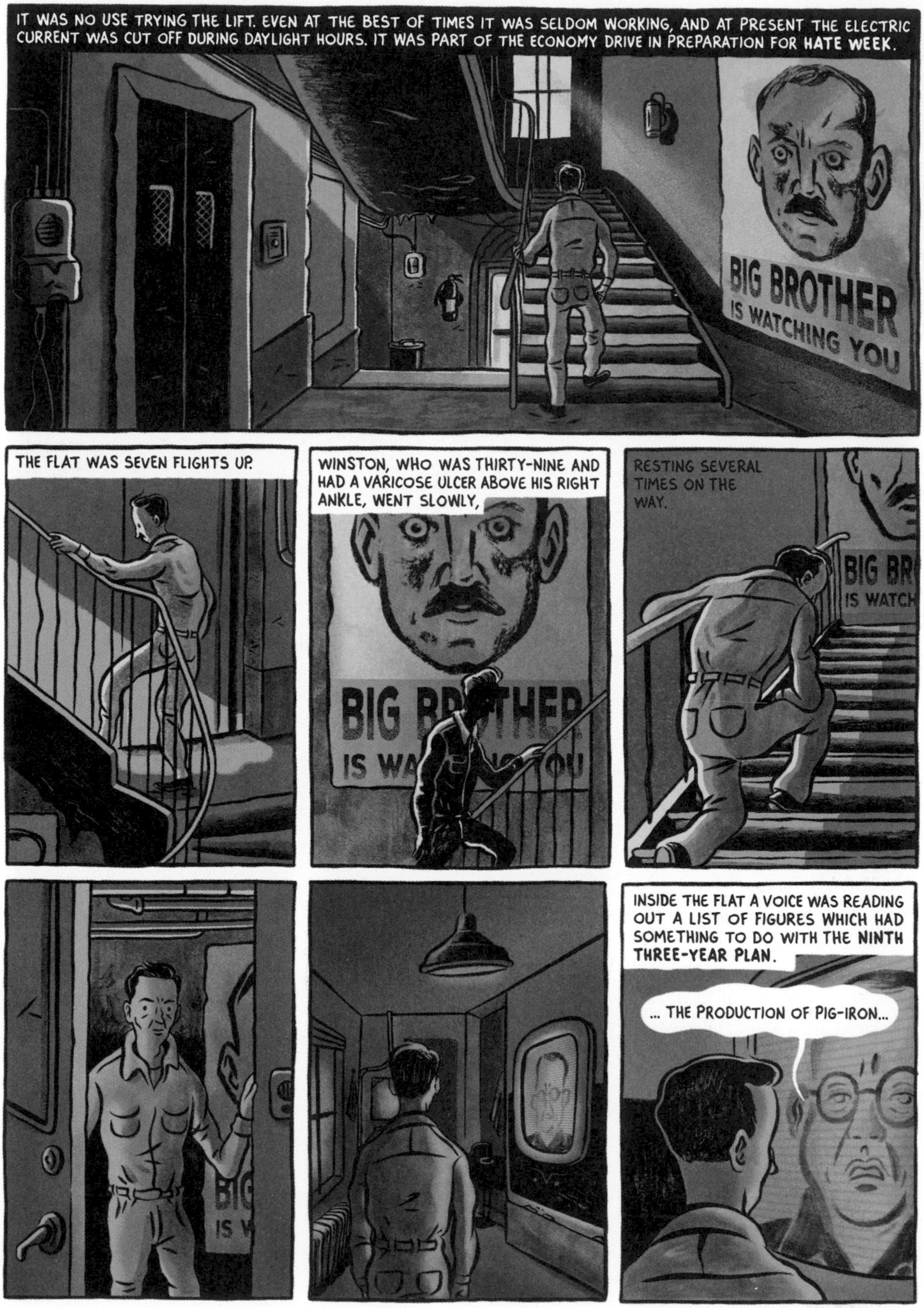
IT WAS NO USE TRYING THE LIFT. EVEN AT THE BEST OF TIMES IT WAS SELDOM WORKING, AND AT PRESENT THE ELECTRIC CURRENT WAS CUT OFF DURING DAYLIGHT HOURS. IT WAS PART OF THE ECONOMY DRIVE IN PREPARATION FOR HATE WEEK.
BIG BROTHER IS WATCHING YOU
THE FLAT WAS SEVEN FLIGHTS UP.
WINSTON, WHO WAS THIRTY-NINE AND HAD A VARICOSE ULCER ABOVE HIS RIGHT ANKLE, WENT SLOWLY,
RESTING SEVERAL TIMES ON THE WAY.
INSIDE THE FLAT A VOICE WAS READING OUT A LIST OF FIGURES WHICH HAD SOMETHING TO DO WITH THE NINTH THREE-YEAR PLAN.
... THE PRODUCTION OF PIG-IRON...

THE INSTRUMENT (THE TELESCREEN, IT WAS CALLED) COULD BE DIMMED, BUT THERE WAS NO WAY OF SHUTTING IT OFF.

ANY SOUND THAT WINSTON MADE, ABOVE THE LEVEL OF A VERY LOW WHISPER, WOULD BE PICKED UP BY IT.

AND SO LONG AS HE REMAINED WITHIN THE FIELD OF VISION WHICH THE METAL PLAQUE COMMANDED, HE COULD BE SEEN AS WELL AS HEARD.

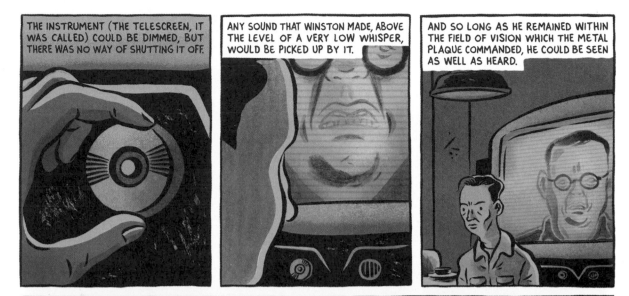

THERE WAS OF COURSE NO WAY OF KNOWING WHETHER YOU WERE BEING WATCHED AT ANY GIVEN MOMENT. HOW OFTEN, OR ON WHAT SYSTEM, THE **THOUGHT POLICE** PLUGGED IN ON ANY INDIVIDUAL WIRE WAS GUESSWORK. IT WAS EVEN CONCEIVABLE THAT THEY WATCHED EVERYBODY ALL THE TIME.

YOU HAD TO LIVE — DID LIVE, FROM HABIT THAT BECAME INSTINCT — IN THE ASSUMPTION THAT EVERY SOUND YOU MADE WAS OVERHEARD.

AND, EXCEPT IN DARKNESS, EVERY MOVEMENT SCRUTINISED.

WINSTON KEPT HIS BACK TURNED TO THE TELESCREEN.

IT WAS SAFER.

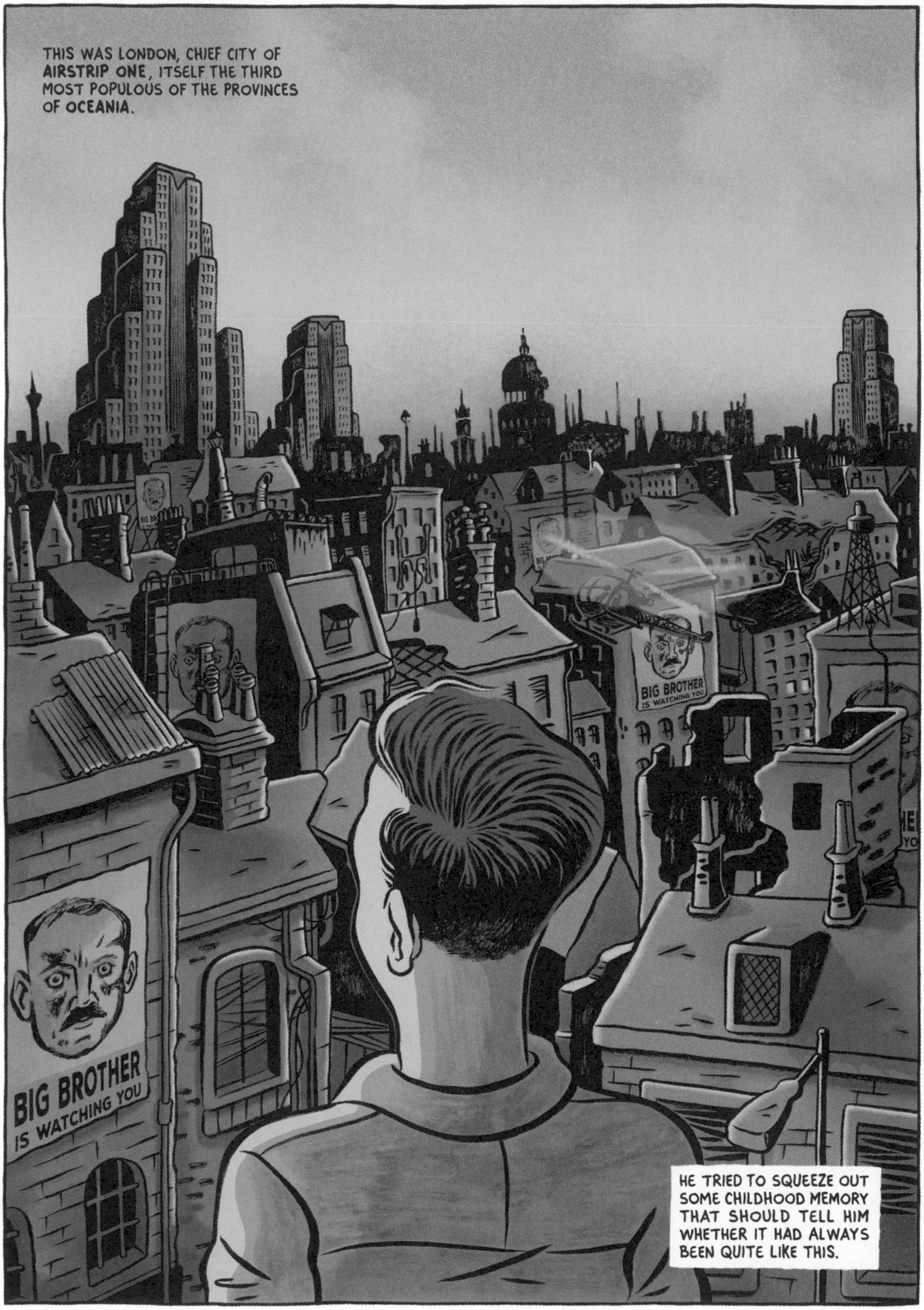
THIS WAS LONDON, CHIEF CITY OF AIRSTRIP ONE, ITSELF THE THIRD MOST POPULOUS OF THE PROVINCES OF OCEANIA.
BIG BROTHER IS WATCHING YOU
BIG BROTHER IS WATCHING YOU
HE TRIED TO SQUEEZE OUT SOME CHILDHOOD MEMORY THAT SHOULD TELL HIM WHETHER IT HAD ALWAYS BEEN QUITE LIKE THIS.

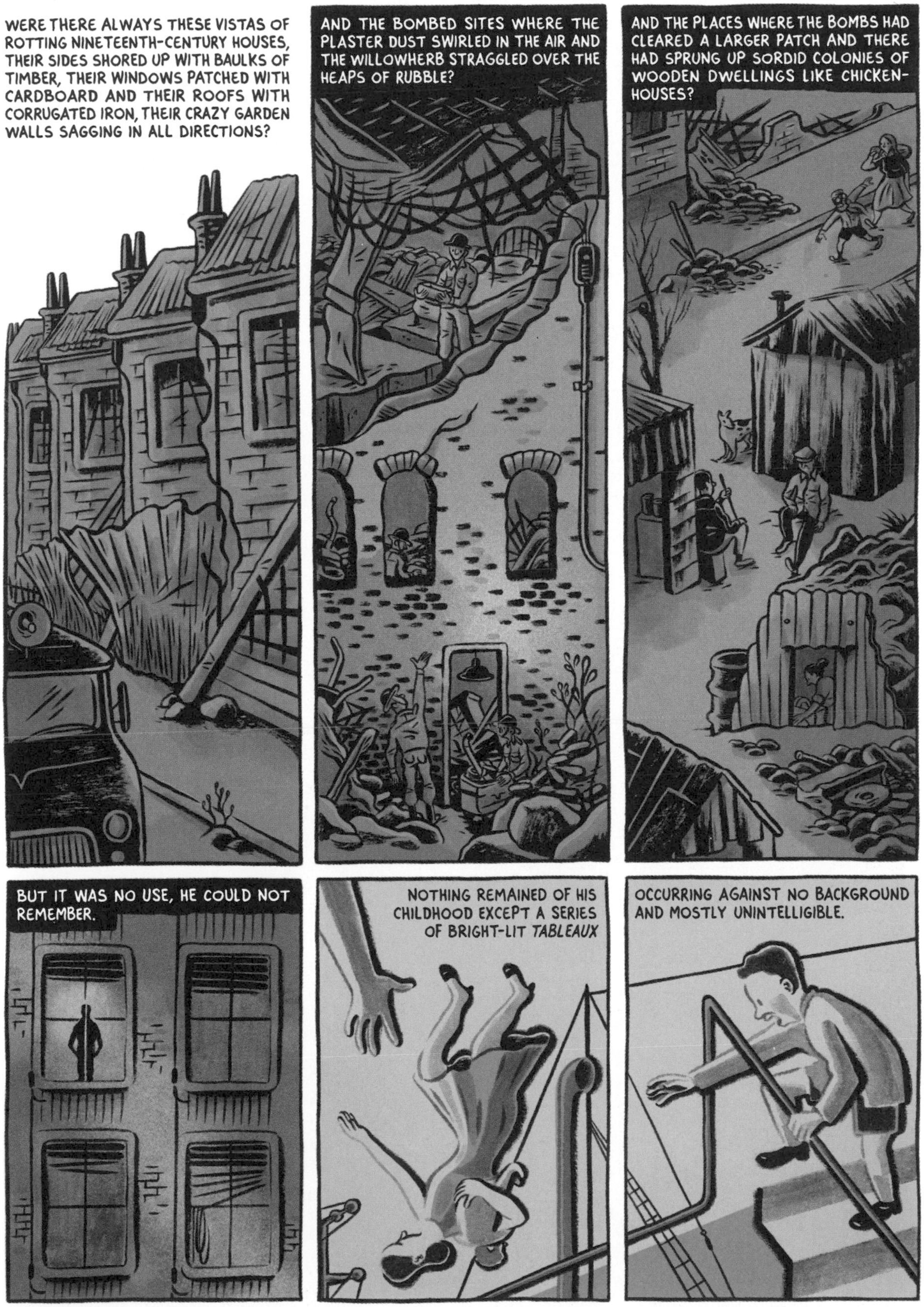
WERE THERE ALWAYS THESE VISTAS OF ROTTING NINETEENTH-CENTURY HOUSES, THEIR SIDES SHORED UP WITH BAULKS OF TIMBER, THEIR WINDOWS PATCHED WITH CARDBOARD AND THEIR ROOFS WITH CORRUGATED IRON, THEIR CRAZY GARDEN WALLS SAGGING IN ALL DIRECTIONS?
AND THE BOMBED SITES WHERE THE PLASTER DUST SWIRLED IN THE AIR AND THE WILLOWHERB STRAGGLED OVER THE HEAPS OF RUBBLE?
AND THE PLACES WHERE THE BOMBS HAD CLEARED A LARGER PATCH AND THERE HAD SPRUNG UP SORDID COLONIES OF WOODEN DWELLINGS LIKE CHICKEN-HOUSES?
BUT IT WAS NO USE, HE COULD NOT REMEMBER.
NOTHING REMAINED OF HIS CHILDHOOD EXCEPT A SERIES OF BRIGHT-LIT *TABLEAUX*
OCCURRING AGAINST NO BACKGROUND AND MOSTLY UNINTELLIGIBLE.

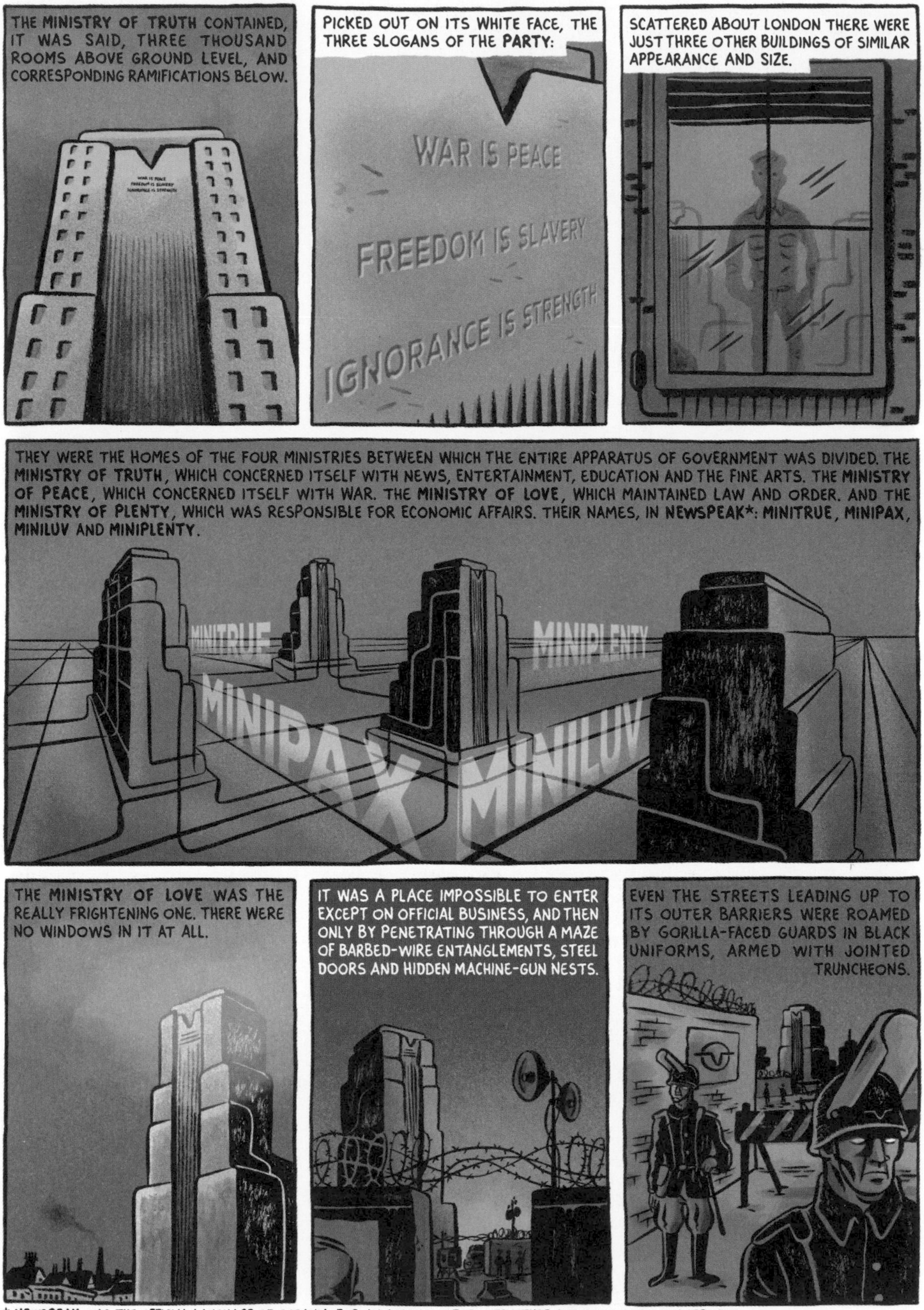
THE MINISTRY OF TRUTH CONTAINED, IT WAS SAID, THREE THOUSAND ROOMS ABOVE GROUND LEVEL, AND CORRESPONDING RAMIFICATIONS BELOW.
PICKED OUT ON ITS WHITE FACE, THE THREE SLOGANS OF THE PARTY:
WAR IS PEACE
FREEDOM IS SLAVERY
IGNORANCE IS STRENGTH
SCATTERED ABOUT LONDON THERE WERE JUST THREE OTHER BUILDINGS OF SIMILAR APPEARANCE AND SIZE.
THEY WERE THE HOMES OF THE FOUR MINISTRIES BETWEEN WHICH THE ENTIRE APPARATUS OF GOVERNMENT WAS DIVIDED. THE MINISTRY OF TRUTH, WHICH CONCERNED ITSELF WITH NEWS, ENTERTAINMENT, EDUCATION AND THE FINE ARTS. THE MINISTRY OF PEACE, WHICH CONCERNED ITSELF WITH WAR. THE MINISTRY OF LOVE, WHICH MAINTAINED LAW AND ORDER. AND THE MINISTRY OF PLENTY, WHICH WAS RESPONSIBLE FOR ECONOMIC AFFAIRS. THEIR NAMES, IN NEWSPEAK*: MINITRUE, MINIPAX, MINILUV AND MINIPLENTY.
MINITRUE
MINIPLENTY
MINIPAX
MINILUV
THE MINISTRY OF LOVE WAS THE REALLY FRIGHTENING ONE. THERE WERE NO WINDOWS IN IT AT ALL.
IT WAS A PLACE IMPOSSIBLE TO ENTER EXCEPT ON OFFICIAL BUSINESS, AND THEN ONLY BY PENETRATING THROUGH A MAZE OF BARBED-WIRE ENTANGLEMENTS, STEEL DOORS AND HIDDEN MACHINE-GUN NESTS.
EVEN THE STREETS LEADING UP TO ITS OUTER BARRIERS WERE ROAMED BY GORILLA-FACED GUARDS IN BLACK UNIFORMS, ARMED WITH JOINTED TRUNCHEONS.

* **NEWSPEAK** WAS THE OFFICIAL LANGUAGE OF OCEANIA. FOR AN ACCOUNT OF ITS STRUCTURE AND ETYMOLOGY SEE APPENDIX.

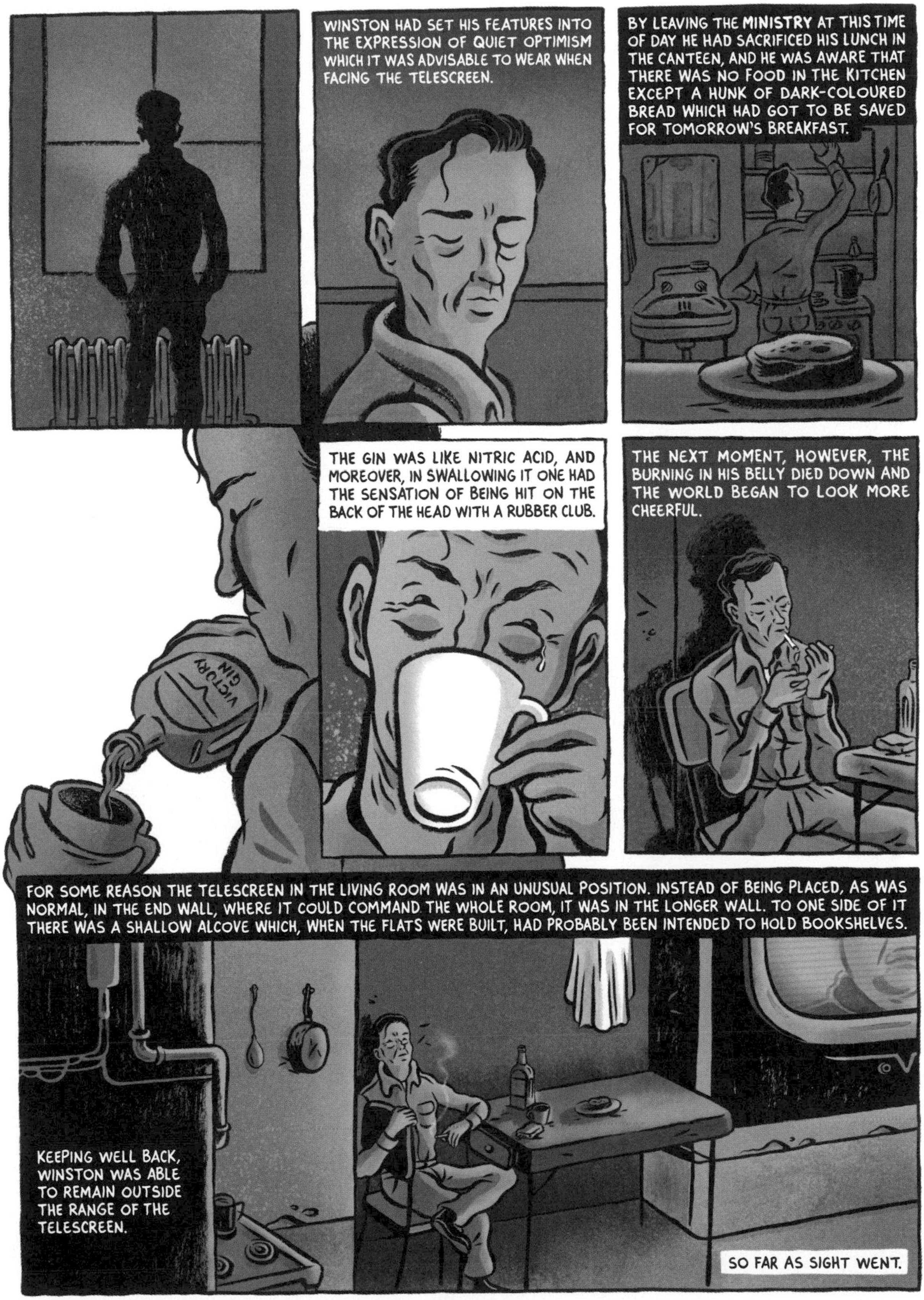
WINSTON HAD SET HIS FEATURES INTO THE EXPRESSION OF QUIET OPTIMISM WHICH IT WAS ADVISABLE TO WEAR WHEN FACING THE TELESCREEN.
BY LEAVING THE MINISTRY AT THIS TIME OF DAY HE HAD SACRIFICED HIS LUNCH IN THE CANTEEN, AND HE WAS AWARE THAT THERE WAS NO FOOD IN THE KITCHEN EXCEPT A HUNK OF DARK-COLOURED BREAD WHICH HAD GOT TO BE SAVED FOR TOMORROW'S BREAKFAST.
VICTORY GIN
THE GIN WAS LIKE NITRIC ACID, AND MOREOVER, IN SWALLOWING IT ONE HAD THE SENSATION OF BEING HIT ON THE BACK OF THE HEAD WITH A RUBBER CLUB.
THE NEXT MOMENT, HOWEVER, THE BURNING IN HIS BELLY DIED DOWN AND THE WORLD BEGAN TO LOOK MORE CHEERFUL.
FOR SOME REASON THE TELESCREEN IN THE LIVING ROOM WAS IN AN UNUSUAL POSITION. INSTEAD OF BEING PLACED, AS WAS NORMAL, IN THE END WALL, WHERE IT COULD COMMAND THE WHOLE ROOM, IT WAS IN THE LONGER WALL. TO ONE SIDE OF IT THERE WAS A SHALLOW ALCOVE WHICH, WHEN THE FLATS WERE BUILT, HAD PROBABLY BEEN INTENDED TO HOLD BOOKSHELVES.
KEEPING WELL BACK, WINSTON WAS ABLE TO REMAIN OUTSIDE THE RANGE OF THE TELESCREEN.
SO FAR AS SIGHT WENT.

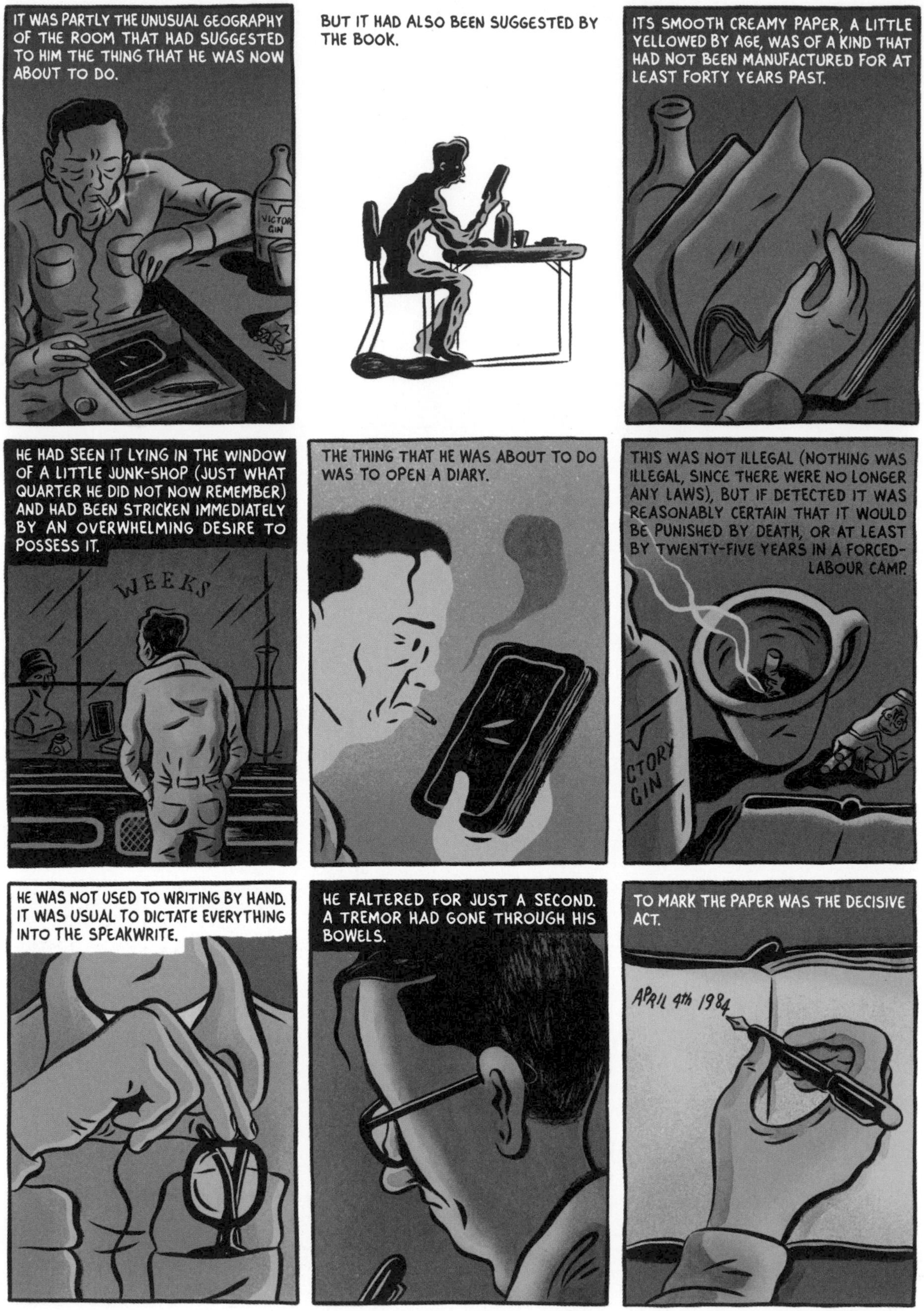
IT WAS PARTLY THE UNUSUAL GEOGRAPHY OF THE ROOM THAT HAD SUGGESTED TO HIM THE THING THAT HE WAS NOW ABOUT TO DO.
VICTORY GIN
BUT IT HAD ALSO BEEN SUGGESTED BY THE BOOK.
ITS SMOOTH CREAMY PAPER, A LITTLE YELLOWED BY AGE, WAS OF A KIND THAT HAD NOT BEEN MANUFACTURED FOR AT LEAST FORTY YEARS PAST.
HE HAD SEEN IT LYING IN THE WINDOW OF A LITTLE JUNK-SHOP (JUST WHAT QUARTER HE DID NOT NOW REMEMBER) AND HAD BEEN STRICKEN IMMEDIATELY BY AN OVERWHELMING DESIRE TO POSSESS IT.
WEEKS
THE THING THAT HE WAS ABOUT TO DO WAS TO OPEN A DIARY.
THIS WAS NOT ILLEGAL (NOTHING WAS ILLEGAL, SINCE THERE WERE NO LONGER ANY LAWS), BUT IF DETECTED IT WAS REASONABLY CERTAIN THAT IT WOULD BE PUNISHED BY DEATH, OR AT LEAST BY TWENTY-FIVE YEARS IN A FORCED-LABOUR CAMP.
CTORY GIN
HE WAS NOT USED TO WRITING BY HAND. IT WAS USUAL TO DICTATE EVERYTHING INTO THE SPEAKWRITE.
HE FALTERED FOR JUST A SECOND. A TREMOR HAD GONE THROUGH HIS BOWELS.
TO MARK THE PAPER WAS THE DECISIVE ACT.
APRIL 4th 1984

A SENSE OF COMPLETE HELPLESSNESS HAD DESCENDED UPON HIM. TO BEGIN WITH HE DID NOT KNOW WITH ANY CERTAINTY THAT THIS *WAS* 1984.

IT WAS NEVER POSSIBLE NOWADAYS TO PIN DOWN ANY DATE WITHIN A YEAR OR TWO.

FOR WHOM WAS HE WRITING THIS DIARY? FOR THE FUTURE, FOR THE UNBORN. HOW COULD YOU COMMUNICATE WITH THE FUTURE?

IT WAS OF ITS NATURE IMPOSSIBLE. EITHER THE FUTURE WOULD RESEMBLE THE PRESENT, IN WHICH CASE IT WOULD NOT LISTEN TO HIM: OR IT WOULD BE DIFFERENT FROM IT, AND HIS PREDICAMENT WOULD BE MEANINGLESS.

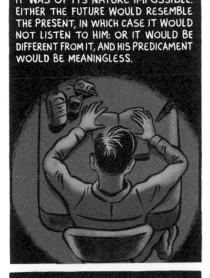

HE SEEMED NOT MERELY TO HAVE LOST THE POWER OF EXPRESSING HIMSELF, BUT WHAT IT WAS THAT HE HAD ORIGINALLY INTENDED TO SAY.

FOR WEEKS PAST HE HAD BEEN MAKING READY FOR THIS MOMENT, AND IT HAD NEVER CROSSED HIS MIND THAT ANYTHING WOULD BE NEEDED EXCEPT COURAGE.

THE ACTUAL WRITING WOULD BE EASY. ALL HE HAD TO DO WAS TO TRANSFER TO PAPER THE INTERMINABLE RESTLESS MONOLOGUE THAT HAD BEEN RUNNING INSIDE HIS HEAD, LITERALLY FOR YEARS.

AT THIS MOMENT, HOWEVER, EVEN THE MONOLOGUE HAD DRIED UP.

SUDDENLY HE BEGAN WRITING IN SHEER PANIC.

April 4th 1984
Last night to the flicks. All war films. One very good of a ship full of refugees being bombed. Audience much amused by shots of a great huge fat man trying to swim away

WINSTON STOPPED WRITING, PARTLY BECAUSE HE WAS SUFFERING FROM CRAMP. HE DID NOT KNOW WHAT HAD MADE HIM POUR OUT THIS STREAM OF RUBBISH.

The helicopter planted a 20 kilo bomb among them
Then there was a wonderful shot of an arm going up up right up into the air
There was a lot of app. lause

BUT THE CURIOUS THING WAS THAT WHILE HE WAS DOING SO A TOTALLY DIFFERENT MEMORY HAD CLARIFIED ITSELF IN HIS MIND.

IT WAS, HE NOW REALISED, BECAUSE OF THIS OTHER INCIDENT THAT HE HAD SUDDENLY DECIDED TO COME HOME AND BEGIN THE DIARY.

IT HAD HAPPENED THAT MORNING. IT WAS NEARLY ELEVEN HUNDRED, AND IN THE **RECORDS DEPARTMENT**, WHERE HE WORKED, THEY WERE DRAGGING THE CHAIRS OUT OF THE CUBICLES AND GROUPING THEM IN THE CENTRE OF THE HALL, IN PREPARATION FOR THE **TWO MINUTES HATE**. TWO PEOPLE, WHOM HE KNEW BY SIGHT, BUT HAD NEVER SPOKEN TO, CAME UNEXPECTEDLY INTO THE ROOM.

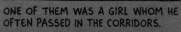

ONE OF THEM WAS A GIRL WHOM HE OFTEN PASSED IN THE CORRIDORS.

HE DID NOT KNOW HER NAME, BUT HE KNEW THAT SHE WORKED IN THE FICTION DEPARTMENT.

PRESUMABLY — SINCE HE HAD SOMETIMES SEEN HER WITH OILY HANDS AND CARRYING A SPANNER — SHE HAD SOME MECHANICAL JOB ON ONE OF THE NOVEL-WRITING MACHINES.

A SASH, EMBLEM OF THE JUNIOR ANTI-SEX LEAGUE, WAS WOUND SEVERAL TIMES ROUND HER WAIST.

WINSTON HAD DISLIKED HER FROM THE VERY FIRST MOMENT OF SEEING HER. IT WAS ALWAYS THE WOMEN, AND ABOVE ALL THE YOUNG ONES, WHO WERE THE MOST BIGOTED ADHERENTS OF THE **PARTY**, THE SWALLOWERS OF SLOGANS, THE AMATEUR SPIES AND NOSERS-OUT OF UNORTHODOXY.

BUT THIS PARTICULAR GIRL GAVE HIM THE IMPRESSION OF BEING MORE DANGEROUS THAN MOST.

HE FELT A PECULIAR UNEASINESS, WHICH HAD FEAR MIXED UP IN IT AS WELL AS HOSTILITY, WHENEVER SHE WAS ANYWHERE NEAR HIM.

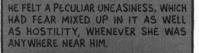

THE OTHER PERSON WAS A MAN NAMED O'BRIEN, HOLDER OF SOME POST SO IMPORTANT AND REMOTE THAT WINSTON HAD ONLY A DIM IDEA OF ITS NATURE.

A MOMENTARY HUSH PASSED OVER THE GROUP OF PEOPLE ROUND THE CHAIRS AS THEY SAW THE BLACK OVERALLS OF AN **INNER PARTY** MEMBER APPROACHING.

WINSTON WAS INTRIGUED BY THE CONTRAST BETWEEN HIS URBANE MANNER AND HIS PRIZEFIGHTER'S PHYSIQUE.

HE BELIEVED THAT HIS POLITICAL ORTHODOXY WAS NOT PERFECT. SOMETHING IN HIS FACE SUGGESTED IT IRRESISTIBLY.

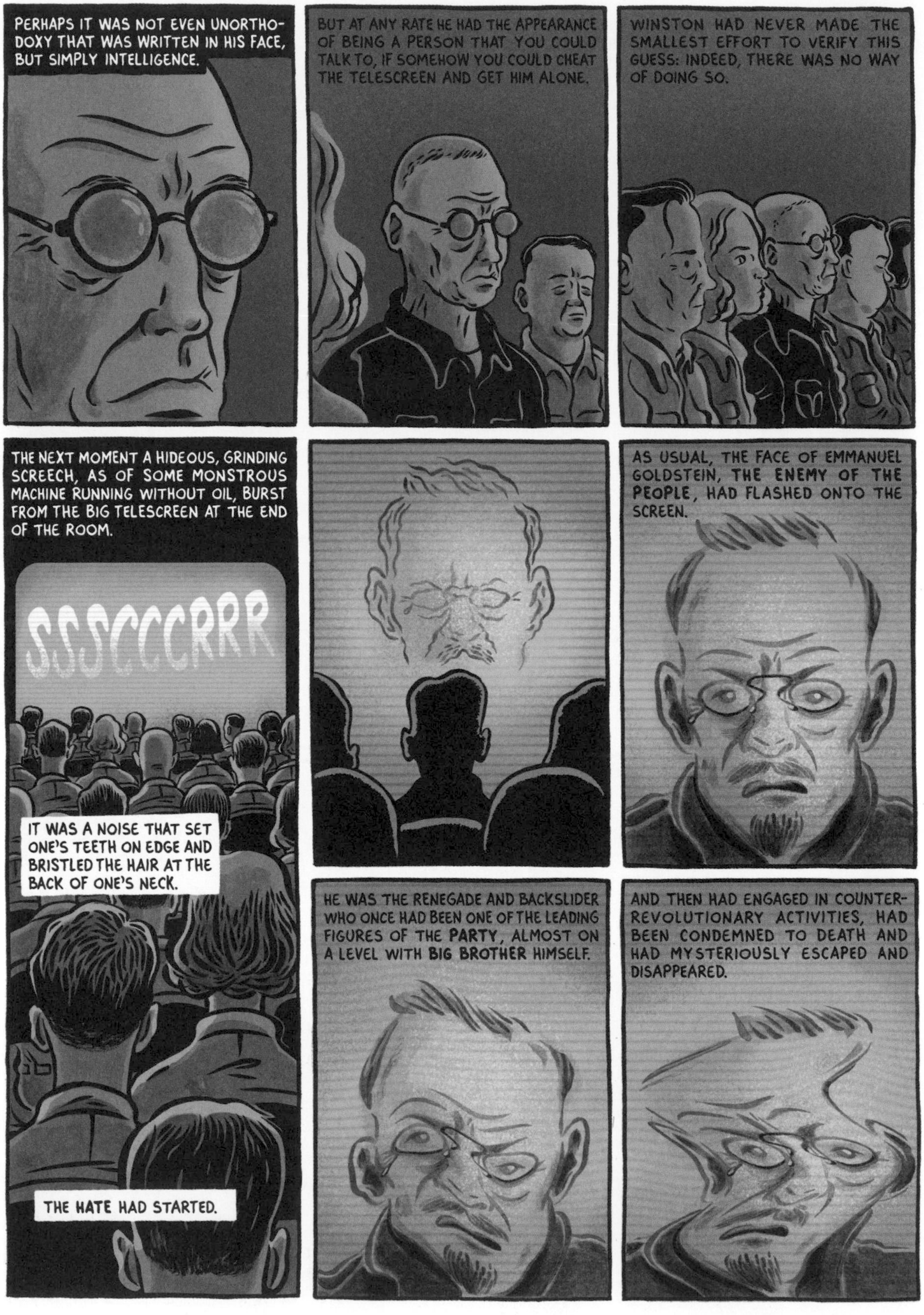
PERHAPS IT WAS NOT EVEN UNORTHODOXY THAT WAS WRITTEN IN HIS FACE, BUT SIMPLY INTELLIGENCE.
BUT AT ANY RATE HE HAD THE APPEARANCE OF BEING A PERSON THAT YOU COULD TALK TO, IF SOMEHOW YOU COULD CHEAT THE TELESCREEN AND GET HIM ALONE.
WINSTON HAD NEVER MADE THE SMALLEST EFFORT TO VERIFY THIS GUESS: INDEED, THERE WAS NO WAY OF DOING SO.
THE NEXT MOMENT A HIDEOUS, GRINDING SCREECH, AS OF SOME MONSTROUS MACHINE RUNNING WITHOUT OIL, BURST FROM THE BIG TELESCREEN AT THE END OF THE ROOM.
SSSCCCRRR
IT WAS A NOISE THAT SET ONE'S TEETH ON EDGE AND BRISTLED THE HAIR AT THE BACK OF ONE'S NECK.
THE HATE HAD STARTED.
AS USUAL, THE FACE OF EMMANUEL GOLDSTEIN, THE ENEMY OF THE PEOPLE, HAD FLASHED ONTO THE SCREEN.
HE WAS THE RENEGADE AND BACKSLIDER WHO ONCE HAD BEEN ONE OF THE LEADING FIGURES OF THE PARTY, ALMOST ON A LEVEL WITH BIG BROTHER HIMSELF.
AND THEN HAD ENGAGED IN COUNTER-REVOLUTIONARY ACTIVITIES, HAD BEEN CONDEMNED TO DEATH AND HAD MYSTERIOUSLY ESCAPED AND DISAPPEARED.

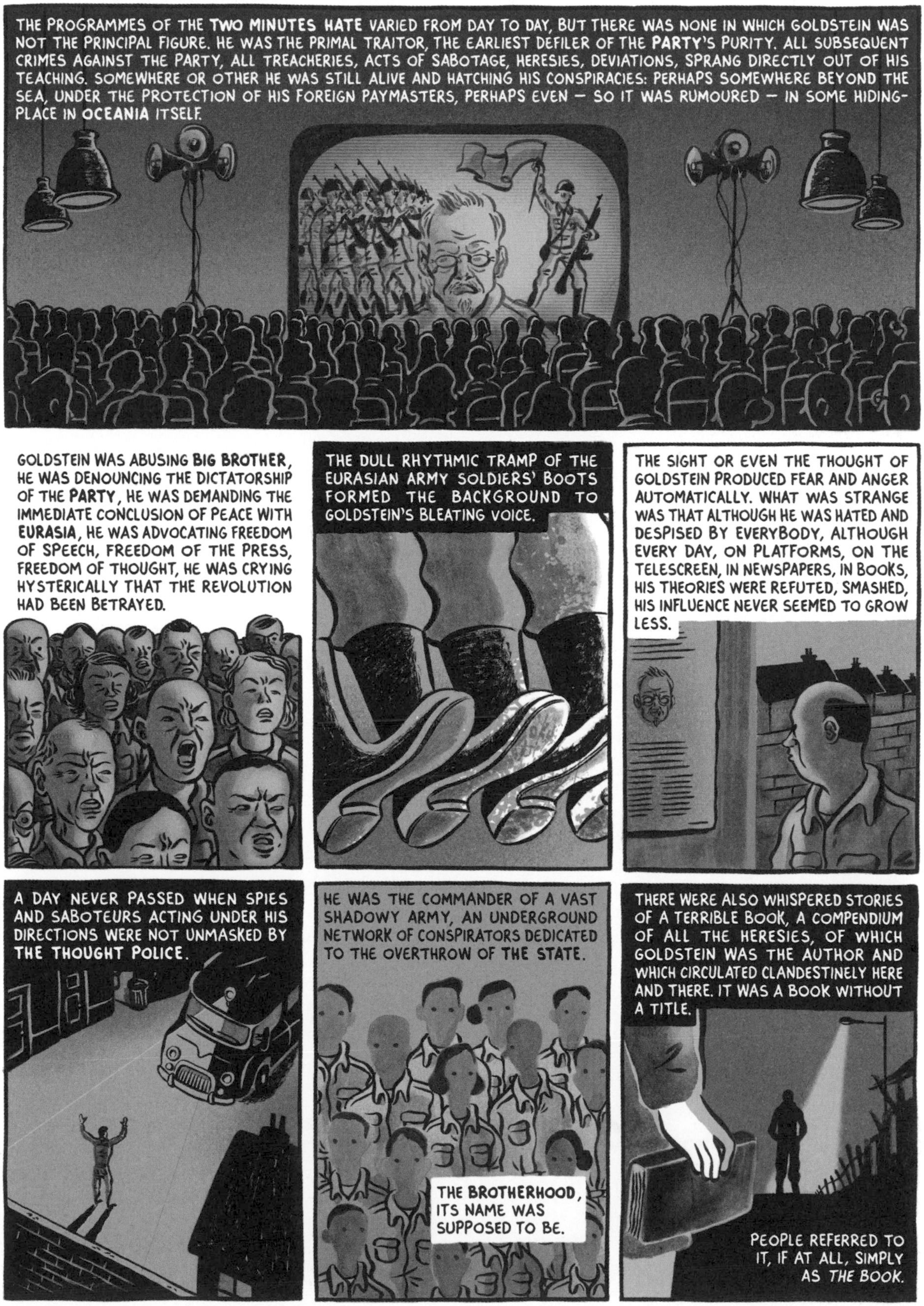
THE PROGRAMMES OF THE TWO MINUTES HATE VARIED FROM DAY TO DAY, BUT THERE WAS NONE IN WHICH GOLDSTEIN WAS NOT THE PRINCIPAL FIGURE. HE WAS THE PRIMAL TRAITOR, THE EARLIEST DEFILER OF THE PARTY'S PURITY. ALL SUBSEQUENT CRIMES AGAINST THE PARTY, ALL TREACHERIES, ACTS OF SABOTAGE, HERESIES, DEVIATIONS, SPRANG DIRECTLY OUT OF HIS TEACHING. SOMEWHERE OR OTHER HE WAS STILL ALIVE AND HATCHING HIS CONSPIRACIES: PERHAPS SOMEWHERE BEYOND THE SEA, UNDER THE PROTECTION OF HIS FOREIGN PAYMASTERS, PERHAPS EVEN — SO IT WAS RUMOURED — IN SOME HIDING-PLACE IN OCEANIA ITSELF.
GOLDSTEIN WAS ABUSING BIG BROTHER, HE WAS DENOUNCING THE DICTATORSHIP OF THE PARTY, HE WAS DEMANDING THE IMMEDIATE CONCLUSION OF PEACE WITH EURASIA, HE WAS ADVOCATING FREEDOM OF SPEECH, FREEDOM OF THE PRESS, FREEDOM OF THOUGHT, HE WAS CRYING HYSTERICALLY THAT THE REVOLUTION HAD BEEN BETRAYED.
THE DULL RHYTHMIC TRAMP OF THE EURASIAN ARMY SOLDIERS' BOOTS FORMED THE BACKGROUND TO GOLDSTEIN'S BLEATING VOICE.
THE SIGHT OR EVEN THE THOUGHT OF GOLDSTEIN PRODUCED FEAR AND ANGER AUTOMATICALLY. WHAT WAS STRANGE WAS THAT ALTHOUGH HE WAS HATED AND DESPISED BY EVERYBODY, ALTHOUGH EVERY DAY, ON PLATFORMS, ON THE TELESCREEN, IN NEWSPAPERS, IN BOOKS, HIS THEORIES WERE REFUTED, SMASHED, HIS INFLUENCE NEVER SEEMED TO GROW LESS.
A DAY NEVER PASSED WHEN SPIES AND SABOTEURS ACTING UNDER HIS DIRECTIONS WERE NOT UNMASKED BY THE THOUGHT POLICE.
HE WAS THE COMMANDER OF A VAST SHADOWY ARMY, AN UNDERGROUND NETWORK OF CONSPIRATORS DEDICATED TO THE OVERTHROW OF THE STATE.
THE BROTHERHOOD, ITS NAME WAS SUPPOSED TO BE.
THERE WERE ALSO WHISPERED STORIES OF A TERRIBLE BOOK, A COMPENDIUM OF ALL THE HERESIES, OF WHICH GOLDSTEIN WAS THE AUTHOR AND WHICH CIRCULATED CLANDESTINELY HERE AND THERE. IT WAS A BOOK WITHOUT A TITLE.
PEOPLE REFERRED TO IT, IF AT ALL, SIMPLY AS THE BOOK.

IN ITS SECOND MINUTE THE **HATE** ROSE TO A FRENZY. PEOPLE WERE LEAPING UP AND DOWN IN THEIR PLACES AND SHOUTING AT THE TOPS OF THEIR VOICES IN AN EFFORT TO DROWN THE MADDENING BLEATING VOICE THAT CAME FROM THE SCREEN.

IN A LUCID MOMENT WINSTON FOUND THAT HE WAS SHOUTING WITH THE OTHERS.

THE HORRIBLE THING ABOUT THE **TWO MINUTES HATE** WAS NOT THAT ONE WAS OBLIGED TO ACT A PART, BUT THAT IT WAS IMPOSSIBLE TO AVOID JOINING IN.

WITHIN THIRTY SECONDS ANY PRETENCE WAS ALWAYS UNNECESSARY. A HIDEOUS ECSTASY OF FEAR AND VINDICTIVENESS, A DESIRE TO KILL, TO TORTURE, TO SMASH FACES IN WITH A SLEDGE-HAMMER, SEEMED TO FLOW THROUGH THE WHOLE GROUP OF PEOPLE LIKE AN ELECTRIC CURRENT, TURNING ONE EVEN AGAINST ONE'S WILL INTO A GRIMACING, SCREAMING LUNATIC.

AND YET THE RAGE THAT ONE FELT WAS AN ABSTRACT, UNDIRECTED EMOTION WHICH COULD BE SWITCHED FROM ONE OBJECT TO ANOTHER LIKE THE FLAME OF A BLOWLAMP.

THUS, AT ONE MOMENT WINSTON'S HATRED WAS NOT TURNED AGAINST GOLDSTEIN AT ALL, BUT, ON THE CONTRARY, AGAINST BIG BROTHER, THE PARTY AND THE THOUGHT POLICE.

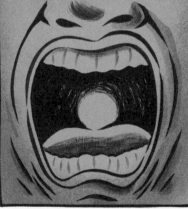

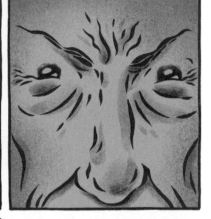

AT SUCH MOMENTS HIS HEART WENT OUT TO THE LONELY, DERIDED HERETIC ON THE SCREEN, SOLE GUARDIAN OF TRUTH AND SANITY IN A WORLD OF LIES.

AND YET THE VERY NEXT INSTANT HE WAS AT ONE WITH THE PEOPLE ABOUT HIM. AT THOSE MOMENTS HIS SECRET LOATHING OF **BIG BROTHER** CHANGED INTO ADORATION, AND GOLDSTEIN SEEMED LIKE SOME SINISTER ENCHANTER, CAPABLE BY THE MERE POWER OF HIS VOICE OF WRECKING THE STRUCTURE OF CIVILISATION.

WINSTON SUCCEEDED IN TRANSFERRING HIS HATRED TO THE DARK-HAIRED GIRL BEHIND HIM. VIVID, BEAUTIFUL HALLUCINATIONS FLASHED THROUGH HIS MIND.

HE WOULD FLOG HER TO DEATH WITH A RUBBER TRUNCHEON.

BETTER THAN BEFORE, HE REALISED WHY IT WAS THAT HE HATED HER. HE HATED HER BECAUSE SHE WAS YOUNG AND PRETTY AND SEXLESS.

BECAUSE ROUND HER SWEET SUPPLE WAIST, WHICH SEEMED TO ASK YOU TO ENCIRCLE IT WITH YOUR ARM, THERE WAS ONLY THE ODIOUS SCARLET SASH, AGGRESSIVE SYMBOL OF CHASTITY.

THE **HATE** ROSE TO ITS CLIMAX. GOLDSTEIN'S FACE MELTED.

IT WAS SUBSTITUTED WITH THE FIGURE OF A EURASIAN SOLDIER...

WHO MELTED INTO THE FACE OF **BIG BROTHER**.

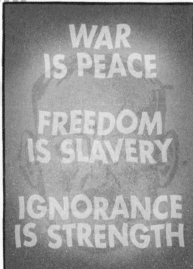

WAR IS PEACE

FREEDOM IS SLAVERY

IGNORANCE IS STRENGTH

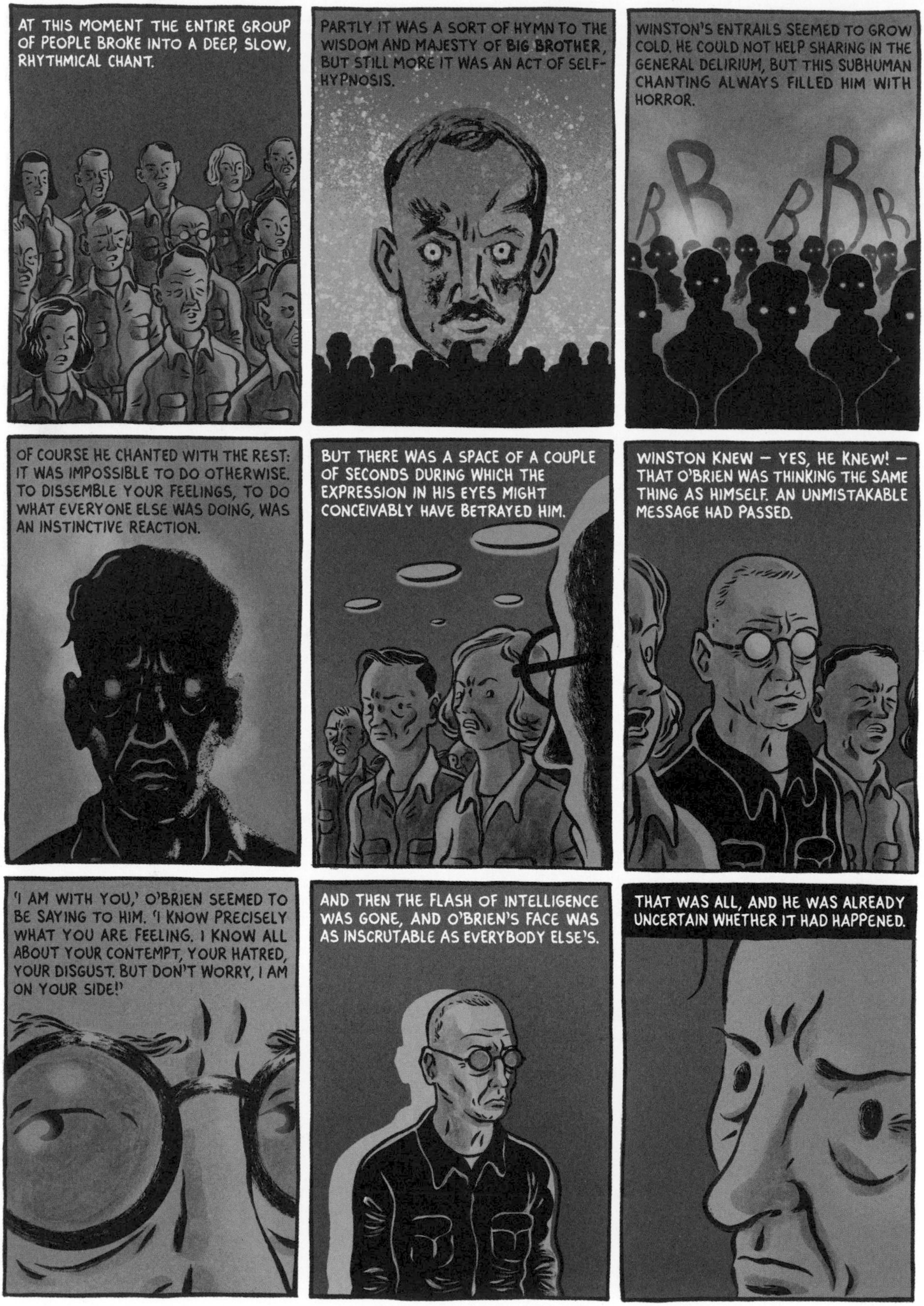
AT THIS MOMENT THE ENTIRE GROUP OF PEOPLE BROKE INTO A DEEP, SLOW, RHYTHMICAL CHANT.
PARTLY IT WAS A SORT OF HYMN TO THE WISDOM AND MAJESTY OF BIG BROTHER, BUT STILL MORE IT WAS AN ACT OF SELF-HYPNOSIS.
WINSTON'S ENTRAILS SEEMED TO GROW COLD. HE COULD NOT HELP SHARING IN THE GENERAL DELIRIUM, BUT THIS SUBHUMAN CHANTING ALWAYS FILLED HIM WITH HORROR.
B B B B B B
OF COURSE HE CHANTED WITH THE REST: IT WAS IMPOSSIBLE TO DO OTHERWISE. TO DISSEMBLE YOUR FEELINGS, TO DO WHAT EVERYONE ELSE WAS DOING, WAS AN INSTINCTIVE REACTION.
BUT THERE WAS A SPACE OF A COUPLE OF SECONDS DURING WHICH THE EXPRESSION IN HIS EYES MIGHT CONCEIVABLY HAVE BETRAYED HIM.
WINSTON KNEW – YES, HE KNEW! – THAT O'BRIEN WAS THINKING THE SAME THING AS HIMSELF. AN UNMISTAKABLE MESSAGE HAD PASSED.
'I AM WITH YOU,' O'BRIEN SEEMED TO BE SAYING TO HIM. 'I KNOW PRECISELY WHAT YOU ARE FEELING. I KNOW ALL ABOUT YOUR CONTEMPT, YOUR HATRED, YOUR DISGUST. BUT DON'T WORRY, I AM ON YOUR SIDE!'
AND THEN THE FLASH OF INTELLIGENCE WAS GONE, AND O'BRIEN'S FACE WAS AS INSCRUTABLE AS EVERYBODY ELSE'S.
THAT WAS ALL, AND HE WAS ALREADY UNCERTAIN WHETHER IT HAD HAPPENED.

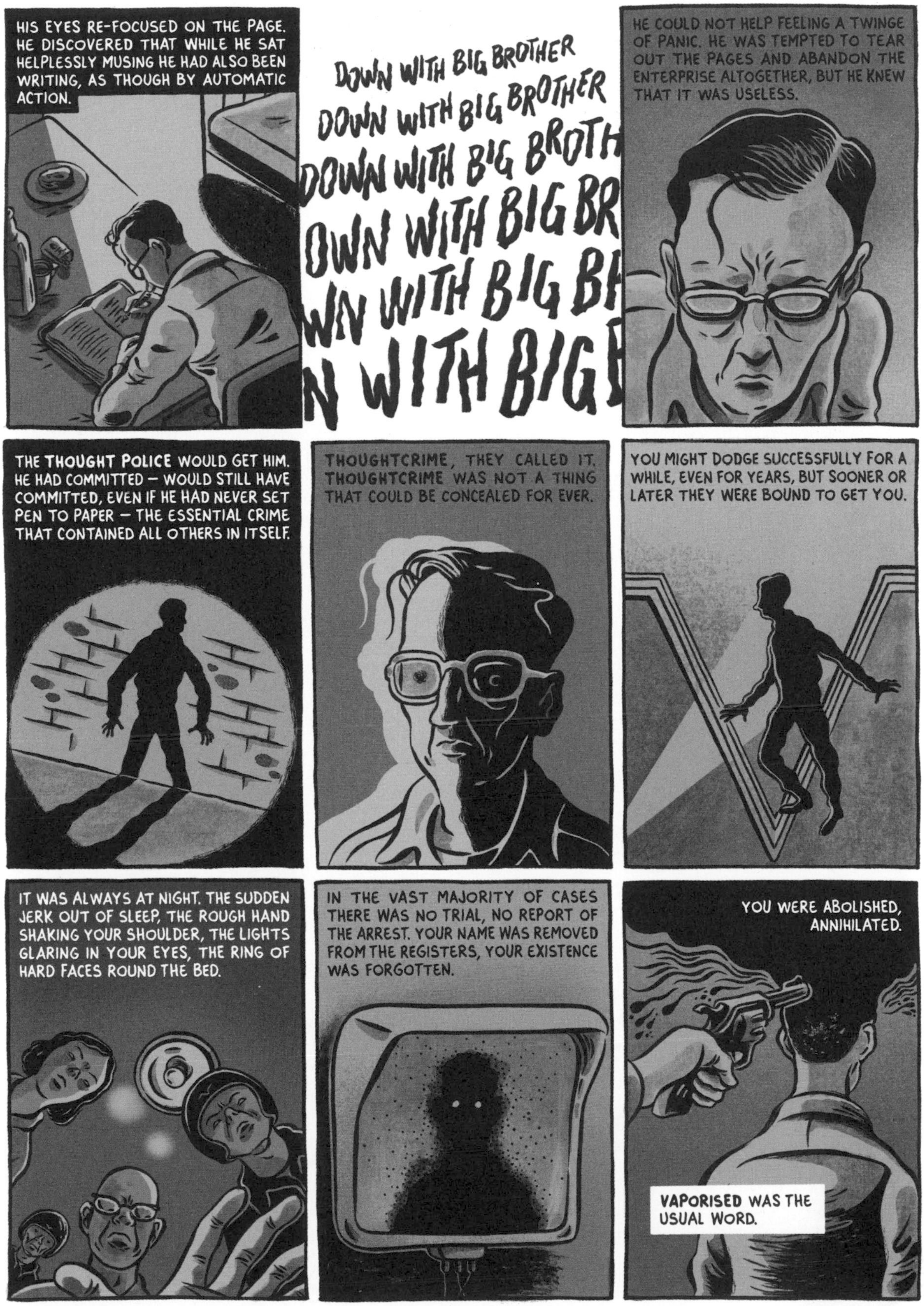
HIS EYES RE-FOCUSED ON THE PAGE. HE DISCOVERED THAT WHILE HE SAT HELPLESSLY MUSING HE HAD ALSO BEEN WRITING, AS THOUGH BY AUTOMATIC ACTION.
DOWN WITH BIG BROTHER
DOWN WITH BIG BROTHER
DOWN WITH BIG BROTH
OWN WITH BIG BR
WN WITH BIG B
N WITH BIG
HE COULD NOT HELP FEELING A TWINGE OF PANIC. HE WAS TEMPTED TO TEAR OUT THE PAGES AND ABANDON THE ENTERPRISE ALTOGETHER, BUT HE KNEW THAT IT WAS USELESS.
THE THOUGHT POLICE WOULD GET HIM. HE HAD COMMITTED — WOULD STILL HAVE COMMITTED, EVEN IF HE HAD NEVER SET PEN TO PAPER — THE ESSENTIAL CRIME THAT CONTAINED ALL OTHERS IN ITSELF.
THOUGHTCRIME, THEY CALLED IT. THOUGHTCRIME WAS NOT A THING THAT COULD BE CONCEALED FOR EVER.
YOU MIGHT DODGE SUCCESSFULLY FOR A WHILE, EVEN FOR YEARS, BUT SOONER OR LATER THEY WERE BOUND TO GET YOU.
IT WAS ALWAYS AT NIGHT. THE SUDDEN JERK OUT OF SLEEP, THE ROUGH HAND SHAKING YOUR SHOULDER, THE LIGHTS GLARING IN YOUR EYES, THE RING OF HARD FACES ROUND THE BED.
IN THE VAST MAJORITY OF CASES THERE WAS NO TRIAL, NO REPORT OF THE ARREST. YOUR NAME WAS REMOVED FROM THE REGISTERS, YOUR EXISTENCE WAS FORGOTTEN.
YOU WERE ABOLISHED, ANNIHILATED.
VAPORISED WAS THE USUAL WORD.

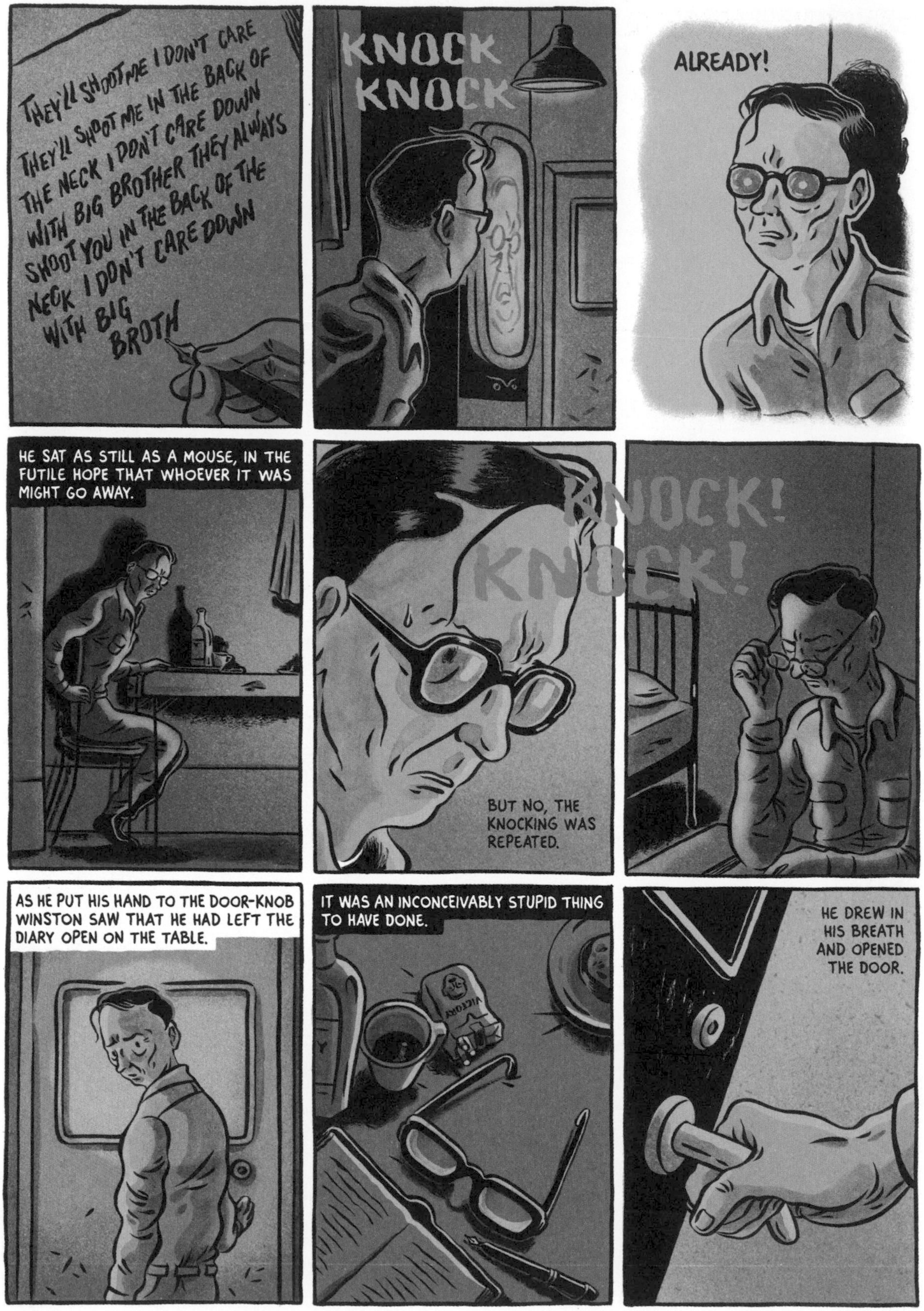
THEY'LL SHOOT ME I DON'T CARE THEY'LL SHOOT ME IN THE BACK OF THE NECK I DON'T CARE DOWN WITH BIG BROTHER THEY ALWAYS SHOOT YOU IN THE BACK OF THE NECK I DON'T CARE DOWN WITH BIG BROTH
KNOCK KNOCK
ALREADY!
HE SAT AS STILL AS A MOUSE, IN THE FUTILE HOPE THAT WHOEVER IT WAS MIGHT GO AWAY.
KNOCK! KNOCK!
BUT NO, THE KNOCKING WAS REPEATED.
AS HE PUT HIS HAND TO THE DOOR-KNOB WINSTON SAW THAT HE HAD LEFT THE DIARY OPEN ON THE TABLE.
IT WAS AN INCONCEIVABLY STUPID THING TO HAVE DONE.
VICTORY
HE DREW IN HIS BREATH AND OPENED THE DOOR.

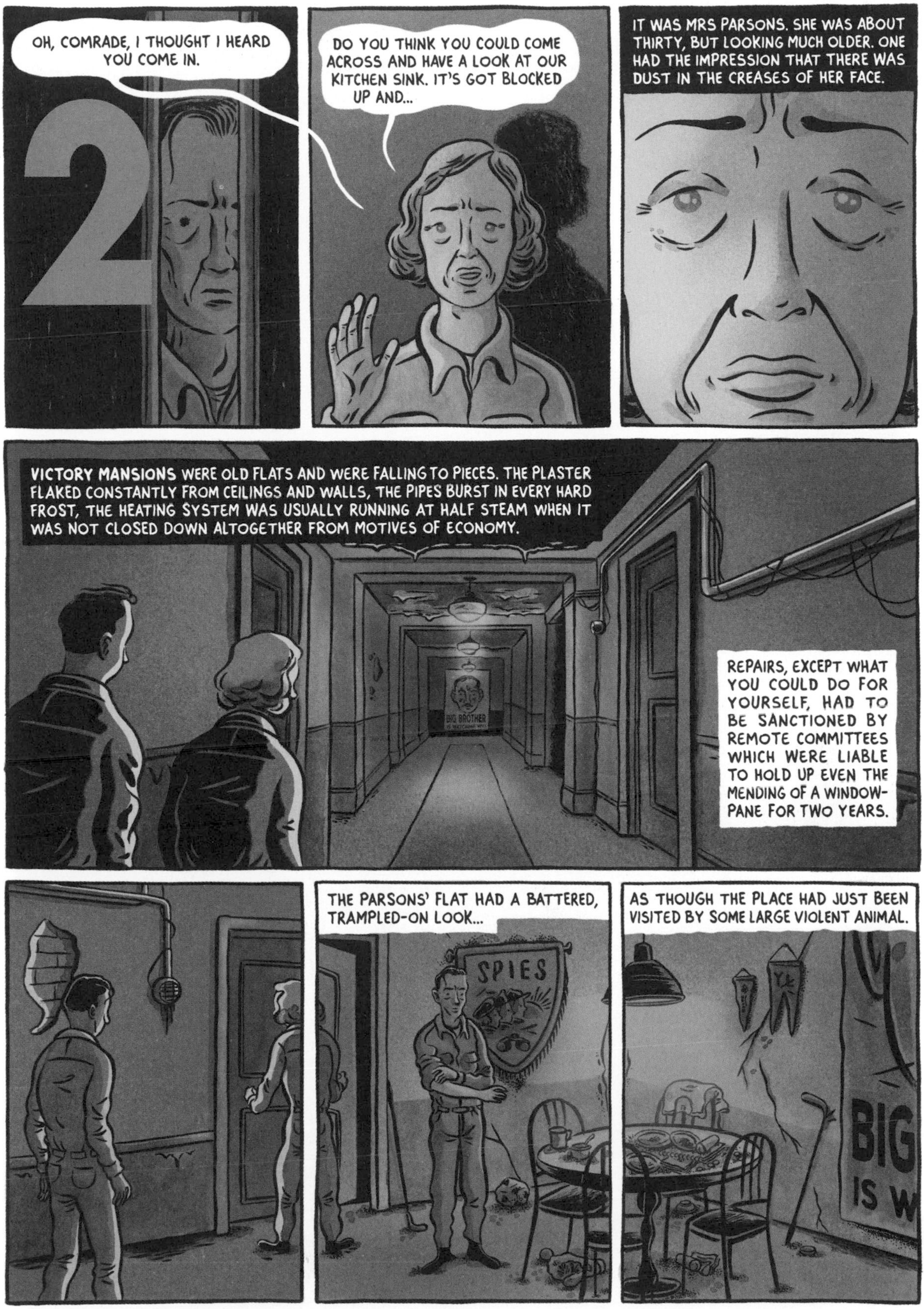
2
OH, COMRADE, I THOUGHT I HEARD YOU COME IN.
DO YOU THINK YOU COULD COME ACROSS AND HAVE A LOOK AT OUR KITCHEN SINK. IT'S GOT BLOCKED UP AND...
IT WAS MRS PARSONS. SHE WAS ABOUT THIRTY, BUT LOOKING MUCH OLDER. ONE HAD THE IMPRESSION THAT THERE WAS DUST IN THE CREASES OF HER FACE.
VICTORY MANSIONS WERE OLD FLATS AND WERE FALLING TO PIECES. THE PLASTER FLAKED CONSTANTLY FROM CEILINGS AND WALLS, THE PIPES BURST IN EVERY HARD FROST, THE HEATING SYSTEM WAS USUALLY RUNNING AT HALF STEAM WHEN IT WAS NOT CLOSED DOWN ALTOGETHER FROM MOTIVES OF ECONOMY.
BIG BROTHER
REPAIRS, EXCEPT WHAT YOU COULD DO FOR YOURSELF, HAD TO BE SANCTIONED BY REMOTE COMMITTEES WHICH WERE LIABLE TO HOLD UP EVEN THE MENDING OF A WINDOW-PANE FOR TWO YEARS.
THE PARSONS' FLAT HAD A BATTERED, TRAMPLED-ON LOOK...
SPIES
AS THOUGH THE PLACE HAD JUST BEEN VISITED BY SOME LARGE VIOLENT ANIMAL.
BIG
IS W

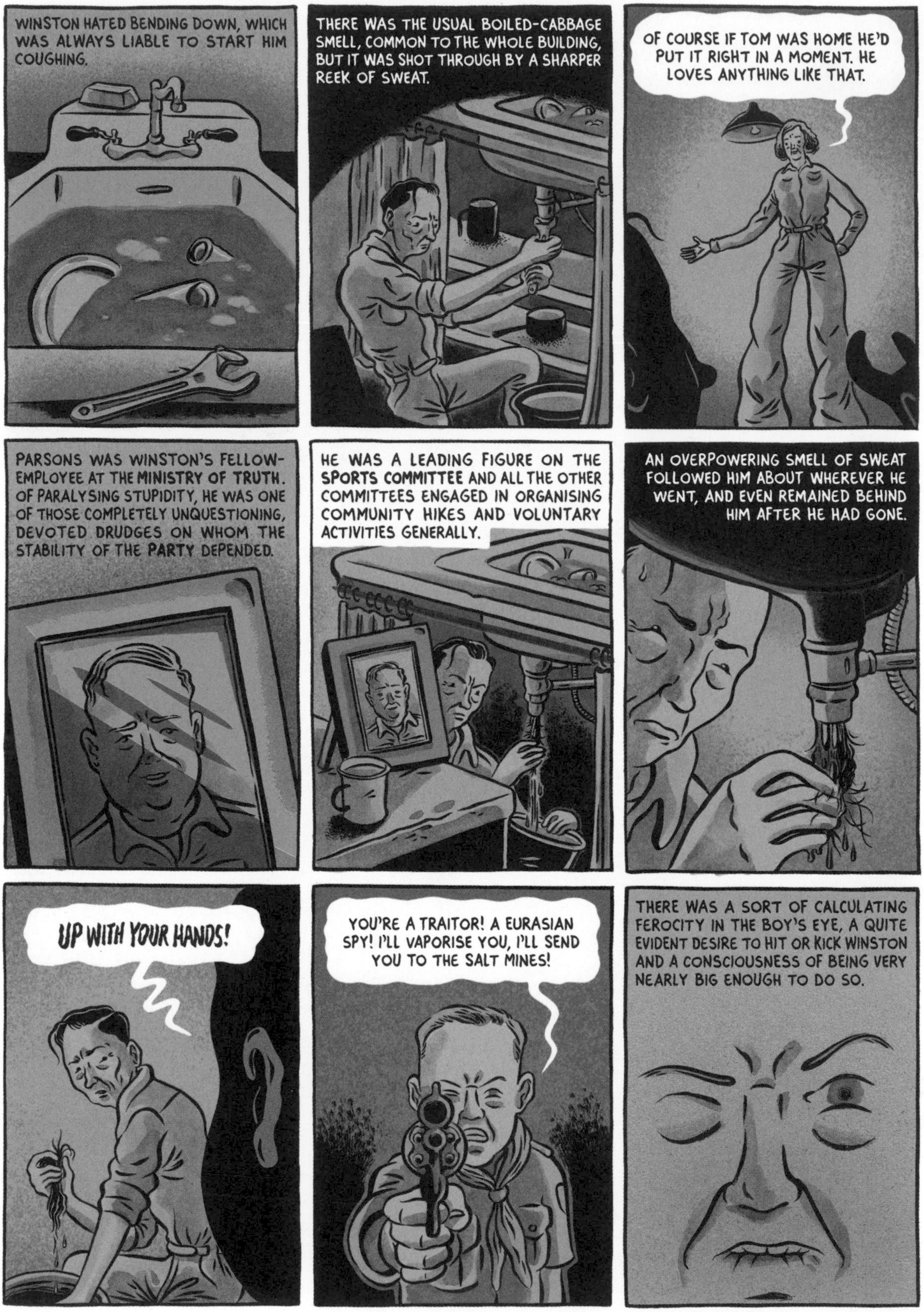
WINSTON HATED BENDING DOWN, WHICH WAS ALWAYS LIABLE TO START HIM COUGHING.
THERE WAS THE USUAL BOILED-CABBAGE SMELL, COMMON TO THE WHOLE BUILDING, BUT IT WAS SHOT THROUGH BY A SHARPER REEK OF SWEAT.
OF COURSE IF TOM WAS HOME HE'D PUT IT RIGHT IN A MOMENT. HE LOVES ANYTHING LIKE THAT.
PARSONS WAS WINSTON'S FELLOW-EMPLOYEE AT THE MINISTRY OF TRUTH. OF PARALYSING STUPIDITY, HE WAS ONE OF THOSE COMPLETELY UNQUESTIONING, DEVOTED DRUDGES ON WHOM THE STABILITY OF THE PARTY DEPENDED.
HE WAS A LEADING FIGURE ON THE SPORTS COMMITTEE AND ALL THE OTHER COMMITTEES ENGAGED IN ORGANISING COMMUNITY HIKES AND VOLUNTARY ACTIVITIES GENERALLY.
AN OVERPOWERING SMELL OF SWEAT FOLLOWED HIM ABOUT WHEREVER HE WENT, AND EVEN REMAINED BEHIND HIM AFTER HE HAD GONE.
UP WITH YOUR HANDS!
YOU'RE A TRAITOR! A EURASIAN SPY! I'LL VAPORISE YOU, I'LL SEND YOU TO THE SALT MINES!
THERE WAS A SORT OF CALCULATING FEROCITY IN THE BOY'S EYE, A QUITE EVIDENT DESIRE TO HIT OR KICK WINSTON AND A CONSCIOUSNESS OF BEING VERY NEARLY BIG ENOUGH TO DO SO.

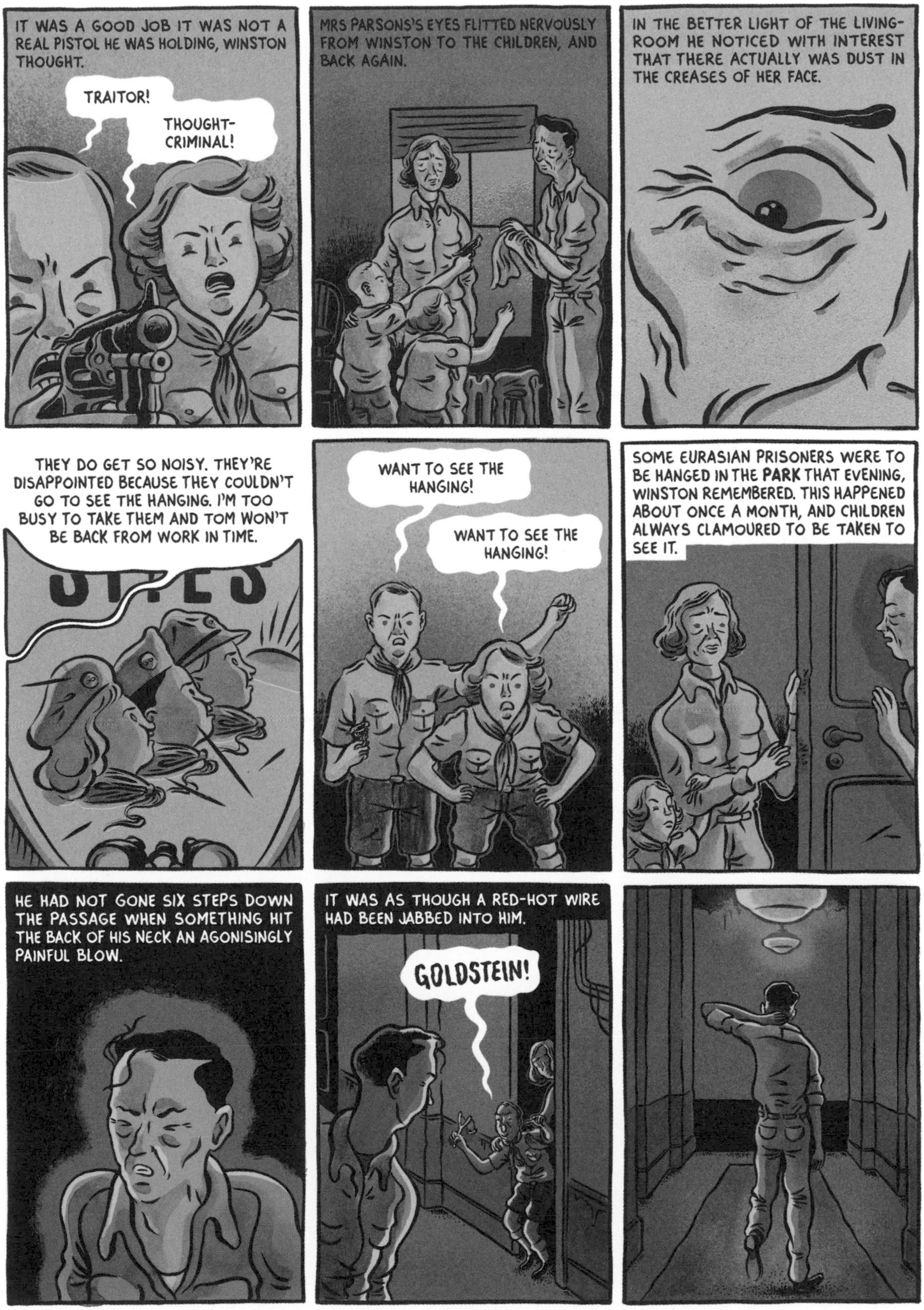
IT WAS A GOOD JOB IT WAS NOT A REAL PISTOL HE WAS HOLDING, WINSTON THOUGHT.
TRAITOR!
THOUGHT-CRIMINAL!
MRS PARSONS'S EYES FLITTED NERVOUSLY FROM WINSTON TO THE CHILDREN, AND BACK AGAIN.
IN THE BETTER LIGHT OF THE LIVING-ROOM HE NOTICED WITH INTEREST THAT THERE ACTUALLY WAS DUST IN THE CREASES OF HER FACE.
THEY DO GET SO NOISY. THEY'RE DISAPPOINTED BECAUSE THEY COULDN'T GO TO SEE THE HANGING. I'M TOO BUSY TO TAKE THEM AND TOM WON'T BE BACK FROM WORK IN TIME.
WANT TO SEE THE HANGING!
WANT TO SEE THE HANGING!
SOME EURASIAN PRISONERS WERE TO BE HANGED IN THE PARK THAT EVENING, WINSTON REMEMBERED. THIS HAPPENED ABOUT ONCE A MONTH, AND CHILDREN ALWAYS CLAMOURED TO BE TAKEN TO SEE IT.
HE HAD NOT GONE SIX STEPS DOWN THE PASSAGE WHEN SOMETHING HIT THE BACK OF HIS NECK AN AGONISINGLY PAINFUL BLOW.
IT WAS AS THOUGH A RED-HOT WIRE HAD BEEN JABBED INTO HIM.
GOLDSTEIN!

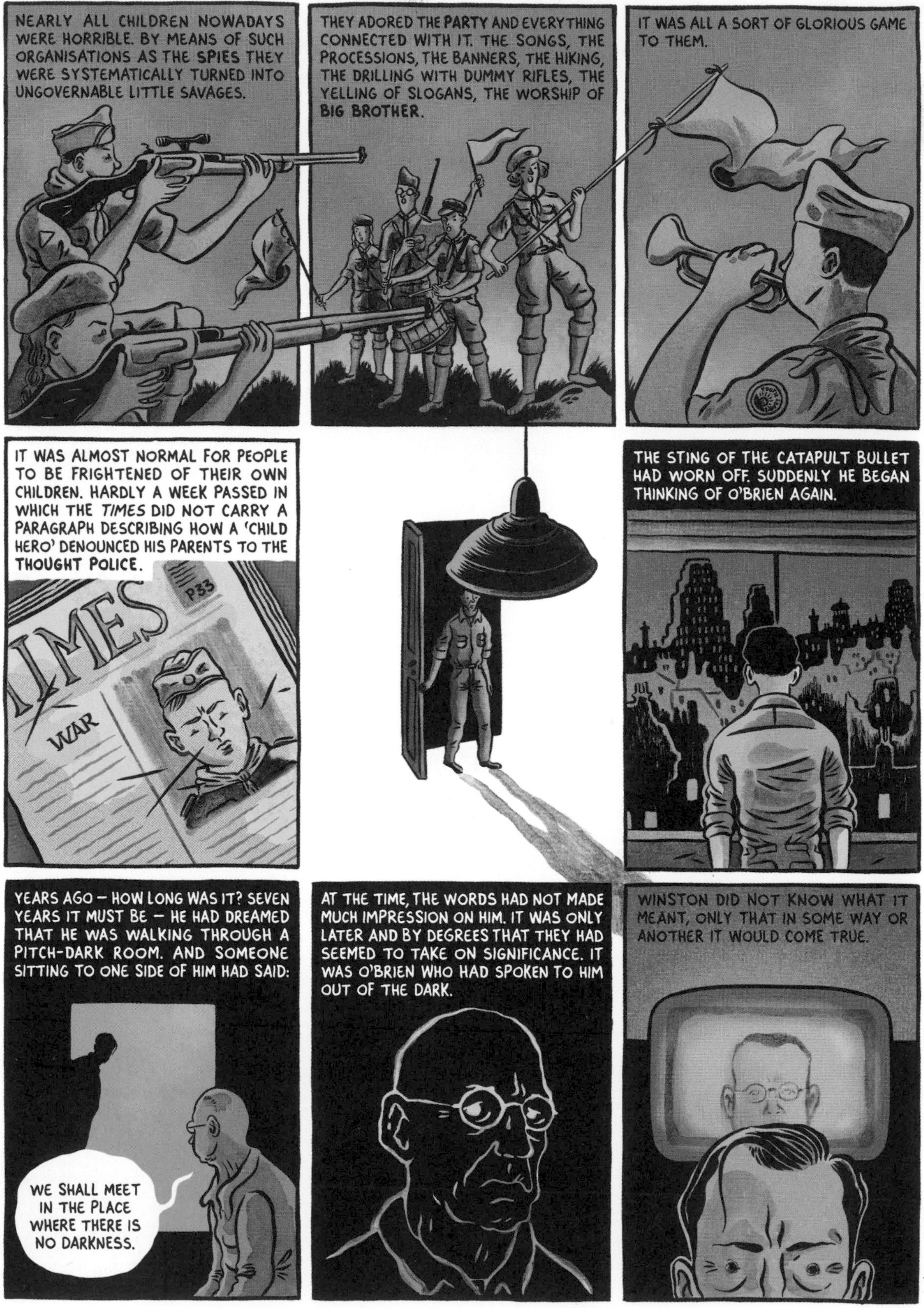
NEARLY ALL CHILDREN NOWADAYS WERE HORRIBLE. BY MEANS OF SUCH ORGANISATIONS AS THE SPIES THEY WERE SYSTEMATICALLY TURNED INTO UNGOVERNABLE LITTLE SAVAGES.
THEY ADORED THE PARTY AND EVERYTHING CONNECTED WITH IT. THE SONGS, THE PROCESSIONS, THE BANNERS, THE HIKING, THE DRILLING WITH DUMMY RIFLES, THE YELLING OF SLOGANS, THE WORSHIP OF BIG BROTHER.
IT WAS ALL A SORT OF GLORIOUS GAME TO THEM.
IT WAS ALMOST NORMAL FOR PEOPLE TO BE FRIGHTENED OF THEIR OWN CHILDREN. HARDLY A WEEK PASSED IN WHICH THE TIMES DID NOT CARRY A PARAGRAPH DESCRIBING HOW A 'CHILD HERO' DENOUNCED HIS PARENTS TO THE THOUGHT POLICE.
IMES
P33
WAR
THE STING OF THE CATAPULT BULLET HAD WORN OFF. SUDDENLY HE BEGAN THINKING OF O'BRIEN AGAIN.
YEARS AGO — HOW LONG WAS IT? SEVEN YEARS IT MUST BE — HE HAD DREAMED THAT HE WAS WALKING THROUGH A PITCH-DARK ROOM. AND SOMEONE SITTING TO ONE SIDE OF HIM HAD SAID:
WE SHALL MEET IN THE PLACE WHERE THERE IS NO DARKNESS.
AT THE TIME, THE WORDS HAD NOT MADE MUCH IMPRESSION ON HIM. IT WAS ONLY LATER AND BY DEGREES THAT THEY HAD SEEMED TO TAKE ON SIGNIFICANCE. IT WAS O'BRIEN WHO HAD SPOKEN TO HIM OUT OF THE DARK.
WINSTON DID NOT KNOW WHAT IT MEANT, ONLY THAT IN SOME WAY OR ANOTHER IT WOULD COME TRUE.

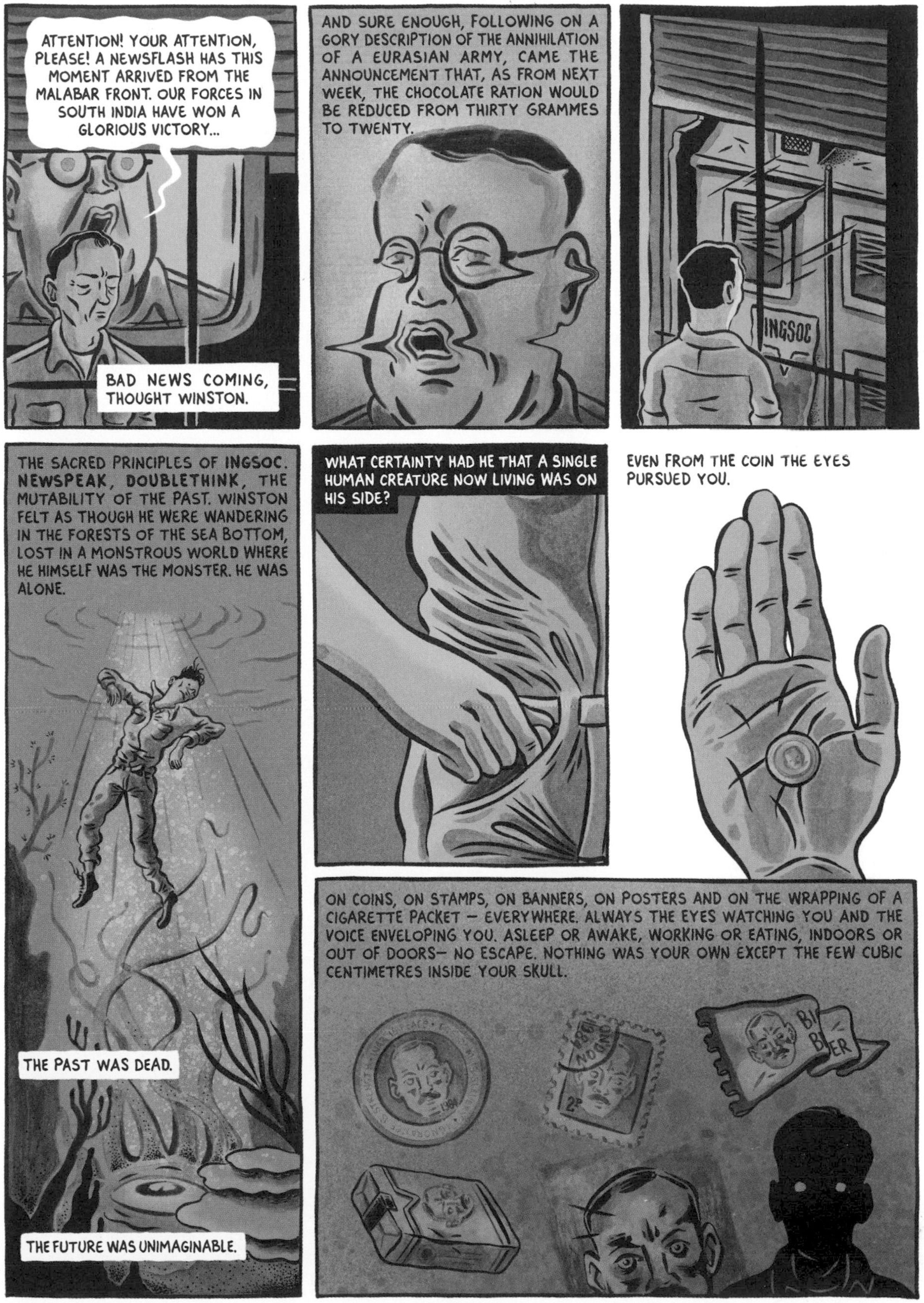
ATTENTION! YOUR ATTENTION, PLEASE! A NEWSFLASH HAS THIS MOMENT ARRIVED FROM THE MALABAR FRONT. OUR FORCES IN SOUTH INDIA HAVE WON A GLORIOUS VICTORY...
BAD NEWS COMING, THOUGHT WINSTON.
AND SURE ENOUGH, FOLLOWING ON A GORY DESCRIPTION OF THE ANNIHILATION OF A EURASIAN ARMY, CAME THE ANNOUNCEMENT THAT, AS FROM NEXT WEEK, THE CHOCOLATE RATION WOULD BE REDUCED FROM THIRTY GRAMMES TO TWENTY.
INGSOC
THE SACRED PRINCIPLES OF INGSOC. NEWSPEAK, DOUBLETHINK, THE MUTABILITY OF THE PAST. WINSTON FELT AS THOUGH HE WERE WANDERING IN THE FORESTS OF THE SEA BOTTOM, LOST IN A MONSTROUS WORLD WHERE HE HIMSELF WAS THE MONSTER. HE WAS ALONE.
THE PAST WAS DEAD.
THE FUTURE WAS UNIMAGINABLE.
WHAT CERTAINTY HAD HE THAT A SINGLE HUMAN CREATURE NOW LIVING WAS ON HIS SIDE?
EVEN FROM THE COIN THE EYES PURSUED YOU.
ON COINS, ON STAMPS, ON BANNERS, ON POSTERS AND ON THE WRAPPING OF A CIGARETTE PACKET — EVERYWHERE. ALWAYS THE EYES WATCHING YOU AND THE VOICE ENVELOPING YOU. ASLEEP OR AWAKE, WORKING OR EATING, INDOORS OR OUT OF DOORS— NO ESCAPE. NOTHING WAS YOUR OWN EXCEPT THE FEW CUBIC CENTIMETRES INSIDE YOUR SKULL.

HE WONDERED AGAIN FOR WHOM HE WAS WRITING THE DIARY, AND IN FRONT OF HIM THERE LAY NOT DEATH BUT ANNIHILATION. THE DIARY WOULD BE REDUCED TO ASHES AND HIMSELF TO VAPOUR.

HOW COULD YOU MAKE APPEAL TO THE FUTURE WHEN NOT A TRACE OF YOU, NOT EVEN AN ANONYMOUS WORD SCRIBBLED ON A PIECE OF PAPER, COULD PHYSICALLY SURVIVE?

TO THE FUTURE OR TO THE PAST, TO A TIME WHEN THOUGHT IS FREE, WHEN MEN ARE DIFFERENT FROM ONE ANOTHER AND DO NOT LIVE ALONE

TO A TIME WHEN TRUTH EXISTS AND WHAT IS DONE CANNOT BE UNDONE: FROM THE AGE OF SOLITUDE, FROM THE AGE OF BIG BROTHER, FROM THE AGE OF DOUBLETHINK, GREETINGS!

HE WAS ALREADY DEAD, HE REFLECTED.

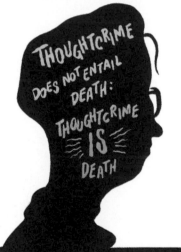

THOUGHTCRIME DOES NOT ENTAIL DEATH: THOUGHTCRIME IS DEATH

NOW THAT HE HAD RECOGNISED HIMSELF AS A DEAD MAN IT BECAME IMPORTANT TO STAY ALIVE AS LONG AS POSSIBLE. TWO FINGERS OF HIS RIGHT HAND WERE INKSTAINED. IT WAS EXACTLY THE KIND OF DETAIL THAT MIGHT BETRAY YOU.

SOME NOSING ZEALOT IN THE **MINISTRY** MIGHT START WONDERING WHY HE HAD BEEN WRITING DURING THE LUNCH INTERVAL, WHY HE HAD USED AN OLD-FASHIONED PEN, *WHAT HE HAD BEEN WRITING.*

HE PUT THE DIARY AWAY IN THE DRAWER. IT WAS QUITE USELESS TO THINK OF HIDING IT, BUT HE COULD AT LEAST MAKE SURE WHETHER OR NOT ITS EXISTENCE HAD BEEN DISCOVERED.

A HAIR LAID ACROSS THE PAGE-ENDS WAS TOO OBVIOUS. WITH THE TIP OF HIS FINGER HE PICKED UP AN IDENTIFIABLE GRAIN OF WHITISH DUST AND DEPOSITED IT ON THE CORNER OF THE COVER,

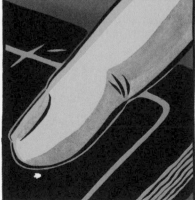

WHERE IT WAS BOUND TO BE SHAKEN OFF IF THE BOOK WAS MOVED.

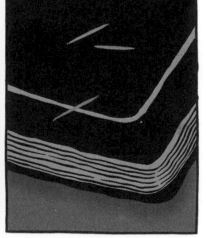

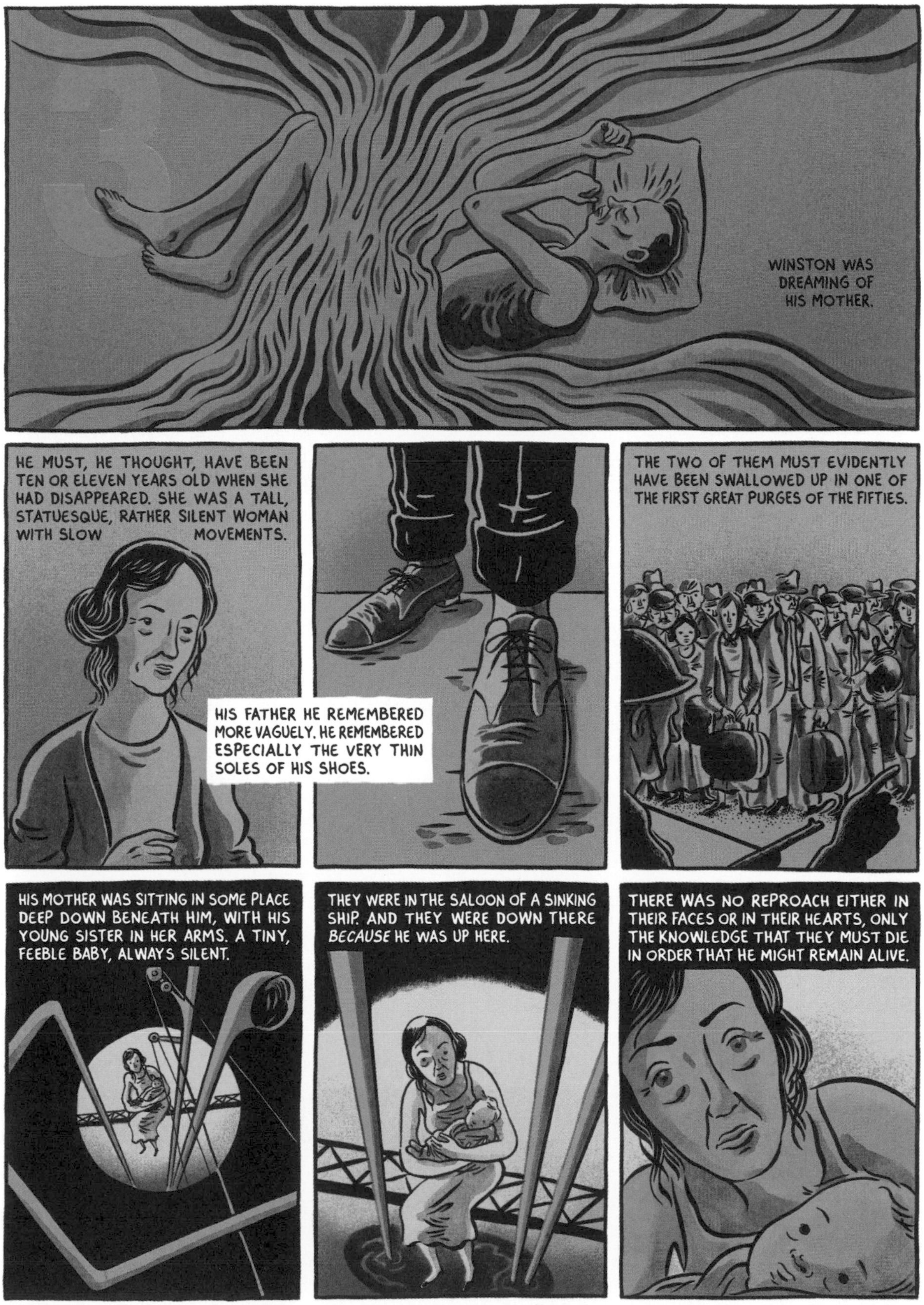
WINSTON WAS DREAMING OF HIS MOTHER.
HE MUST, HE THOUGHT, HAVE BEEN TEN OR ELEVEN YEARS OLD WHEN SHE HAD DISAPPEARED. SHE WAS A TALL, STATUESQUE, RATHER SILENT WOMAN WITH SLOW MOVEMENTS.
HIS FATHER HE REMEMBERED MORE VAGUELY. HE REMEMBERED ESPECIALLY THE VERY THIN SOLES OF HIS SHOES.
THE TWO OF THEM MUST EVIDENTLY HAVE BEEN SWALLOWED UP IN ONE OF THE FIRST GREAT PURGES OF THE FIFTIES.
HIS MOTHER WAS SITTING IN SOME PLACE DEEP DOWN BENEATH HIM, WITH HIS YOUNG SISTER IN HER ARMS. A TINY, FEEBLE BABY, ALWAYS SILENT.
THEY WERE IN THE SALOON OF A SINKING SHIP. AND THEY WERE DOWN THERE *BECAUSE* HE WAS UP HERE.
THERE WAS NO REPROACH EITHER IN THEIR FACES OR IN THEIR HEARTS, ONLY THE KNOWLEDGE THAT THEY MUST DIE IN ORDER THAT HE MIGHT REMAIN ALIVE.

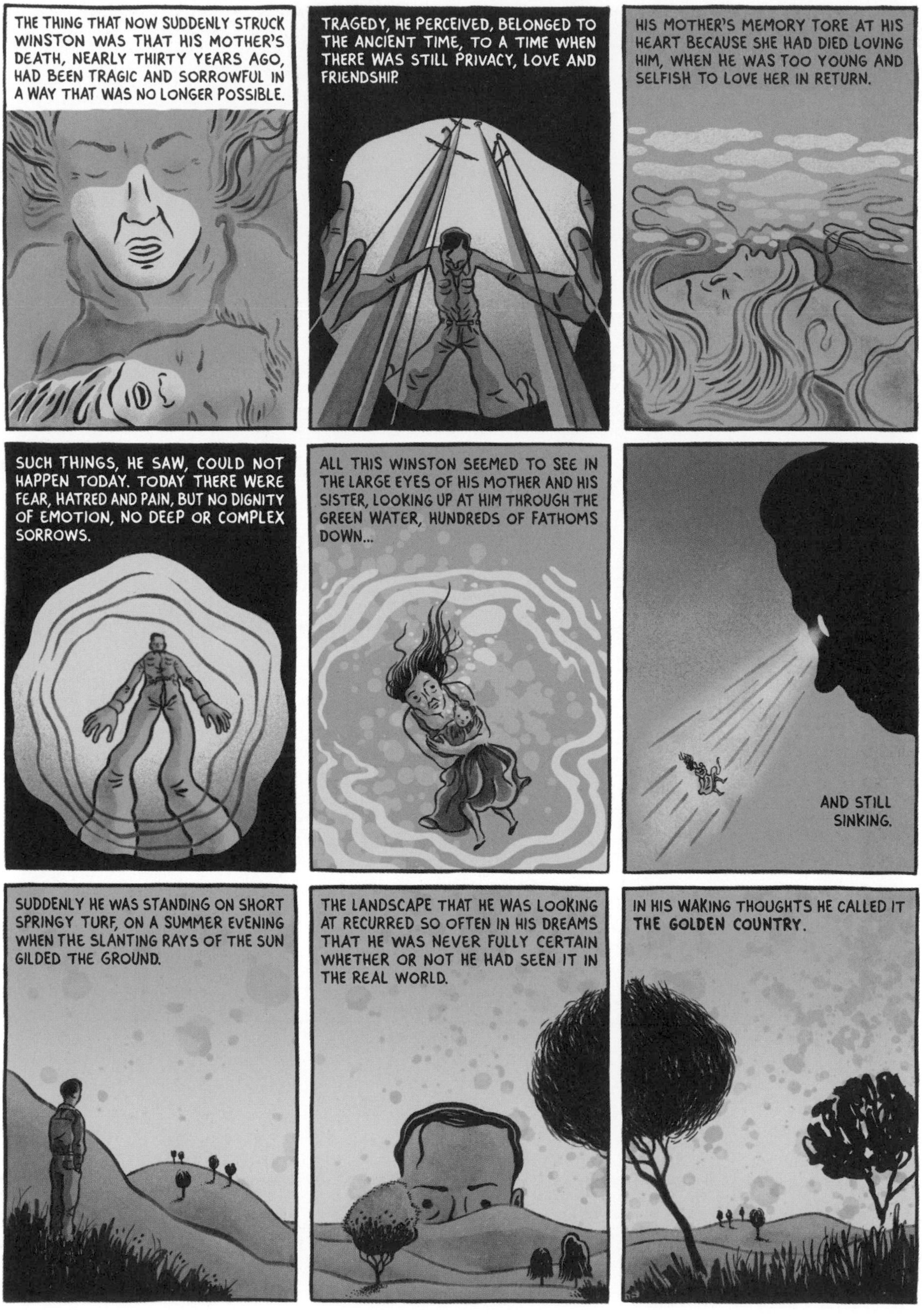
THE THING THAT NOW SUDDENLY STRUCK WINSTON WAS THAT HIS MOTHER'S DEATH, NEARLY THIRTY YEARS AGO, HAD BEEN TRAGIC AND SORROWFUL IN A WAY THAT WAS NO LONGER POSSIBLE.
TRAGEDY, HE PERCEIVED, BELONGED TO THE ANCIENT TIME, TO A TIME WHEN THERE WAS STILL PRIVACY, LOVE AND FRIENDSHIP.
HIS MOTHER'S MEMORY TORE AT HIS HEART BECAUSE SHE HAD DIED LOVING HIM, WHEN HE WAS TOO YOUNG AND SELFISH TO LOVE HER IN RETURN.
SUCH THINGS, HE SAW, COULD NOT HAPPEN TODAY. TODAY THERE WERE FEAR, HATRED AND PAIN, BUT NO DIGNITY OF EMOTION, NO DEEP OR COMPLEX SORROWS.
ALL THIS WINSTON SEEMED TO SEE IN THE LARGE EYES OF HIS MOTHER AND HIS SISTER, LOOKING UP AT HIM THROUGH THE GREEN WATER, HUNDREDS OF FATHOMS DOWN...
AND STILL SINKING.
SUDDENLY HE WAS STANDING ON SHORT SPRINGY TURF, ON A SUMMER EVENING WHEN THE SLANTING RAYS OF THE SUN GILDED THE GROUND.
THE LANDSCAPE THAT HE WAS LOOKING AT RECURRED SO OFTEN IN HIS DREAMS THAT HE WAS NEVER FULLY CERTAIN WHETHER OR NOT HE HAD SEEN IT IN THE REAL WORLD.
IN HIS WAKING THOUGHTS HE CALLED IT THE GOLDEN COUNTRY.

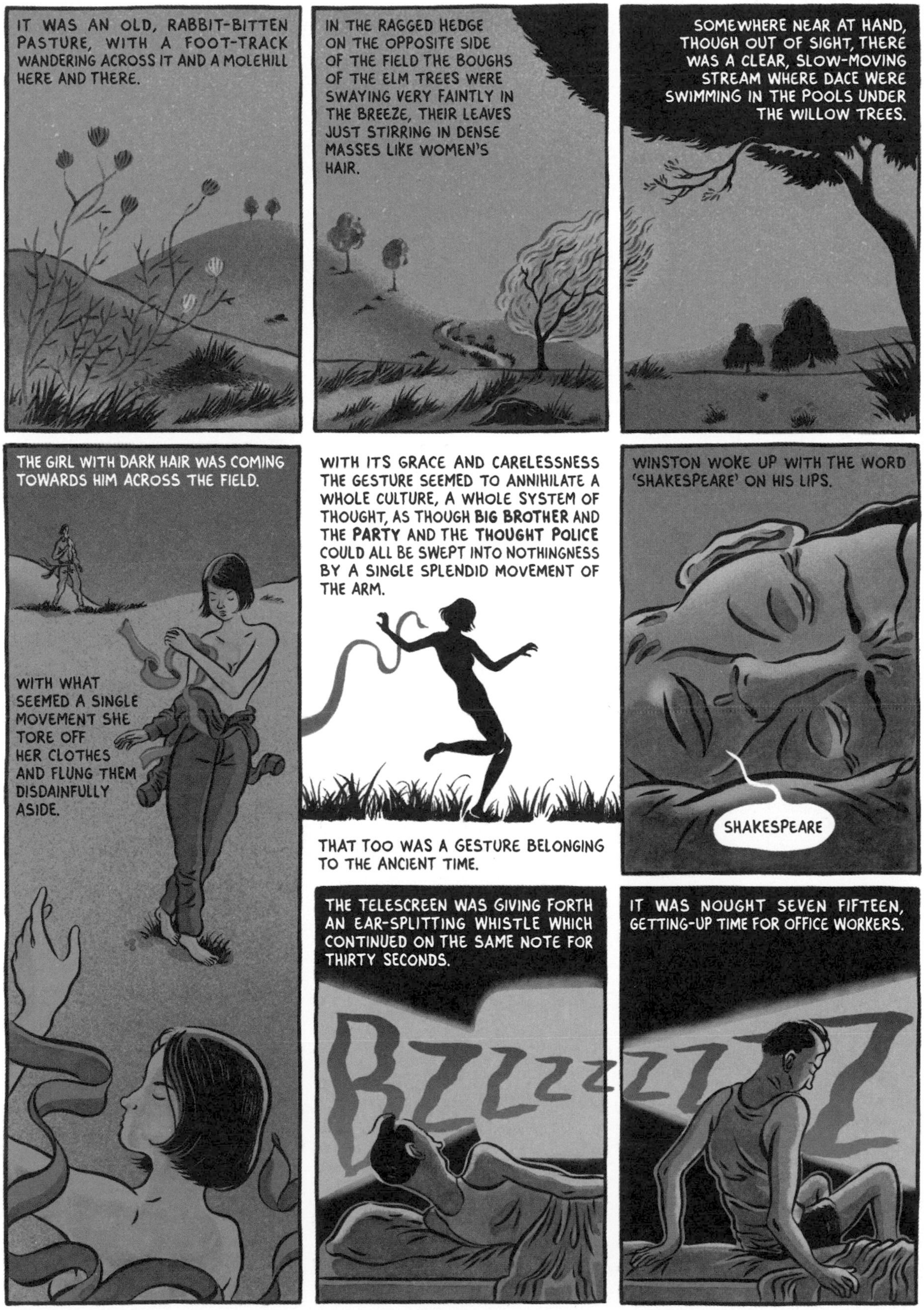
IT WAS AN OLD, RABBIT-BITTEN PASTURE, WITH A FOOT-TRACK WANDERING ACROSS IT AND A MOLEHILL HERE AND THERE.
IN THE RAGGED HEDGE ON THE OPPOSITE SIDE OF THE FIELD THE BOUGHS OF THE ELM TREES WERE SWAYING VERY FAINTLY IN THE BREEZE, THEIR LEAVES JUST STIRRING IN DENSE MASSES LIKE WOMEN'S HAIR.
SOMEWHERE NEAR AT HAND, THOUGH OUT OF SIGHT, THERE WAS A CLEAR, SLOW-MOVING STREAM WHERE DACE WERE SWIMMING IN THE POOLS UNDER THE WILLOW TREES.
THE GIRL WITH DARK HAIR WAS COMING TOWARDS HIM ACROSS THE FIELD.
WITH WHAT SEEMED A SINGLE MOVEMENT SHE TORE OFF HER CLOTHES AND FLUNG THEM DISDAINFULLY ASIDE.
WITH ITS GRACE AND CARELESSNESS THE GESTURE SEEMED TO ANNIHILATE A WHOLE CULTURE, A WHOLE SYSTEM OF THOUGHT, AS THOUGH **BIG BROTHER** AND THE **PARTY** AND THE **THOUGHT POLICE** COULD ALL BE SWEPT INTO NOTHINGNESS BY A SINGLE SPLENDID MOVEMENT OF THE ARM.
THAT TOO WAS A GESTURE BELONGING TO THE ANCIENT TIME.
WINSTON WOKE UP WITH THE WORD 'SHAKESPEARE' ON HIS LIPS.
SHAKESPEARE
THE TELESCREEN WAS GIVING FORTH AN EAR-SPLITTING WHISTLE WHICH CONTINUED ON THE SAME NOTE FOR THIRTY SECONDS.
BZZZZZZZ
IT WAS NOUGHT SEVEN FIFTEEN, GETTING-UP TIME FOR OFFICE WORKERS.

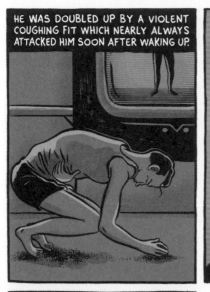

HE WAS DOUBLED UP BY A VIOLENT COUGHING FIT WHICH NEARLY ALWAYS ATTACKED HIM SOON AFTER WAKING UP.

THIRTY TO FORTY GROUP! TAKE YOUR PLACES, PLEASE. THIRTIES TO FORTIES!

ARMS BENDING AND STRETCHING! ONE, TWO, THREE, FOUR! COME ON, COMRADES, PUT A BIT OF LIFE INTO IT!

WINSTON WAS WEARING ON HIS FACE THE LOOK OF GRIM ENJOYMENT WHICH WAS CONSIDERED PROPER DURING THE **PHYSICAL JERKS.**

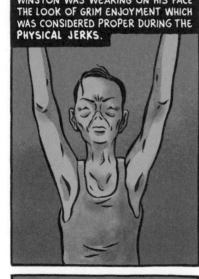

HE WAS STRUGGLING TO THINK HIS WAY BACKWARD INTO THE DIM PERIOD OF HIS EARLY CHILDHOOD.

IT WAS EXTRAORDINARILY DIFFICULT. WHEN THERE WERE NO EXTERNAL RECORDS THAT YOU COULD REFER TO, EVEN THE OUTLINE OF YOUR OWN LIFE LOST ITS SHARPNESS.

EVERYTHING HAD BEEN DIFFERENT THEN. EVEN THE NAMES OF COUNTRIES, AND THEIR SHAPES ON THE MAP, HAD BEEN DIFFERENT.

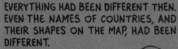

AIRSTRIP ONE, FOR INSTANCE, HAD NOT BEEN SO CALLED IN THOSE DAYS: IT HAD BEEN CALLED ENGLAND OR BRITAIN.

GREAT BRITAIN

THOUGH LONDON, HE FELT FAIRLY CERTAIN, HAD ALWAYS BEEN CALLED LONDON.

LONDON

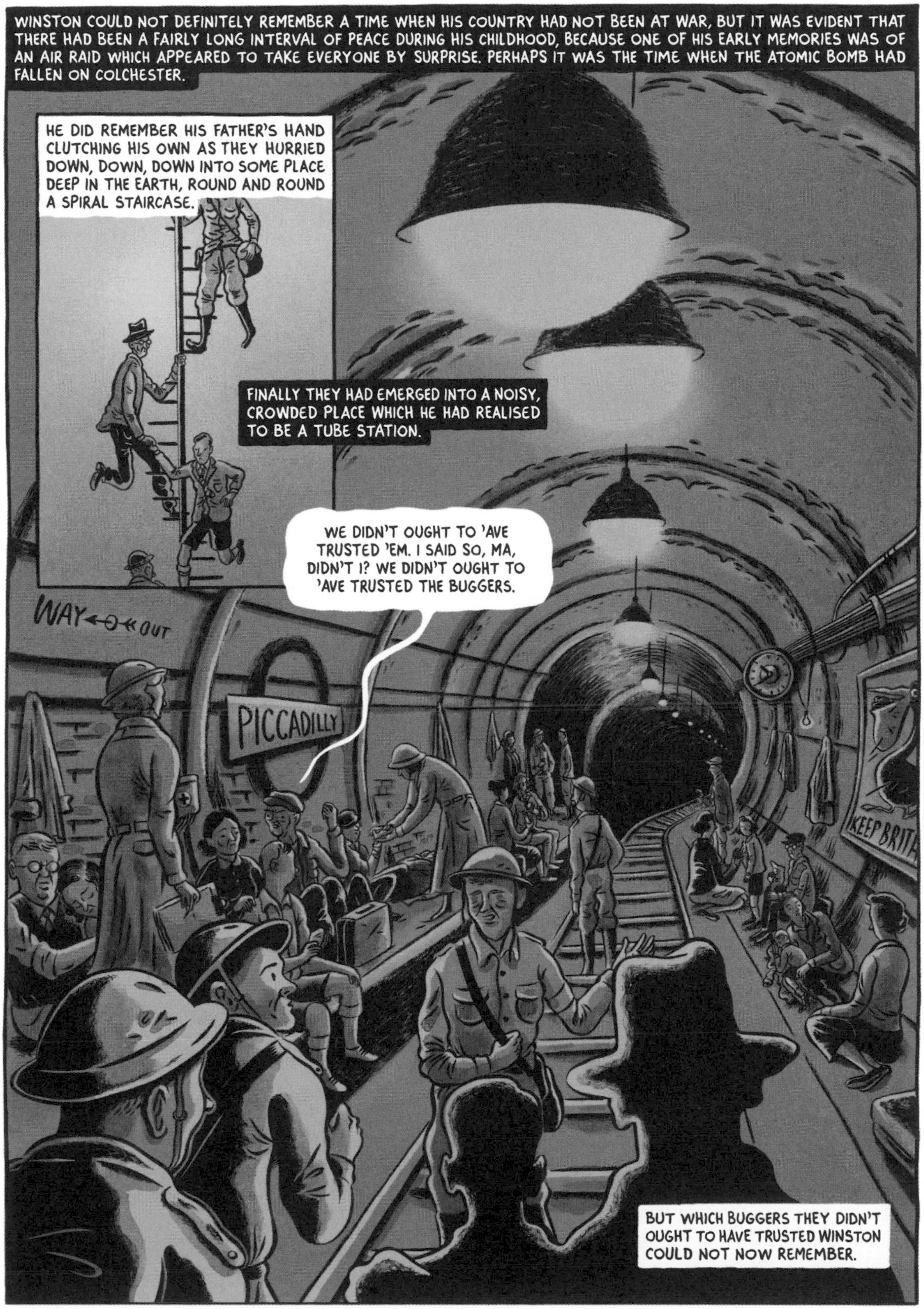
WINSTON COULD NOT DEFINITELY REMEMBER A TIME WHEN HIS COUNTRY HAD NOT BEEN AT WAR, BUT IT WAS EVIDENT THAT THERE HAD BEEN A FAIRLY LONG INTERVAL OF PEACE DURING HIS CHILDHOOD, BECAUSE ONE OF HIS EARLY MEMORIES WAS OF AN AIR RAID WHICH APPEARED TO TAKE EVERYONE BY SURPRISE. PERHAPS IT WAS THE TIME WHEN THE ATOMIC BOMB HAD FALLEN ON COLCHESTER.
HE DID REMEMBER HIS FATHER'S HAND CLUTCHING HIS OWN AS THEY HURRIED DOWN, DOWN, DOWN INTO SOME PLACE DEEP IN THE EARTH, ROUND AND ROUND A SPIRAL STAIRCASE.
FINALLY THEY HAD EMERGED INTO A NOISY, CROWDED PLACE WHICH HE HAD REALISED TO BE A TUBE STATION.
WE DIDN'T OUGHT TO 'AVE TRUSTED 'EM. I SAID SO, MA, DIDN'T I? WE DIDN'T OUGHT TO 'AVE TRUSTED THE BUGGERS.
WAY OUT
PICCADILLY
KEEP BRITA
BUT WHICH BUGGERS THEY DIDN'T OUGHT TO HAVE TRUSTED WINSTON COULD NOT NOW REMEMBER.

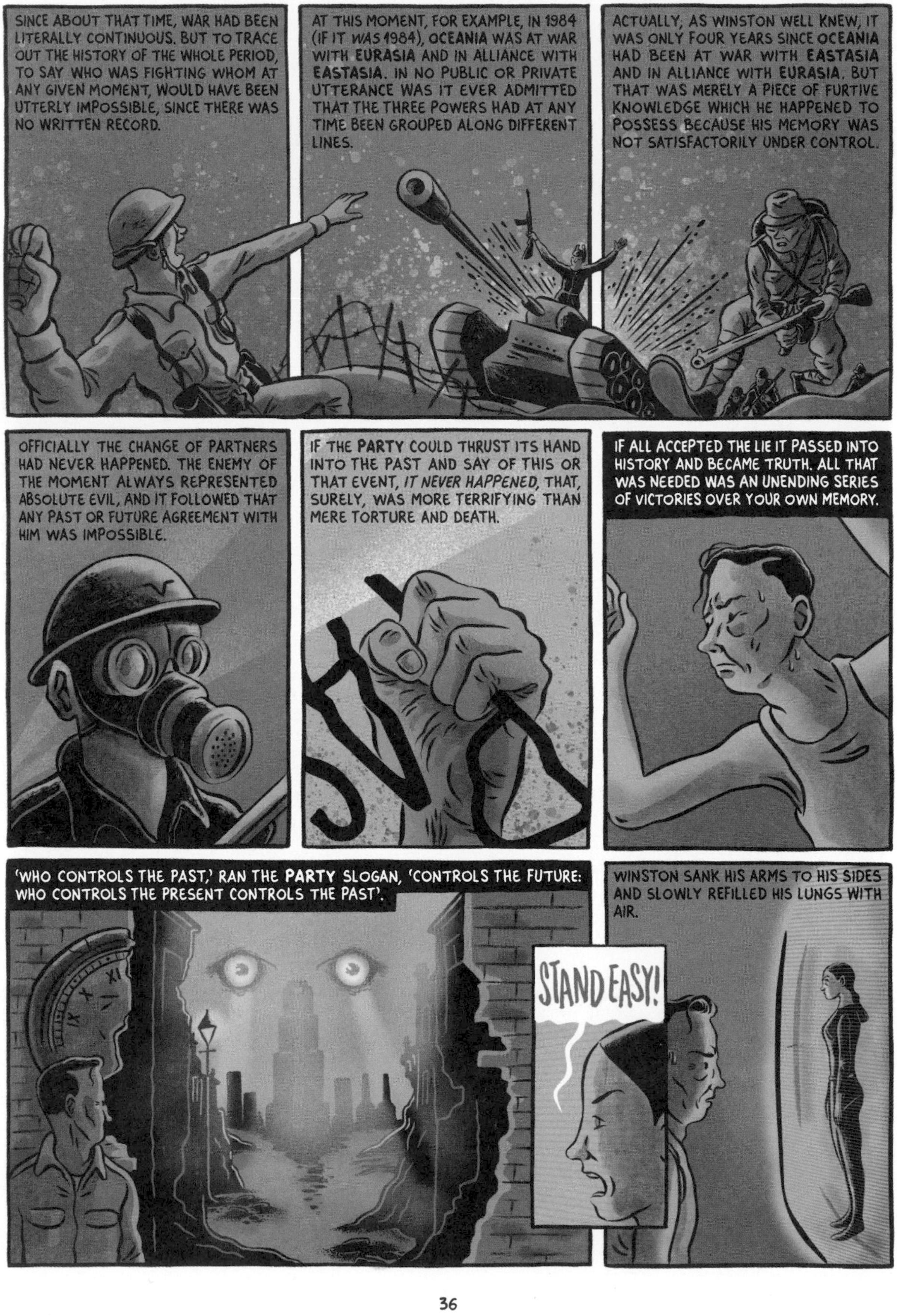
SINCE ABOUT THAT TIME, WAR HAD BEEN LITERALLY CONTINUOUS. BUT TO TRACE OUT THE HISTORY OF THE WHOLE PERIOD, TO SAY WHO WAS FIGHTING WHOM AT ANY GIVEN MOMENT, WOULD HAVE BEEN UTTERLY IMPOSSIBLE, SINCE THERE WAS NO WRITTEN RECORD.
AT THIS MOMENT, FOR EXAMPLE, IN 1984 (IF IT *WAS* 1984), **OCEANIA** WAS AT WAR WITH **EURASIA** AND IN ALLIANCE WITH **EASTASIA**. IN NO PUBLIC OR PRIVATE UTTERANCE WAS IT EVER ADMITTED THAT THE THREE POWERS HAD AT ANY TIME BEEN GROUPED ALONG DIFFERENT LINES.
ACTUALLY, AS WINSTON WELL KNEW, IT WAS ONLY FOUR YEARS SINCE **OCEANIA** HAD BEEN AT WAR WITH **EASTASIA** AND IN ALLIANCE WITH **EURASIA**. BUT THAT WAS MERELY A PIECE OF FURTIVE KNOWLEDGE WHICH HE HAPPENED TO POSSESS BECAUSE HIS MEMORY WAS NOT SATISFACTORILY UNDER CONTROL.
OFFICIALLY THE CHANGE OF PARTNERS HAD NEVER HAPPENED. THE ENEMY OF THE MOMENT ALWAYS REPRESENTED ABSOLUTE EVIL, AND IT FOLLOWED THAT ANY PAST OR FUTURE AGREEMENT WITH HIM WAS IMPOSSIBLE.
IF THE **PARTY** COULD THRUST ITS HAND INTO THE PAST AND SAY OF THIS OR THAT EVENT, *IT NEVER HAPPENED*, THAT, SURELY, WAS MORE TERRIFYING THAN MERE TORTURE AND DEATH.
IF ALL ACCEPTED THE LIE IT PASSED INTO HISTORY AND BECAME TRUTH. ALL THAT WAS NEEDED WAS AN UNENDING SERIES OF VICTORIES OVER YOUR OWN MEMORY.
'WHO CONTROLS THE PAST,' RAN THE **PARTY** SLOGAN, 'CONTROLS THE FUTURE: WHO CONTROLS THE PRESENT CONTROLS THE PAST'.
WINSTON SANK HIS ARMS TO HIS SIDES AND SLOWLY REFILLED HIS LUNGS WITH AIR.
STAND EASY!

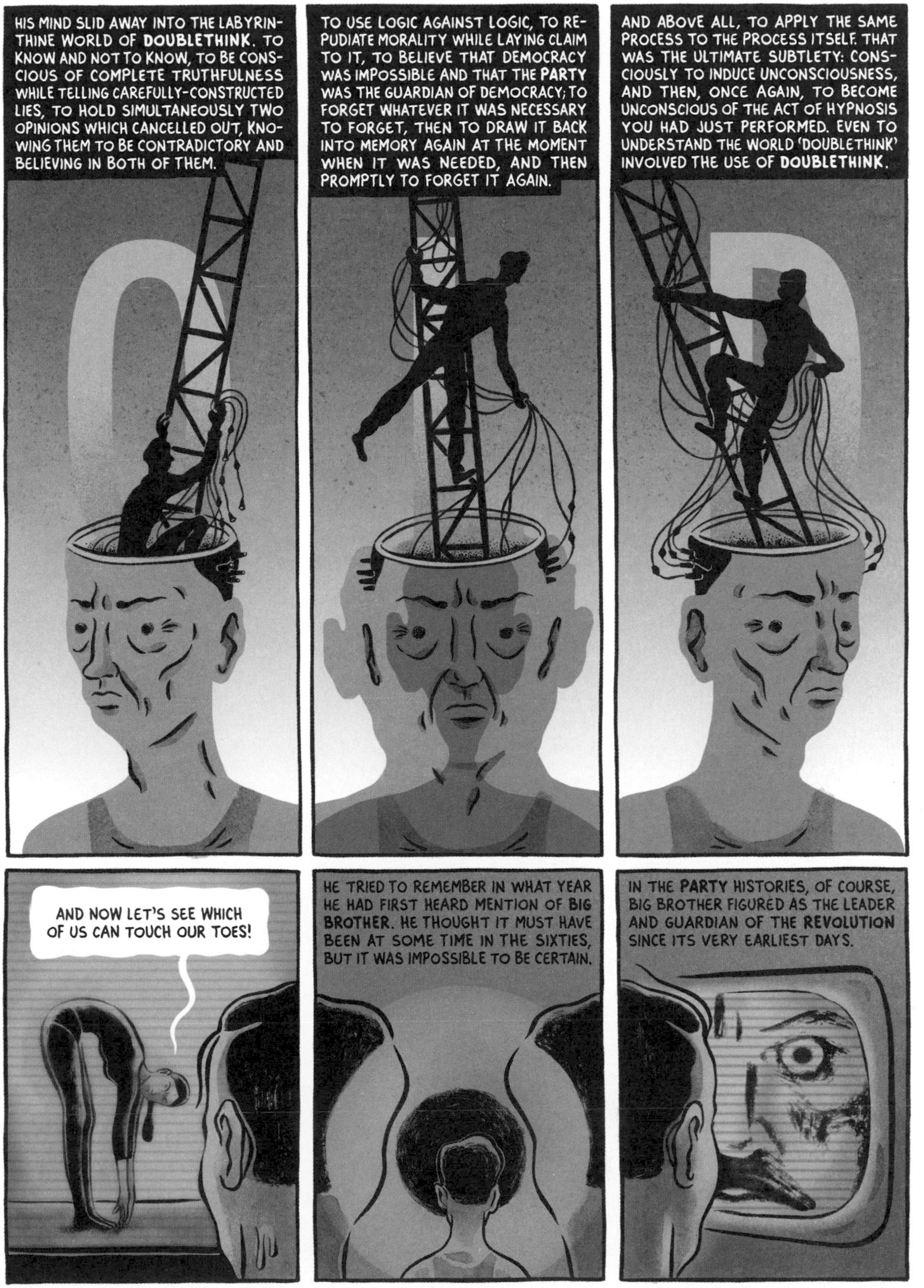

HIS MIND SLID AWAY INTO THE LABYRIN-
THINE WORLD OF **DOUBLETHINK**. TO
KNOW AND NOT TO KNOW, TO BE CONS-
CIOUS OF COMPLETE TRUTHFULNESS
WHILE TELLING CAREFULLY-CONSTRUCTED
LIES, TO HOLD SIMULTANEOUSLY TWO
OPINIONS WHICH CANCELLED OUT, KNO-
WING THEM TO BE CONTRADICTORY AND
BELIEVING IN BOTH OF THEM.

TO USE LOGIC AGAINST LOGIC, TO RE-
PUDIATE MORALITY WHILE LAYING CLAIM
TO IT, TO BELIEVE THAT DEMOCRACY
WAS IMPOSSIBLE AND THAT THE **PARTY**
WAS THE GUARDIAN OF DEMOCRACY; TO
FORGET WHATEVER IT WAS NECESSARY
TO FORGET, THEN TO DRAW IT BACK
INTO MEMORY AGAIN AT THE MOMENT
WHEN IT WAS NEEDED, AND THEN
PROMPTLY TO FORGET IT AGAIN.

AND ABOVE ALL, TO APPLY THE SAME
PROCESS TO THE PROCESS ITSELF. THAT
WAS THE ULTIMATE SUBTLETY: CONS-
CIOUSLY TO INDUCE UNCONSCIOUSNESS,
AND THEN, ONCE AGAIN, TO BECOME
UNCONSCIOUS OF THE ACT OF HYPNOSIS
YOU HAD JUST PERFORMED. EVEN TO
UNDERSTAND THE WORLD 'DOUBLETHINK'
INVOLVED THE USE OF **DOUBLETHINK**.

> AND NOW LET'S SEE WHICH
> OF US CAN TOUCH OUR TOES!

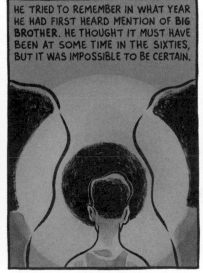

HE TRIED TO REMEMBER IN WHAT YEAR
HE HAD FIRST HEARD MENTION OF BIG
BROTHER. HE THOUGHT IT MUST HAVE
BEEN AT SOME TIME IN THE SIXTIES,
BUT IT WAS IMPOSSIBLE TO BE CERTAIN.

IN THE **PARTY** HISTORIES, OF COURSE,
BIG BROTHER FIGURED AS THE LEADER
AND GUARDIAN OF THE **REVOLUTION**
SINCE ITS VERY EARLIEST DAYS.

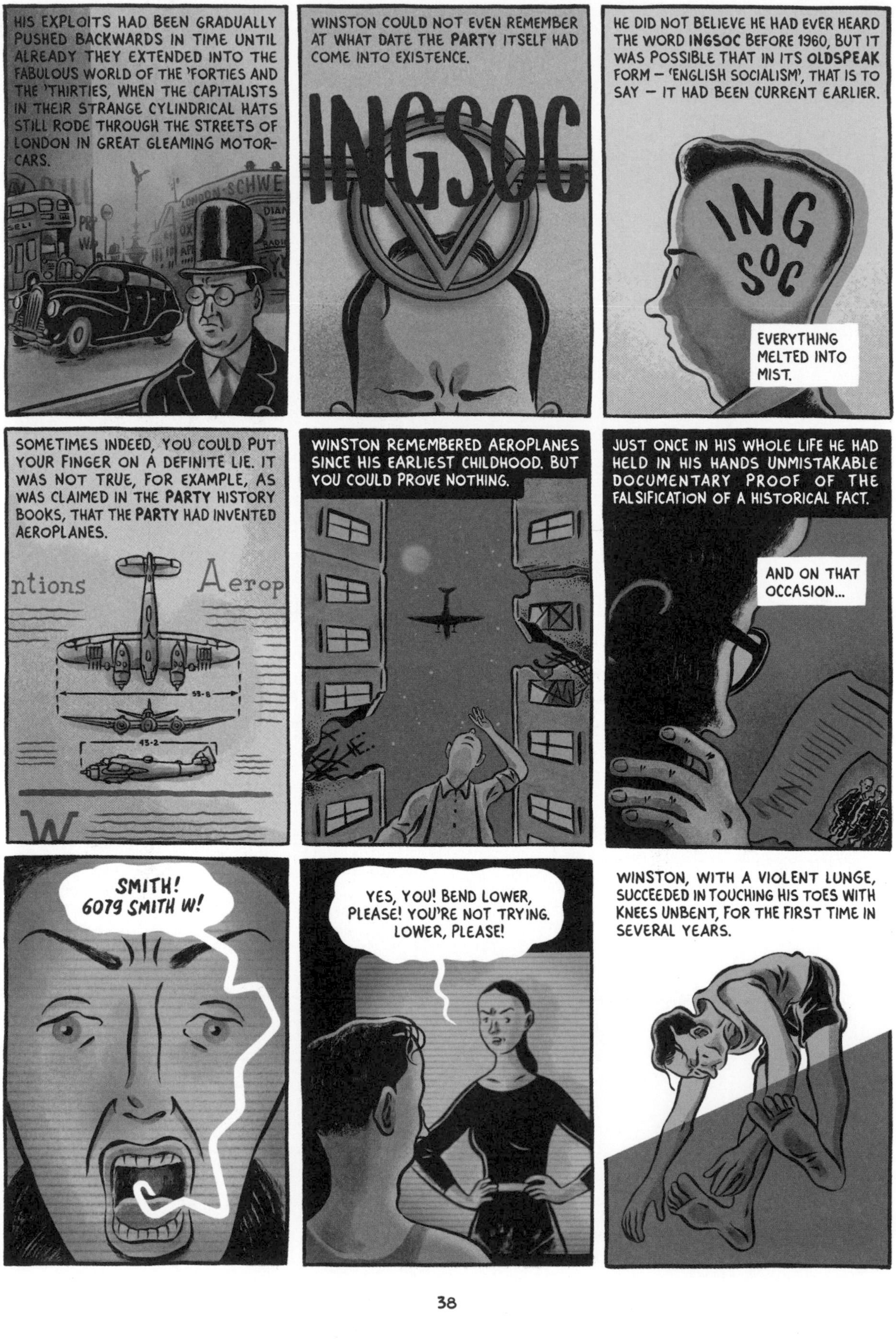
HIS EXPLOITS HAD BEEN GRADUALLY PUSHED BACKWARDS IN TIME UNTIL ALREADY THEY EXTENDED INTO THE FABULOUS WORLD OF THE 'FORTIES AND THE 'THIRTIES, WHEN THE CAPITALISTS IN THEIR STRANGE CYLINDRICAL HATS STILL RODE THROUGH THE STREETS OF LONDON IN GREAT GLEAMING MOTOR-CARS.
WINSTON COULD NOT EVEN REMEMBER AT WHAT DATE THE **PARTY** ITSELF HAD COME INTO EXISTENCE.
INGSOC
HE DID NOT BELIEVE HE HAD EVER HEARD THE WORD **INGSOC** BEFORE 1960, BUT IT WAS POSSIBLE THAT IN ITS **OLDSPEAK** FORM — 'ENGLISH SOCIALISM', THAT IS TO SAY — IT HAD BEEN CURRENT EARLIER.
ING SOC
EVERYTHING MELTED INTO MIST.
SOMETIMES INDEED, YOU COULD PUT YOUR FINGER ON A DEFINITE LIE. IT WAS NOT TRUE, FOR EXAMPLE, AS WAS CLAIMED IN THE **PARTY** HISTORY BOOKS, THAT THE **PARTY** HAD INVENTED AEROPLANES.
ntions
Aerop
WINSTON REMEMBERED AEROPLANES SINCE HIS EARLIEST CHILDHOOD. BUT YOU COULD PROVE NOTHING.
JUST ONCE IN HIS WHOLE LIFE HE HAD HELD IN HIS HANDS UNMISTAKABLE DOCUMENTARY PROOF OF THE FALSIFICATION OF A HISTORICAL FACT.
AND ON THAT OCCASION...
SMITH! 6079 SMITH W!
YES, YOU! BEND LOWER, PLEASE! YOU'RE NOT TRYING. LOWER, PLEASE!
WINSTON, WITH A VIOLENT LUNGE, SUCCEEDED IN TOUCHING HIS TOES WITH KNEES UNBENT, FOR THE FIRST TIME IN SEVERAL YEARS.

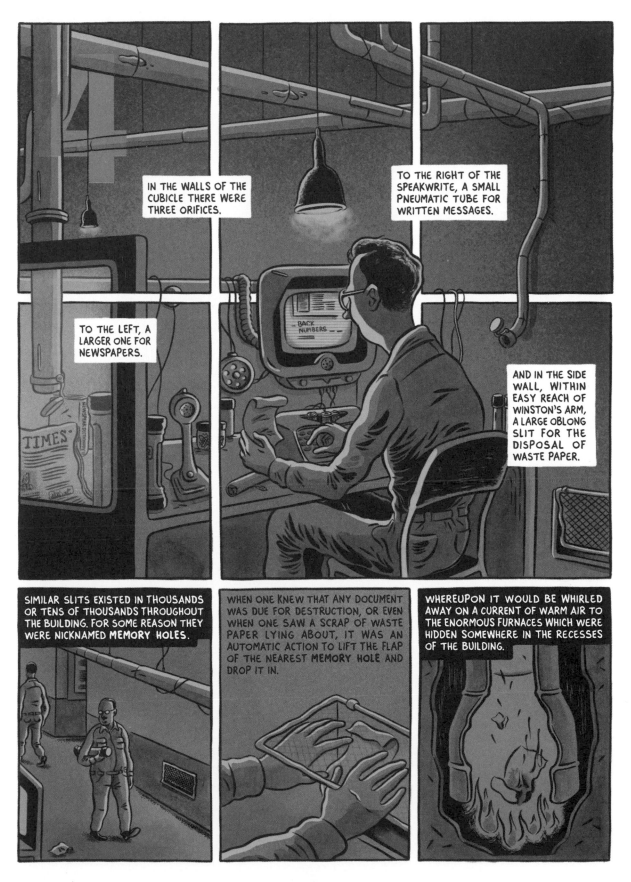

IN THE WALLS OF THE CUBICLE THERE WERE THREE ORIFICES.

TO THE RIGHT OF THE SPEAKWRITE, A SMALL PNEUMATIC TUBE FOR WRITTEN MESSAGES.

TO THE LEFT, A LARGER ONE FOR NEWSPAPERS.

AND IN THE SIDE WALL, WITHIN EASY REACH OF WINSTON'S ARM, A LARGE OBLONG SLIT FOR THE DISPOSAL OF WASTE PAPER.

SIMILAR SLITS EXISTED IN THOUSANDS OR TENS OF THOUSANDS THROUGHOUT THE BUILDING. FOR SOME REASON THEY WERE NICKNAMED **MEMORY HOLES**.

WHEN ONE KNEW THAT ANY DOCUMENT WAS DUE FOR DESTRUCTION, OR EVEN WHEN ONE SAW A SCRAP OF WASTE PAPER LYING ABOUT, IT WAS AN AUTOMATIC ACTION TO LIFT THE FLAP OF THE NEAREST MEMORY HOLE AND DROP IT IN.

WHEREUPON IT WOULD BE WHIRLED AWAY ON A CURRENT OF WARM AIR TO THE ENORMOUS FURNACES WHICH WERE HIDDEN SOMEWHERE IN THE RECESSES OF THE BUILDING.

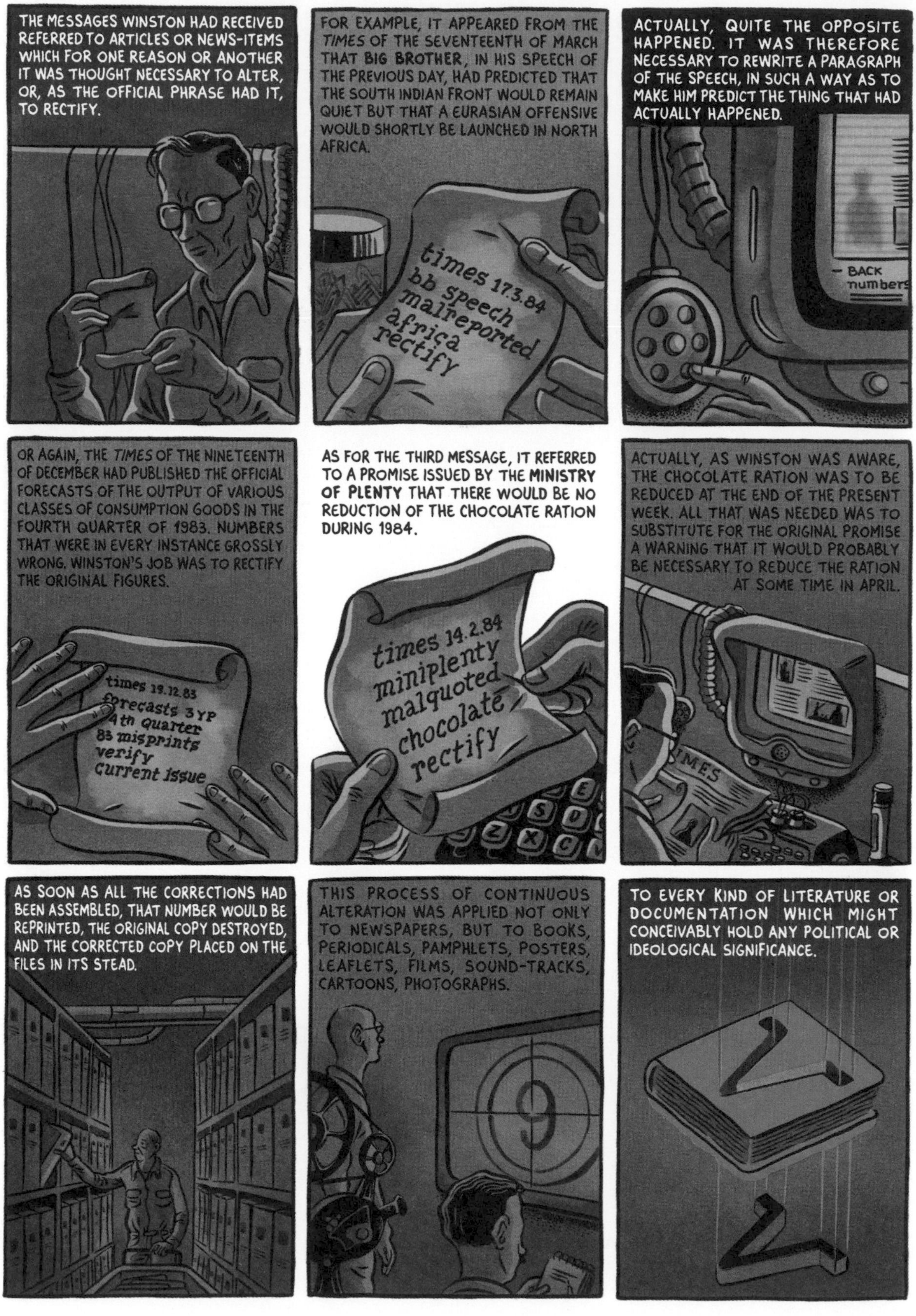
THE MESSAGES WINSTON HAD RECEIVED REFERRED TO ARTICLES OR NEWS-ITEMS WHICH FOR ONE REASON OR ANOTHER IT WAS THOUGHT NECESSARY TO ALTER, OR, AS THE OFFICIAL PHRASE HAD IT, TO RECTIFY.
FOR EXAMPLE, IT APPEARED FROM THE *TIMES* OF THE SEVENTEENTH OF MARCH THAT **BIG BROTHER**, IN HIS SPEECH OF THE PREVIOUS DAY, HAD PREDICTED THAT THE SOUTH INDIAN FRONT WOULD REMAIN QUIET BUT THAT A EURASIAN OFFENSIVE WOULD SHORTLY BE LAUNCHED IN NORTH AFRICA.
times 17.3.84 bb speech malreported africa rectify
ACTUALLY, QUITE THE OPPOSITE HAPPENED. IT WAS THEREFORE NECESSARY TO REWRITE A PARAGRAPH OF THE SPEECH, IN SUCH A WAY AS TO MAKE HIM PREDICT THE THING THAT HAD ACTUALLY HAPPENED.
– BACK numbers
OR AGAIN, THE *TIMES* OF THE NINETEENTH OF DECEMBER HAD PUBLISHED THE OFFICIAL FORECASTS OF THE OUTPUT OF VARIOUS CLASSES OF CONSUMPTION GOODS IN THE FOURTH QUARTER OF 1983. NUMBERS THAT WERE IN EVERY INSTANCE GROSSLY WRONG. WINSTON'S JOB WAS TO RECTIFY THE ORIGINAL FIGURES.
times 19.12.83 forecasts 3 YP 4th quarter 83 misprints verify current issue
AS FOR THE THIRD MESSAGE, IT REFERRED TO A PROMISE ISSUED BY THE **MINISTRY OF PLENTY** THAT THERE WOULD BE NO REDUCTION OF THE CHOCOLATE RATION DURING 1984.
times 14.2.84 miniplenty malquoted chocolate rectify
ACTUALLY, AS WINSTON WAS AWARE, THE CHOCOLATE RATION WAS TO BE REDUCED AT THE END OF THE PRESENT WEEK. ALL THAT WAS NEEDED WAS TO SUBSTITUTE FOR THE ORIGINAL PROMISE A WARNING THAT IT WOULD PROBABLY BE NECESSARY TO REDUCE THE RATION AT SOME TIME IN APRIL.
AS SOON AS ALL THE CORRECTIONS HAD BEEN ASSEMBLED, THAT NUMBER WOULD BE REPRINTED, THE ORIGINAL COPY DESTROYED, AND THE CORRECTED COPY PLACED ON THE FILES IN ITS STEAD.
THIS PROCESS OF CONTINUOUS ALTERATION WAS APPLIED NOT ONLY TO NEWSPAPERS, BUT TO BOOKS, PERIODICALS, PAMPHLETS, POSTERS, LEAFLETS, FILMS, SOUND-TRACKS, CARTOONS, PHOTOGRAPHS.
9
TO EVERY KIND OF LITERATURE OR DOCUMENTATION WHICH MIGHT CONCEIVABLY HOLD ANY POLITICAL OR IDEOLOGICAL SIGNIFICANCE.

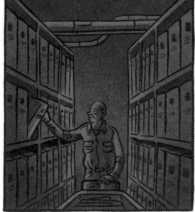

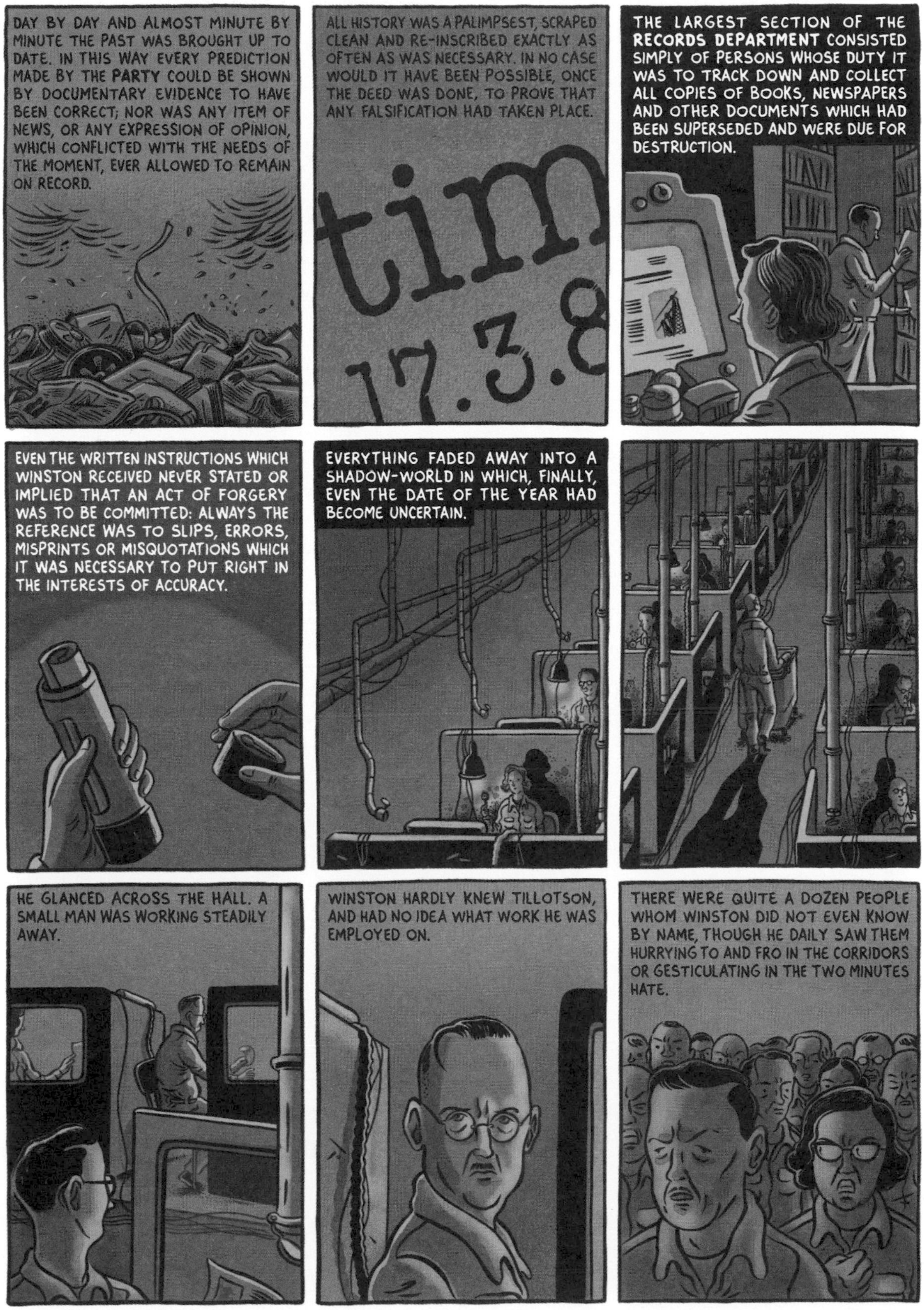
DAY BY DAY AND ALMOST MINUTE BY MINUTE THE PAST WAS BROUGHT UP TO DATE. IN THIS WAY EVERY PREDICTION MADE BY THE **PARTY** COULD BE SHOWN BY DOCUMENTARY EVIDENCE TO HAVE BEEN CORRECT; NOR WAS ANY ITEM OF NEWS, OR ANY EXPRESSION OF OPINION, WHICH CONFLICTED WITH THE NEEDS OF THE MOMENT, EVER ALLOWED TO REMAIN ON RECORD.
ALL HISTORY WAS A PALIMPSEST, SCRAPED CLEAN AND RE-INSCRIBED EXACTLY AS OFTEN AS WAS NECESSARY. IN NO CASE WOULD IT HAVE BEEN POSSIBLE, ONCE THE DEED WAS DONE, TO PROVE THAT ANY FALSIFICATION HAD TAKEN PLACE.
tim
17.3.8
THE LARGEST SECTION OF THE **RECORDS DEPARTMENT** CONSISTED SIMPLY OF PERSONS WHOSE DUTY IT WAS TO TRACK DOWN AND COLLECT ALL COPIES OF BOOKS, NEWSPAPERS AND OTHER DOCUMENTS WHICH HAD BEEN SUPERSEDED AND WERE DUE FOR DESTRUCTION.
EVEN THE WRITTEN INSTRUCTIONS WHICH WINSTON RECEIVED NEVER STATED OR IMPLIED THAT AN ACT OF FORGERY WAS TO BE COMMITTED: ALWAYS THE REFERENCE WAS TO SLIPS, ERRORS, MISPRINTS OR MISQUOTATIONS WHICH IT WAS NECESSARY TO PUT RIGHT IN THE INTERESTS OF ACCURACY.
EVERYTHING FADED AWAY INTO A SHADOW-WORLD IN WHICH, FINALLY, EVEN THE DATE OF THE YEAR HAD BECOME UNCERTAIN.
HE GLANCED ACROSS THE HALL. A SMALL MAN WAS WORKING STEADILY AWAY.
WINSTON HARDLY KNEW TILLOTSON, AND HAD NO IDEA WHAT WORK HE WAS EMPLOYED ON.
THERE WERE QUITE A DOZEN PEOPLE WHOM WINSTON DID NOT EVEN KNOW BY NAME, THOUGH HE DAILY SAW THEM HURRYING TO AND FRO IN THE CORRIDORS OR GESTICULATING IN THE TWO MINUTES HATE.

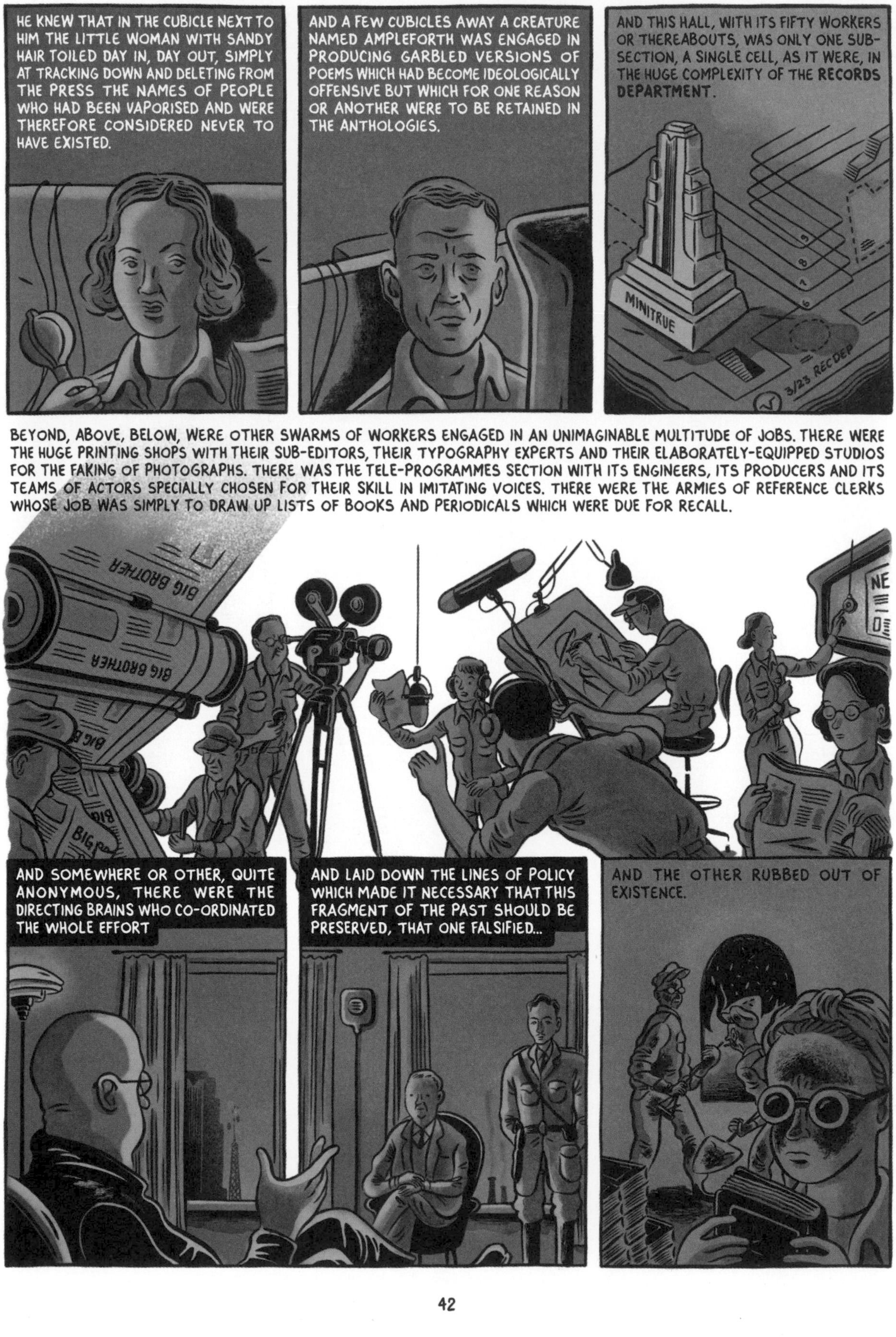
HE KNEW THAT IN THE CUBICLE NEXT TO HIM THE LITTLE WOMAN WITH SANDY HAIR TOILED DAY IN, DAY OUT, SIMPLY AT TRACKING DOWN AND DELETING FROM THE PRESS THE NAMES OF PEOPLE WHO HAD BEEN VAPORISED AND WERE THEREFORE CONSIDERED NEVER TO HAVE EXISTED.
AND A FEW CUBICLES AWAY A CREATURE NAMED AMPLEFORTH WAS ENGAGED IN PRODUCING GARBLED VERSIONS OF POEMS WHICH HAD BECOME IDEOLOGICALLY OFFENSIVE BUT WHICH FOR ONE REASON OR ANOTHER WERE TO BE RETAINED IN THE ANTHOLOGIES.
AND THIS HALL, WITH ITS FIFTY WORKERS OR THEREABOUTS, WAS ONLY ONE SUB-SECTION, A SINGLE CELL, AS IT WERE, IN THE HUGE COMPLEXITY OF THE **RECORDS DEPARTMENT**.
MINITRUE
3/23 REC DEP
BEYOND, ABOVE, BELOW, WERE OTHER SWARMS OF WORKERS ENGAGED IN AN UNIMAGINABLE MULTITUDE OF JOBS. THERE WERE THE HUGE PRINTING SHOPS WITH THEIR SUB-EDITORS, THEIR TYPOGRAPHY EXPERTS AND THEIR ELABORATELY-EQUIPPED STUDIOS FOR THE FAKING OF PHOTOGRAPHS. THERE WAS THE TELE-PROGRAMMES SECTION WITH ITS ENGINEERS, ITS PRODUCERS AND ITS TEAMS OF ACTORS SPECIALLY CHOSEN FOR THEIR SKILL IN IMITATING VOICES. THERE WERE THE ARMIES OF REFERENCE CLERKS WHOSE JOB WAS SIMPLY TO DRAW UP LISTS OF BOOKS AND PERIODICALS WHICH WERE DUE FOR RECALL.
BIG BROTHER
BIG BROTHER
AND SOMEWHERE OR OTHER, QUITE ANONYMOUS, THERE WERE THE DIRECTING BRAINS WHO CO-ORDINATED THE WHOLE EFFORT
AND LAID DOWN THE LINES OF POLICY WHICH MADE IT NECESSARY THAT THIS FRAGMENT OF THE PAST SHOULD BE PRESERVED, THAT ONE FALSIFIED...
AND THE OTHER RUBBED OUT OF EXISTENCE.

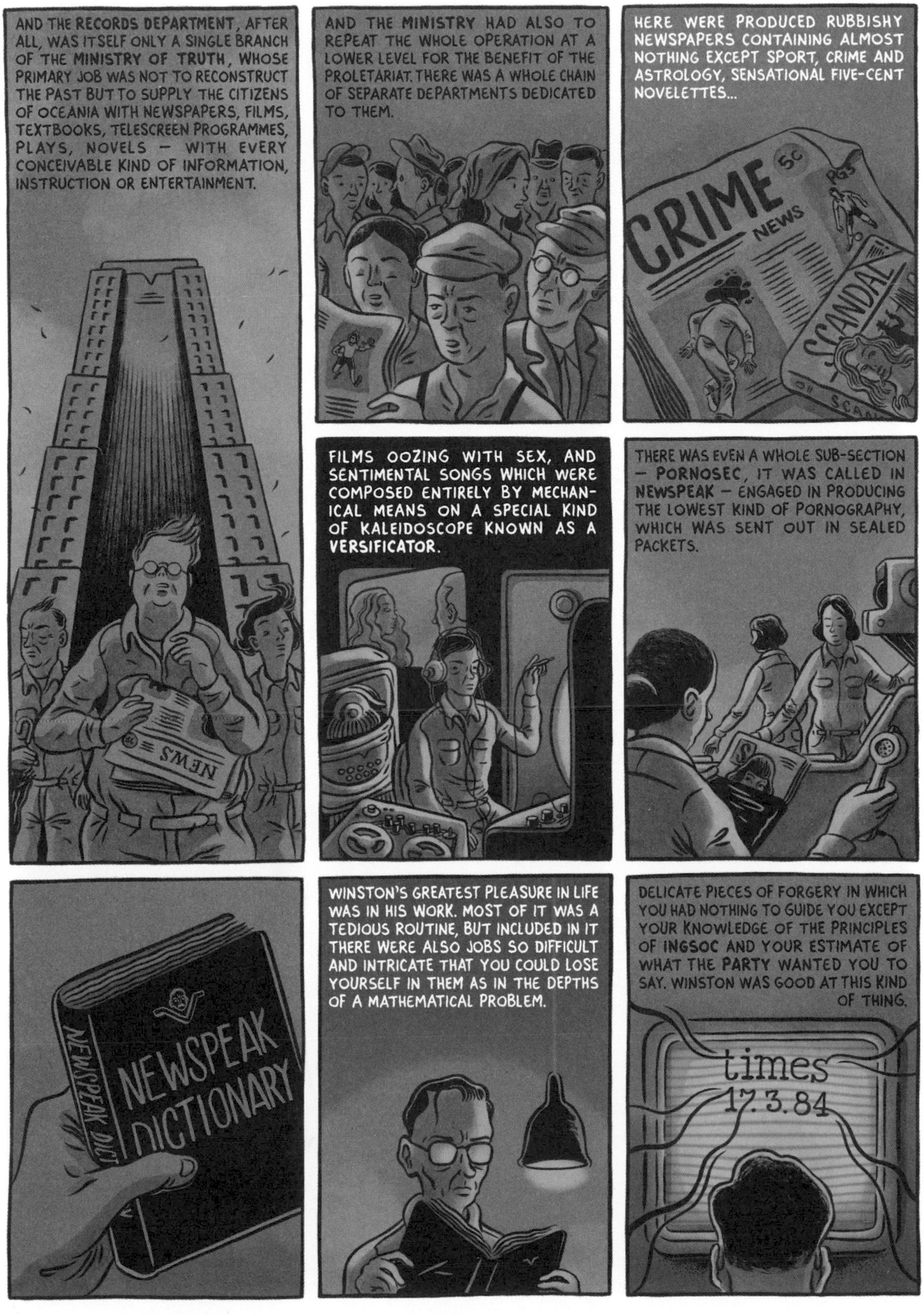
AND THE RECORDS DEPARTMENT, AFTER ALL, WAS ITSELF ONLY A SINGLE BRANCH OF THE MINISTRY OF TRUTH, WHOSE PRIMARY JOB WAS NOT TO RECONSTRUCT THE PAST BUT TO SUPPLY THE CITIZENS OF OCEANIA WITH NEWSPAPERS, FILMS, TEXTBOOKS, TELESCREEN PROGRAMMES, PLAYS, NOVELS — WITH EVERY CONCEIVABLE KIND OF INFORMATION, INSTRUCTION OR ENTERTAINMENT.
AND THE MINISTRY HAD ALSO TO REPEAT THE WHOLE OPERATION AT A LOWER LEVEL FOR THE BENEFIT OF THE PROLETARIAT. THERE WAS A WHOLE CHAIN OF SEPARATE DEPARTMENTS DEDICATED TO THEM.
HERE WERE PRODUCED RUBBISHY NEWSPAPERS CONTAINING ALMOST NOTHING EXCEPT SPORT, CRIME AND ASTROLOGY, SENSATIONAL FIVE-CENT NOVELETTES...
CRIME NEWS
5c
SCANDAL
FILMS OOZING WITH SEX, AND SENTIMENTAL SONGS WHICH WERE COMPOSED ENTIRELY BY MECHANICAL MEANS ON A SPECIAL KIND OF KALEIDOSCOPE KNOWN AS A VERSIFICATOR.
THERE WAS EVEN A WHOLE SUB-SECTION — PORNOSEC, IT WAS CALLED IN NEWSPEAK — ENGAGED IN PRODUCING THE LOWEST KIND OF PORNOGRAPHY, WHICH WAS SENT OUT IN SEALED PACKETS.
NEWSPEAK DICTIONARY
NEWSPEAK DICT
WINSTON'S GREATEST PLEASURE IN LIFE WAS IN HIS WORK. MOST OF IT WAS A TEDIOUS ROUTINE, BUT INCLUDED IN IT THERE WERE ALSO JOBS SO DIFFICULT AND INTRICATE THAT YOU COULD LOSE YOURSELF IN THEM AS IN THE DEPTHS OF A MATHEMATICAL PROBLEM.
DELICATE PIECES OF FORGERY IN WHICH YOU HAD NOTHING TO GUIDE YOU EXCEPT YOUR KNOWLEDGE OF THE PRINCIPLES OF INGSOC AND YOUR ESTIMATE OF WHAT THE PARTY WANTED YOU TO SAY. WINSTON WAS GOOD AT THIS KIND OF THING.
times
17.3.84

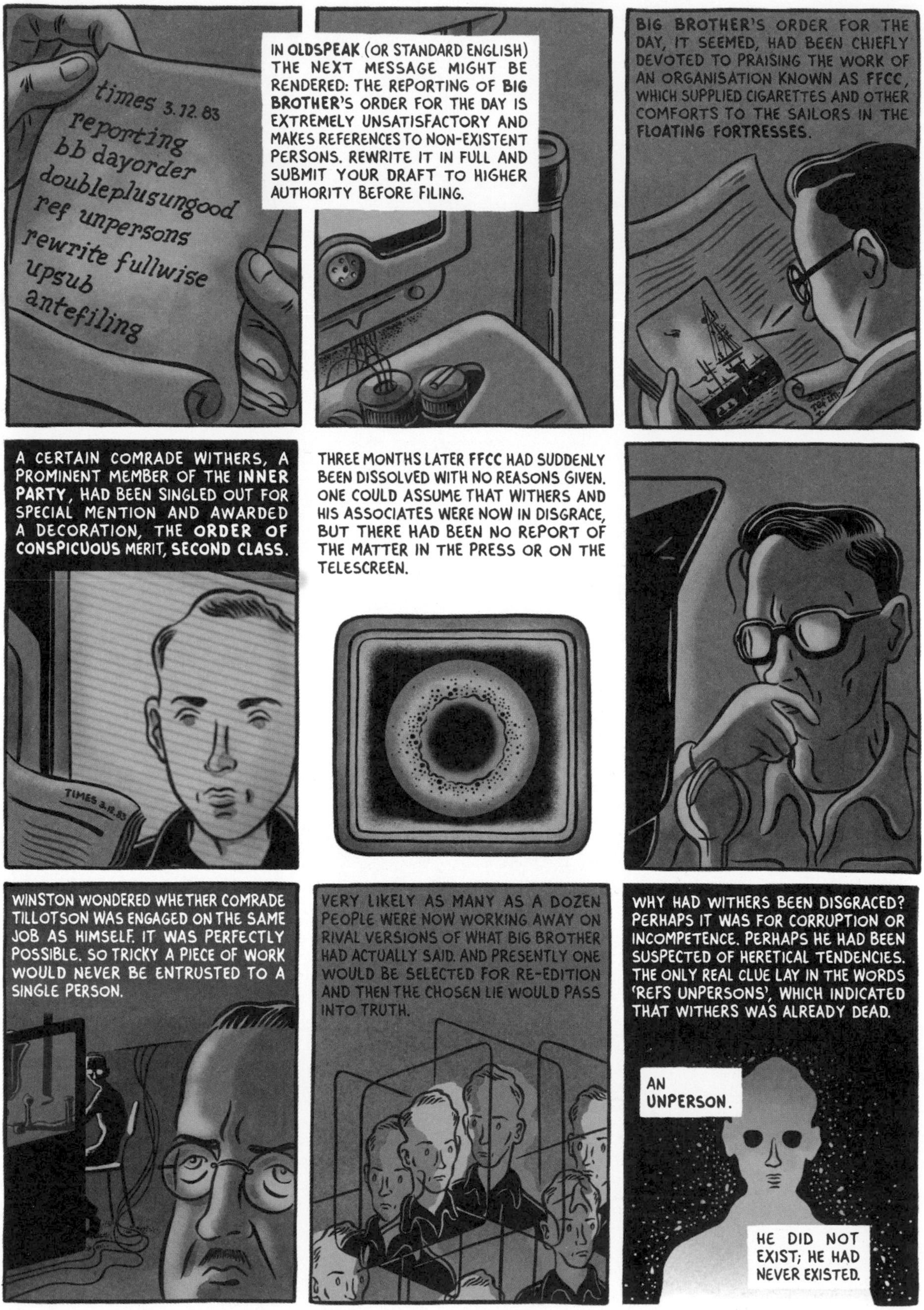
times 3.12.83
reporting
bb dayorder
doubleplusungood
ref unpersons
rewrite fullwise
upsub
antefiling
IN OLDSPEAK (OR STANDARD ENGLISH) THE NEXT MESSAGE MIGHT BE RENDERED: THE REPORTING OF BIG BROTHER'S ORDER FOR THE DAY IS EXTREMELY UNSATISFACTORY AND MAKES REFERENCES TO NON-EXISTENT PERSONS. REWRITE IT IN FULL AND SUBMIT YOUR DRAFT TO HIGHER AUTHORITY BEFORE FILING.
BIG BROTHER'S ORDER FOR THE DAY, IT SEEMED, HAD BEEN CHIEFLY DEVOTED TO PRAISING THE WORK OF AN ORGANISATION KNOWN AS FFCC, WHICH SUPPLIED CIGARETTES AND OTHER COMFORTS TO THE SAILORS IN THE FLOATING FORTRESSES.
A CERTAIN COMRADE WITHERS, A PROMINENT MEMBER OF THE INNER PARTY, HAD BEEN SINGLED OUT FOR SPECIAL MENTION AND AWARDED A DECORATION, THE ORDER OF CONSPICUOUS MERIT, SECOND CLASS.
TIMES 3.12.83
THREE MONTHS LATER FFCC HAD SUDDENLY BEEN DISSOLVED WITH NO REASONS GIVEN. ONE COULD ASSUME THAT WITHERS AND HIS ASSOCIATES WERE NOW IN DISGRACE, BUT THERE HAD BEEN NO REPORT OF THE MATTER IN THE PRESS OR ON THE TELESCREEN.
WINSTON WONDERED WHETHER COMRADE TILLOTSON WAS ENGAGED ON THE SAME JOB AS HIMSELF. IT WAS PERFECTLY POSSIBLE. SO TRICKY A PIECE OF WORK WOULD NEVER BE ENTRUSTED TO A SINGLE PERSON.
VERY LIKELY AS MANY AS A DOZEN PEOPLE WERE NOW WORKING AWAY ON RIVAL VERSIONS OF WHAT BIG BROTHER HAD ACTUALLY SAID. AND PRESENTLY ONE WOULD BE SELECTED FOR RE-EDITION AND THEN THE CHOSEN LIE WOULD PASS INTO TRUTH.
WHY HAD WITHERS BEEN DISGRACED? PERHAPS IT WAS FOR CORRUPTION OR INCOMPETENCE. PERHAPS HE HAD BEEN SUSPECTED OF HERETICAL TENDENCIES. THE ONLY REAL CLUE LAY IN THE WORDS 'REFS UNPERSONS', WHICH INDICATED THAT WITHERS WAS ALREADY DEAD.
AN UNPERSON.
HE DID NOT EXIST; HE HAD NEVER EXISTED.

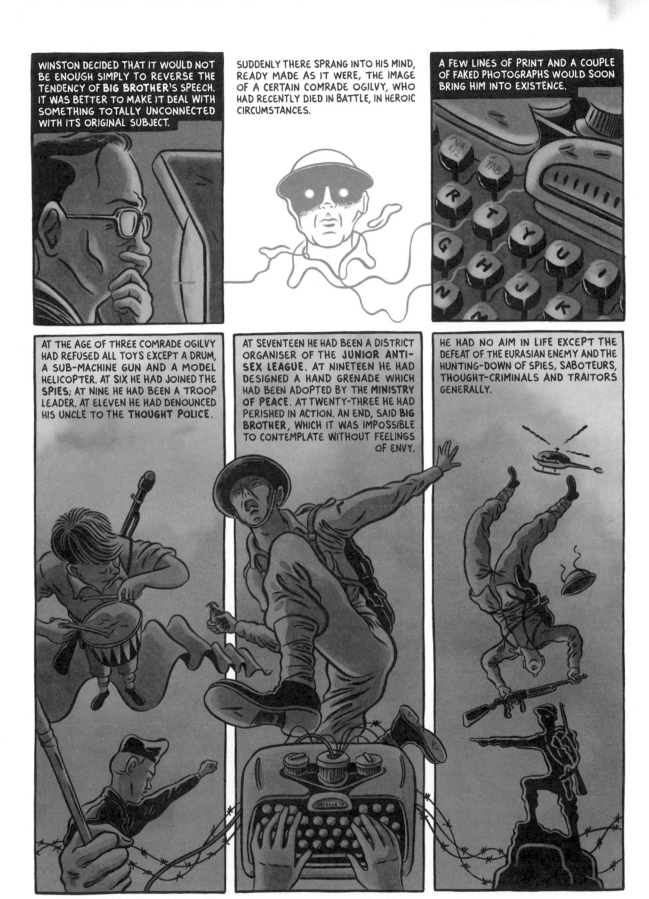

WINSTON DECIDED THAT IT WOULD NOT BE ENOUGH SIMPLY TO REVERSE THE TENDENCY OF **BIG BROTHER**'S SPEECH. IT WAS BETTER TO MAKE IT DEAL WITH SOMETHING TOTALLY UNCONNECTED WITH ITS ORIGINAL SUBJECT.

SUDDENLY THERE SPRANG INTO HIS MIND, READY MADE AS IT WERE, THE IMAGE OF A CERTAIN COMRADE OGILVY, WHO HAD RECENTLY DIED IN BATTLE, IN HEROIC CIRCUMSTANCES.

A FEW LINES OF PRINT AND A COUPLE OF FAKED PHOTOGRAPHS WOULD SOON BRING HIM INTO EXISTENCE.

AT THE AGE OF THREE COMRADE OGILVY HAD REFUSED ALL TOYS EXCEPT A DRUM, A SUB-MACHINE GUN AND A MODEL HELICOPTER. AT SIX HE HAD JOINED THE **SPIES**; AT NINE HE HAD BEEN A TROOP LEADER. AT ELEVEN HE HAD DENOUNCED HIS UNCLE TO THE **THOUGHT POLICE**.

AT SEVENTEEN HE HAD BEEN A DISTRICT ORGANISER OF THE **JUNIOR ANTI-SEX LEAGUE**. AT NINETEEN HE HAD DESIGNED A HAND GRENADE WHICH HAD BEEN ADOPTED BY THE **MINISTRY OF PEACE**. AT TWENTY-THREE HE HAD PERISHED IN ACTION. AN END, SAID **BIG BROTHER**, WHICH IT WAS IMPOSSIBLE TO CONTEMPLATE WITHOUT FEELINGS OF ENVY.

HE HAD NO AIM IN LIFE EXCEPT THE DEFEAT OF THE EURASIAN ENEMY AND THE HUNTING-DOWN OF SPIES, SABOTEURS, THOUGHT-CRIMINALS AND TRAITORS GENERALLY.

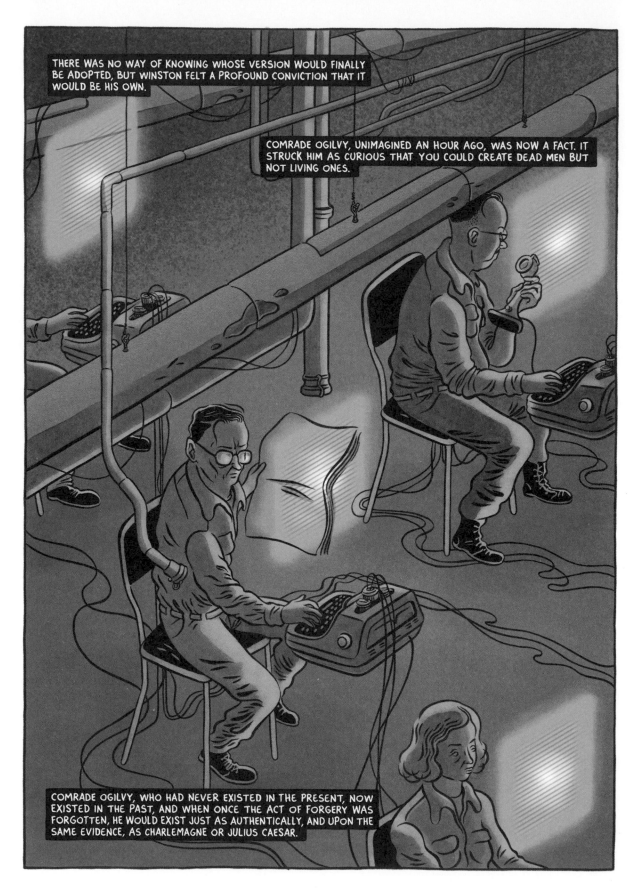

THERE WAS NO WAY OF KNOWING WHOSE VERSION WOULD FINALLY BE ADOPTED, BUT WINSTON FELT A PROFOUND CONVICTION THAT IT WOULD BE HIS OWN.

COMRADE OGILVY, UNIMAGINED AN HOUR AGO, WAS NOW A FACT. IT STRUCK HIM AS CURIOUS THAT YOU COULD CREATE DEAD MEN BUT NOT LIVING ONES.

COMRADE OGILVY, WHO HAD NEVER EXISTED IN THE PRESENT, NOW EXISTED IN THE PAST, AND WHEN ONCE THE ACT OF FORGERY WAS FORGOTTEN, HE WOULD EXIST JUST AS AUTHENTICALLY, AND UPON THE SAME EVIDENCE, AS CHARLEMAGNE OR JULIUS CAESAR.

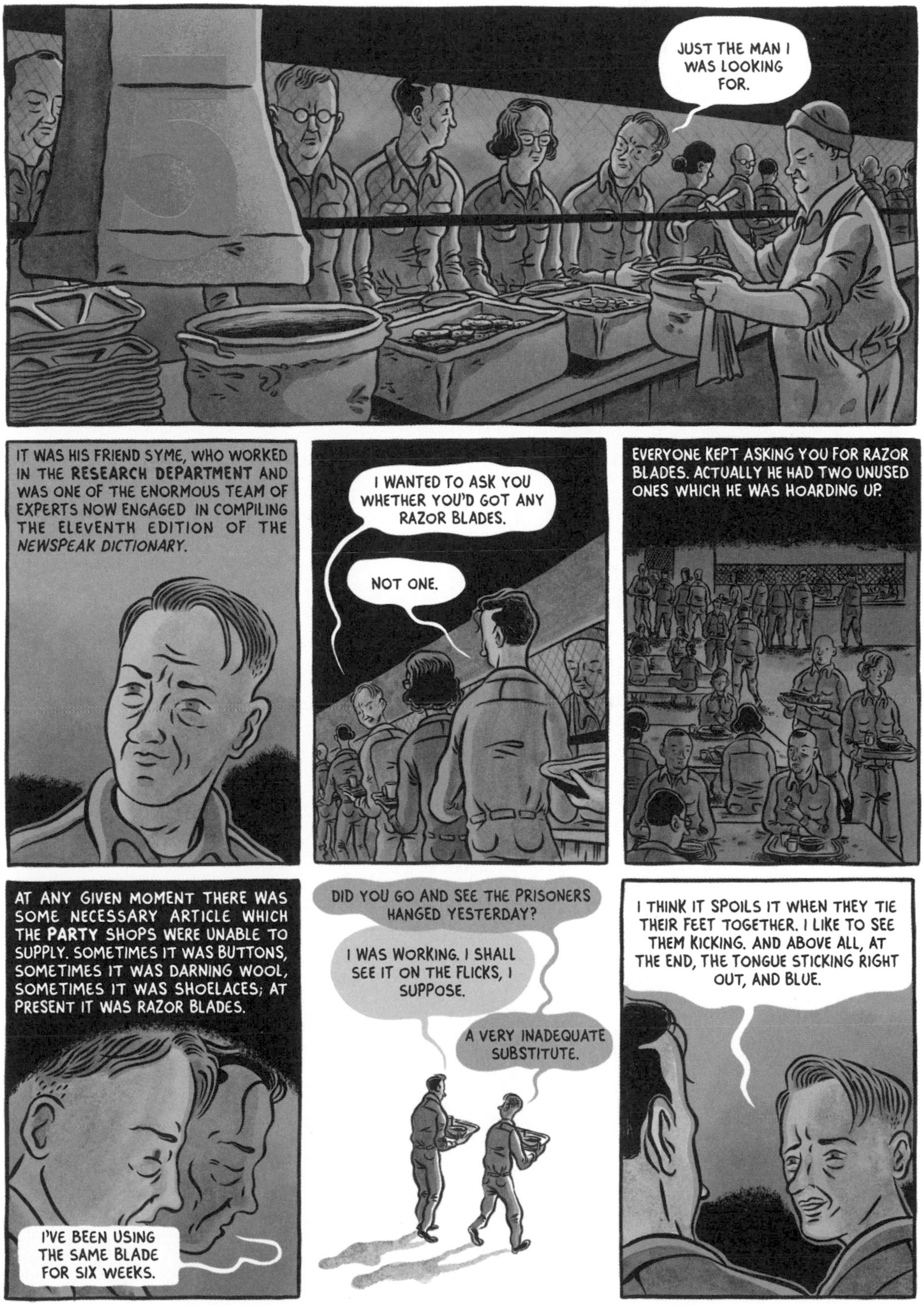
JUST THE MAN I WAS LOOKING FOR.
IT WAS HIS FRIEND SYME, WHO WORKED IN THE RESEARCH DEPARTMENT AND WAS ONE OF THE ENORMOUS TEAM OF EXPERTS NOW ENGAGED IN COMPILING THE ELEVENTH EDITION OF THE NEWSPEAK DICTIONARY.
I WANTED TO ASK YOU WHETHER YOU'D GOT ANY RAZOR BLADES.
NOT ONE.
EVERYONE KEPT ASKING YOU FOR RAZOR BLADES. ACTUALLY HE HAD TWO UNUSED ONES WHICH HE WAS HOARDING UP.
AT ANY GIVEN MOMENT THERE WAS SOME NECESSARY ARTICLE WHICH THE PARTY SHOPS WERE UNABLE TO SUPPLY. SOMETIMES IT WAS BUTTONS, SOMETIMES IT WAS DARNING WOOL, SOMETIMES IT WAS SHOELACES; AT PRESENT IT WAS RAZOR BLADES.
I'VE BEEN USING THE SAME BLADE FOR SIX WEEKS.
DID YOU GO AND SEE THE PRISONERS HANGED YESTERDAY?
I WAS WORKING. I SHALL SEE IT ON THE FLICKS, I SUPPOSE.
A VERY INADEQUATE SUBSTITUTE.
I THINK IT SPOILS IT WHEN THEY TIE THEIR FEET TOGETHER. I LIKE TO SEE THEM KICKING. AND ABOVE ALL, AT THE END, THE TONGUE STICKING RIGHT OUT, AND BLUE.

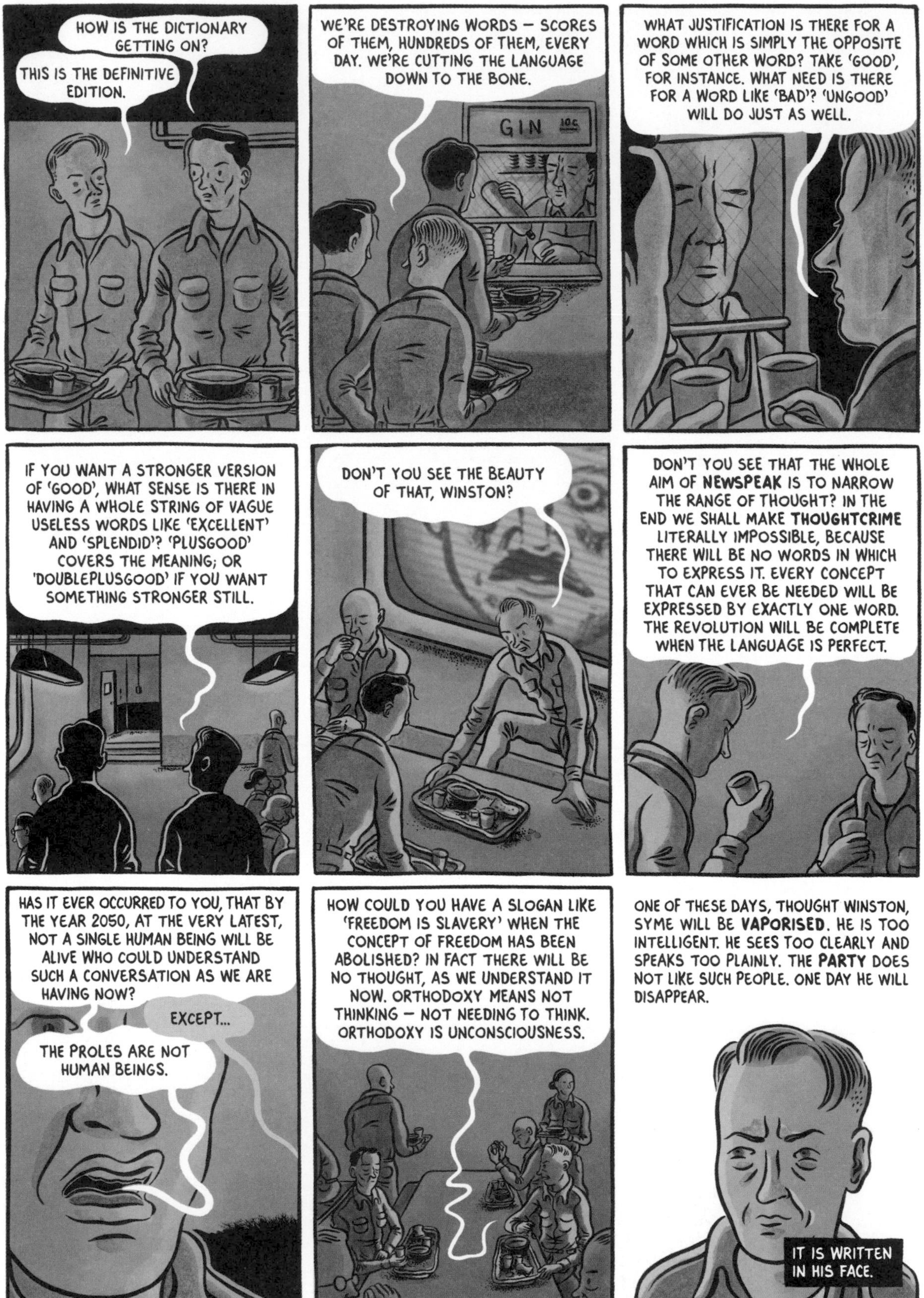
HOW IS THE DICTIONARY GETTING ON?
THIS IS THE DEFINITIVE EDITION.
WE'RE DESTROYING WORDS – SCORES OF THEM, HUNDREDS OF THEM, EVERY DAY. WE'RE CUTTING THE LANGUAGE DOWN TO THE BONE.
GIN 10¢
WHAT JUSTIFICATION IS THERE FOR A WORD WHICH IS SIMPLY THE OPPOSITE OF SOME OTHER WORD? TAKE 'GOOD', FOR INSTANCE. WHAT NEED IS THERE FOR A WORD LIKE 'BAD'? 'UNGOOD' WILL DO JUST AS WELL.
IF YOU WANT A STRONGER VERSION OF 'GOOD', WHAT SENSE IS THERE IN HAVING A WHOLE STRING OF VAGUE USELESS WORDS LIKE 'EXCELLENT' AND 'SPLENDID'? 'PLUSGOOD' COVERS THE MEANING; OR 'DOUBLEPLUSGOOD' IF YOU WANT SOMETHING STRONGER STILL.
DON'T YOU SEE THE BEAUTY OF THAT, WINSTON?
DON'T YOU SEE THAT THE WHOLE AIM OF NEWSPEAK IS TO NARROW THE RANGE OF THOUGHT? IN THE END WE SHALL MAKE THOUGHTCRIME LITERALLY IMPOSSIBLE, BECAUSE THERE WILL BE NO WORDS IN WHICH TO EXPRESS IT. EVERY CONCEPT THAT CAN EVER BE NEEDED WILL BE EXPRESSED BY EXACTLY ONE WORD. THE REVOLUTION WILL BE COMPLETE WHEN THE LANGUAGE IS PERFECT.
HAS IT EVER OCCURRED TO YOU, THAT BY THE YEAR 2050, AT THE VERY LATEST, NOT A SINGLE HUMAN BEING WILL BE ALIVE WHO COULD UNDERSTAND SUCH A CONVERSATION AS WE ARE HAVING NOW?
EXCEPT...
THE PROLES ARE NOT HUMAN BEINGS.
HOW COULD YOU HAVE A SLOGAN LIKE 'FREEDOM IS SLAVERY' WHEN THE CONCEPT OF FREEDOM HAS BEEN ABOLISHED? IN FACT THERE WILL BE NO THOUGHT, AS WE UNDERSTAND IT NOW. ORTHODOXY MEANS NOT THINKING – NOT NEEDING TO THINK. ORTHODOXY IS UNCONSCIOUSNESS.
ONE OF THESE DAYS, THOUGHT WINSTON, SYME WILL BE VAPORISED. HE IS TOO INTELLIGENT. HE SEES TOO CLEARLY AND SPEAKS TOO PLAINLY. THE PARTY DOES NOT LIKE SUCH PEOPLE. ONE DAY HE WILL DISAPPEAR.
IT IS WRITTEN IN HIS FACE.

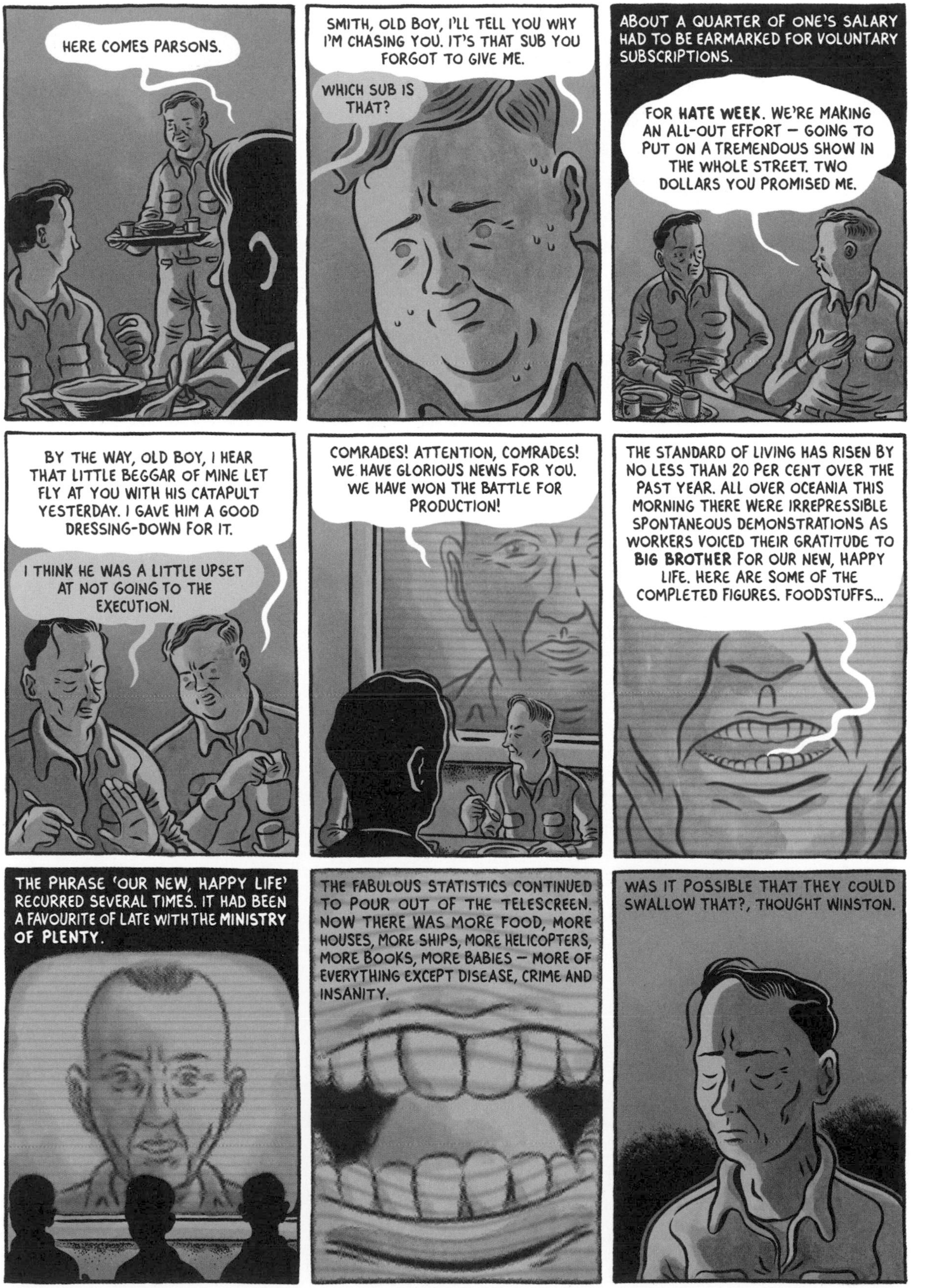
HERE COMES PARSONS.
SMITH, OLD BOY, I'LL TELL YOU WHY I'M CHASING YOU. IT'S THAT SUB YOU FORGOT TO GIVE ME.
WHICH SUB IS THAT?
ABOUT A QUARTER OF ONE'S SALARY HAD TO BE EARMARKED FOR VOLUNTARY SUBSCRIPTIONS.
FOR HATE WEEK. WE'RE MAKING AN ALL-OUT EFFORT – GOING TO PUT ON A TREMENDOUS SHOW IN THE WHOLE STREET. TWO DOLLARS YOU PROMISED ME.
BY THE WAY, OLD BOY, I HEAR THAT LITTLE BEGGAR OF MINE LET FLY AT YOU WITH HIS CATAPULT YESTERDAY. I GAVE HIM A GOOD DRESSING-DOWN FOR IT.
I THINK HE WAS A LITTLE UPSET AT NOT GOING TO THE EXECUTION.
COMRADES! ATTENTION, COMRADES! WE HAVE GLORIOUS NEWS FOR YOU. WE HAVE WON THE BATTLE FOR PRODUCTION!
THE STANDARD OF LIVING HAS RISEN BY NO LESS THAN 20 PER CENT OVER THE PAST YEAR. ALL OVER OCEANIA THIS MORNING THERE WERE IRREPRESSIBLE SPONTANEOUS DEMONSTRATIONS AS WORKERS VOICED THEIR GRATITUDE TO BIG BROTHER FOR OUR NEW, HAPPY LIFE. HERE ARE SOME OF THE COMPLETED FIGURES. FOODSTUFFS...
THE PHRASE 'OUR NEW, HAPPY LIFE' RECURRED SEVERAL TIMES. IT HAD BEEN A FAVOURITE OF LATE WITH THE MINISTRY OF PLENTY.
THE FABULOUS STATISTICS CONTINUED TO POUR OUT OF THE TELESCREEN. NOW THERE WAS MORE FOOD, MORE HOUSES, MORE SHIPS, MORE HELICOPTERS, MORE BOOKS, MORE BABIES – MORE OF EVERYTHING EXCEPT DISEASE, CRIME AND INSANITY.
WAS IT POSSIBLE THAT THEY COULD SWALLOW THAT?, THOUGHT WINSTON.

HAD LIFE ALWAYS BEEN LIKE THIS? HAD FOOD ALWAYS TASTED LIKE THIS? HE LOOKED ROUND THE CANTEEN. BATTERED METAL TABLES AND CHAIRS, BENT SPOONS, DENTED TRAYS, COARSE WHITE MUGS; ALL SURFACES GREASY.

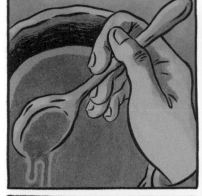

A SOURISH, COMPOSITE SMELL OF BAD GIN AND BAD COFFEE AND METALLIC STEW AND DIRTY CLOTHES.

ALWAYS IN YOUR STOMACH AND IN YOUR SKIN THERE WAS A SORT OF PROTEST, A FEELING THAT YOU HAD BEEN CHEATED OF SOMETHING THAT YOU HAD A RIGHT TO.

THERE HAD NEVER BEEN QUITE ENOUGH TO EAT, ONE HAD NEVER HAD SOCKS OR UNDERCLOTHES THAT WERE NOT FULL OF HOLES, FURNITURE HAD ALWAYS BEEN RICKETY, ROOMS UNDERHEATED, TUBE TRAINS CROWDED, WATER COLD, SOAP GRITTY. NOTHING WAS CHEAP AND PLENTIFUL EXCEPT SYNTHETIC GIN. WHY SHOULD ONE FEEL IT TO BE INTOLERABLE UNLESS ONE HAD SOME KIND OF ANCESTRAL MEMORY THAT THINGS HAD ONCE BEEN DIFFERENT?

NEARLY EVERYONE WAS UGLY, AND WOULD STILL HAVE BEEN UGLY EVEN IF DRESSED OTHERWISE THAN IN THE UNIFORM BLUE OVERALLS.

HOW EASY IT WAS, THOUGHT WINSTON, IF YOU DID NOT LOOK ABOUT YOU, TO BELIEVE THAT THE PHYSICAL TYPE SET UP BY THE **PARTY** AS AN IDEAL — TALL MUSCULAR YOUTHS AND DEEP-BOSOMED MAIDENS, BLOND-HAIRED, VITAL, SUNBURNT, CAREFREE — EXISTED AND EVEN PREDOMINATED.

ACTUALLY, SO FAR AS HE COULD JUDGE, THE MAJORITY OF PEOPLE IN **AIRSTRIP ONE** WERE SMALL AND ILL-FAVOURED.

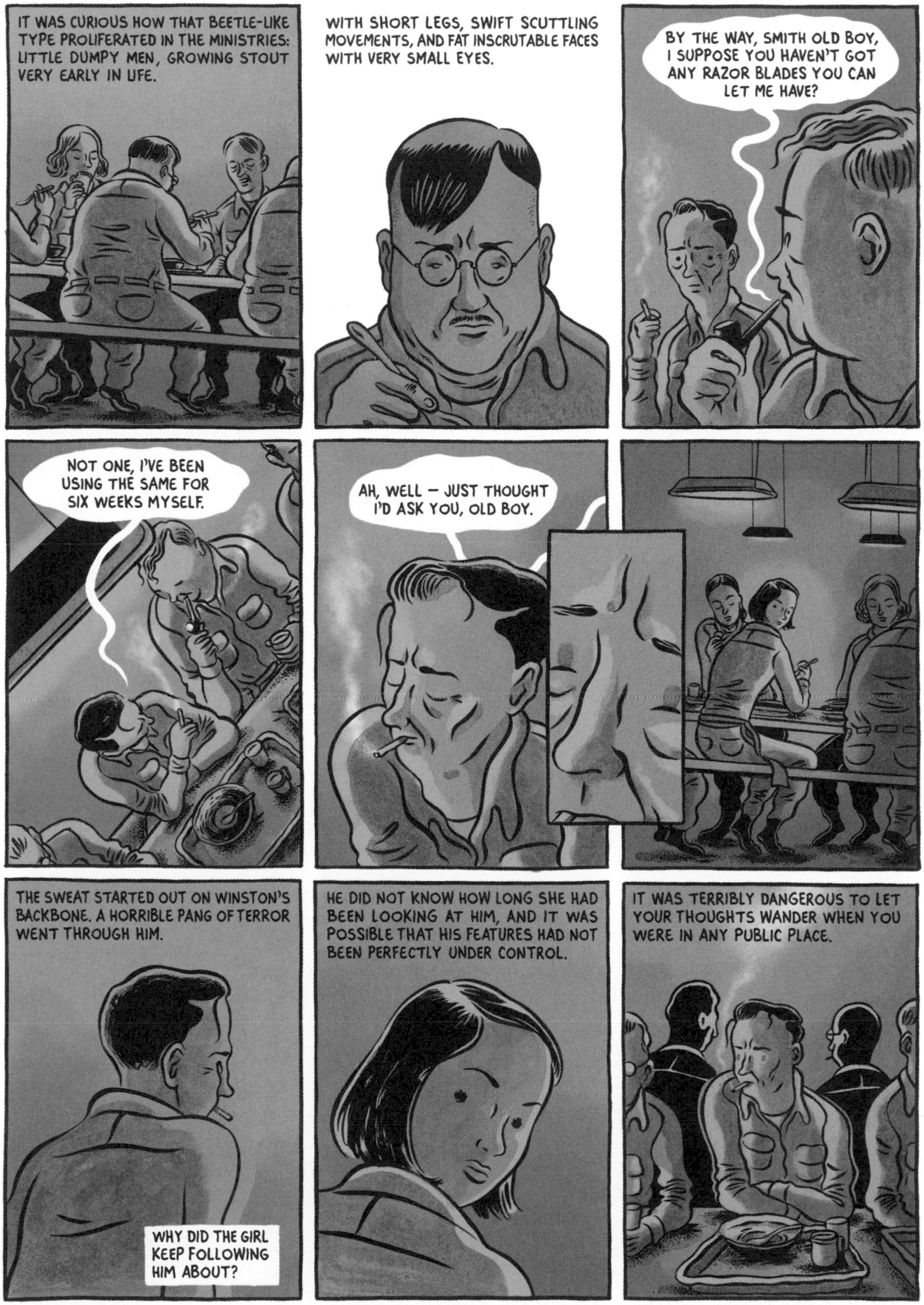
IT WAS CURIOUS HOW THAT BEETLE-LIKE TYPE PROLIFERATED IN THE MINISTRIES: LITTLE DUMPY MEN, GROWING STOUT VERY EARLY IN LIFE.
WITH SHORT LEGS, SWIFT SCUTTLING MOVEMENTS, AND FAT INSCRUTABLE FACES WITH VERY SMALL EYES.
BY THE WAY, SMITH OLD BOY, I SUPPOSE YOU HAVEN'T GOT ANY RAZOR BLADES YOU CAN LET ME HAVE?
NOT ONE, I'VE BEEN USING THE SAME FOR SIX WEEKS MYSELF.
AH, WELL — JUST THOUGHT I'D ASK YOU, OLD BOY.
THE SWEAT STARTED OUT ON WINSTON'S BACKBONE. A HORRIBLE PANG OF TERROR WENT THROUGH HIM.
WHY DID THE GIRL KEEP FOLLOWING HIM ABOUT?
HE DID NOT KNOW HOW LONG SHE HAD BEEN LOOKING AT HIM, AND IT WAS POSSIBLE THAT HIS FEATURES HAD NOT BEEN PERFECTLY UNDER CONTROL.
IT WAS TERRIBLY DANGEROUS TO LET YOUR THOUGHTS WANDER WHEN YOU WERE IN ANY PUBLIC PLACE.

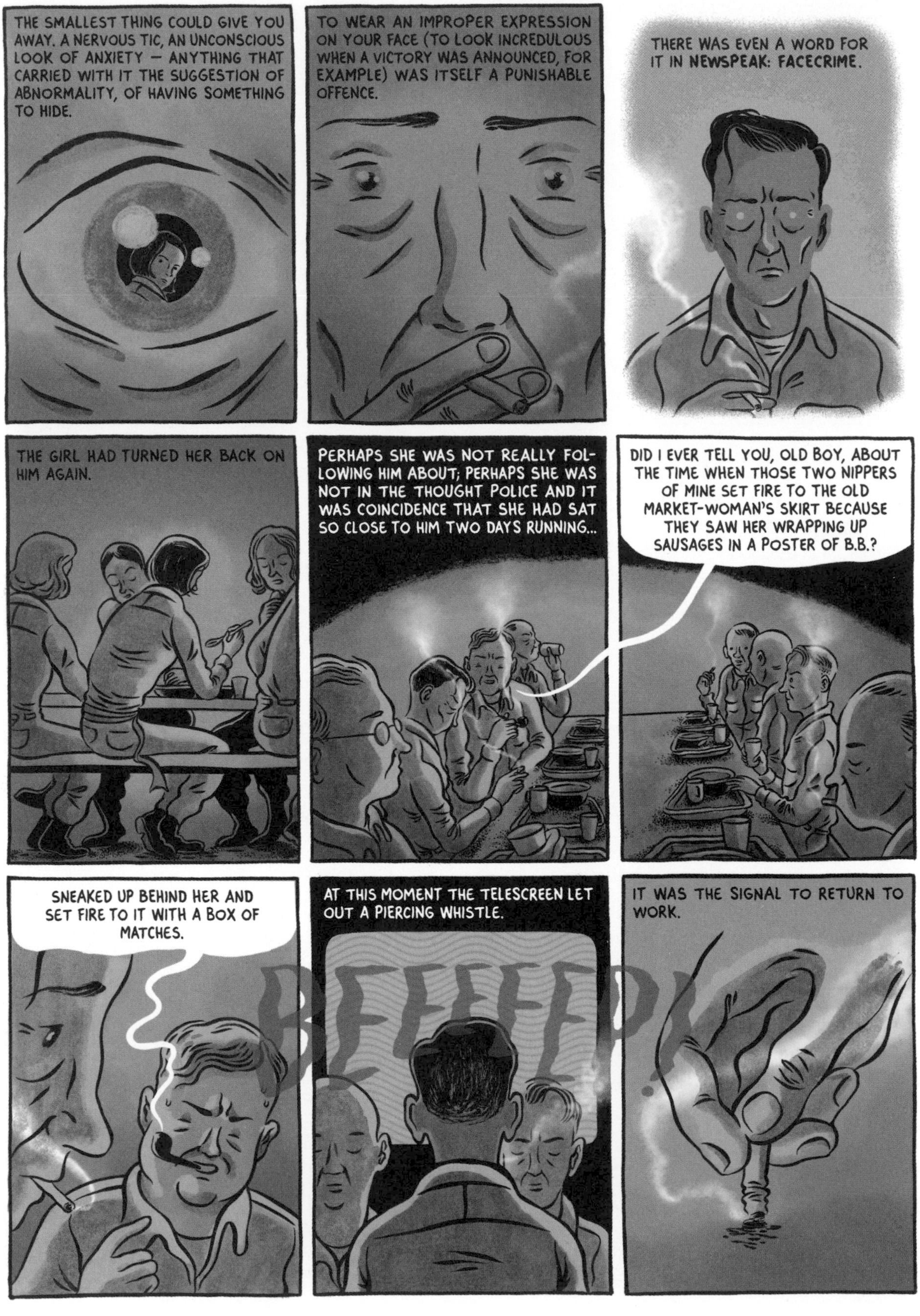
THE SMALLEST THING COULD GIVE YOU AWAY. A NERVOUS TIC, AN UNCONSCIOUS LOOK OF ANXIETY — ANYTHING THAT CARRIED WITH IT THE SUGGESTION OF ABNORMALITY, OF HAVING SOMETHING TO HIDE.
TO WEAR AN IMPROPER EXPRESSION ON YOUR FACE (TO LOOK INCREDULOUS WHEN A VICTORY WAS ANNOUNCED, FOR EXAMPLE) WAS ITSELF A PUNISHABLE OFFENCE.
THERE WAS EVEN A WORD FOR IT IN NEWSPEAK: FACECRIME.
THE GIRL HAD TURNED HER BACK ON HIM AGAIN.
PERHAPS SHE WAS NOT REALLY FOLLOWING HIM ABOUT; PERHAPS SHE WAS NOT IN THE THOUGHT POLICE AND IT WAS COINCIDENCE THAT SHE HAD SAT SO CLOSE TO HIM TWO DAYS RUNNING...
DID I EVER TELL YOU, OLD BOY, ABOUT THE TIME WHEN THOSE TWO NIPPERS OF MINE SET FIRE TO THE OLD MARKET-WOMAN'S SKIRT BECAUSE THEY SAW HER WRAPPING UP SAUSAGES IN A POSTER OF B.B.?
SNEAKED UP BEHIND HER AND SET FIRE TO IT WITH A BOX OF MATCHES.
AT THIS MOMENT THE TELESCREEN LET OUT A PIERCING WHISTLE.
BEEEEEP!
IT WAS THE SIGNAL TO RETURN TO WORK.

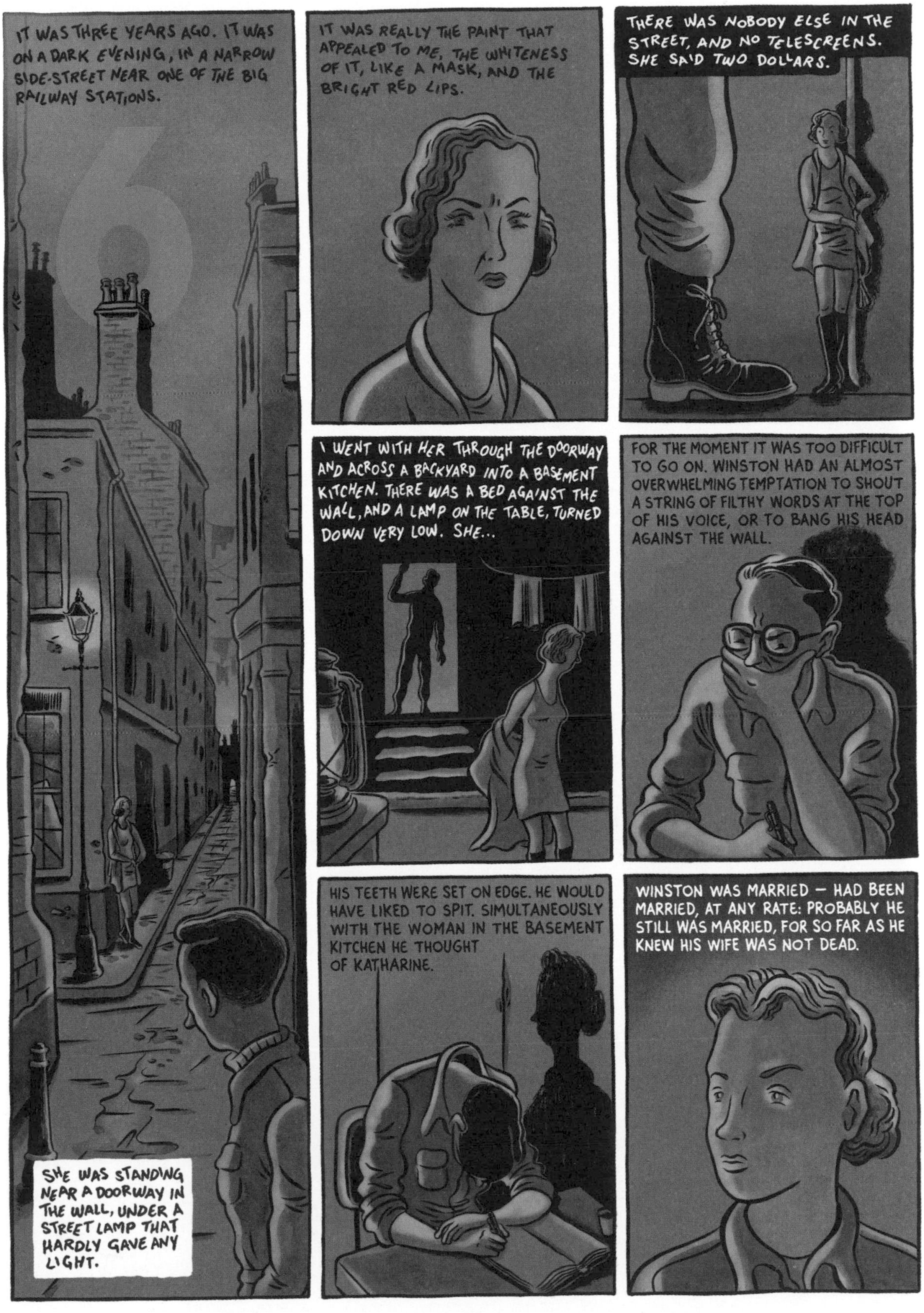
IT WAS THREE YEARS AGO. IT WAS ON A DARK EVENING, IN A NARROW SIDE-STREET NEAR ONE OF THE BIG RAILWAY STATIONS.
SHE WAS STANDING NEAR A DOORWAY IN THE WALL, UNDER A STREET LAMP THAT HARDLY GAVE ANY LIGHT.
IT WAS REALLY THE PAINT THAT APPEALED TO ME, THE WHITENESS OF IT, LIKE A MASK, AND THE BRIGHT RED LIPS.
THERE WAS NOBODY ELSE IN THE STREET, AND NO TELESCREENS. SHE SAID TWO DOLLARS.
I WENT WITH HER THROUGH THE DOORWAY AND ACROSS A BACKYARD INTO A BASEMENT KITCHEN. THERE WAS A BED AGAINST THE WALL, AND A LAMP ON THE TABLE, TURNED DOWN VERY LOW. SHE...
FOR THE MOMENT IT WAS TOO DIFFICULT TO GO ON. WINSTON HAD AN ALMOST OVERWHELMING TEMPTATION TO SHOUT A STRING OF FILTHY WORDS AT THE TOP OF HIS VOICE, OR TO BANG HIS HEAD AGAINST THE WALL.
HIS TEETH WERE SET ON EDGE. HE WOULD HAVE LIKED TO SPIT. SIMULTANEOUSLY WITH THE WOMAN IN THE BASEMENT KITCHEN HE THOUGHT OF KATHARINE.
WINSTON WAS MARRIED — HAD BEEN MARRIED, AT ANY RATE: PROBABLY HE STILL WAS MARRIED, FOR SO FAR AS HE KNEW HIS WIFE WAS NOT DEAD.

HE SEEMED TO BREATHE AGAIN THE WARM STUFFY ODOUR OF THE BASEMENT KITCHEN.

AN ODOUR COMPOUNDED OF BUGS AND DIRTY CLOTHES AND VILLAINOUS CHEAP SCENT, BUT NEVERTHELESS ALLURING, BECAUSE NO WOMAN OF THE **PARTY** EVER USED SCENT.

ONLY THE PROLES USED SCENT.

THAT WOMAN HAD BEEN HIS FIRST LAPSE IN TWO YEARS OR THEREABOUTS. IT WAS FORBIDDEN, OF COURSE, BUT IT WAS EASY ENOUGH, PROVIDED THAT YOU COULD AVOID BEING CAUGHT IN THE ACT.

TACITLY THE **PARTY** WAS EVEN INCLINED TO ENCOURAGE PROSTITUTION, AS AN OUTLET FOR INSTINCTS WHICH COULD NOT BE ALTOGETHER SUPPRESSED.

MERE DEBAUCHERY DID NOT MATTER VERY MUCH, SO LONG AS IT WAS FURTIVE AND JOYLESS. THE UNFORGIVABLE CRIME WAS PROMISCUITY BETWEEN **PARTY** MEMBERS.

THE AIM WAS NOT MERELY TO PREVENT MEN AND WOMEN FROM FORMING LOYALTIES WHICH IT MIGHT NOT BE ABLE TO CONTROL.

ITS REAL, UNDECLARED PURPOSE WAS TO REMOVE ALL PLEASURE FROM THE SEXUAL ACT, WHICH SHOULD BE LOOKED ON AS A SLIGHTLY DISGUSTING MINOR OPERATION, LIKE HAVING AN ENEMA.

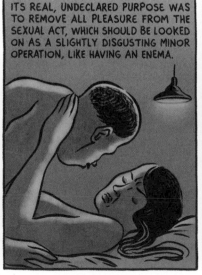

THE ONLY RECOGNISED PURPOSE OF MARRIAGE WAS TO BEGET CHILDREN FOR THE SERVICE OF THE **PARTY**.

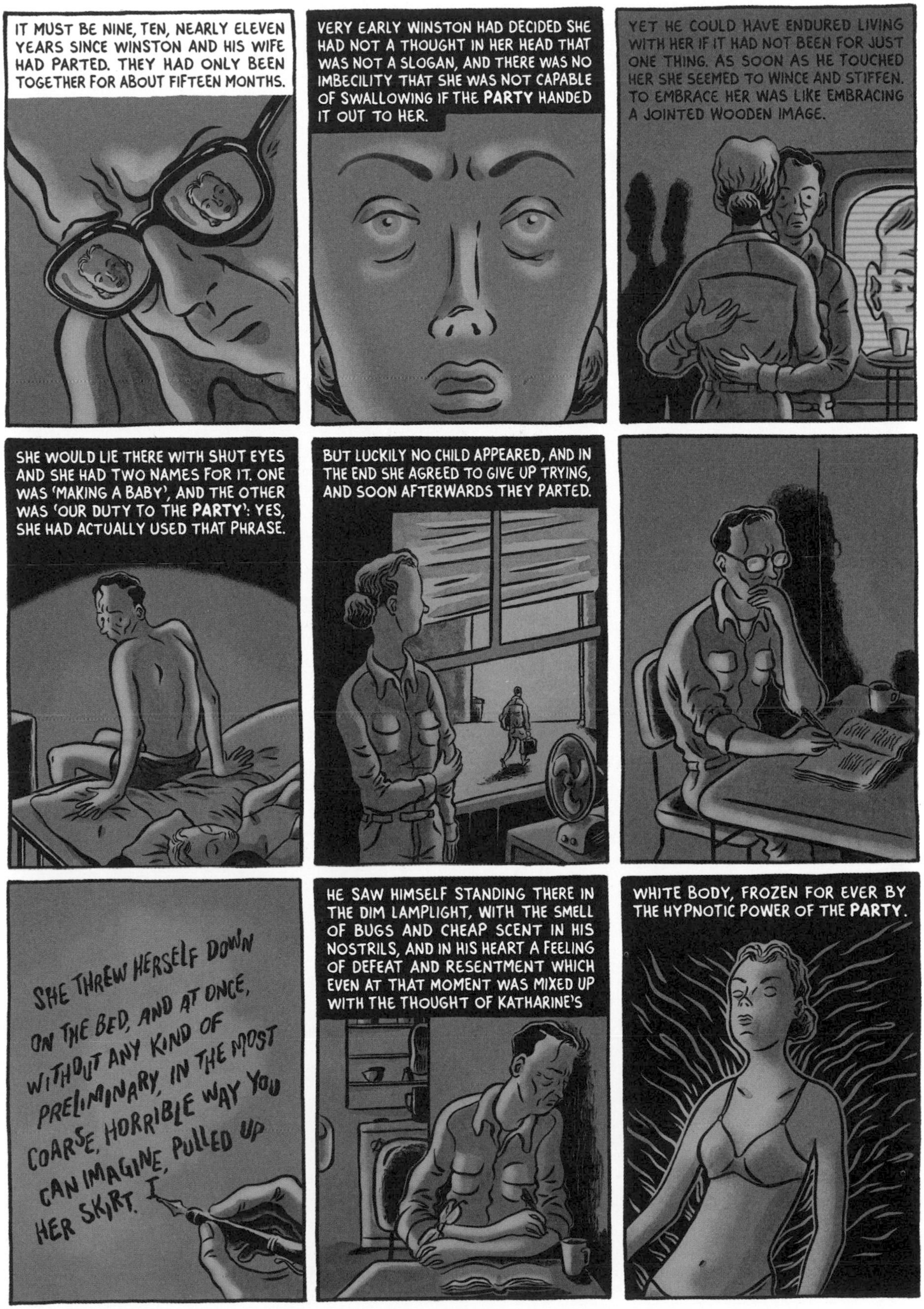
IT MUST BE NINE, TEN, NEARLY ELEVEN YEARS SINCE WINSTON AND HIS WIFE HAD PARTED. THEY HAD ONLY BEEN TOGETHER FOR ABOUT FIFTEEN MONTHS.
VERY EARLY WINSTON HAD DECIDED SHE HAD NOT A THOUGHT IN HER HEAD THAT WAS NOT A SLOGAN, AND THERE WAS NO IMBECILITY THAT SHE WAS NOT CAPABLE OF SWALLOWING IF THE PARTY HANDED IT OUT TO HER.
YET HE COULD HAVE ENDURED LIVING WITH HER IF IT HAD NOT BEEN FOR JUST ONE THING. AS SOON AS HE TOUCHED HER SHE SEEMED TO WINCE AND STIFFEN. TO EMBRACE HER WAS LIKE EMBRACING A JOINTED WOODEN IMAGE.
SHE WOULD LIE THERE WITH SHUT EYES AND SHE HAD TWO NAMES FOR IT. ONE WAS 'MAKING A BABY', AND THE OTHER WAS 'OUR DUTY TO THE PARTY': YES, SHE HAD ACTUALLY USED THAT PHRASE.
BUT LUCKILY NO CHILD APPEARED, AND IN THE END SHE AGREED TO GIVE UP TRYING, AND SOON AFTERWARDS THEY PARTED.
SHE THREW HERSELF DOWN ON THE BED, AND AT ONCE, WITHOUT ANY KIND OF PRELIMINARY, IN THE MOST COARSE, HORRIBLE WAY YOU CAN IMAGINE, PULLED UP HER SKIRT. I
HE SAW HIMSELF STANDING THERE IN THE DIM LAMPLIGHT, WITH THE SMELL OF BUGS AND CHEAP SCENT IN HIS NOSTRILS, AND IN HIS HEART A FEELING OF DEFEAT AND RESENTMENT WHICH EVEN AT THAT MOMENT WAS MIXED UP WITH THE THOUGHT OF KATHARINE'S
WHITE BODY, FROZEN FOR EVER BY THE HYPNOTIC POWER OF THE PARTY.

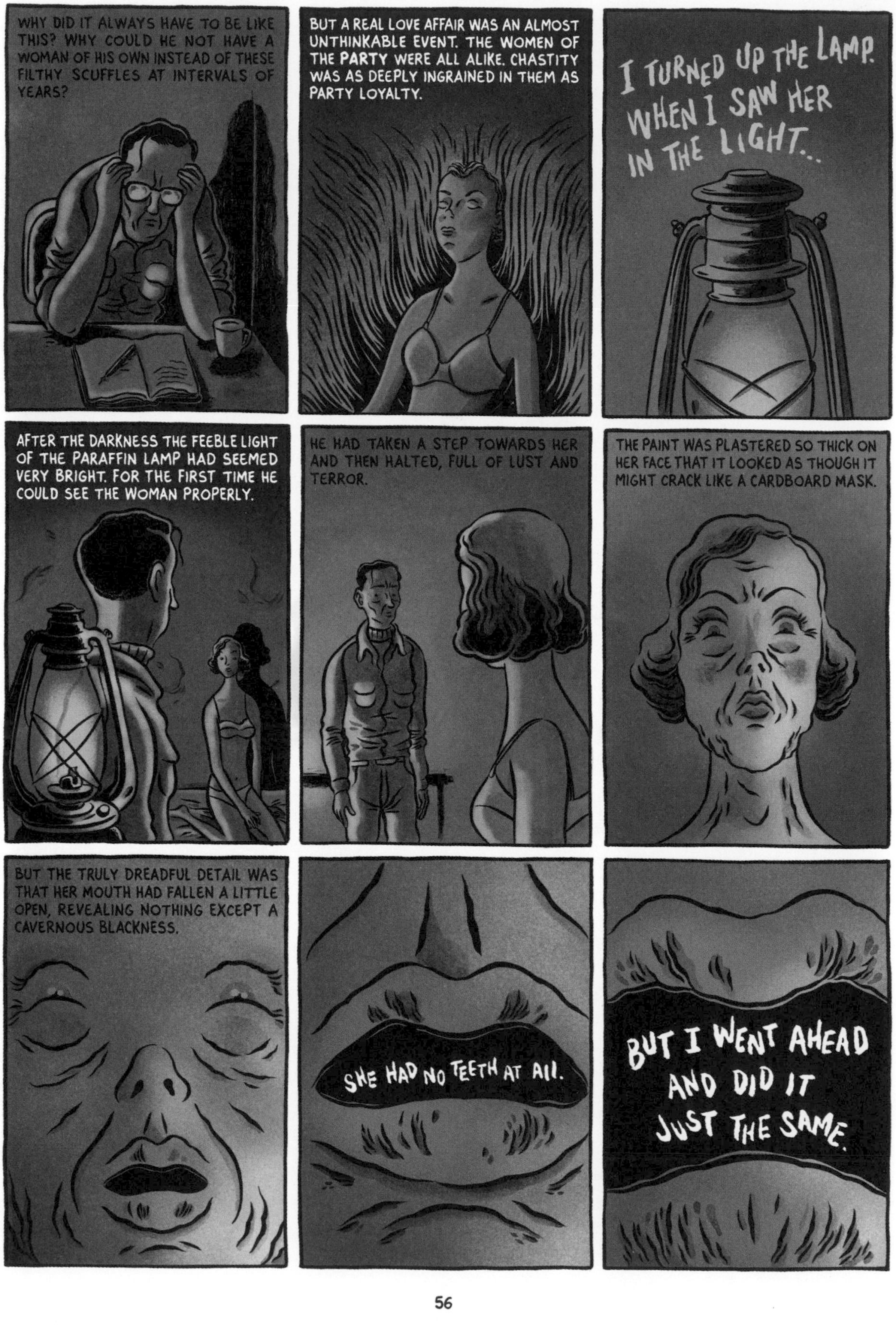
WHY DID IT ALWAYS HAVE TO BE LIKE THIS? WHY COULD HE NOT HAVE A WOMAN OF HIS OWN INSTEAD OF THESE FILTHY SCUFFLES AT INTERVALS OF YEARS?
BUT A REAL LOVE AFFAIR WAS AN ALMOST UNTHINKABLE EVENT. THE WOMEN OF THE PARTY WERE ALL ALIKE. CHASTITY WAS AS DEEPLY INGRAINED IN THEM AS PARTY LOYALTY.
I TURNED UP THE LAMP. WHEN I SAW HER IN THE LIGHT...
AFTER THE DARKNESS THE FEEBLE LIGHT OF THE PARAFFIN LAMP HAD SEEMED VERY BRIGHT. FOR THE FIRST TIME HE COULD SEE THE WOMAN PROPERLY.
HE HAD TAKEN A STEP TOWARDS HER AND THEN HALTED, FULL OF LUST AND TERROR.
THE PAINT WAS PLASTERED SO THICK ON HER FACE THAT IT LOOKED AS THOUGH IT MIGHT CRACK LIKE A CARDBOARD MASK.
BUT THE TRULY DREADFUL DETAIL WAS THAT HER MOUTH HAD FALLEN A LITTLE OPEN, REVEALING NOTHING EXCEPT A CAVERNOUS BLACKNESS.
SHE HAD NO TEETH AT ALL.
BUT I WENT AHEAD AND DID IT JUST THE SAME.

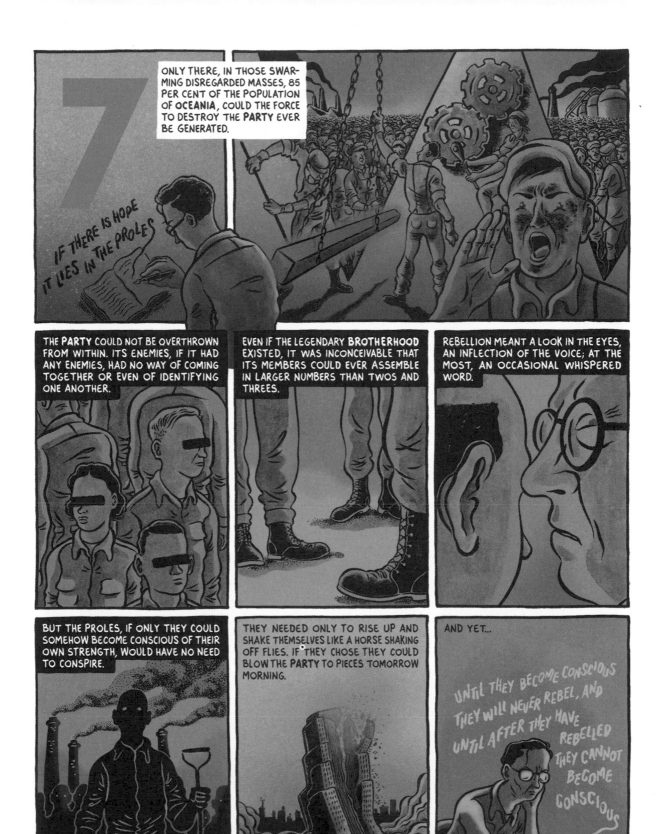

7

ONLY THERE, IN THOSE SWARMING DISREGARDED MASSES, 85 PER CENT OF THE POPULATION OF **OCEANIA**, COULD THE FORCE TO DESTROY THE **PARTY** EVER BE GENERATED.

IF THERE IS HOPE IT LIES IN THE PROLES

THE **PARTY** COULD NOT BE OVERTHROWN FROM WITHIN. ITS ENEMIES, IF IT HAD ANY ENEMIES, HAD NO WAY OF COMING TOGETHER OR EVEN OF IDENTIFYING ONE ANOTHER.

EVEN IF THE LEGENDARY **BROTHERHOOD** EXISTED, IT WAS INCONCEIVABLE THAT ITS MEMBERS COULD EVER ASSEMBLE IN LARGER NUMBERS THAN TWOS AND THREES.

REBELLION MEANT A LOOK IN THE EYES, AN INFLECTION OF THE VOICE; AT THE MOST, AN OCCASIONAL WHISPERED WORD.

BUT THE PROLES, IF ONLY THEY COULD SOMEHOW BECOME CONSCIOUS OF THEIR OWN STRENGTH, WOULD HAVE NO NEED TO CONSPIRE.

THEY NEEDED ONLY TO RISE UP AND SHAKE THEMSELVES LIKE A HORSE SHAKING OFF FLIES. IF THEY CHOSE THEY COULD BLOW THE **PARTY** TO PIECES TOMORROW MORNING.

AND YET...

UNTIL THEY BECOME CONSCIOUS THEY WILL NEVER REBEL, AND UNTIL AFTER THEY HAVE REBELLED THEY CANNOT BECOME CONSCIOUS

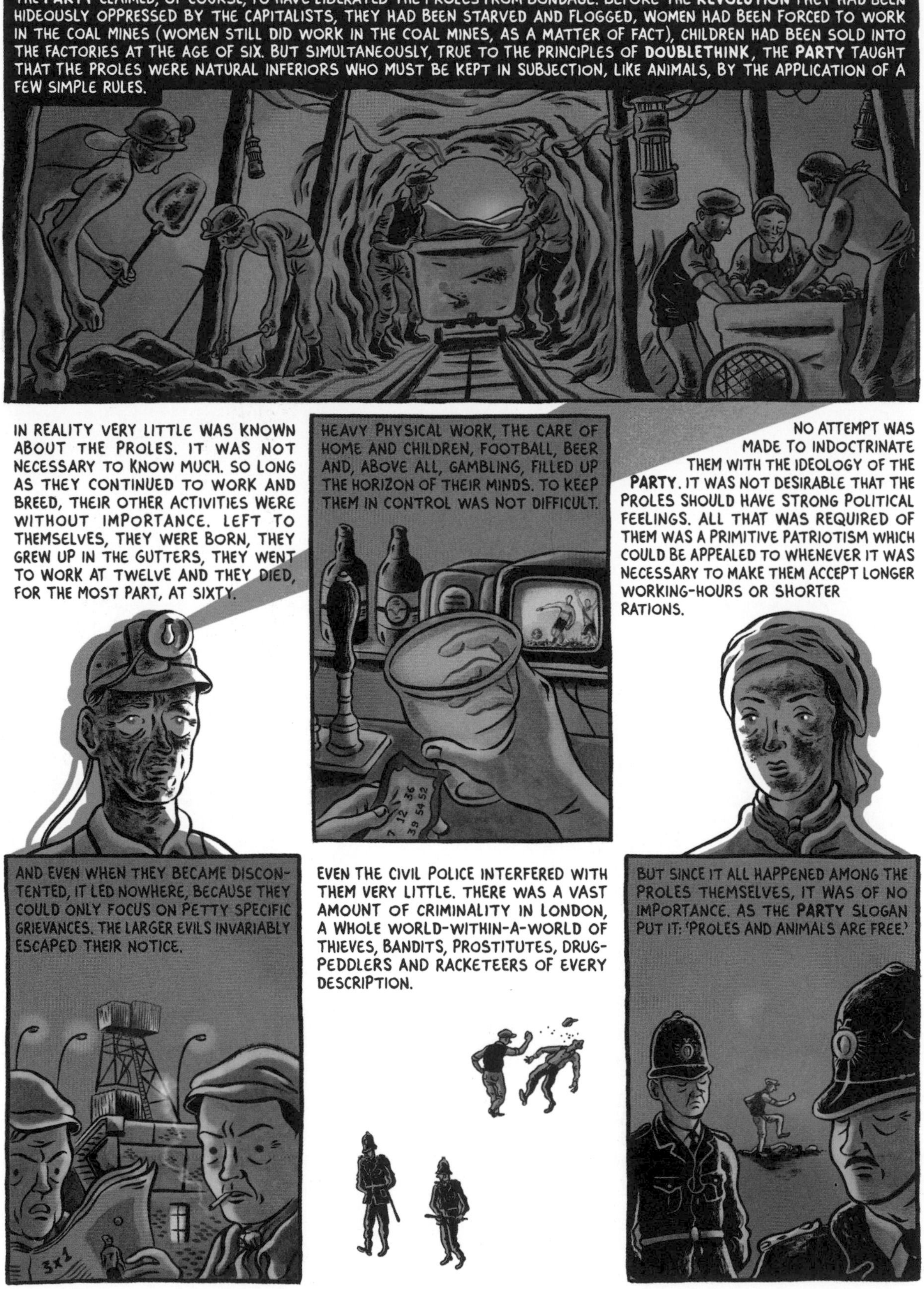
THE PARTY CLAIMED, OF COURSE, TO HAVE LIBERATED THE PROLES FROM BONDAGE. BEFORE THE REVOLUTION THEY HAD BEEN HIDEOUSLY OPPRESSED BY THE CAPITALISTS, THEY HAD BEEN STARVED AND FLOGGED, WOMEN HAD BEEN FORCED TO WORK IN THE COAL MINES (WOMEN STILL DID WORK IN THE COAL MINES, AS A MATTER OF FACT), CHILDREN HAD BEEN SOLD INTO THE FACTORIES AT THE AGE OF SIX. BUT SIMULTANEOUSLY, TRUE TO THE PRINCIPLES OF DOUBLETHINK, THE PARTY TAUGHT THAT THE PROLES WERE NATURAL INFERIORS WHO MUST BE KEPT IN SUBJECTION, LIKE ANIMALS, BY THE APPLICATION OF A FEW SIMPLE RULES.
IN REALITY VERY LITTLE WAS KNOWN ABOUT THE PROLES. IT WAS NOT NECESSARY TO KNOW MUCH. SO LONG AS THEY CONTINUED TO WORK AND BREED, THEIR OTHER ACTIVITIES WERE WITHOUT IMPORTANCE. LEFT TO THEMSELVES, THEY WERE BORN, THEY GREW UP IN THE GUTTERS, THEY WENT TO WORK AT TWELVE AND THEY DIED, FOR THE MOST PART, AT SIXTY.
HEAVY PHYSICAL WORK, THE CARE OF HOME AND CHILDREN, FOOTBALL, BEER AND, ABOVE ALL, GAMBLING, FILLED UP THE HORIZON OF THEIR MINDS. TO KEEP THEM IN CONTROL WAS NOT DIFFICULT.
7 12 36 39 54 52
NO ATTEMPT WAS MADE TO INDOCTRINATE THEM WITH THE IDEOLOGY OF THE PARTY. IT WAS NOT DESIRABLE THAT THE PROLES SHOULD HAVE STRONG POLITICAL FEELINGS. ALL THAT WAS REQUIRED OF THEM WAS A PRIMITIVE PATRIOTISM WHICH COULD BE APPEALED TO WHENEVER IT WAS NECESSARY TO MAKE THEM ACCEPT LONGER WORKING-HOURS OR SHORTER RATIONS.
AND EVEN WHEN THEY BECAME DISCONTENTED, IT LED NOWHERE, BECAUSE THEY COULD ONLY FOCUS ON PETTY SPECIFIC GRIEVANCES. THE LARGER EVILS INVARIABLY ESCAPED THEIR NOTICE.
3x1
EVEN THE CIVIL POLICE INTERFERED WITH THEM VERY LITTLE. THERE WAS A VAST AMOUNT OF CRIMINALITY IN LONDON, A WHOLE WORLD-WITHIN-A-WORLD OF THIEVES, BANDITS, PROSTITUTES, DRUG-PEDDLERS AND RACKETEERS OF EVERY DESCRIPTION.
BUT SINCE IT ALL HAPPENED AMONG THE PROLES THEMSELVES, IT WAS OF NO IMPORTANCE. AS THE PARTY SLOGAN PUT IT: 'PROLES AND ANIMALS ARE FREE.'

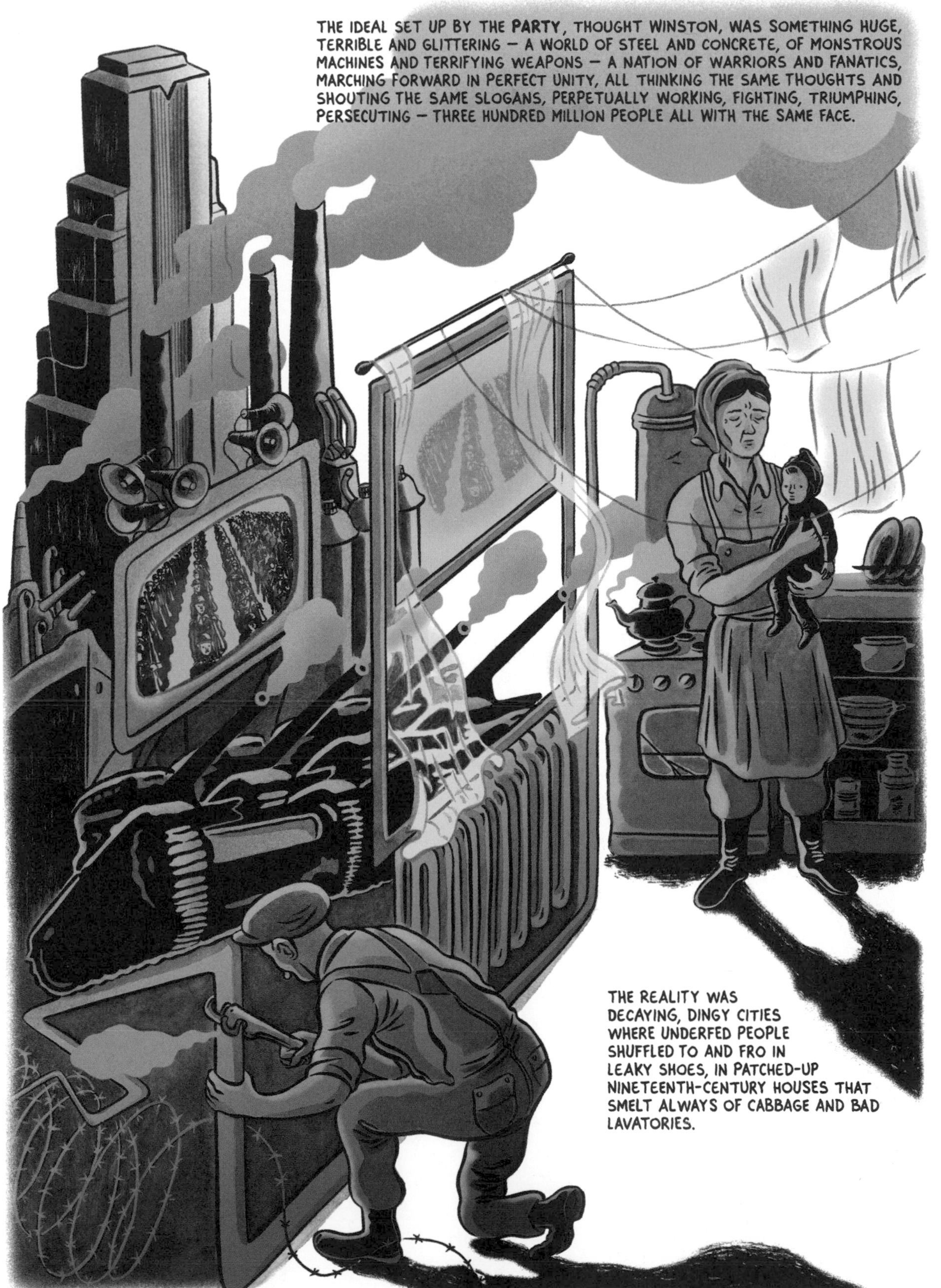
THE IDEAL SET UP BY THE PARTY, THOUGHT WINSTON, WAS SOMETHING HUGE, TERRIBLE AND GLITTERING — A WORLD OF STEEL AND CONCRETE, OF MONSTROUS MACHINES AND TERRIFYING WEAPONS — A NATION OF WARRIORS AND FANATICS, MARCHING FORWARD IN PERFECT UNITY, ALL THINKING THE SAME THOUGHTS AND SHOUTING THE SAME SLOGANS, PERPETUALLY WORKING, FIGHTING, TRIUMPHING, PERSECUTING — THREE HUNDRED MILLION PEOPLE ALL WITH THE SAME FACE.
THE REALITY WAS DECAYING, DINGY CITIES WHERE UNDERFED PEOPLE SHUFFLED TO AND FRO IN LEAKY SHOES, IN PATCHED-UP NINETEENTH-CENTURY HOUSES THAT SMELT ALWAYS OF CABBAGE AND BAD LAVATORIES.

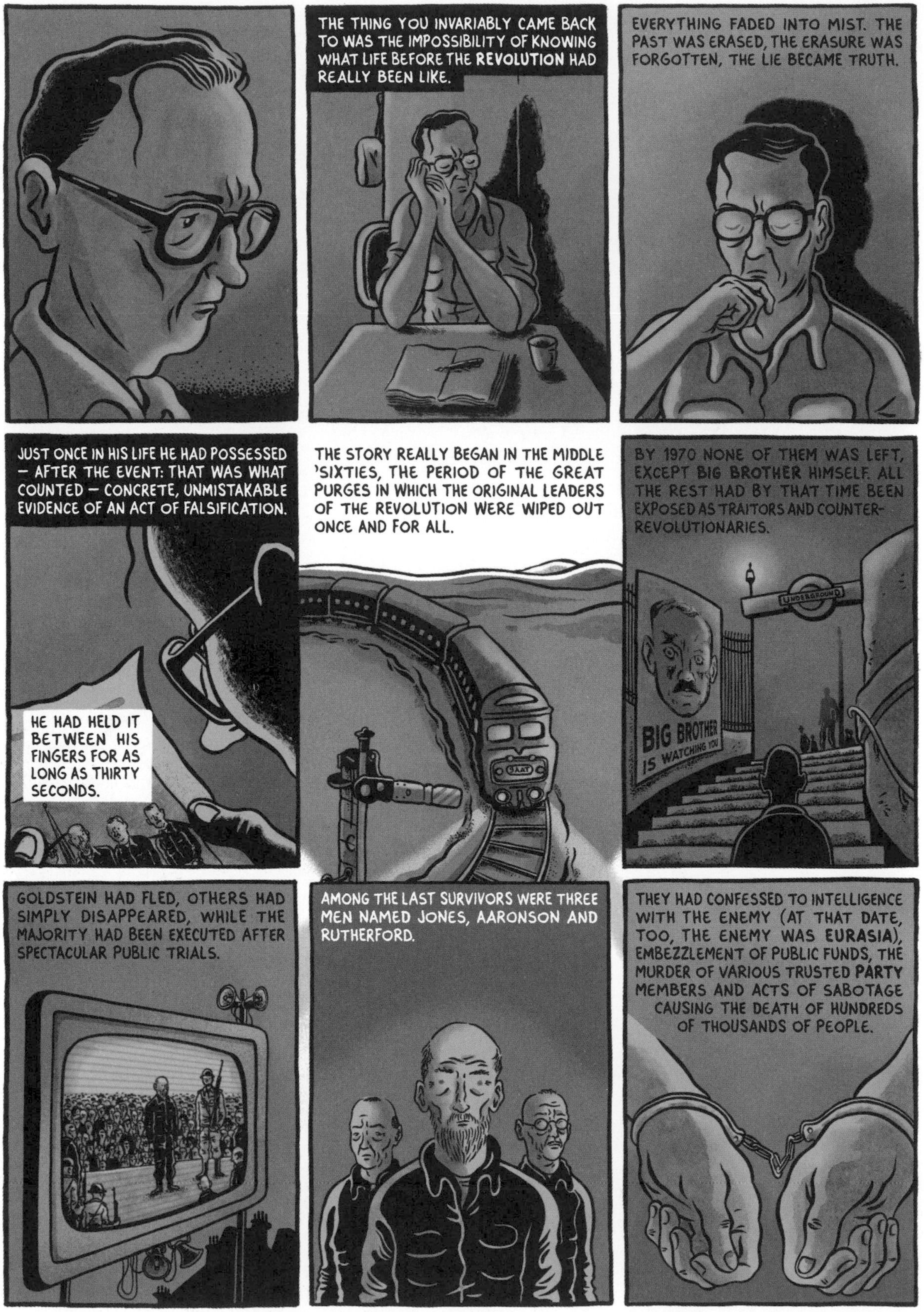

THE THING YOU INVARIABLY CAME BACK TO WAS THE IMPOSSIBILITY OF KNOWING WHAT LIFE BEFORE THE REVOLUTION HAD REALLY BEEN LIKE.
EVERYTHING FADED INTO MIST. THE PAST WAS ERASED, THE ERASURE WAS FORGOTTEN, THE LIE BECAME TRUTH.
JUST ONCE IN HIS LIFE HE HAD POSSESSED — AFTER THE EVENT: THAT WAS WHAT COUNTED — CONCRETE, UNMISTAKABLE EVIDENCE OF AN ACT OF FALSIFICATION.
HE HAD HELD IT BETWEEN HIS FINGERS FOR AS LONG AS THIRTY SECONDS.
THE STORY REALLY BEGAN IN THE MIDDLE 'SIXTIES, THE PERIOD OF THE GREAT PURGES IN WHICH THE ORIGINAL LEADERS OF THE REVOLUTION WERE WIPED OUT ONCE AND FOR ALL.
BY 1970 NONE OF THEM WAS LEFT, EXCEPT BIG BROTHER HIMSELF. ALL THE REST HAD BY THAT TIME BEEN EXPOSED AS TRAITORS AND COUNTER-REVOLUTIONARIES.
UNDERGROUND
BIG BROTHER IS WATCHING YOU
GOLDSTEIN HAD FLED, OTHERS HAD SIMPLY DISAPPEARED, WHILE THE MAJORITY HAD BEEN EXECUTED AFTER SPECTACULAR PUBLIC TRIALS.
AMONG THE LAST SURVIVORS WERE THREE MEN NAMED JONES, AARONSON AND RUTHERFORD.
THEY HAD CONFESSED TO INTELLIGENCE WITH THE ENEMY (AT THAT DATE, TOO, THE ENEMY WAS EURASIA), EMBEZZLEMENT OF PUBLIC FUNDS, THE MURDER OF VARIOUS TRUSTED PARTY MEMBERS AND ACTS OF SABOTAGE CAUSING THE DEATH OF HUNDREDS OF THOUSANDS OF PEOPLE.

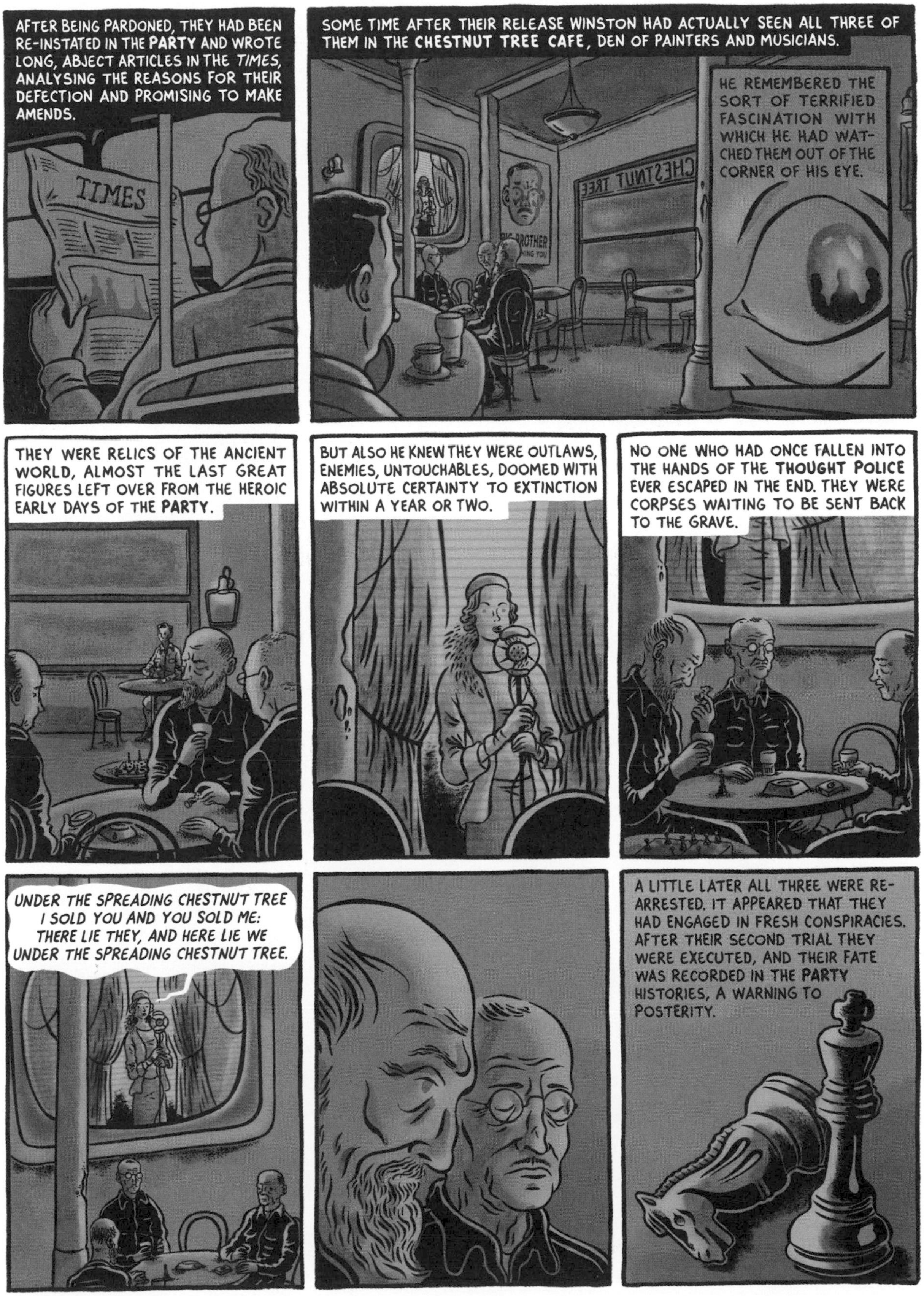
AFTER BEING PARDONED, THEY HAD BEEN RE-INSTATED IN THE PARTY AND WROTE LONG, ABJECT ARTICLES IN THE TIMES, ANALYSING THE REASONS FOR THEIR DEFECTION AND PROMISING TO MAKE AMENDS.
TIMES
SOME TIME AFTER THEIR RELEASE WINSTON HAD ACTUALLY SEEN ALL THREE OF THEM IN THE CHESTNUT TREE CAFE, DEN OF PAINTERS AND MUSICIANS.
HE REMEMBERED THE SORT OF TERRIFIED FASCINATION WITH WHICH HE HAD WATCHED THEM OUT OF THE CORNER OF HIS EYE.
THEY WERE RELICS OF THE ANCIENT WORLD, ALMOST THE LAST GREAT FIGURES LEFT OVER FROM THE HEROIC EARLY DAYS OF THE PARTY.
BUT ALSO HE KNEW THEY WERE OUTLAWS, ENEMIES, UNTOUCHABLES, DOOMED WITH ABSOLUTE CERTAINTY TO EXTINCTION WITHIN A YEAR OR TWO.
NO ONE WHO HAD ONCE FALLEN INTO THE HANDS OF THE THOUGHT POLICE EVER ESCAPED IN THE END. THEY WERE CORPSES WAITING TO BE SENT BACK TO THE GRAVE.
UNDER THE SPREADING CHESTNUT TREE I SOLD YOU AND YOU SOLD ME: THERE LIE THEY, AND HERE LIE WE UNDER THE SPREADING CHESTNUT TREE.
A LITTLE LATER ALL THREE WERE RE-ARRESTED. IT APPEARED THAT THEY HAD ENGAGED IN FRESH CONSPIRACIES. AFTER THEIR SECOND TRIAL THEY WERE EXECUTED, AND THEIR FATE WAS RECORDED IN THE PARTY HISTORIES, A WARNING TO POSTERITY.

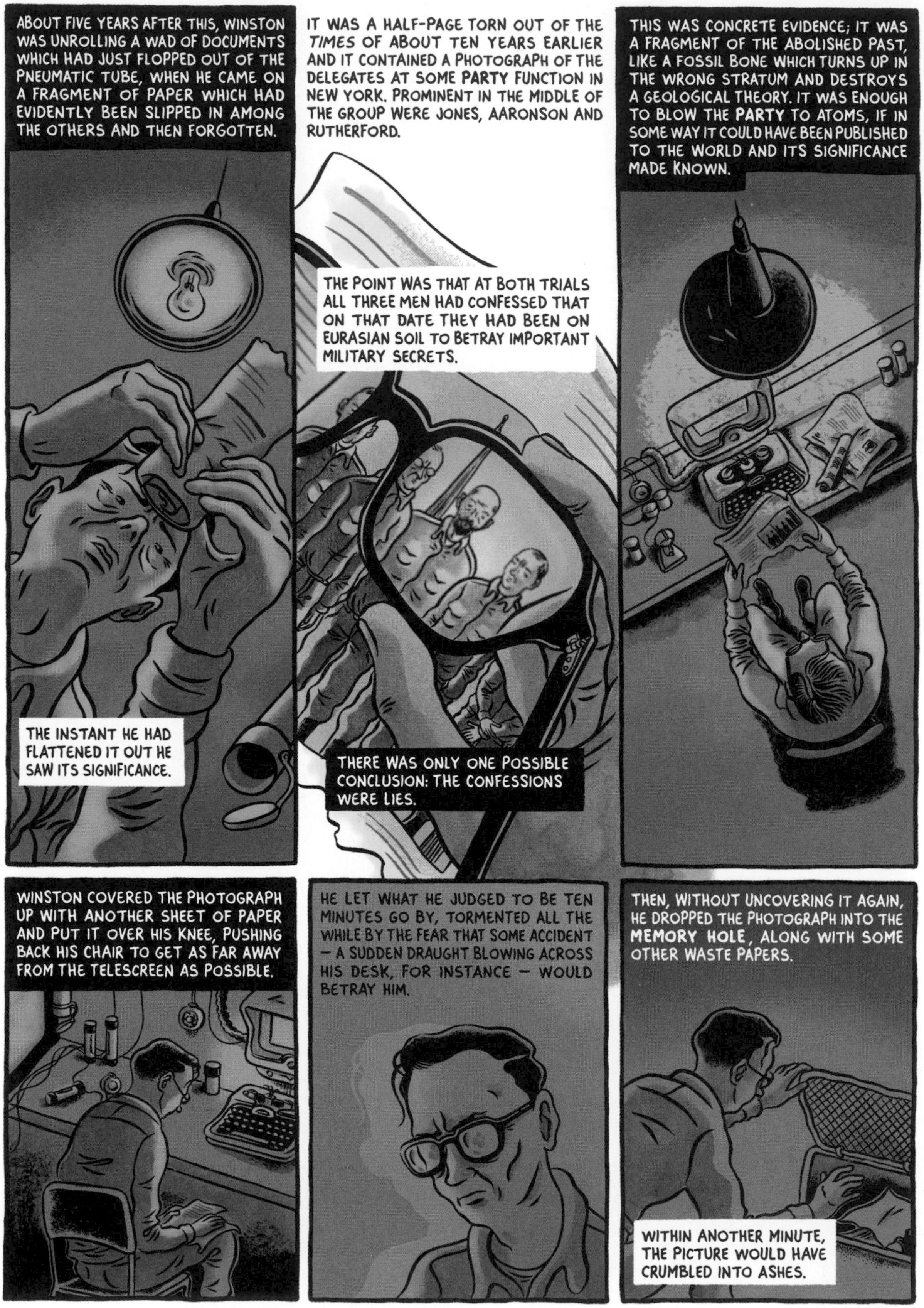
ABOUT FIVE YEARS AFTER THIS, WINSTON WAS UNROLLING A WAD OF DOCUMENTS WHICH HAD JUST FLOPPED OUT OF THE PNEUMATIC TUBE, WHEN HE CAME ON A FRAGMENT OF PAPER WHICH HAD EVIDENTLY BEEN SLIPPED IN AMONG THE OTHERS AND THEN FORGOTTEN.
THE INSTANT HE HAD FLATTENED IT OUT HE SAW ITS SIGNIFICANCE.
IT WAS A HALF-PAGE TORN OUT OF THE *TIMES* OF ABOUT TEN YEARS EARLIER AND IT CONTAINED A PHOTOGRAPH OF THE DELEGATES AT SOME **PARTY** FUNCTION IN NEW YORK. PROMINENT IN THE MIDDLE OF THE GROUP WERE JONES, AARONSON AND RUTHERFORD.
THE POINT WAS THAT AT BOTH TRIALS ALL THREE MEN HAD CONFESSED THAT ON THAT DATE THEY HAD BEEN ON EURASIAN SOIL TO BETRAY IMPORTANT MILITARY SECRETS.
THERE WAS ONLY ONE POSSIBLE CONCLUSION: THE CONFESSIONS WERE LIES.
THIS WAS CONCRETE EVIDENCE; IT WAS A FRAGMENT OF THE ABOLISHED PAST, LIKE A FOSSIL BONE WHICH TURNS UP IN THE WRONG STRATUM AND DESTROYS A GEOLOGICAL THEORY. IT WAS ENOUGH TO BLOW THE **PARTY** TO ATOMS, IF IN SOME WAY IT COULD HAVE BEEN PUBLISHED TO THE WORLD AND ITS SIGNIFICANCE MADE KNOWN.
WINSTON COVERED THE PHOTOGRAPH UP WITH ANOTHER SHEET OF PAPER AND PUT IT OVER HIS KNEE, PUSHING BACK HIS CHAIR TO GET AS FAR AWAY FROM THE TELESCREEN AS POSSIBLE.
HE LET WHAT HE JUDGED TO BE TEN MINUTES GO BY, TORMENTED ALL THE WHILE BY THE FEAR THAT SOME ACCIDENT – A SUDDEN DRAUGHT BLOWING ACROSS HIS DESK, FOR INSTANCE – WOULD BETRAY HIM.
THEN, WITHOUT UNCOVERING IT AGAIN, HE DROPPED THE PHOTOGRAPH INTO THE **MEMORY HOLE**, ALONG WITH SOME OTHER WASTE PAPERS.
WITHIN ANOTHER MINUTE, THE PICTURE WOULD HAVE CRUMBLED INTO ASHES.

WHAT MOST AFFLICTED HIM WITH THE SENSE OF NIGHTMARE WAS THAT HE HAD NEVER CLEARLY UNDERSTOOD WHY THE HUGE IMPOSTURE WAS UNDERTAKEN.
THE IMMEDIATE ADVANTAGES OF FALSIFYING THE PAST WERE OBVIOUS, BUT THE ULTIMATE MOTIVE WAS MYSTERIOUS.
I UNDERSTAND HOW: I DO NOT UNDERSTAND WHY
HE WONDERED, AS HE HAD MANY TIMES WONDERED BEFORE, WHETHER HE HIMSELF WAS A LUNATIC. PERHAPS A LUNATIC WAS SIMPLY A MINORITY OF ONE.
AT ONE TIME IT HAD BEEN A SIGN OF MADNESS TO BELIEVE THAT THE EARTH GOES ROUND THE SUN: TODAY, TO BELIEVE THAT THE PAST IS UNALTERABLE.
HE MIGHT BE ALONE IN HOLDING THAT BELIEF, AND IF ALONE, THEN A LUNATIC. BUT THE THOUGHT OF BEING A LUNATIC DID NOT GREATLY TROUBLE HIM: THE HORROR WAS THAT HE MIGHT ALSO BE WRONG.
THE HYPNOTIC EYES GAZED INTO HIS OWN. IT WAS AS THOUGH SOME HUGE FORCE PENETRATED INSIDE YOUR SKULL, BATTERING AGAINST YOUR BRAIN, FRIGHTENING YOU OUT OF YOUR BELIEFS.
WAR IS PEACE · FREEDOM IS SLAVERY · RANCE IS STRENGTH ·
1984
IN THE END THE PARTY WOULD ANNOUNCE THAT TWO AND TWO MADE FIVE, AND YOU WOULD HAVE TO BELIEVE IT. AND WHAT WAS TERRIFYING WAS NOT THAT THEY WOULD KILL YOU FOR THINKING OTHERWISE, BUT THAT THEY MIGHT BE RIGHT.
FOR, AFTER ALL, HOW DO WE KNOW THAT TWO AND TWO MAKE FOUR? OR THAT THE FORCE OF GRAVITY WORKS? OR THAT THE PAST IS UNCHANGEABLE?
IF BOTH THE PAST AND THE EXTERNAL WORLD EXIST ONLY IN THE MIND, AND IF THE MIND ITSELF IS CONTROLLABLE – WHAT THEN?

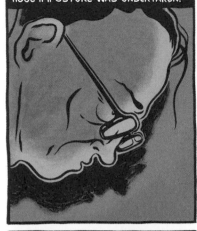

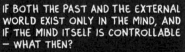

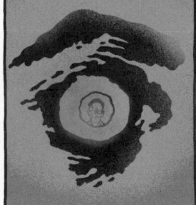

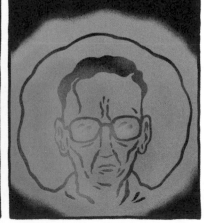

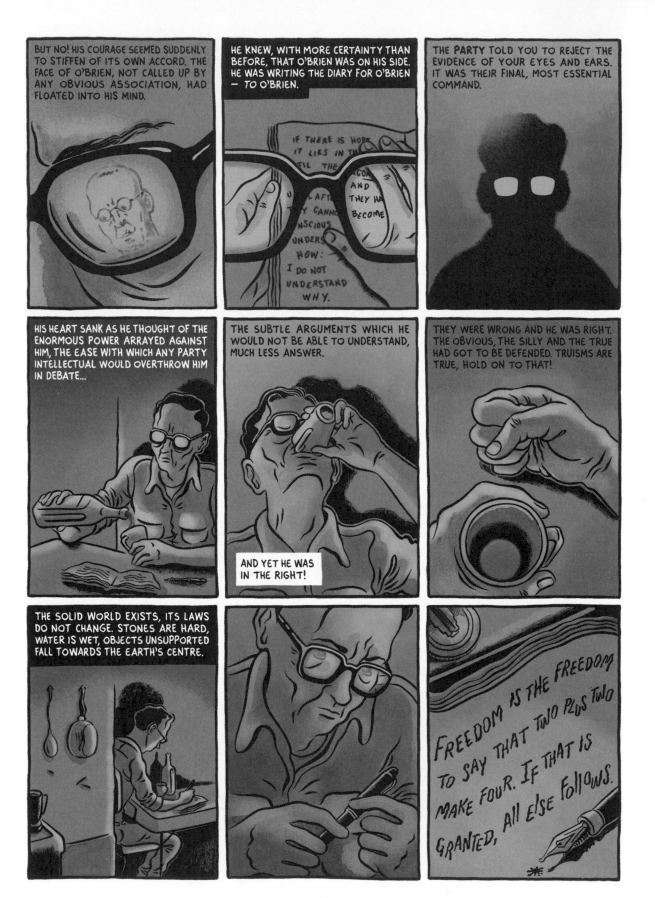

BUT NO! HIS COURAGE SEEMED SUDDENLY TO STIFFEN OF ITS OWN ACCORD. THE FACE OF O'BRIEN, NOT CALLED UP BY ANY OBVIOUS ASSOCIATION, HAD FLOATED INTO HIS MIND.

HE KNEW, WITH MORE CERTAINTY THAN BEFORE, THAT O'BRIEN WAS ON HIS SIDE. HE WAS WRITING THE DIARY FOR O'BRIEN — TO O'BRIEN.

IF THERE IS HOPE IT LIES IN TH...

AND THEY HAVE BECOME

...L AFTE...
...Y CANNO...
...SCIOUS...
UNDERS...
HOW:
I DO NOT
UNDERSTAND
WHY.

THE PARTY TOLD YOU TO REJECT THE EVIDENCE OF YOUR EYES AND EARS. IT WAS THEIR FINAL, MOST ESSENTIAL COMMAND.

HIS HEART SANK AS HE THOUGHT OF THE ENORMOUS POWER ARRAYED AGAINST HIM, THE EASE WITH WHICH ANY PARTY INTELLECTUAL WOULD OVERTHROW HIM IN DEBATE...

THE SUBTLE ARGUMENTS WHICH HE WOULD NOT BE ABLE TO UNDERSTAND, MUCH LESS ANSWER.

AND YET HE WAS IN THE RIGHT!

THEY WERE WRONG AND HE WAS RIGHT. THE OBVIOUS, THE SILLY AND THE TRUE HAD GOT TO BE DEFENDED. TRUISMS ARE TRUE, HOLD ON TO THAT!

THE SOLID WORLD EXISTS, ITS LAWS DO NOT CHANGE. STONES ARE HARD, WATER IS WET, OBJECTS UNSUPPORTED FALL TOWARDS THE EARTH'S CENTRE.

FREEDOM IS THE FREEDOM TO SAY THAT TWO PLUS TWO MAKE FOUR. IF THAT IS GRANTED, ALL ELSE FOLLOWS.

WINSTON HAD WALKED SEVERAL KILOMETRES OVER PAVEMENTS, AND HIS VARICOSE ULCER WAS THROBBING.

THIS WAS THE SECOND TIME IN THREE WEEKS THAT HE HAD MISSED AN EVENING AT THE **COMMUNITY CENTRE**: A RASH ACT, SINCE YOU COULD BE CERTAIN THAT THE NUMBER OF YOUR ATTENDANCES AT THE CENTRE WAS CAREFULLY CHECKED.

IN PRINCIPLE A **PARTY** MEMBER HAD NO SPARE TIME, AND WAS NEVER ALONE EXCEPT IN BED.

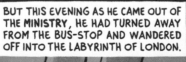

TO DO ANYTHING THAT SUGGESTED A TASTE FOR SOLITUDE, EVEN TO GO FOR A WALK BY YOURSELF, WAS ALWAYS SLIGHTLY DANGEROUS.

THERE WAS A WORD FOR IT IN **NEWSPEAK**: **OWNLIFE**, IT WAS CALLED, MEANING INDIVIDUALISM AND ECCENTRICITY.

BUT THIS EVENING AS HE CAME OUT OF THE **MINISTRY**, HE HAD TURNED AWAY FROM THE BUS-STOP AND WANDERED OFF INTO THE LABYRINTH OF LONDON.

FIRST SOUTH, THEN EAST, THEN NORTH AGAIN, LOSING HIMSELF AMONG UNKNOWN STREETS AND HARDLY BOTHERING IN WHICH DIRECTION HE WAS GOING.

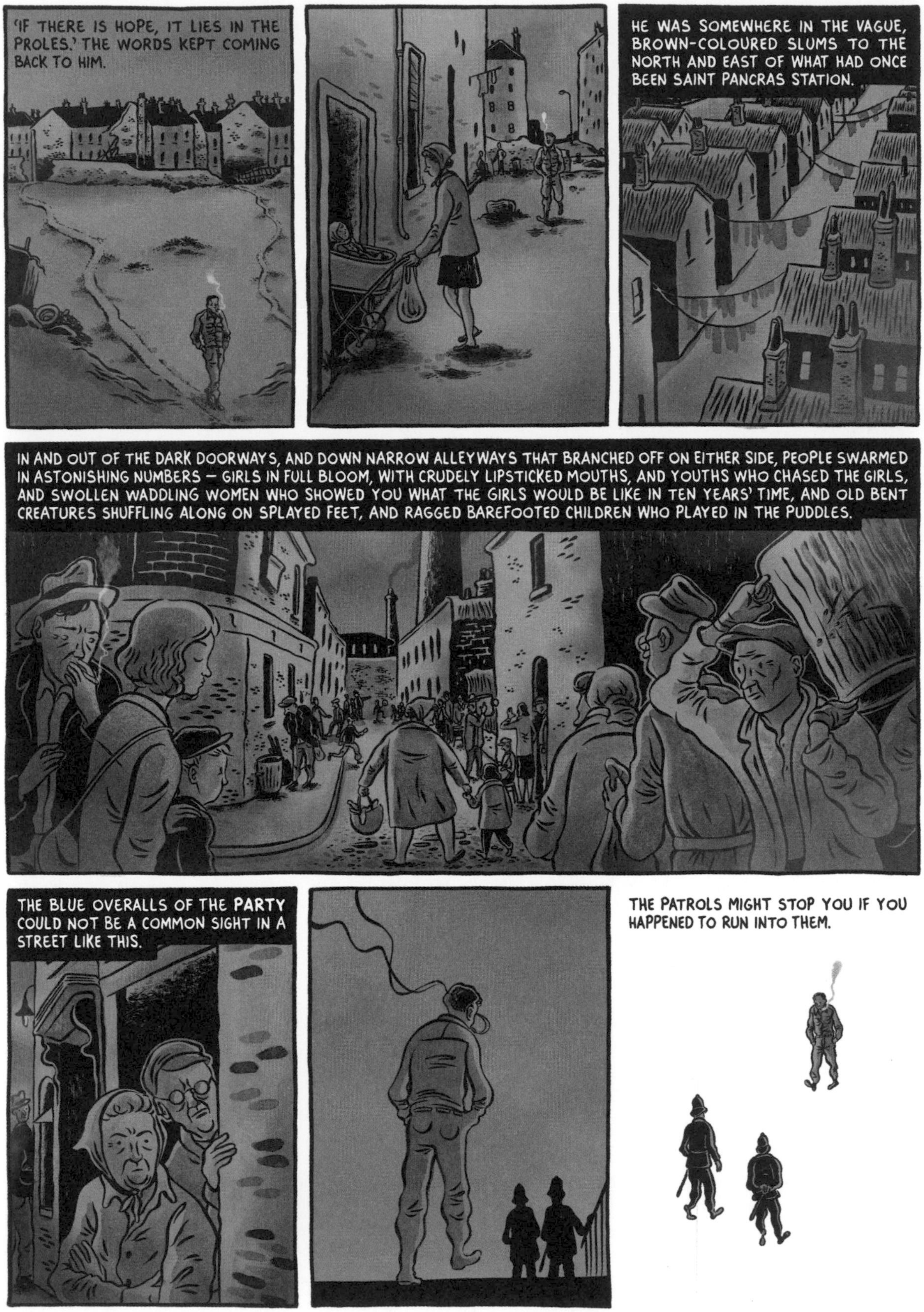

'IF THERE IS HOPE, IT LIES IN THE PROLES.' THE WORDS KEPT COMING BACK TO HIM.
HE WAS SOMEWHERE IN THE VAGUE, BROWN-COLOURED SLUMS TO THE NORTH AND EAST OF WHAT HAD ONCE BEEN SAINT PANCRAS STATION.
IN AND OUT OF THE DARK DOORWAYS, AND DOWN NARROW ALLEYWAYS THAT BRANCHED OFF ON EITHER SIDE, PEOPLE SWARMED IN ASTONISHING NUMBERS – GIRLS IN FULL BLOOM, WITH CRUDELY LIPSTICKED MOUTHS, AND YOUTHS WHO CHASED THE GIRLS, AND SWOLLEN WADDLING WOMEN WHO SHOWED YOU WHAT THE GIRLS WOULD BE LIKE IN TEN YEARS' TIME, AND OLD BENT CREATURES SHUFFLING ALONG ON SPLAYED FEET, AND RAGGED BAREFOOTED CHILDREN WHO PLAYED IN THE PUDDLES.
THE BLUE OVERALLS OF THE **PARTY** COULD NOT BE A COMMON SIGHT IN A STREET LIKE THIS.
THE PATROLS MIGHT STOP YOU IF YOU HAPPENED TO RUN INTO THEM.

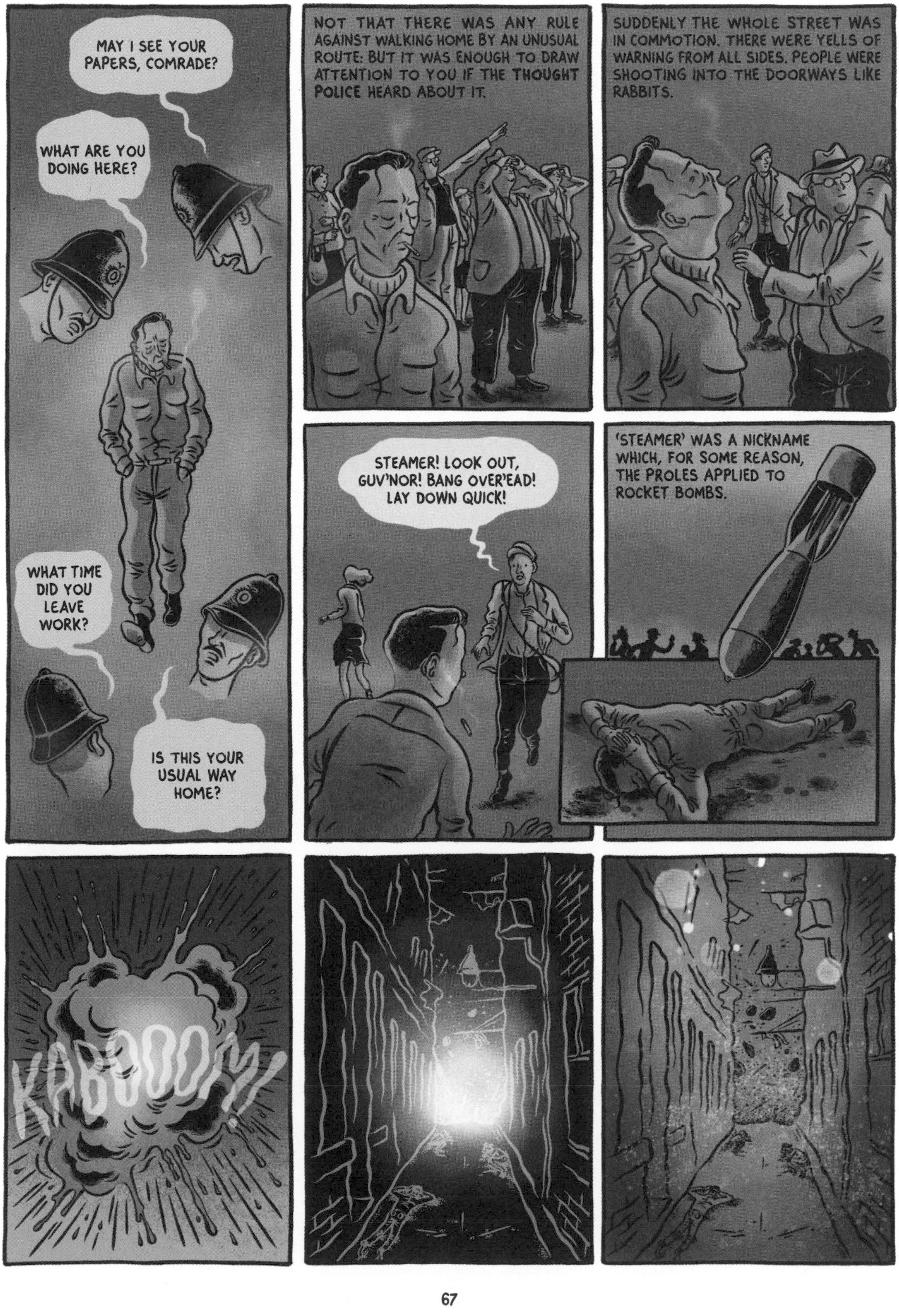

MAY I SEE YOUR PAPERS, COMRADE?
WHAT ARE YOU DOING HERE?
WHAT TIME DID YOU LEAVE WORK?
IS THIS YOUR USUAL WAY HOME?
NOT THAT THERE WAS ANY RULE AGAINST WALKING HOME BY AN UNUSUAL ROUTE: BUT IT WAS ENOUGH TO DRAW ATTENTION TO YOU IF THE THOUGHT POLICE HEARD ABOUT IT.
SUDDENLY THE WHOLE STREET WAS IN COMMOTION. THERE WERE YELLS OF WARNING FROM ALL SIDES. PEOPLE WERE SHOOTING INTO THE DOORWAYS LIKE RABBITS.
STEAMER! LOOK OUT, GUV'NOR! BANG OVER'EAD! LAY DOWN QUICK!
'STEAMER' WAS A NICKNAME WHICH, FOR SOME REASON, THE PROLES APPLIED TO ROCKET BOMBS.
KABOOOM!

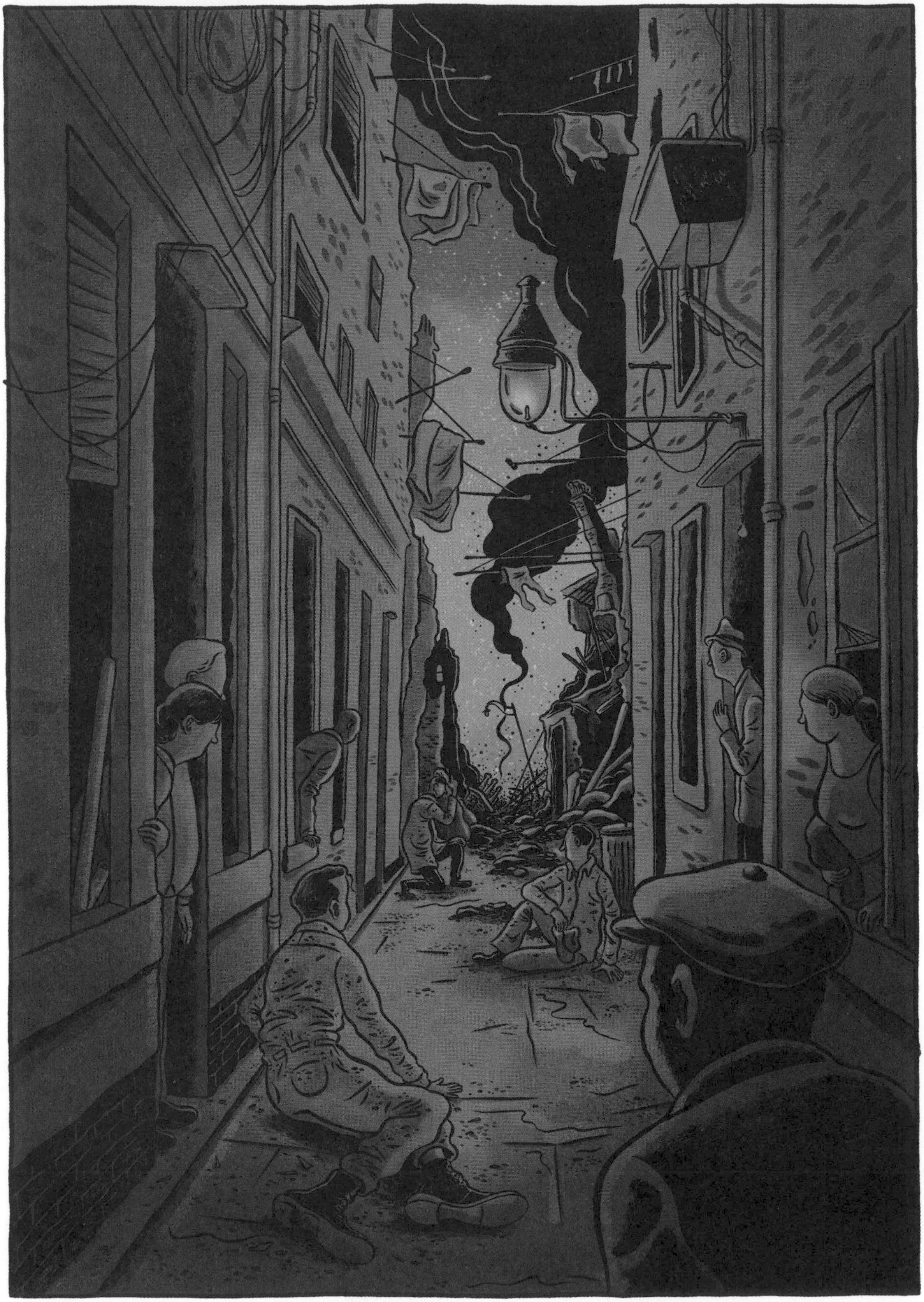

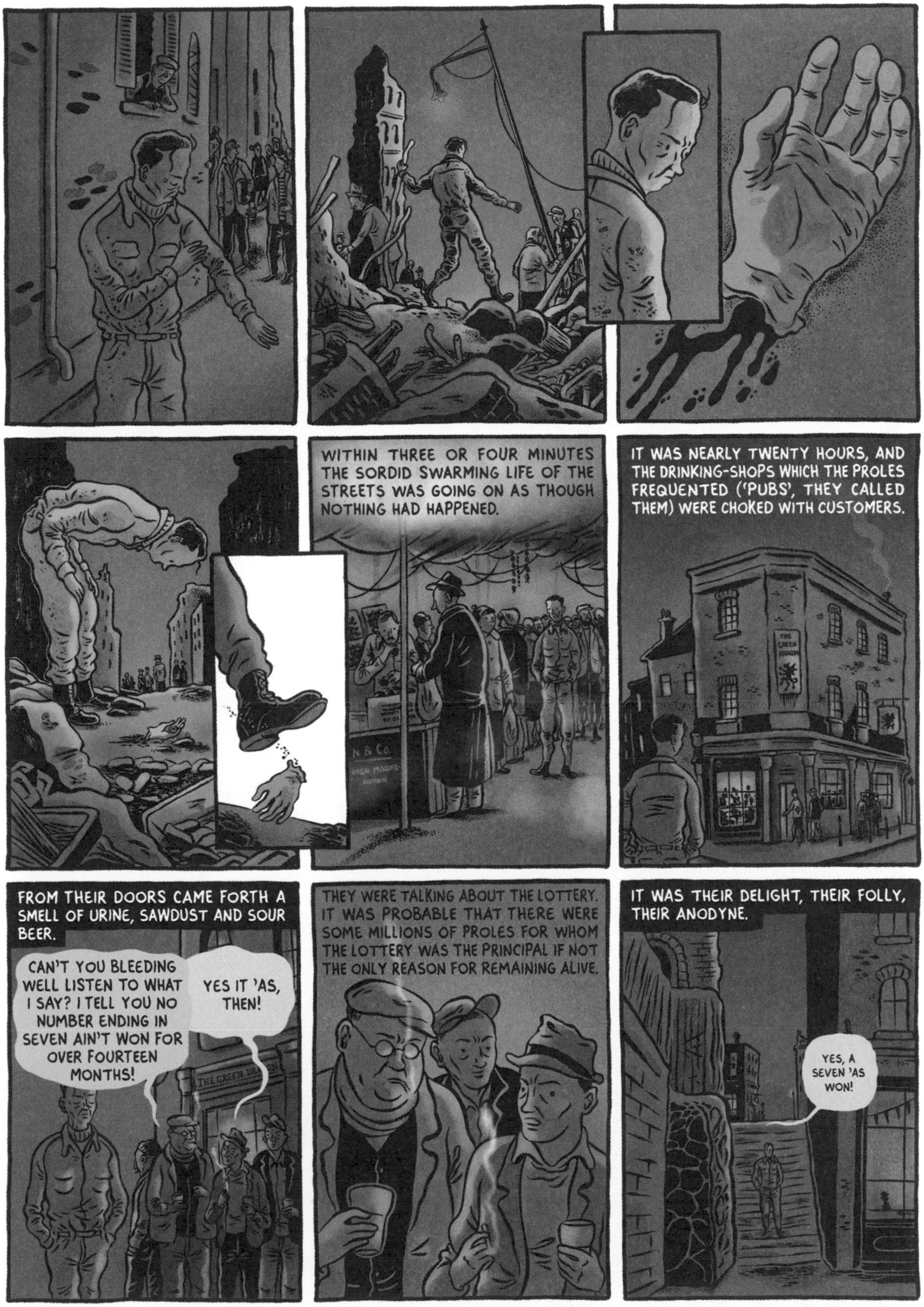
WITHIN THREE OR FOUR MINUTES THE SORDID SWARMING LIFE OF THE STREETS WAS GOING ON AS THOUGH NOTHING HAD HAPPENED.
IT WAS NEARLY TWENTY HOURS, AND THE DRINKING-SHOPS WHICH THE PROLES FREQUENTED ('PUBS', THEY CALLED THEM) WERE CHOKED WITH CUSTOMERS.
FROM THEIR DOORS CAME FORTH A SMELL OF URINE, SAWDUST AND SOUR BEER.
CAN'T YOU BLEEDING WELL LISTEN TO WHAT I SAY? I TELL YOU NO NUMBER ENDING IN SEVEN AIN'T WON FOR OVER FOURTEEN MONTHS!
YES IT 'AS, THEN!
THEY WERE TALKING ABOUT THE LOTTERY. IT WAS PROBABLE THAT THERE WERE SOME MILLIONS OF PROLES FOR WHOM THE LOTTERY WAS THE PRINCIPAL IF NOT THE ONLY REASON FOR REMAINING ALIVE.
IT WAS THEIR DELIGHT, THEIR FOLLY, THEIR ANODYNE.
YES, A SEVEN 'AS WON!

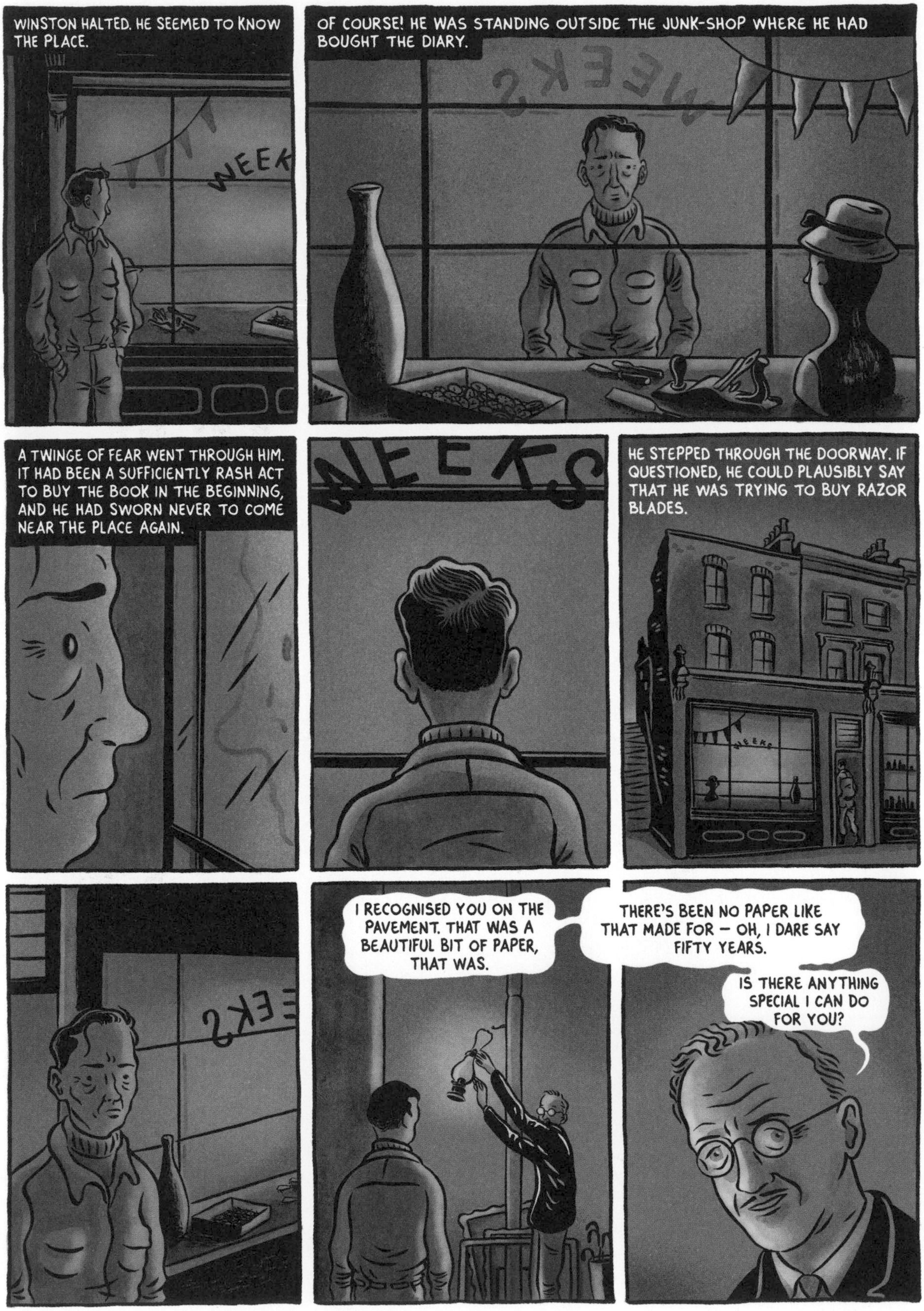

WINSTON HALTED. HE SEEMED TO KNOW THE PLACE.
WEEK
OF COURSE! HE WAS STANDING OUTSIDE THE JUNK-SHOP WHERE HE HAD BOUGHT THE DIARY.
A TWINGE OF FEAR WENT THROUGH HIM. IT HAD BEEN A SUFFICIENTLY RASH ACT TO BUY THE BOOK IN THE BEGINNING, AND HE HAD SWORN NEVER TO COME NEAR THE PLACE AGAIN.
WEEKS
HE STEPPED THROUGH THE DOORWAY. IF QUESTIONED, HE COULD PLAUSIBLY SAY THAT HE WAS TRYING TO BUY RAZOR BLADES.
I RECOGNISED YOU ON THE PAVEMENT. THAT WAS A BEAUTIFUL BIT OF PAPER, THAT WAS.
THERE'S BEEN NO PAPER LIKE THAT MADE FOR — OH, I DARE SAY FIFTY YEARS.
IS THERE ANYTHING SPECIAL I CAN DO FOR YOU?

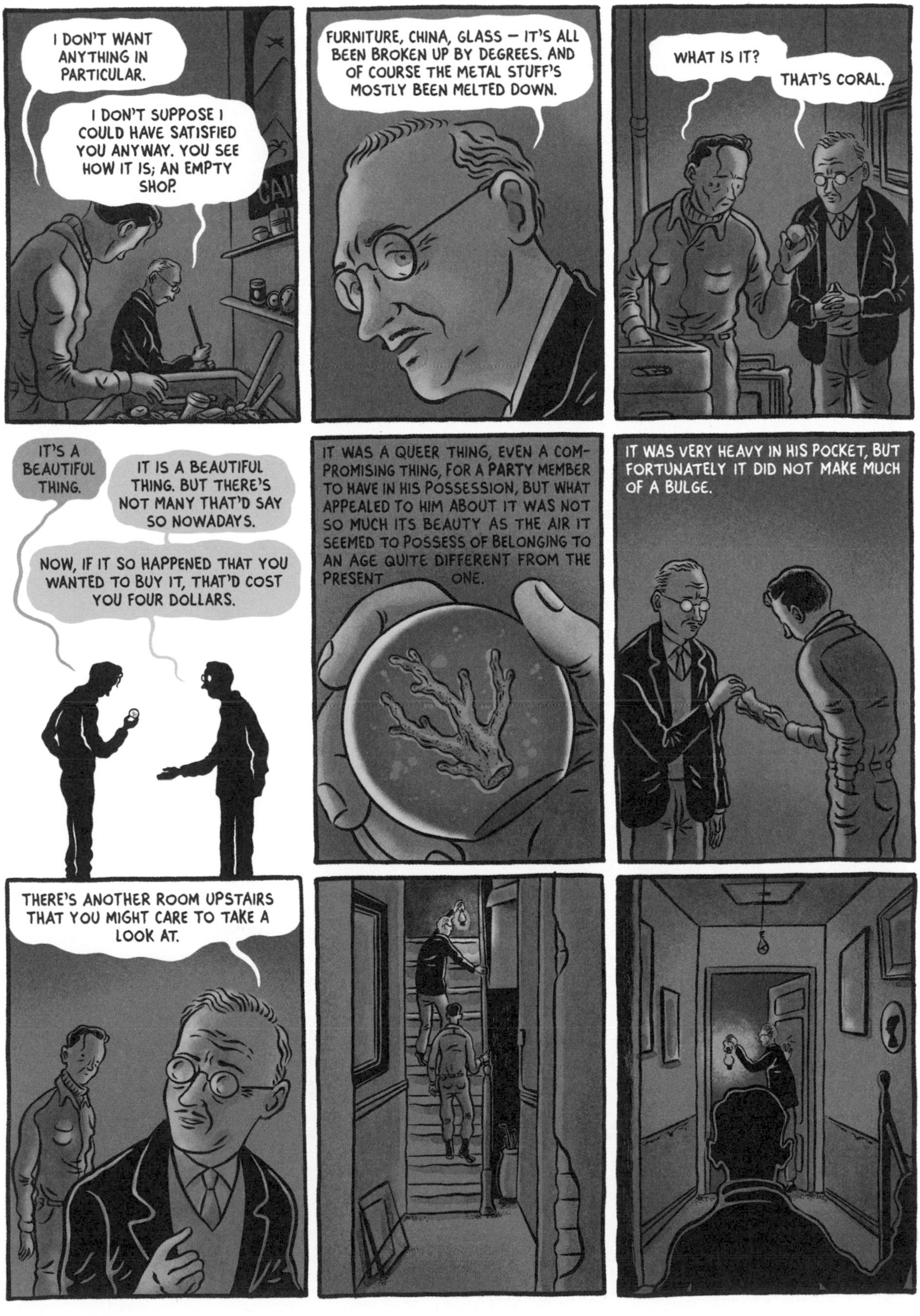
I DON'T WANT ANYTHING IN PARTICULAR.
I DON'T SUPPOSE I COULD HAVE SATISFIED YOU ANYWAY. YOU SEE HOW IT IS; AN EMPTY SHOP.
FURNITURE, CHINA, GLASS — IT'S ALL BEEN BROKEN UP BY DEGREES. AND OF COURSE THE METAL STUFF'S MOSTLY BEEN MELTED DOWN.
WHAT IS IT?
THAT'S CORAL.
IT'S A BEAUTIFUL THING.
IT IS A BEAUTIFUL THING. BUT THERE'S NOT MANY THAT'D SAY SO NOWADAYS.
NOW, IF IT SO HAPPENED THAT YOU WANTED TO BUY IT, THAT'D COST YOU FOUR DOLLARS.
IT WAS A QUEER THING, EVEN A COMPROMISING THING, FOR A PARTY MEMBER TO HAVE IN HIS POSSESSION, BUT WHAT APPEALED TO HIM ABOUT IT WAS NOT SO MUCH ITS BEAUTY AS THE AIR IT SEEMED TO POSSESS OF BELONGING TO AN AGE QUITE DIFFERENT FROM THE PRESENT ONE.
IT WAS VERY HEAVY IN HIS POCKET, BUT FORTUNATELY IT DID NOT MAKE MUCH OF A BULGE.
THERE'S ANOTHER ROOM UPSTAIRS THAT YOU MIGHT CARE TO TAKE A LOOK AT.

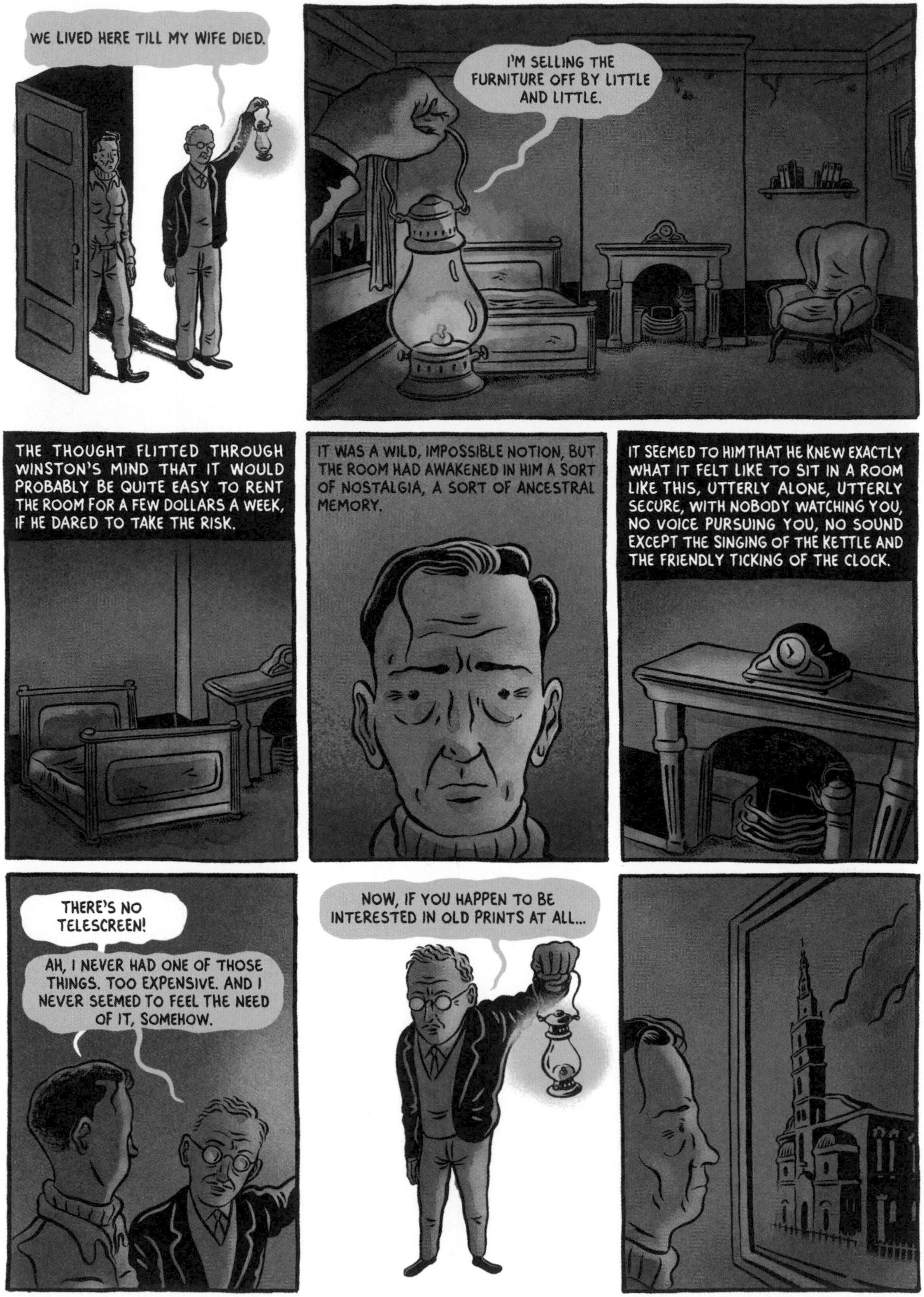
WE LIVED HERE TILL MY WIFE DIED.
I'M SELLING THE FURNITURE OFF BY LITTLE AND LITTLE.
THE THOUGHT FLITTED THROUGH WINSTON'S MIND THAT IT WOULD PROBABLY BE QUITE EASY TO RENT THE ROOM FOR A FEW DOLLARS A WEEK, IF HE DARED TO TAKE THE RISK.
IT WAS A WILD, IMPOSSIBLE NOTION, BUT THE ROOM HAD AWAKENED IN HIM A SORT OF NOSTALGIA, A SORT OF ANCESTRAL MEMORY.
IT SEEMED TO HIM THAT HE KNEW EXACTLY WHAT IT FELT LIKE TO SIT IN A ROOM LIKE THIS, UTTERLY ALONE, UTTERLY SECURE, WITH NOBODY WATCHING YOU, NO VOICE PURSUING YOU, NO SOUND EXCEPT THE SINGING OF THE KETTLE AND THE FRIENDLY TICKING OF THE CLOCK.
THERE'S NO TELESCREEN!
AH, I NEVER HAD ONE OF THOSE THINGS. TOO EXPENSIVE. AND I NEVER SEEMED TO FEEL THE NEED OF IT, SOMEHOW.
NOW, IF YOU HAPPEN TO BE INTERESTED IN OLD PRINTS AT ALL...

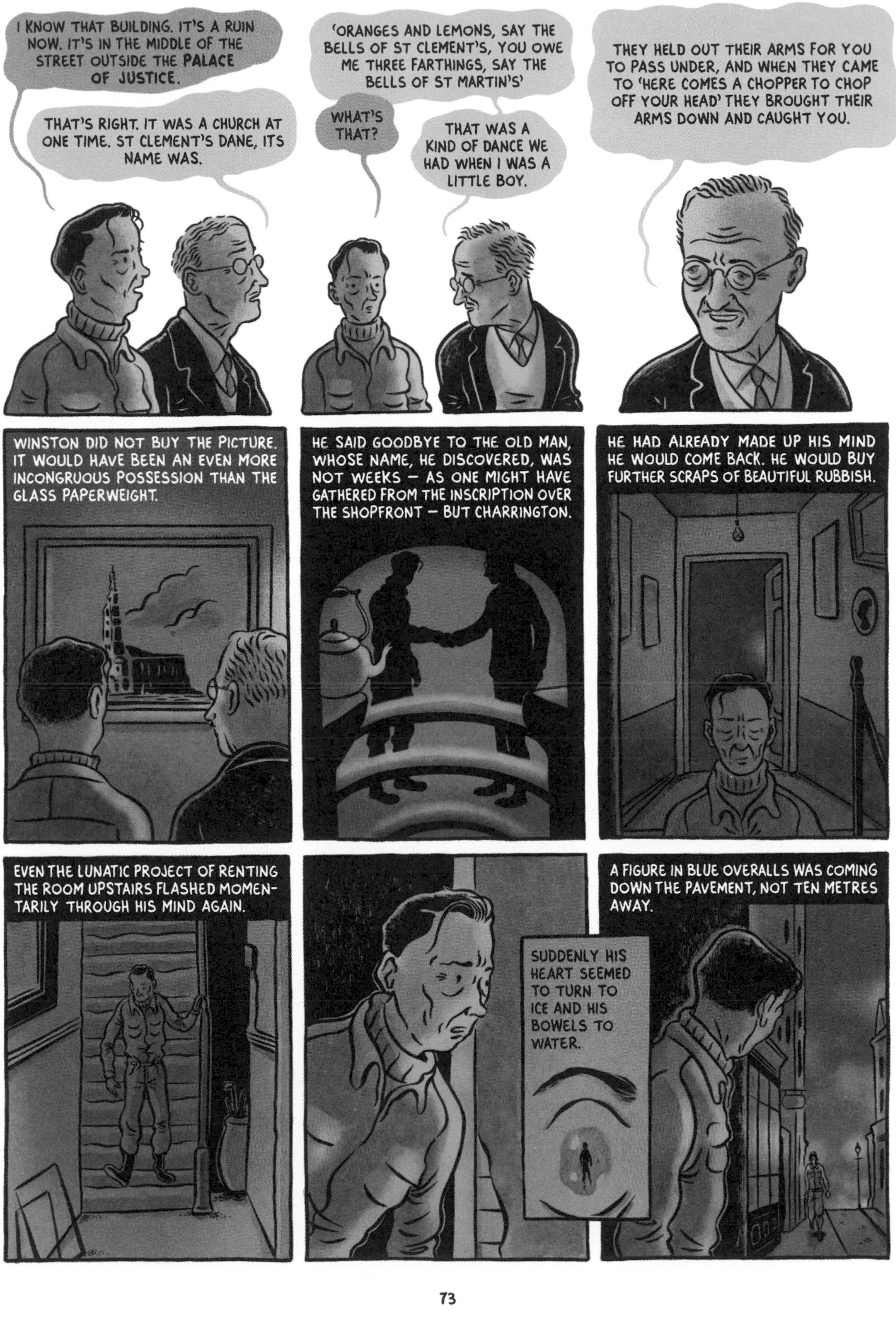
I KNOW THAT BUILDING. IT'S A RUIN NOW. IT'S IN THE MIDDLE OF THE STREET OUTSIDE THE PALACE OF JUSTICE.
THAT'S RIGHT. IT WAS A CHURCH AT ONE TIME. ST CLEMENT'S DANE, ITS NAME WAS.
'ORANGES AND LEMONS, SAY THE BELLS OF ST CLEMENT'S, YOU OWE ME THREE FARTHINGS, SAY THE BELLS OF ST MARTIN'S'
WHAT'S THAT?
THAT WAS A KIND OF DANCE WE HAD WHEN I WAS A LITTLE BOY.
THEY HELD OUT THEIR ARMS FOR YOU TO PASS UNDER, AND WHEN THEY CAME TO 'HERE COMES A CHOPPER TO CHOP OFF YOUR HEAD' THEY BROUGHT THEIR ARMS DOWN AND CAUGHT YOU.
WINSTON DID NOT BUY THE PICTURE. IT WOULD HAVE BEEN AN EVEN MORE INCONGRUOUS POSSESSION THAN THE GLASS PAPERWEIGHT.
HE SAID GOODBYE TO THE OLD MAN, WHOSE NAME, HE DISCOVERED, WAS NOT WEEKS – AS ONE MIGHT HAVE GATHERED FROM THE INSCRIPTION OVER THE SHOPFRONT – BUT CHARRINGTON.
HE HAD ALREADY MADE UP HIS MIND HE WOULD COME BACK. HE WOULD BUY FURTHER SCRAPS OF BEAUTIFUL RUBBISH.
EVEN THE LUNATIC PROJECT OF RENTING THE ROOM UPSTAIRS FLASHED MOMENTARILY THROUGH HIS MIND AGAIN.
SUDDENLY HIS HEART SEEMED TO TURN TO ICE AND HIS BOWELS TO WATER.
A FIGURE IN BLUE OVERALLS WAS COMING DOWN THE PAVEMENT, NOT TEN METRES AWAY.

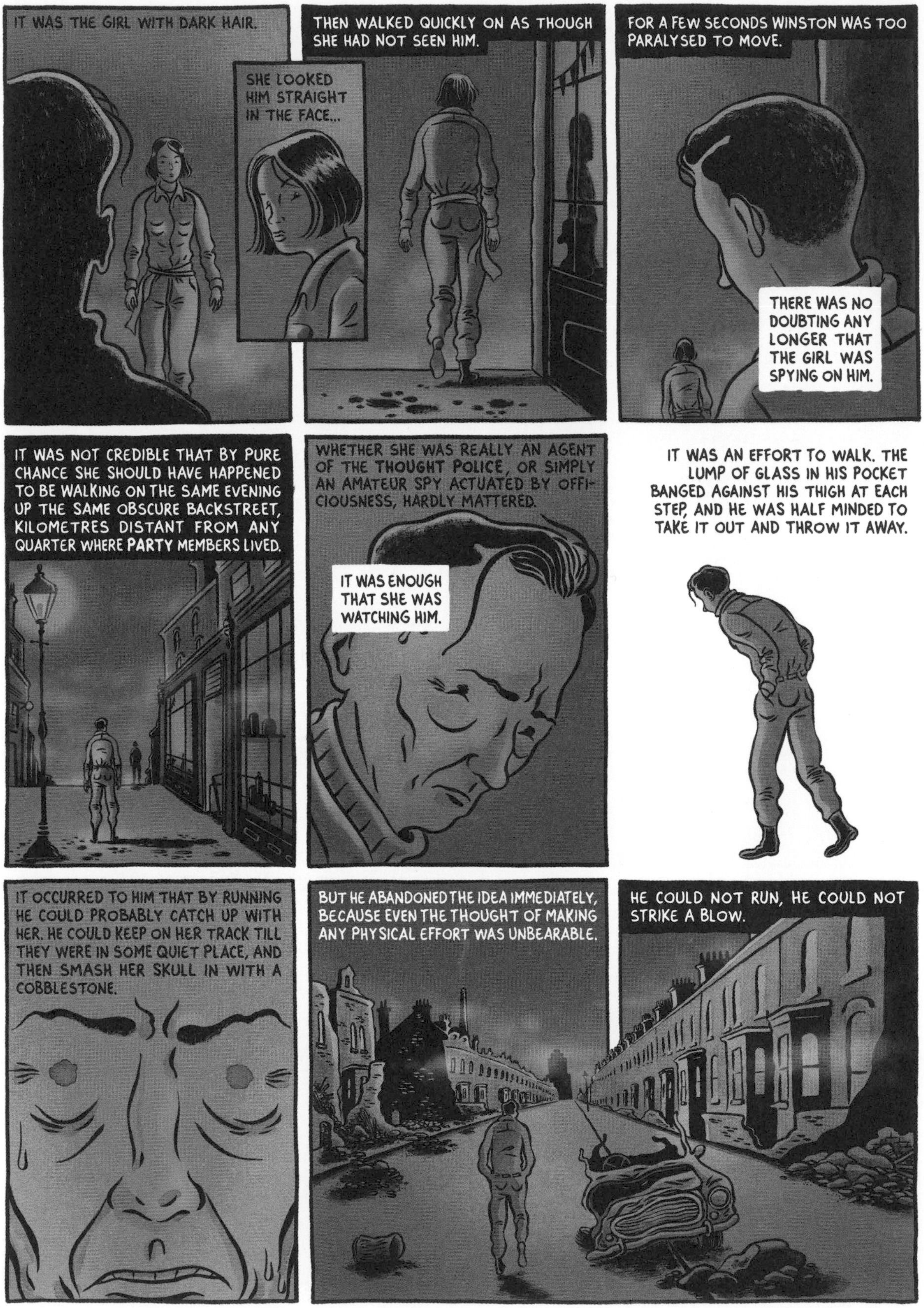
IT WAS THE GIRL WITH DARK HAIR.
SHE LOOKED HIM STRAIGHT IN THE FACE...
THEN WALKED QUICKLY ON AS THOUGH SHE HAD NOT SEEN HIM.
FOR A FEW SECONDS WINSTON WAS TOO PARALYSED TO MOVE.
THERE WAS NO DOUBTING ANY LONGER THAT THE GIRL WAS SPYING ON HIM.
IT WAS NOT CREDIBLE THAT BY PURE CHANCE SHE SHOULD HAVE HAPPENED TO BE WALKING ON THE SAME EVENING UP THE SAME OBSCURE BACKSTREET, KILOMETRES DISTANT FROM ANY QUARTER WHERE PARTY MEMBERS LIVED.
WHETHER SHE WAS REALLY AN AGENT OF THE THOUGHT POLICE, OR SIMPLY AN AMATEUR SPY ACTUATED BY OFFICIOUSNESS, HARDLY MATTERED.
IT WAS ENOUGH THAT SHE WAS WATCHING HIM.
IT WAS AN EFFORT TO WALK. THE LUMP OF GLASS IN HIS POCKET BANGED AGAINST HIS THIGH AT EACH STEP, AND HE WAS HALF MINDED TO TAKE IT OUT AND THROW IT AWAY.
IT OCCURRED TO HIM THAT BY RUNNING HE COULD PROBABLY CATCH UP WITH HER. HE COULD KEEP ON HER TRACK TILL THEY WERE IN SOME QUIET PLACE, AND THEN SMASH HER SKULL IN WITH A COBBLESTONE.
BUT HE ABANDONED THE IDEA IMMEDIATELY, BECAUSE EVEN THE THOUGHT OF MAKING ANY PHYSICAL EFFORT WAS UNBEARABLE.
HE COULD NOT RUN, HE COULD NOT STRIKE A BLOW.

IT WAS AFTER TWENTY-TWO HOURS WHEN HE GOT BACK TO THE FLAT. THE LIGHTS WOULD BE SWITCHED OFF AT THE MAIN AT TWENTY-THREE THIRTY.

IT WAS AT NIGHT THAT THEY CAME FOR YOU, ALWAYS AT NIGHT. THE PROPER THING WAS TO KILL YOURSELF BEFORE THEY GOT YOU.

MANY OF THE DISAPPEARANCES WERE ACTUALLY SUICIDES.

WINSTON THOUGHT OF THE BIOLOGICAL USELESSNESS OF PAIN AND FEAR. HE MIGHT HAVE SILENCED THE GIRL IF ONLY HE HAD ACTED QUICKLY ENOUGH.

BUT PRECISELY BECAUSE OF THE EXTREMITY OF HIS DANGER HE HAD LOST THE POWER TO ACT.

AND IT IS THE SAME, HE PERCEIVED, IN ALL SEEMINGLY HEROIC OR TRAGIC SITUATIONS.

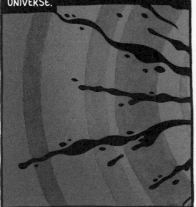

ON THE BATTLEFIELD, IN THE TORTURE CHAMBER, ON A SINKING SHIP, THE ISSUES THAT YOU ARE FIGHTING FOR ARE ALWAYS FORGOTTEN, BECAUSE THE BODY SWELLS UP UNTIL IT FILLS THE UNIVERSE.

AND EVEN WHEN YOU ARE NOT PARALYSED BY FRIGHT OR SCREAMING WITH PAIN, LIFE IS A MOMENT-TO-MOMENT STRUGGLE AGAINST HUNGER OR COLD OR SLEEPLESSNESS.

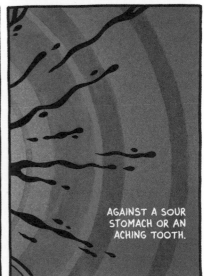

AGAINST A SOUR STOMACH OR AN ACHING TOOTH.

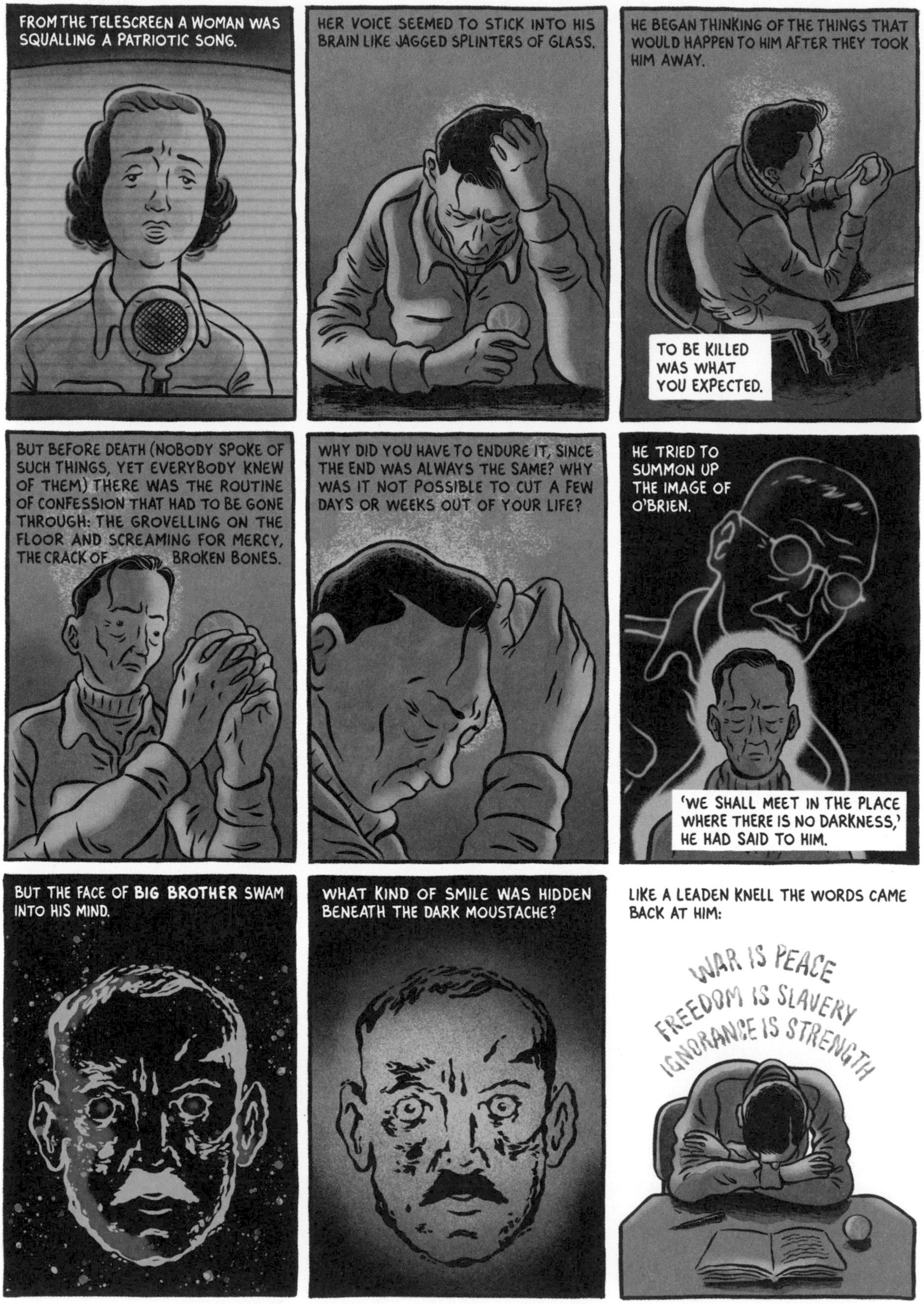
FROM THE TELESCREEN A WOMAN WAS SQUALLING A PATRIOTIC SONG.
HER VOICE SEEMED TO STICK INTO HIS BRAIN LIKE JAGGED SPLINTERS OF GLASS.
HE BEGAN THINKING OF THE THINGS THAT WOULD HAPPEN TO HIM AFTER THEY TOOK HIM AWAY.
TO BE KILLED WAS WHAT YOU EXPECTED.
BUT BEFORE DEATH (NOBODY SPOKE OF SUCH THINGS, YET EVERYBODY KNEW OF THEM) THERE WAS THE ROUTINE OF CONFESSION THAT HAD TO BE GONE THROUGH: THE GROVELLING ON THE FLOOR AND SCREAMING FOR MERCY, THE CRACK OF BROKEN BONES.
WHY DID YOU HAVE TO ENDURE IT, SINCE THE END WAS ALWAYS THE SAME? WHY WAS IT NOT POSSIBLE TO CUT A FEW DAYS OR WEEKS OUT OF YOUR LIFE?
HE TRIED TO SUMMON UP THE IMAGE OF O'BRIEN.
'WE SHALL MEET IN THE PLACE WHERE THERE IS NO DARKNESS,' HE HAD SAID TO HIM.
BUT THE FACE OF BIG BROTHER SWAM INTO HIS MIND.
WHAT KIND OF SMILE WAS HIDDEN BENEATH THE DARK MOUSTACHE?
LIKE A LEADEN KNELL THE WORDS CAME BACK AT HIM:
WAR IS PEACE
FREEDOM IS SLAVERY
IGNORANCE IS STRENGTH

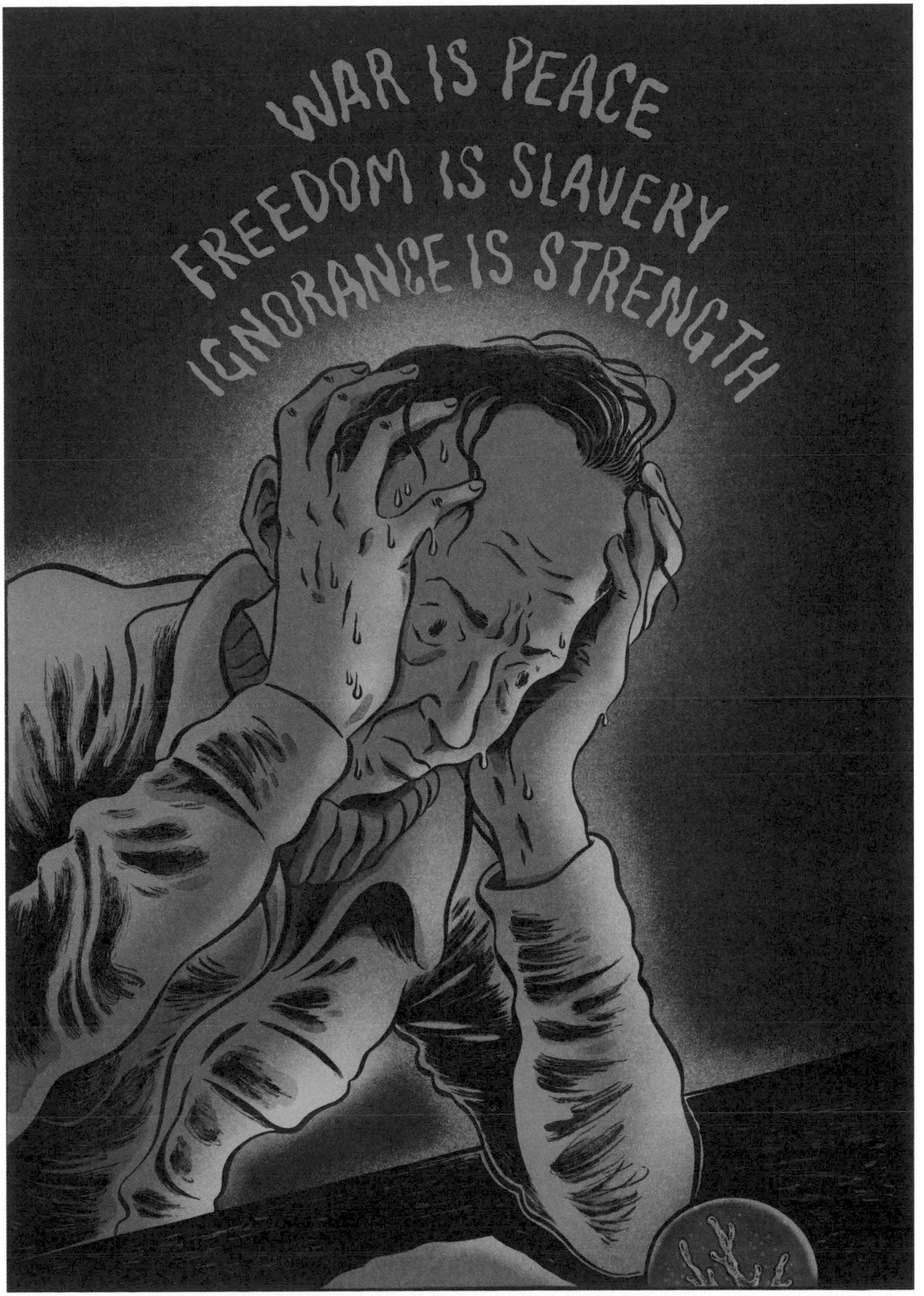
WAR IS PEACE
FREEDOM IS SLAVERY
IGNORANCE IS STRENGTH

PART 2

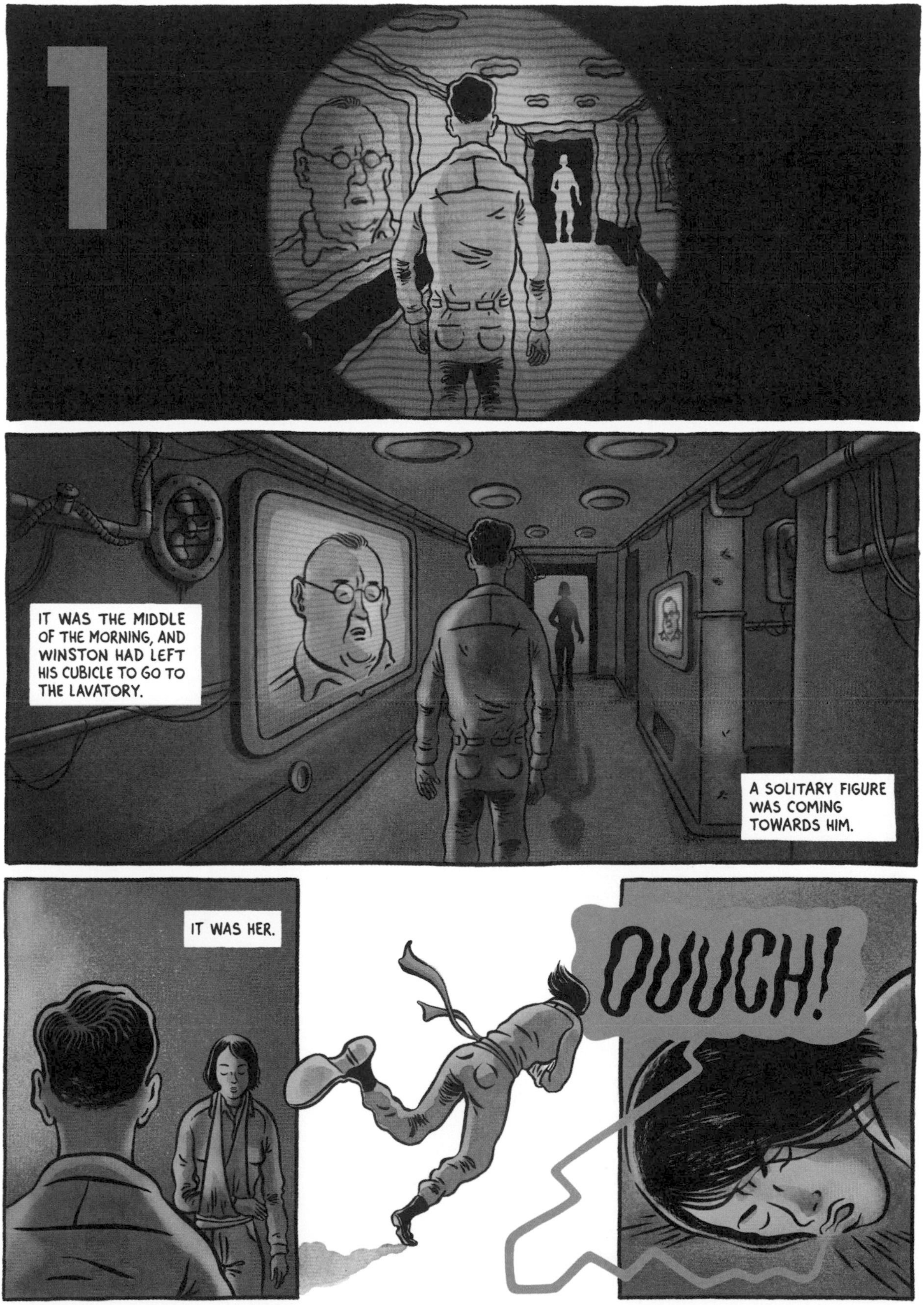
1
IT WAS THE MIDDLE OF THE MORNING, AND WINSTON HAD LEFT HIS CUBICLE TO GO TO THE LAVATORY.
A SOLITARY FIGURE WAS COMING TOWARDS HIM.
IT WAS HER.
OUUCH!

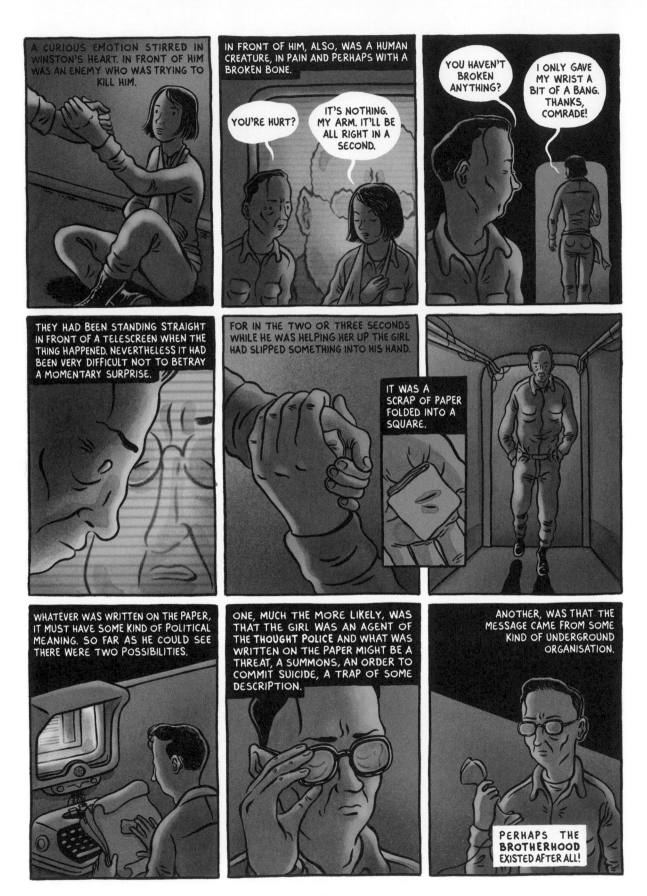

A CURIOUS EMOTION STIRRED IN WINSTON'S HEART. IN FRONT OF HIM WAS AN ENEMY WHO WAS TRYING TO KILL HIM.

IN FRONT OF HIM, ALSO, WAS A HUMAN CREATURE, IN PAIN AND PERHAPS WITH A BROKEN BONE.

YOU'RE HURT?

IT'S NOTHING. MY ARM. IT'LL BE ALL RIGHT IN A SECOND.

YOU HAVEN'T BROKEN ANYTHING?

I ONLY GAVE MY WRIST A BIT OF A BANG. THANKS, COMRADE!

THEY HAD BEEN STANDING STRAIGHT IN FRONT OF A TELESCREEN WHEN THE THING HAPPENED. NEVERTHELESS IT HAD BEEN VERY DIFFICULT NOT TO BETRAY A MOMENTARY SURPRISE.

FOR IN THE TWO OR THREE SECONDS WHILE HE WAS HELPING HER UP THE GIRL HAD SLIPPED SOMETHING INTO HIS HAND.

IT WAS A SCRAP OF PAPER FOLDED INTO A SQUARE.

WHATEVER WAS WRITTEN ON THE PAPER, IT MUST HAVE SOME KIND OF POLITICAL MEANING. SO FAR AS HE COULD SEE THERE WERE TWO POSSIBILITIES.

ONE, MUCH THE MORE LIKELY, WAS THAT THE GIRL WAS AN AGENT OF THE THOUGHT POLICE AND WHAT WAS WRITTEN ON THE PAPER MIGHT BE A THREAT, A SUMMONS, AN ORDER TO COMMIT SUICIDE, A TRAP OF SOME DESCRIPTION.

ANOTHER, WAS THAT THE MESSAGE CAME FROM SOME KIND OF UNDERGROUND ORGANISATION.

PERHAPS THE BROTHERHOOD EXISTED AFTER ALL!

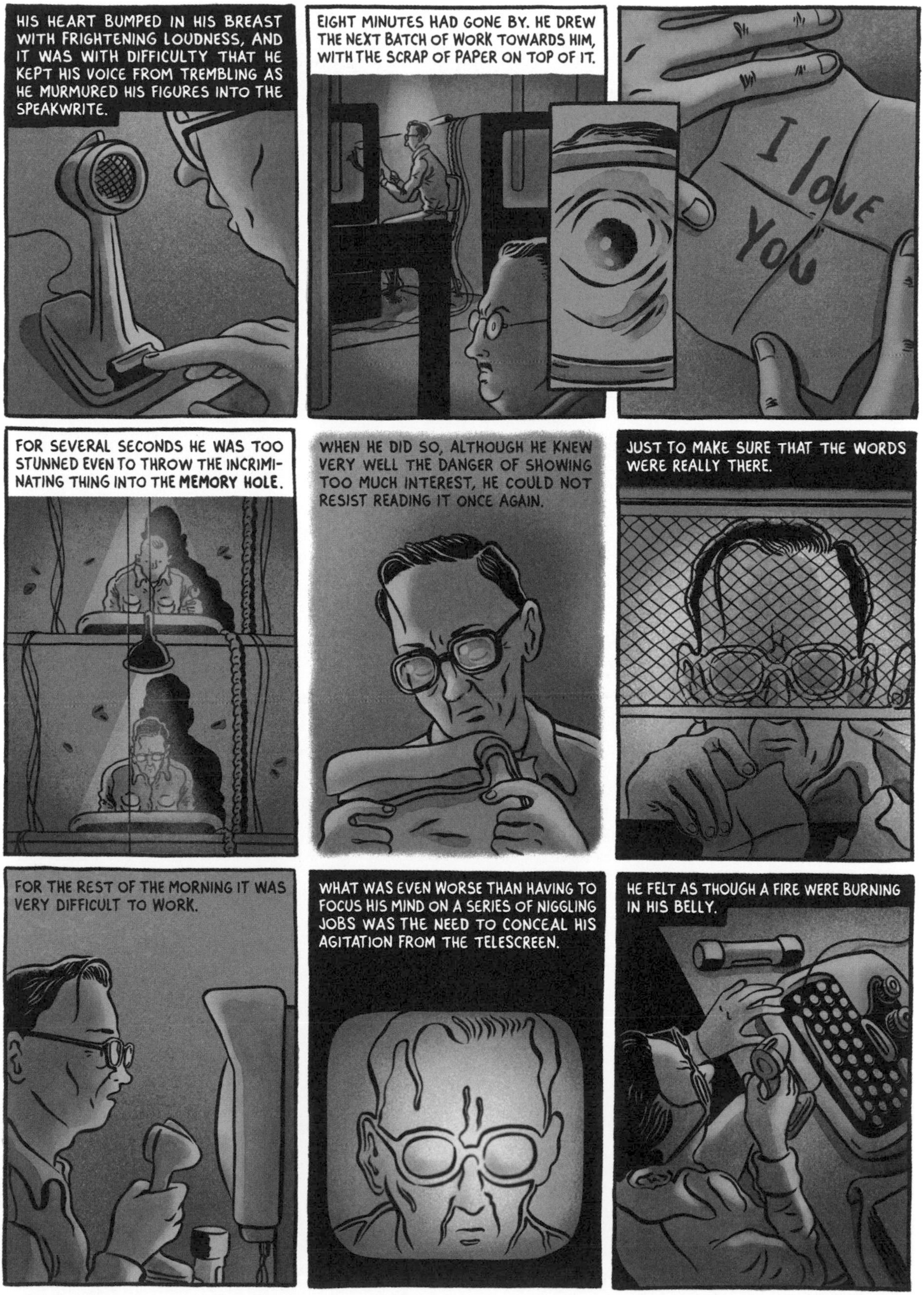
HIS HEART BUMPED IN HIS BREAST WITH FRIGHTENING LOUDNESS, AND IT WAS WITH DIFFICULTY THAT HE KEPT HIS VOICE FROM TREMBLING AS HE MURMURED HIS FIGURES INTO THE SPEAKWRITE.
EIGHT MINUTES HAD GONE BY. HE DREW THE NEXT BATCH OF WORK TOWARDS HIM, WITH THE SCRAP OF PAPER ON TOP OF IT.
I LOVE YOU
FOR SEVERAL SECONDS HE WAS TOO STUNNED EVEN TO THROW THE INCRIMINATING THING INTO THE MEMORY HOLE.
WHEN HE DID SO, ALTHOUGH HE KNEW VERY WELL THE DANGER OF SHOWING TOO MUCH INTEREST, HE COULD NOT RESIST READING IT ONCE AGAIN.
JUST TO MAKE SURE THAT THE WORDS WERE REALLY THERE.
FOR THE REST OF THE MORNING IT WAS VERY DIFFICULT TO WORK.
WHAT WAS EVEN WORSE THAN HAVING TO FOCUS HIS MIND ON A SERIES OF NIGGLING JOBS WAS THE NEED TO CONCEAL HIS AGITATION FROM THE TELESCREEN.
HE FELT AS THOUGH A FIRE WERE BURNING IN HIS BELLY.

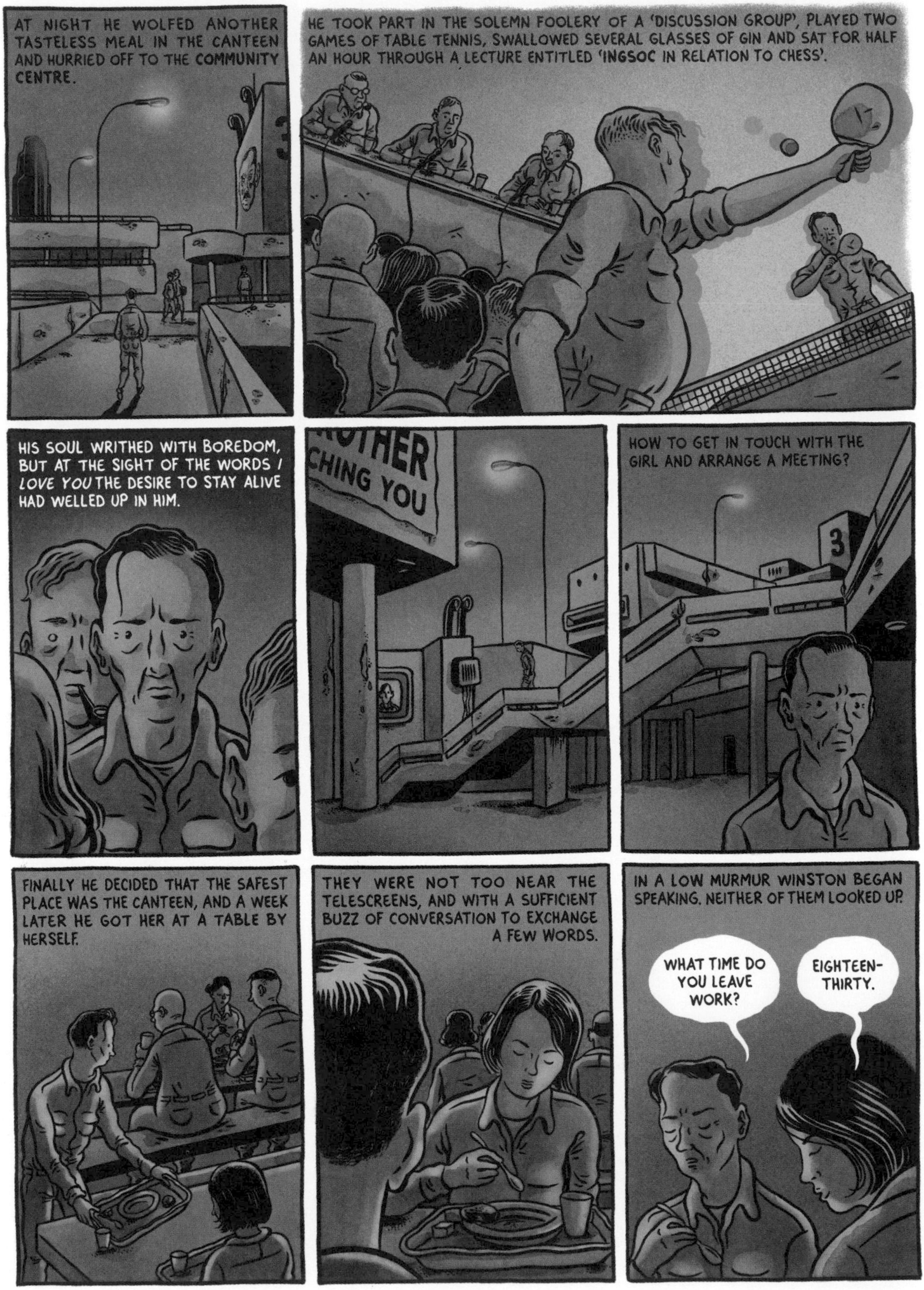

AT NIGHT HE WOLFED ANOTHER TASTELESS MEAL IN THE CANTEEN AND HURRIED OFF TO THE COMMUNITY CENTRE.
HE TOOK PART IN THE SOLEMN FOOLERY OF A 'DISCUSSION GROUP', PLAYED TWO GAMES OF TABLE TENNIS, SWALLOWED SEVERAL GLASSES OF GIN AND SAT FOR HALF AN HOUR THROUGH A LECTURE ENTITLED 'INGSOC IN RELATION TO CHESS'.
HIS SOUL WRITHED WITH BOREDOM, BUT AT THE SIGHT OF THE WORDS *I LOVE YOU* THE DESIRE TO STAY ALIVE HAD WELLED UP IN HIM.
CHING YOU
HOW TO GET IN TOUCH WITH THE GIRL AND ARRANGE A MEETING?
3
FINALLY HE DECIDED THAT THE SAFEST PLACE WAS THE CANTEEN, AND A WEEK LATER HE GOT HER AT A TABLE BY HERSELF.
THEY WERE NOT TOO NEAR THE TELESCREENS, AND WITH A SUFFICIENT BUZZ OF CONVERSATION TO EXCHANGE A FEW WORDS.
IN A LOW MURMUR WINSTON BEGAN SPEAKING. NEITHER OF THEM LOOKED UP.
WHAT TIME DO YOU LEAVE WORK?
EIGHTEEN-THIRTY.

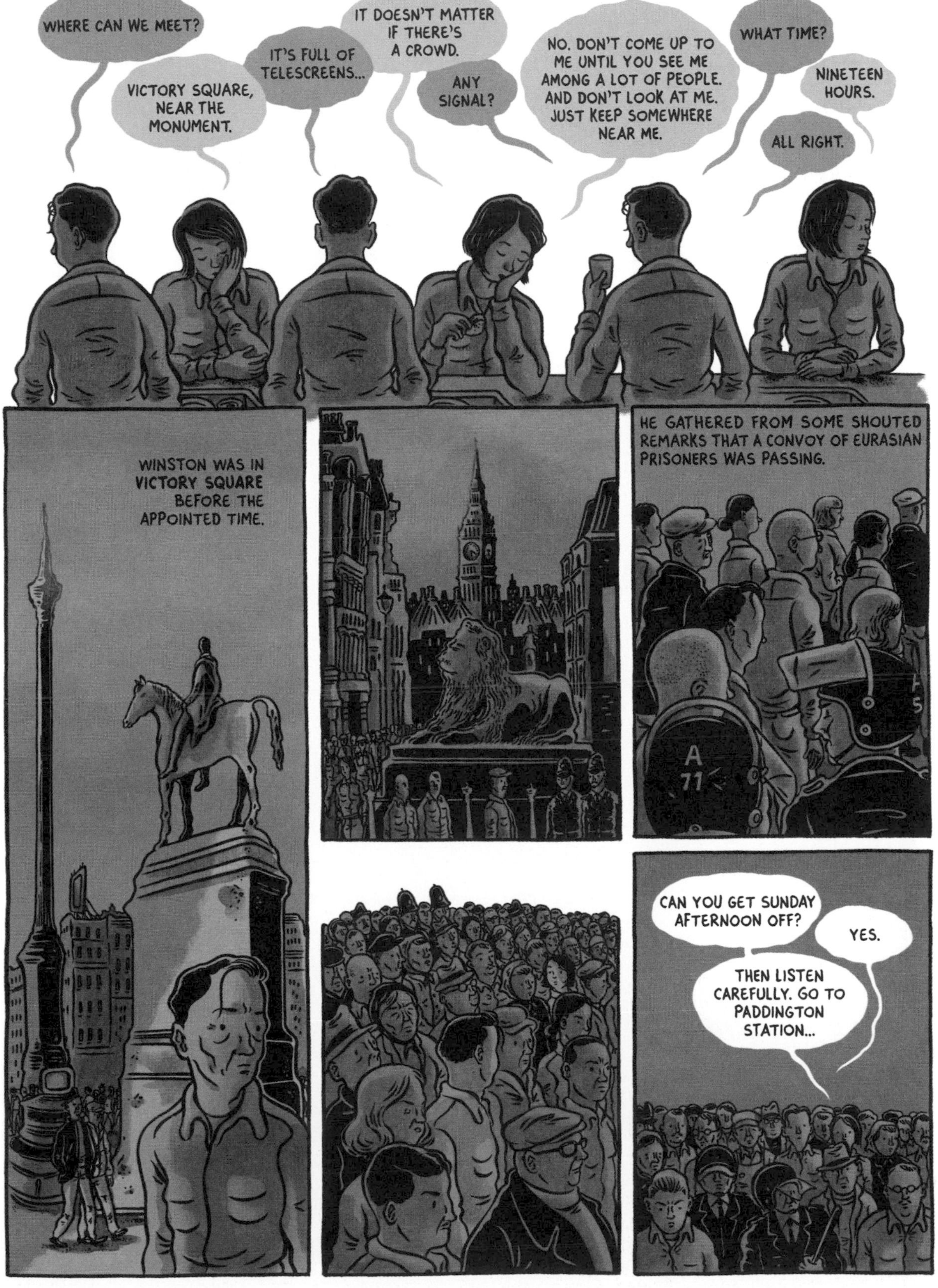
WHERE CAN WE MEET?
VICTORY SQUARE, NEAR THE MONUMENT.
IT'S FULL OF TELESCREENS...
IT DOESN'T MATTER IF THERE'S A CROWD.
ANY SIGNAL?
NO. DON'T COME UP TO ME UNTIL YOU SEE ME AMONG A LOT OF PEOPLE. AND DON'T LOOK AT ME. JUST KEEP SOMEWHERE NEAR ME.
WHAT TIME?
NINETEEN HOURS.
ALL RIGHT.
WINSTON WAS IN **VICTORY SQUARE** BEFORE THE APPOINTED TIME.
HE GATHERED FROM SOME SHOUTED REMARKS THAT A CONVOY OF EURASIAN PRISONERS WAS PASSING.
A 71
CAN YOU GET SUNDAY AFTERNOON OFF?
YES.
THEN LISTEN CAREFULLY. GO TO PADDINGTON STATION...

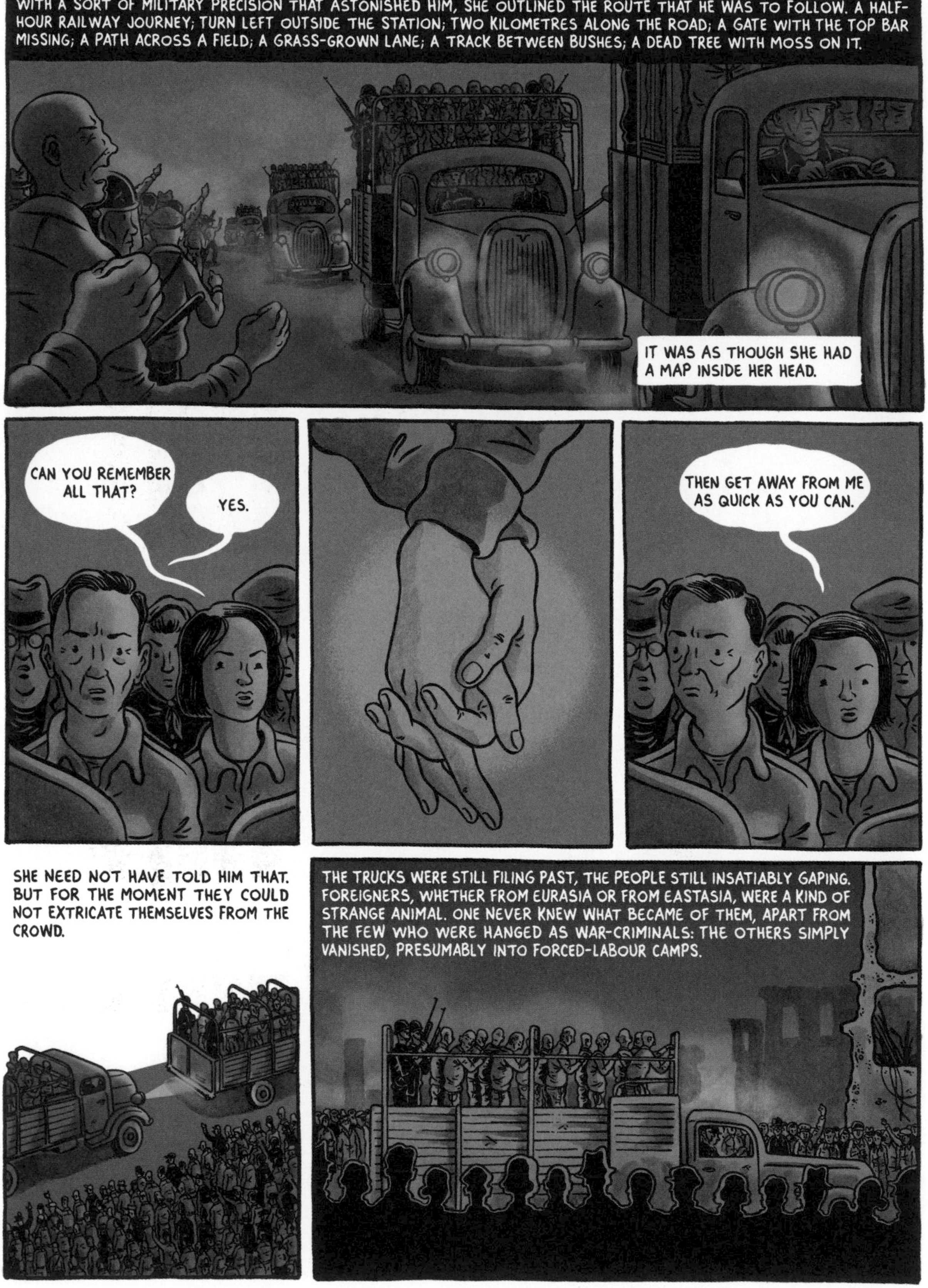
WITH A SORT OF MILITARY PRECISION THAT ASTONISHED HIM, SHE OUTLINED THE ROUTE THAT HE WAS TO FOLLOW. A HALF-HOUR RAILWAY JOURNEY; TURN LEFT OUTSIDE THE STATION; TWO KILOMETRES ALONG THE ROAD; A GATE WITH THE TOP BAR MISSING; A PATH ACROSS A FIELD; A GRASS-GROWN LANE; A TRACK BETWEEN BUSHES; A DEAD TREE WITH MOSS ON IT.
IT WAS AS THOUGH SHE HAD A MAP INSIDE HER HEAD.
CAN YOU REMEMBER ALL THAT?
YES.
THEN GET AWAY FROM ME AS QUICK AS YOU CAN.
SHE NEED NOT HAVE TOLD HIM THAT. BUT FOR THE MOMENT THEY COULD NOT EXTRICATE THEMSELVES FROM THE CROWD.
THE TRUCKS WERE STILL FILING PAST, THE PEOPLE STILL INSATIABLY GAPING. FOREIGNERS, WHETHER FROM EURASIA OR FROM EASTASIA, WERE A KIND OF STRANGE ANIMAL. ONE NEVER KNEW WHAT BECAME OF THEM, APART FROM THE FEW WHO WERE HANGED AS WAR-CRIMINALS: THE OTHERS SIMPLY VANISHED, PRESUMABLY INTO FORCED-LABOUR CAMPS.

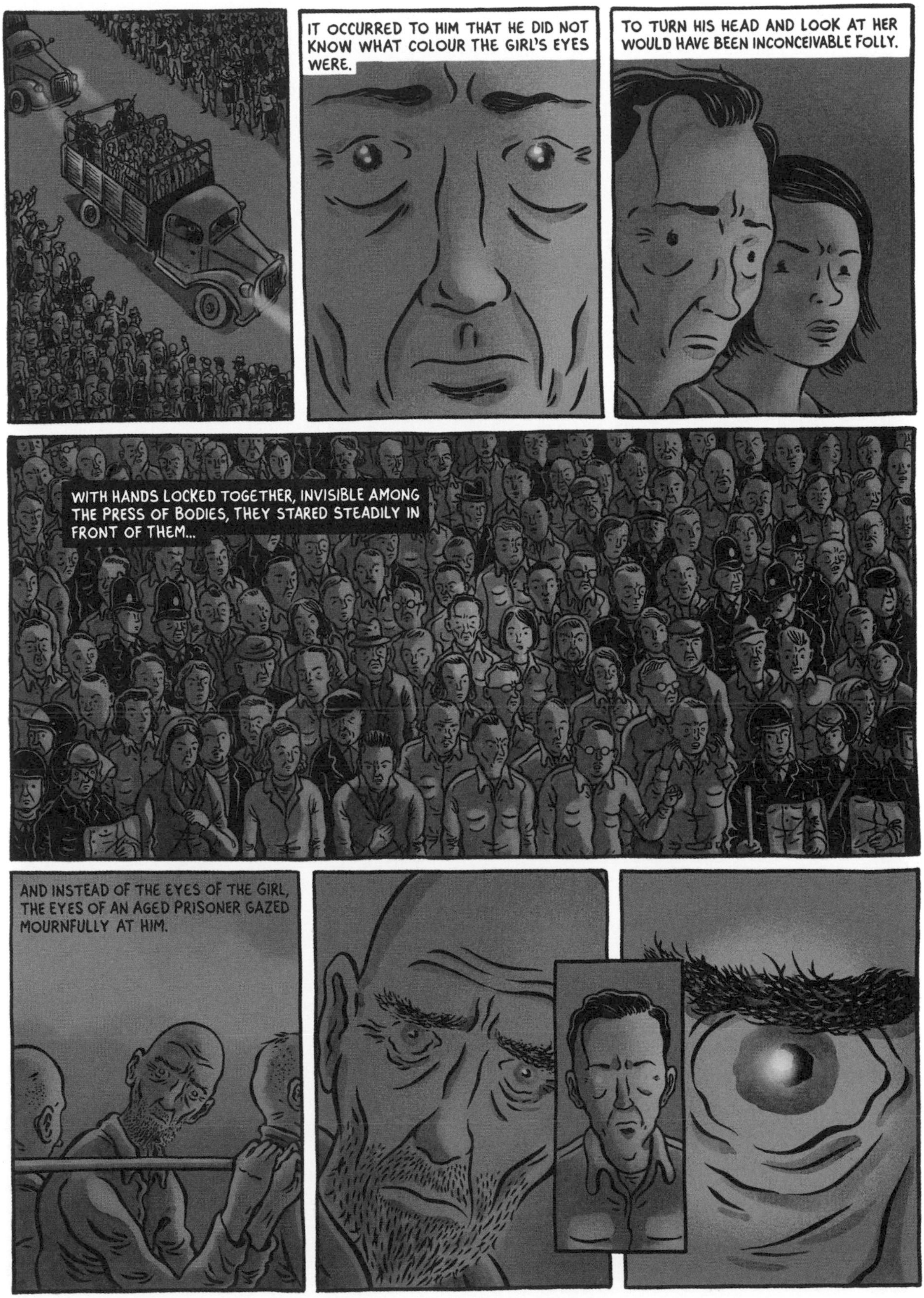
IT OCCURRED TO HIM THAT HE DID NOT KNOW WHAT COLOUR THE GIRL'S EYES WERE.
TO TURN HIS HEAD AND LOOK AT HER WOULD HAVE BEEN INCONCEIVABLE FOLLY.
WITH HANDS LOCKED TOGETHER, INVISIBLE AMONG THE PRESS OF BODIES, THEY STARED STEADILY IN FRONT OF THEM...
AND INSTEAD OF THE EYES OF THE GIRL, THE EYES OF AN AGED PRISONER GAZED MOURNFULLY AT HIM.

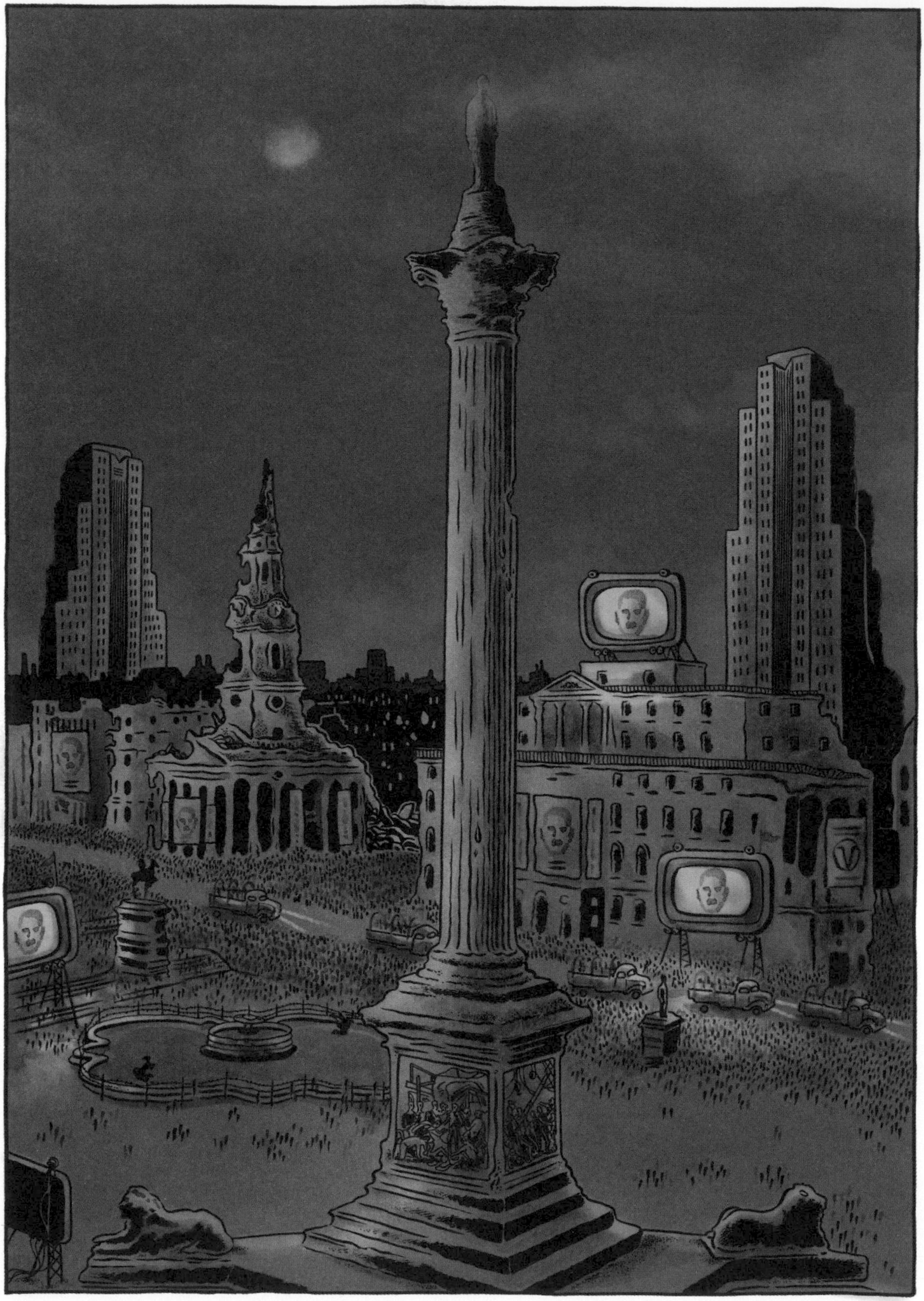

2

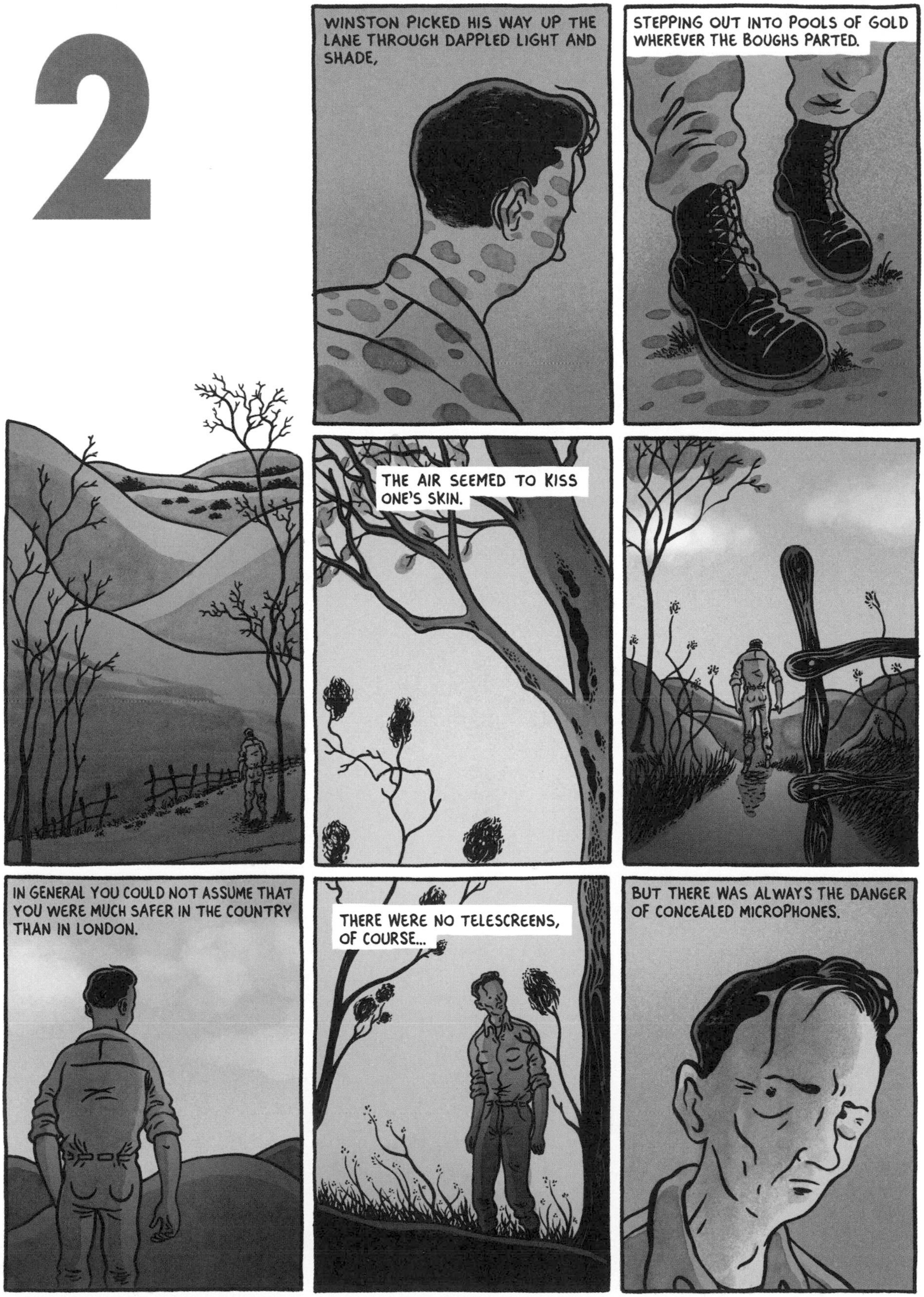
WINSTON PICKED HIS WAY UP THE LANE THROUGH DAPPLED LIGHT AND SHADE,
STEPPING OUT INTO POOLS OF GOLD WHEREVER THE BOUGHS PARTED.
THE AIR SEEMED TO KISS ONE'S SKIN.
IN GENERAL YOU COULD NOT ASSUME THAT YOU WERE MUCH SAFER IN THE COUNTRY THAN IN LONDON.
THERE WERE NO TELESCREENS, OF COURSE...
BUT THERE WAS ALWAYS THE DANGER OF CONCEALED MICROPHONES.

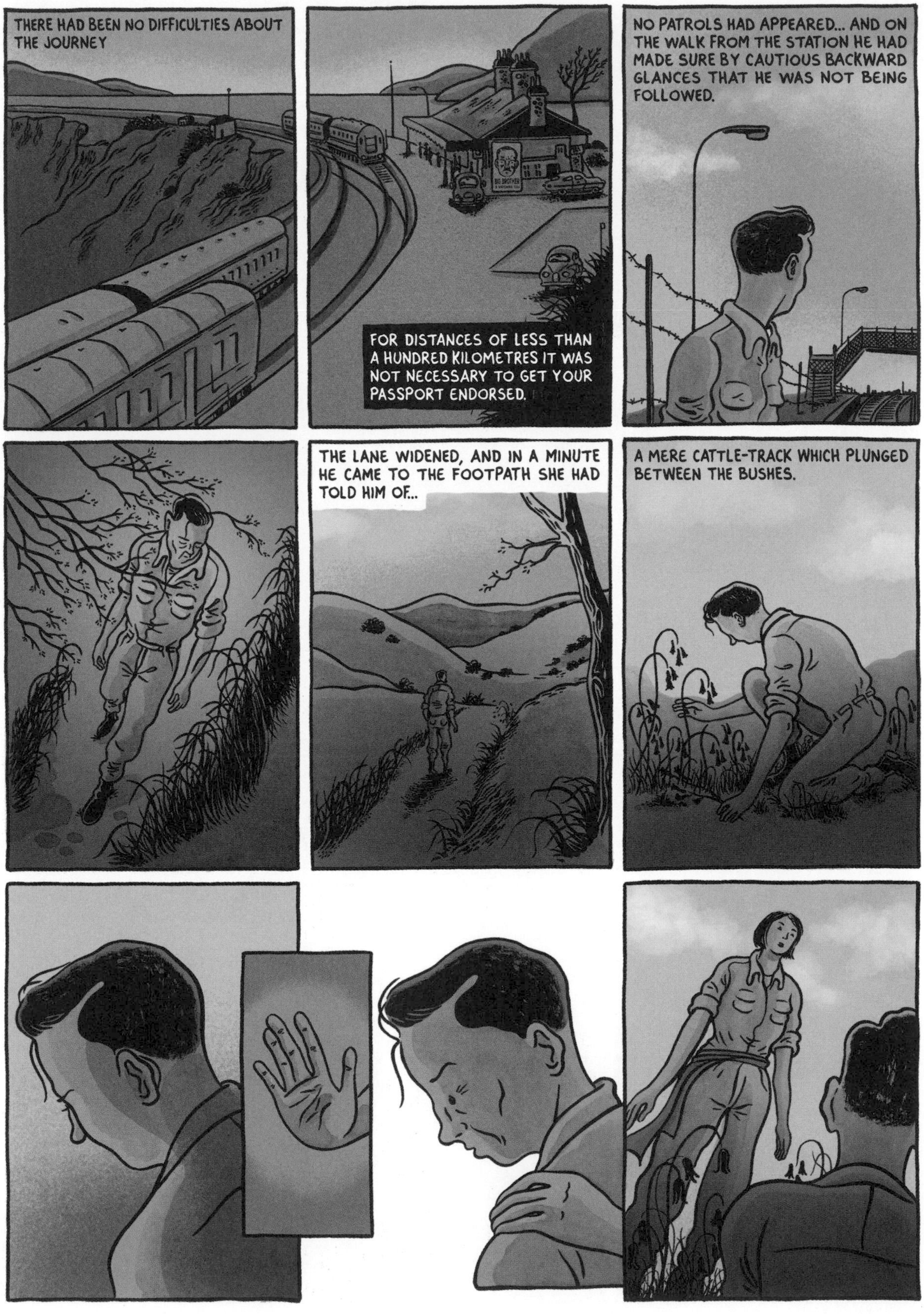
THERE HAD BEEN NO DIFFICULTIES ABOUT THE JOURNEY
FOR DISTANCES OF LESS THAN A HUNDRED KILOMETRES IT WAS NOT NECESSARY TO GET YOUR PASSPORT ENDORSED.
BIG BROTHER
NO PATROLS HAD APPEARED... AND ON THE WALK FROM THE STATION HE HAD MADE SURE BY CAUTIOUS BACKWARD GLANCES THAT HE WAS NOT BEING FOLLOWED.
THE LANE WIDENED, AND IN A MINUTE HE CAME TO THE FOOTPATH SHE HAD TOLD HIM OF...
A MERE CATTLE-TRACK WHICH PLUNGED BETWEEN THE BUSHES.

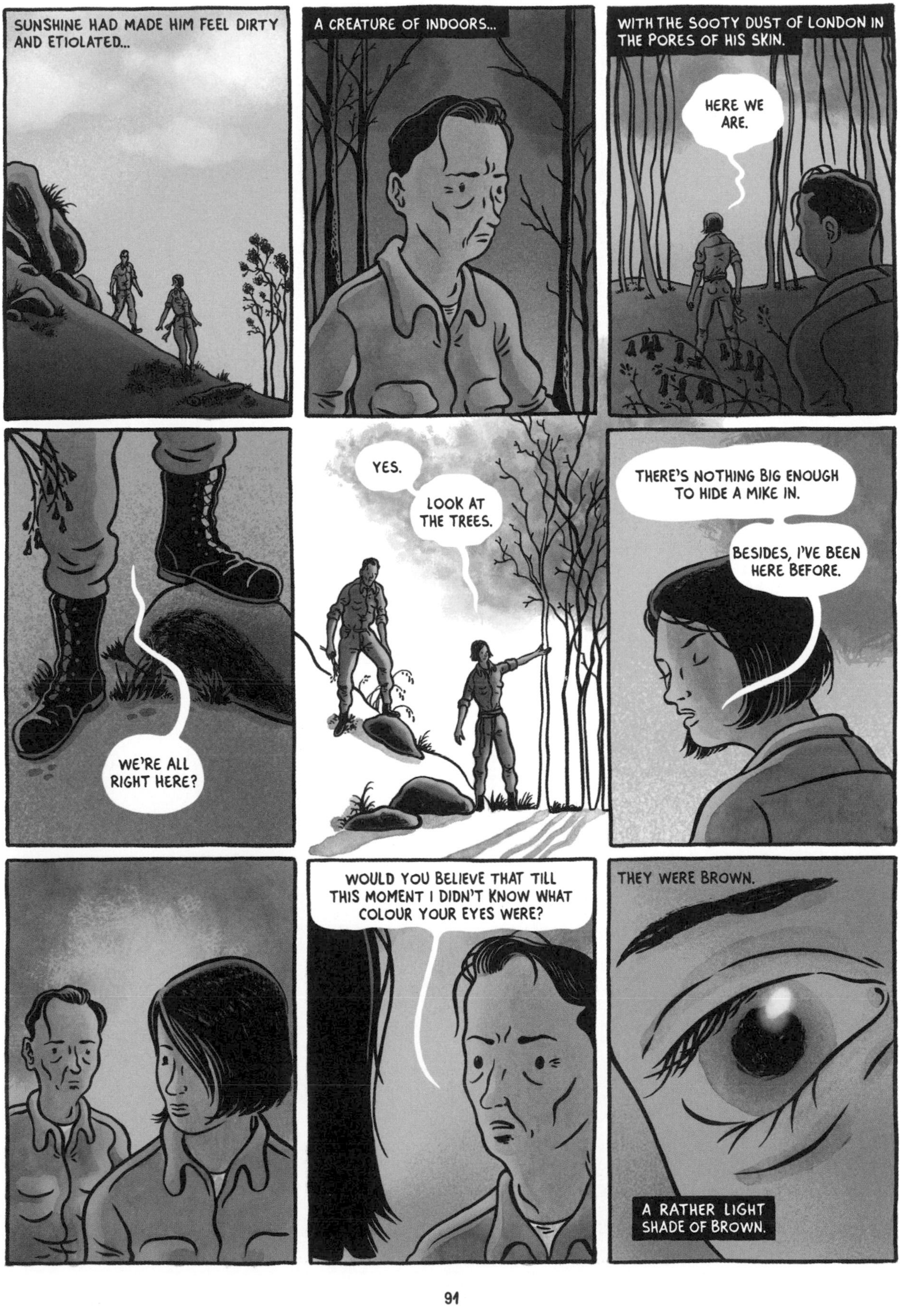
SUNSHINE HAD MADE HIM FEEL DIRTY AND ETIOLATED...
A CREATURE OF INDOORS...
WITH THE SOOTY DUST OF LONDON IN THE PORES OF HIS SKIN.
HERE WE ARE.
WE'RE ALL RIGHT HERE?
YES.
LOOK AT THE TREES.
THERE'S NOTHING BIG ENOUGH TO HIDE A MIKE IN.
BESIDES, I'VE BEEN HERE BEFORE.
WOULD YOU BELIEVE THAT TILL THIS MOMENT I DIDN'T KNOW WHAT COLOUR YOUR EYES WERE?
THEY WERE BROWN.
A RATHER LIGHT SHADE OF BROWN.

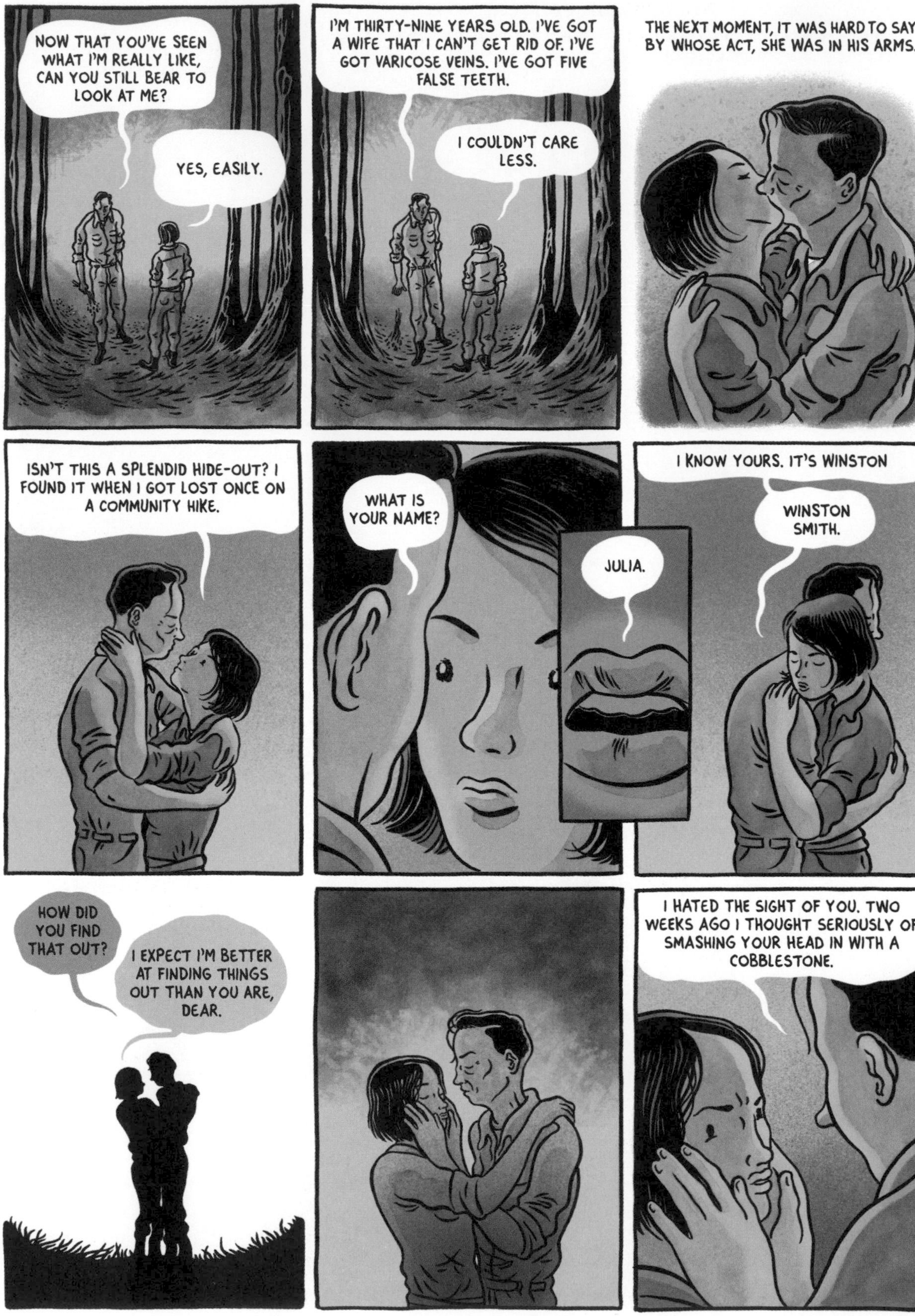
NOW THAT YOU'VE SEEN WHAT I'M REALLY LIKE, CAN YOU STILL BEAR TO LOOK AT ME?
YES, EASILY.
I'M THIRTY-NINE YEARS OLD. I'VE GOT A WIFE THAT I CAN'T GET RID OF. I'VE GOT VARICOSE VEINS. I'VE GOT FIVE FALSE TEETH.
I COULDN'T CARE LESS.
THE NEXT MOMENT, IT WAS HARD TO SAY BY WHOSE ACT, SHE WAS IN HIS ARMS.
ISN'T THIS A SPLENDID HIDE-OUT? I FOUND IT WHEN I GOT LOST ONCE ON A COMMUNITY HIKE.
WHAT IS YOUR NAME?
JULIA.
I KNOW YOURS. IT'S WINSTON
WINSTON SMITH.
HOW DID YOU FIND THAT OUT?
I EXPECT I'M BETTER AT FINDING THINGS OUT THAN YOU ARE, DEAR.
I HATED THE SIGHT OF YOU. TWO WEEKS AGO I THOUGHT SERIOUSLY OF SMASHING YOUR HEAD IN WITH A COBBLESTONE.

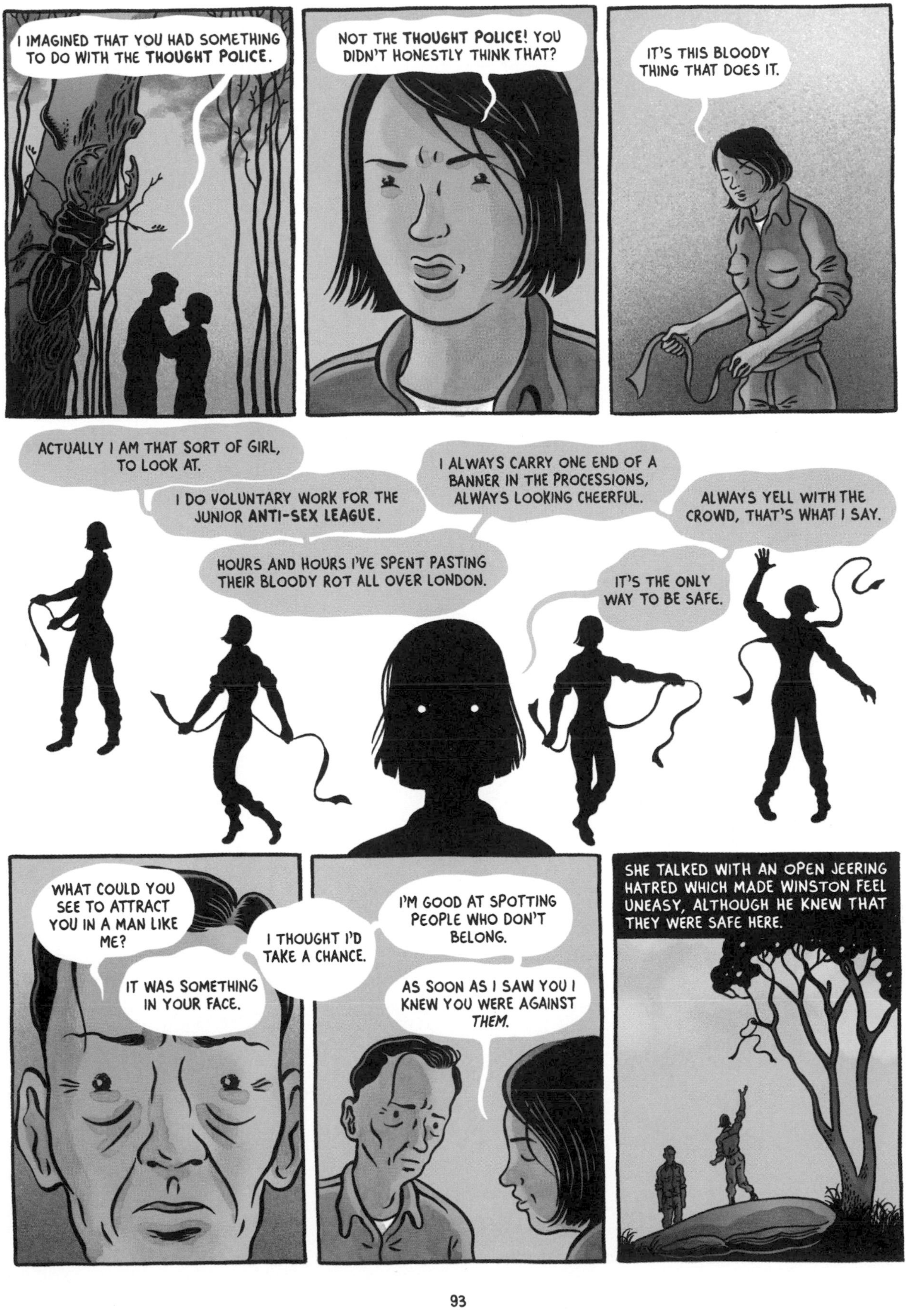
I IMAGINED THAT YOU HAD SOMETHING TO DO WITH THE THOUGHT POLICE.
NOT THE THOUGHT POLICE! YOU DIDN'T HONESTLY THINK THAT?
IT'S THIS BLOODY THING THAT DOES IT.
ACTUALLY I AM THAT SORT OF GIRL, TO LOOK AT.
I DO VOLUNTARY WORK FOR THE JUNIOR ANTI-SEX LEAGUE.
HOURS AND HOURS I'VE SPENT PASTING THEIR BLOODY ROT ALL OVER LONDON.
I ALWAYS CARRY ONE END OF A BANNER IN THE PROCESSIONS, ALWAYS LOOKING CHEERFUL.
ALWAYS YELL WITH THE CROWD, THAT'S WHAT I SAY.
IT'S THE ONLY WAY TO BE SAFE.
WHAT COULD YOU SEE TO ATTRACT YOU IN A MAN LIKE ME?
IT WAS SOMETHING IN YOUR FACE.
I THOUGHT I'D TAKE A CHANCE.
I'M GOOD AT SPOTTING PEOPLE WHO DON'T BELONG.
AS SOON AS I SAW YOU I KNEW YOU WERE AGAINST *THEM*.
SHE TALKED WITH AN OPEN JEERING HATRED WHICH MADE WINSTON FEEL UNEASY, ALTHOUGH HE KNEW THAT THEY WERE SAFE HERE.

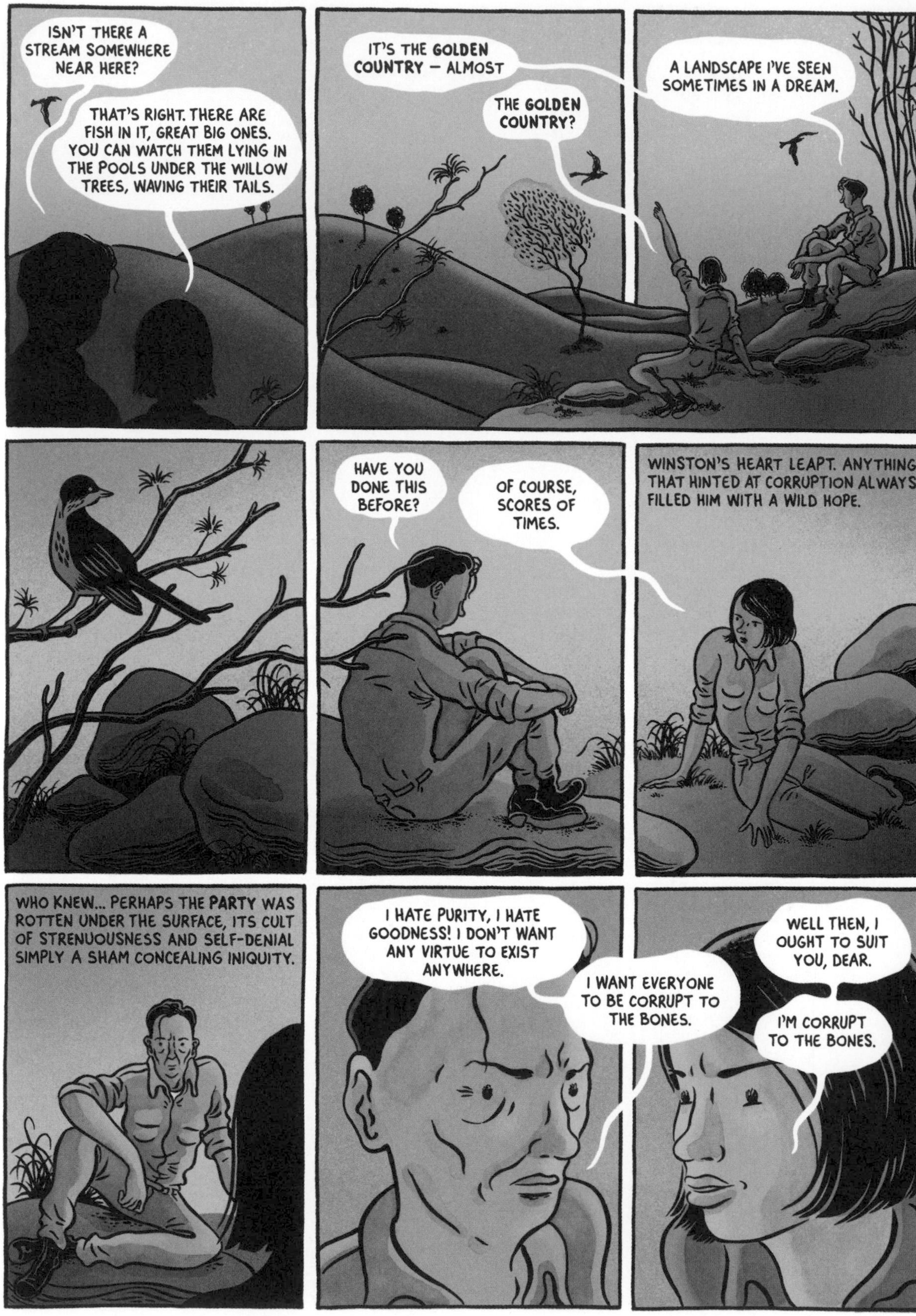
ISN'T THERE A STREAM SOMEWHERE NEAR HERE?
THAT'S RIGHT. THERE ARE FISH IN IT, GREAT BIG ONES. YOU CAN WATCH THEM LYING IN THE POOLS UNDER THE WILLOW TREES, WAVING THEIR TAILS.
IT'S THE GOLDEN COUNTRY — ALMOST
THE GOLDEN COUNTRY?
A LANDSCAPE I'VE SEEN SOMETIMES IN A DREAM.
HAVE YOU DONE THIS BEFORE?
OF COURSE, SCORES OF TIMES.
WINSTON'S HEART LEAPT. ANYTHING THAT HINTED AT CORRUPTION ALWAYS FILLED HIM WITH A WILD HOPE.
WHO KNEW... PERHAPS THE PARTY WAS ROTTEN UNDER THE SURFACE, ITS CULT OF STRENUOUSNESS AND SELF-DENIAL SIMPLY A SHAM CONCEALING INIQUITY.
I HATE PURITY, I HATE GOODNESS! I DON'T WANT ANY VIRTUE TO EXIST ANYWHERE.
I WANT EVERYONE TO BE CORRUPT TO THE BONES.
WELL THEN, I OUGHT TO SUIT YOU, DEAR.
I'M CORRUPT TO THE BONES.

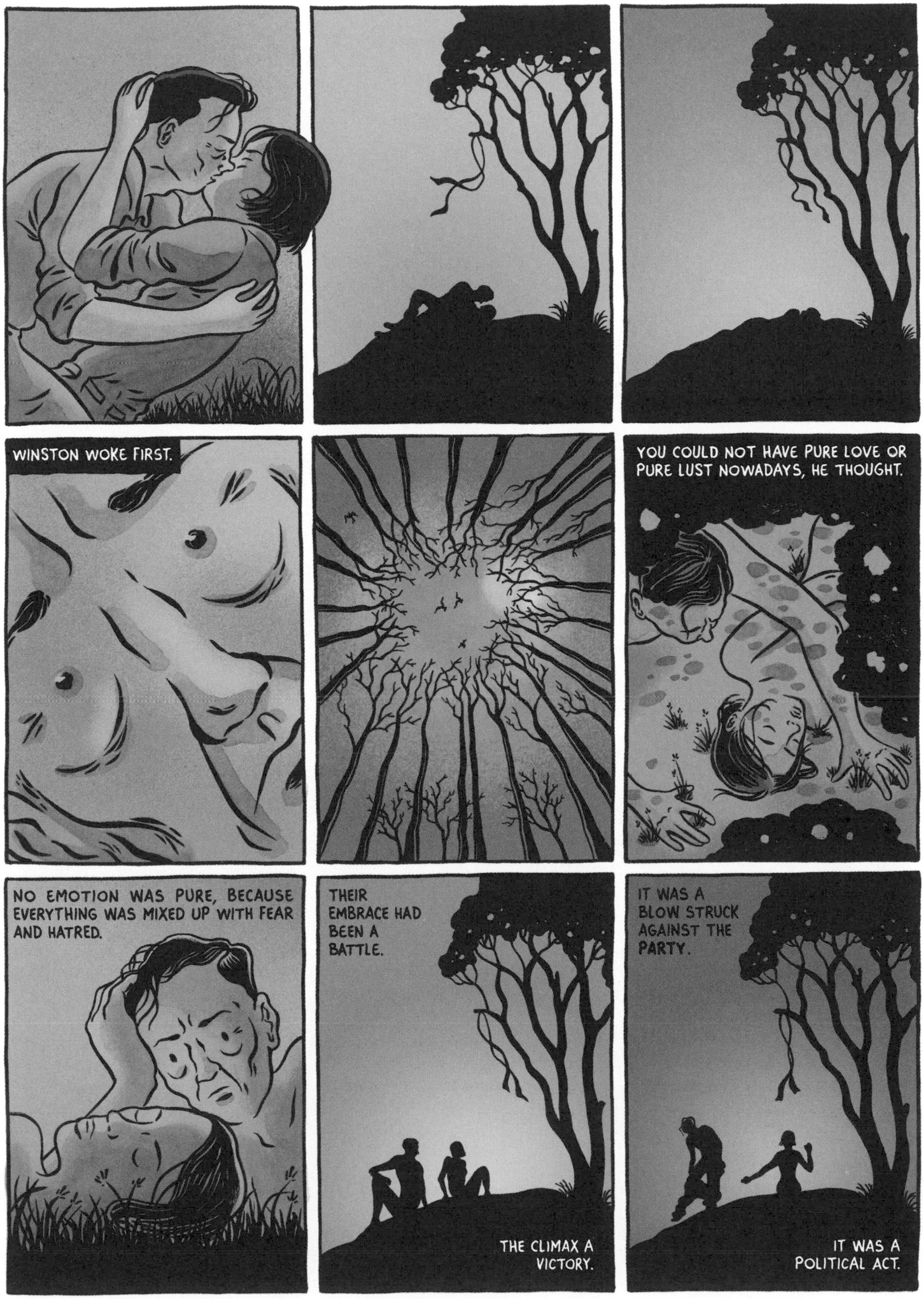
WINSTON WOKE FIRST.
YOU COULD NOT HAVE PURE LOVE OR PURE LUST NOWADAYS, HE THOUGHT.
NO EMOTION WAS PURE, BECAUSE EVERYTHING WAS MIXED UP WITH FEAR AND HATRED.
THEIR EMBRACE HAD BEEN A BATTLE.
THE CLIMAX A VICTORY.
IT WAS A BLOW STRUCK AGAINST THE PARTY.
IT WAS A POLITICAL ACT.

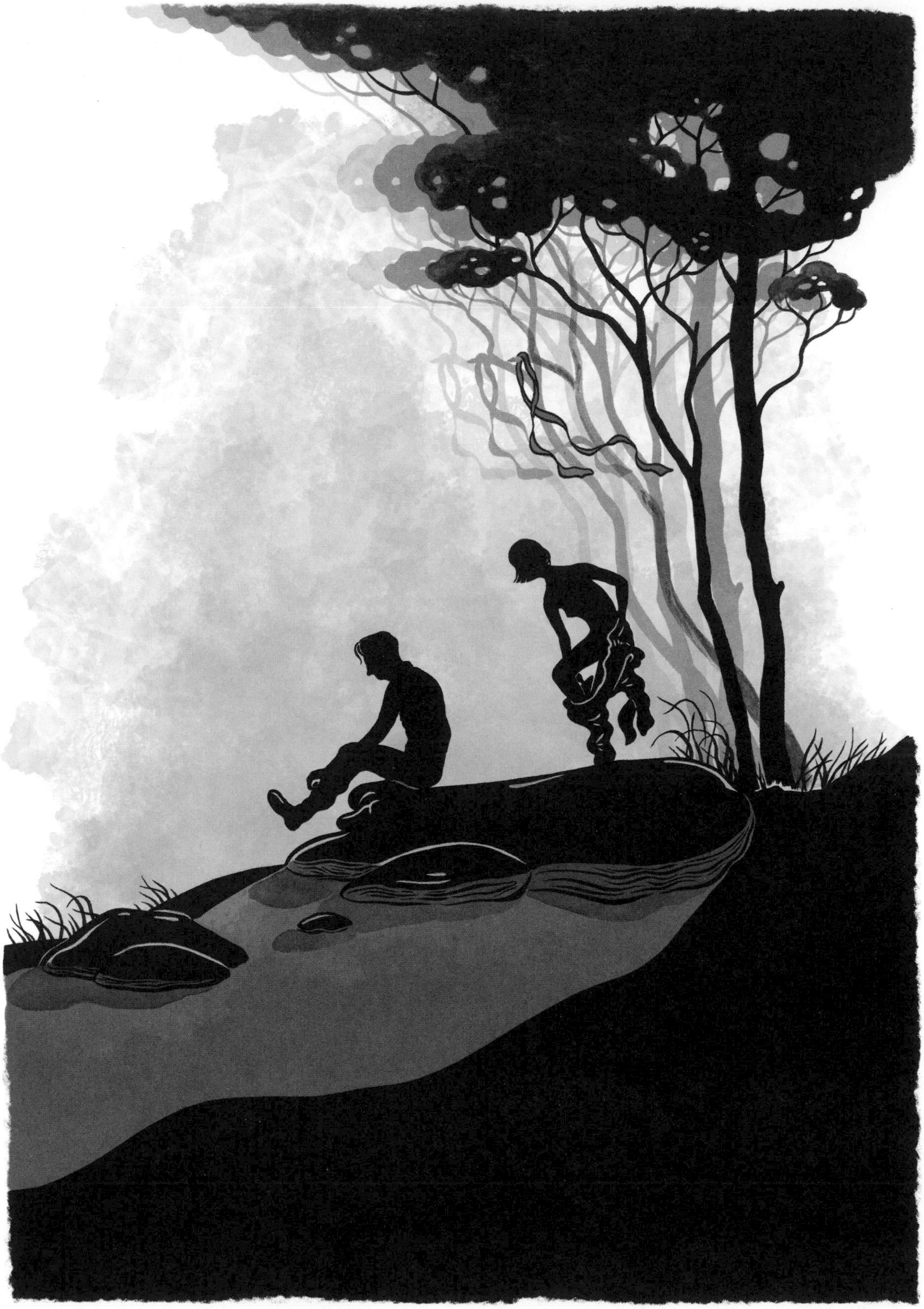

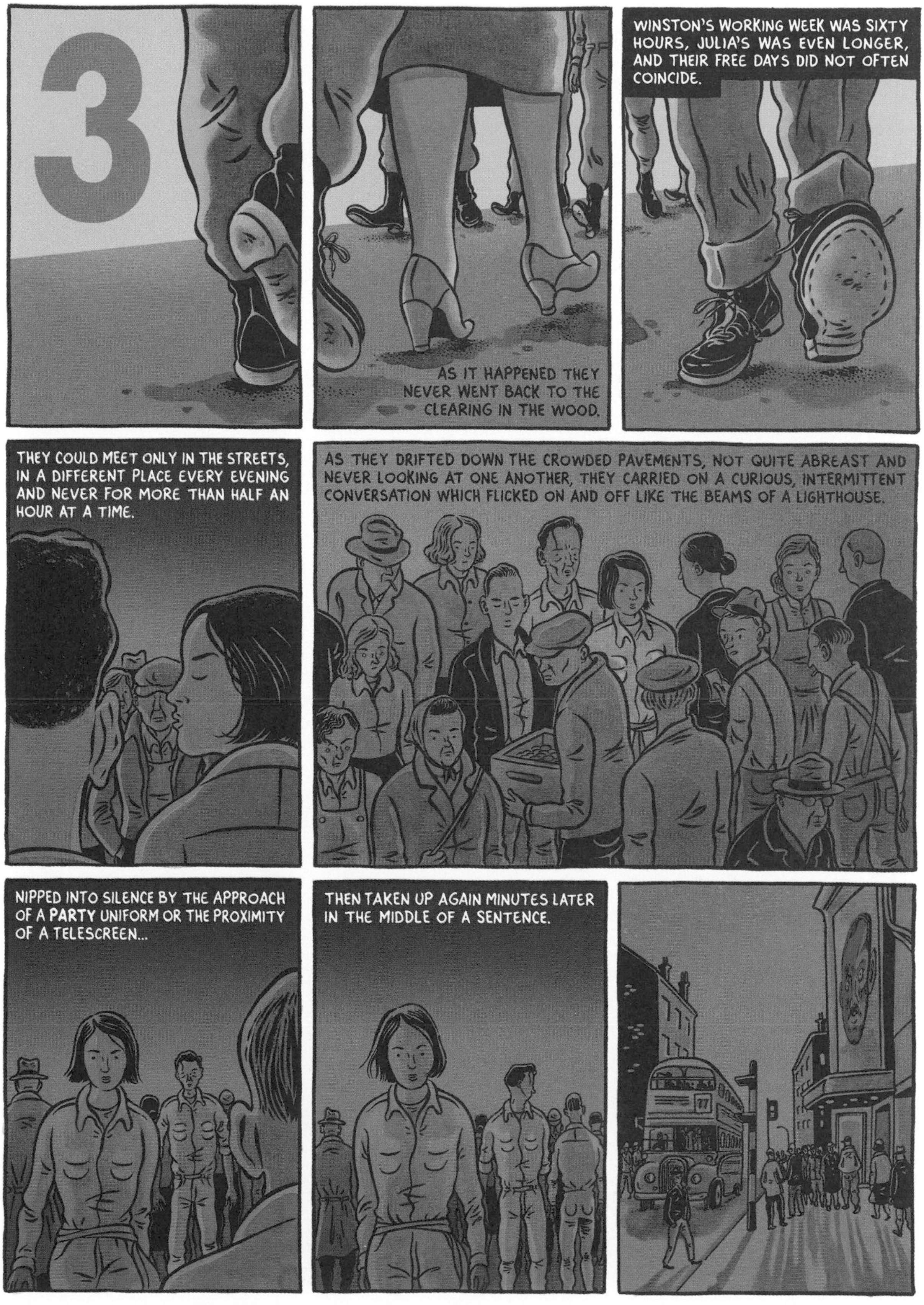
3
AS IT HAPPENED THEY NEVER WENT BACK TO THE CLEARING IN THE WOOD.
WINSTON'S WORKING WEEK WAS SIXTY HOURS, JULIA'S WAS EVEN LONGER, AND THEIR FREE DAYS DID NOT OFTEN COINCIDE.
THEY COULD MEET ONLY IN THE STREETS, IN A DIFFERENT PLACE EVERY EVENING AND NEVER FOR MORE THAN HALF AN HOUR AT A TIME.
AS THEY DRIFTED DOWN THE CROWDED PAVEMENTS, NOT QUITE ABREAST AND NEVER LOOKING AT ONE ANOTHER, THEY CARRIED ON A CURIOUS, INTERMITTENT CONVERSATION WHICH FLICKED ON AND OFF LIKE THE BEAMS OF A LIGHTHOUSE.
NIPPED INTO SILENCE BY THE APPROACH OF A PARTY UNIFORM OR THE PROXIMITY OF A TELESCREEN...
THEN TAKEN UP AGAIN MINUTES LATER IN THE MIDDLE OF A SENTENCE.
77

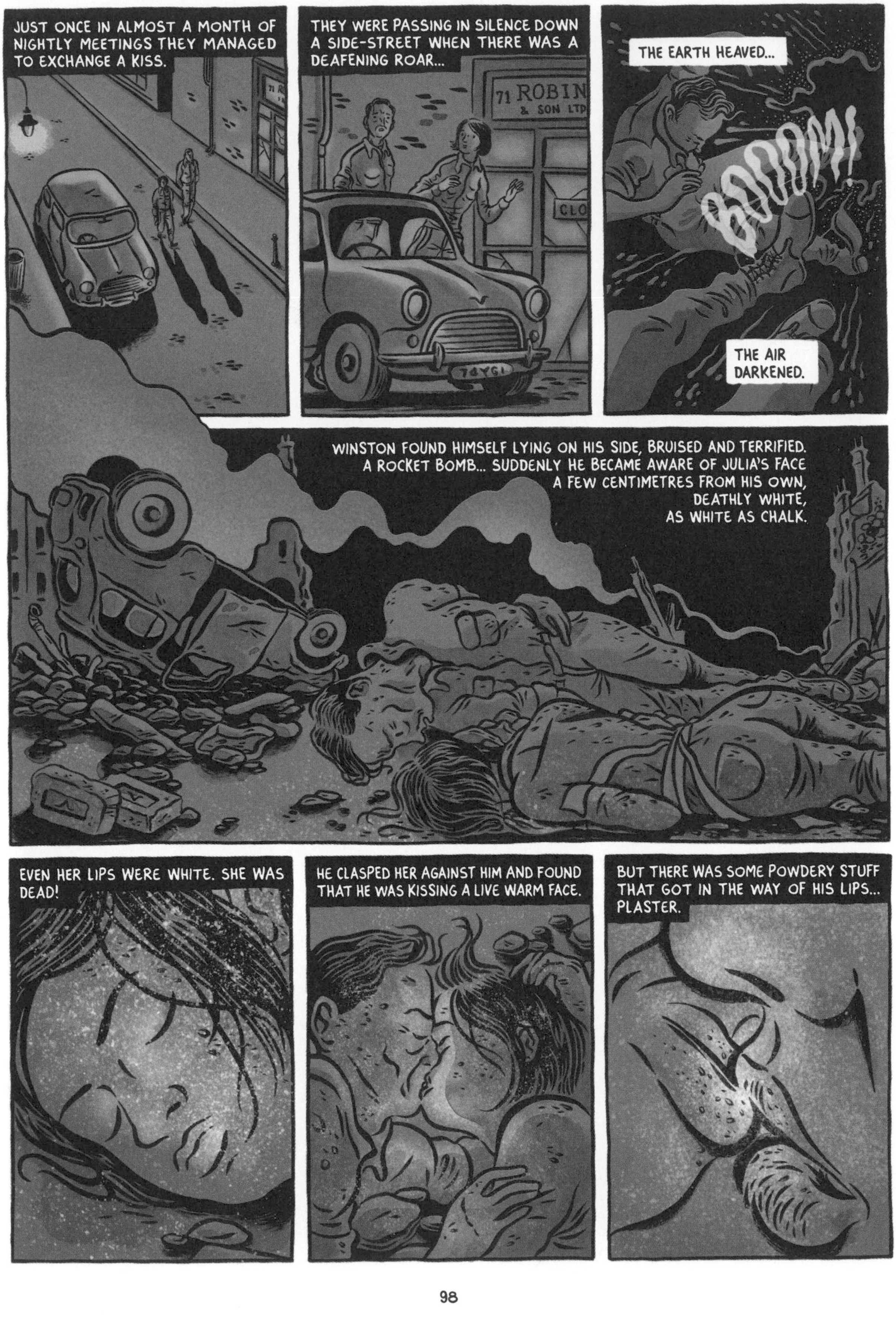
JUST ONCE IN ALMOST A MONTH OF NIGHTLY MEETINGS THEY MANAGED TO EXCHANGE A KISS.
THEY WERE PASSING IN SILENCE DOWN A SIDE-STREET WHEN THERE WAS A DEAFENING ROAR...
71 ROBIN & SON LTD
THE EARTH HEAVED...
BOOOM!
THE AIR DARKENED.
WINSTON FOUND HIMSELF LYING ON HIS SIDE, BRUISED AND TERRIFIED. A ROCKET BOMB... SUDDENLY HE BECAME AWARE OF JULIA'S FACE A FEW CENTIMETRES FROM HIS OWN, DEATHLY WHITE, AS WHITE AS CHALK.
EVEN HER LIPS WERE WHITE. SHE WAS DEAD!
HE CLASPED HER AGAINST HIM AND FOUND THAT HE WAS KISSING A LIVE WARM FACE.
BUT THERE WAS SOME POWDERY STUFF THAT GOT IN THE WAY OF HIS LIPS... PLASTER.

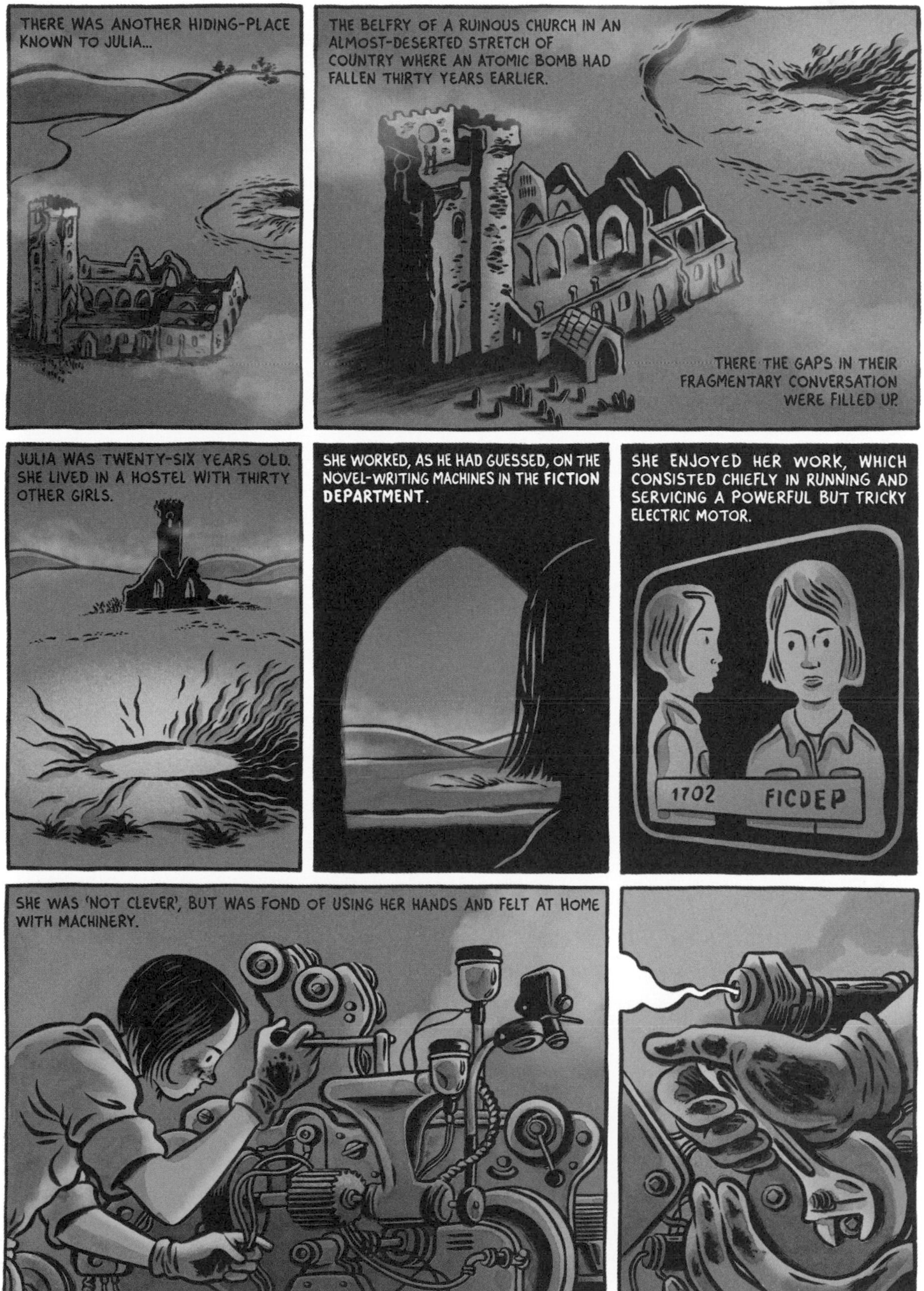
THERE WAS ANOTHER HIDING-PLACE KNOWN TO JULIA...
THE BELFRY OF A RUINOUS CHURCH IN AN ALMOST-DESERTED STRETCH OF COUNTRY WHERE AN ATOMIC BOMB HAD FALLEN THIRTY YEARS EARLIER.
THERE THE GAPS IN THEIR FRAGMENTARY CONVERSATION WERE FILLED UP.
JULIA WAS TWENTY-SIX YEARS OLD. SHE LIVED IN A HOSTEL WITH THIRTY OTHER GIRLS.
SHE WORKED, AS HE HAD GUESSED, ON THE NOVEL-WRITING MACHINES IN THE FICTION DEPARTMENT.
SHE ENJOYED HER WORK, WHICH CONSISTED CHIEFLY IN RUNNING AND SERVICING A POWERFUL BUT TRICKY ELECTRIC MOTOR.
1702
FICDEP
SHE WAS 'NOT CLEVER', BUT WAS FOND OF USING HER HANDS AND FELT AT HOME WITH MACHINERY.

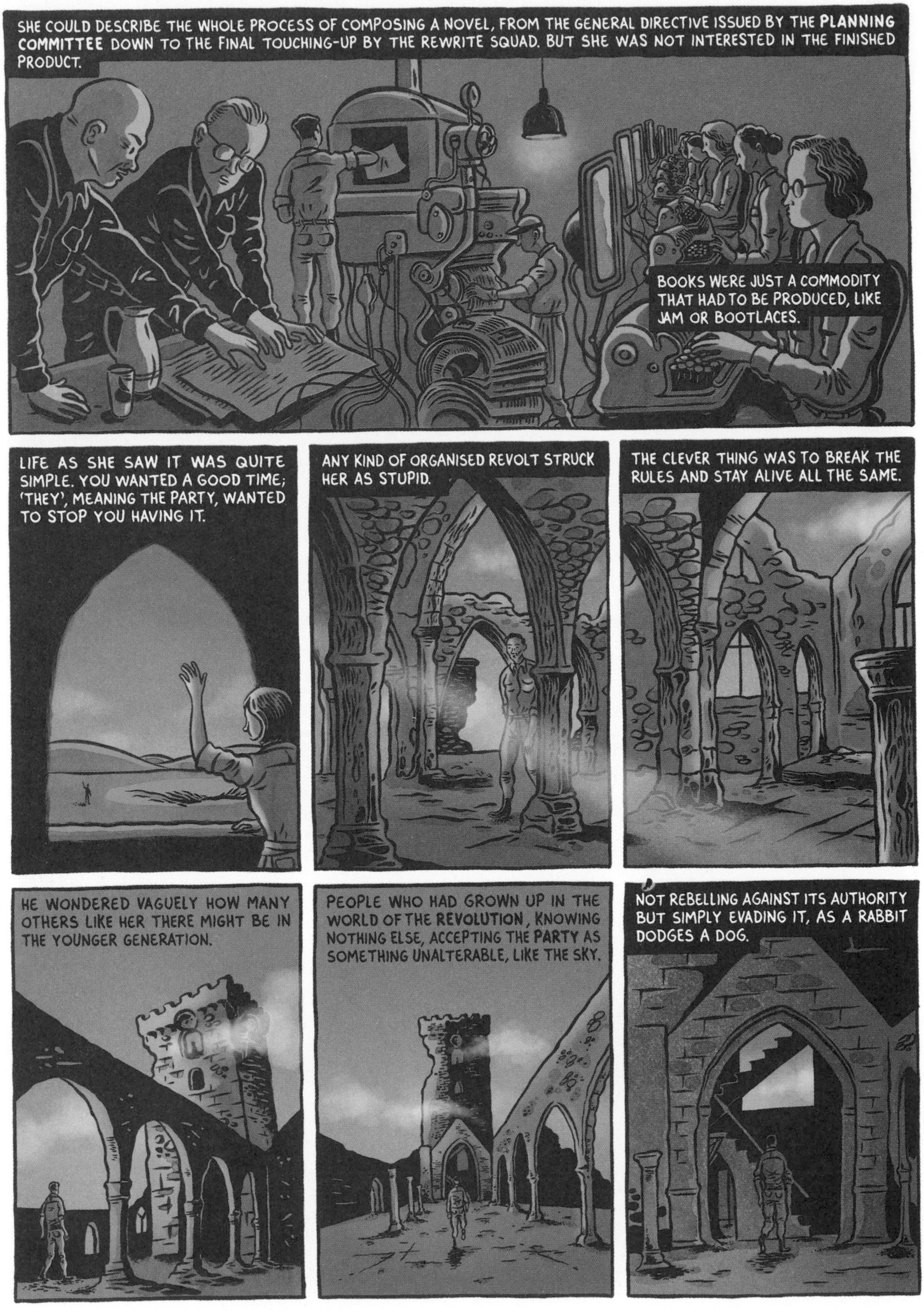
SHE COULD DESCRIBE THE WHOLE PROCESS OF COMPOSING A NOVEL, FROM THE GENERAL DIRECTIVE ISSUED BY THE PLANNING COMMITTEE DOWN TO THE FINAL TOUCHING-UP BY THE REWRITE SQUAD. BUT SHE WAS NOT INTERESTED IN THE FINISHED PRODUCT.
BOOKS WERE JUST A COMMODITY THAT HAD TO BE PRODUCED, LIKE JAM OR BOOTLACES.
LIFE AS SHE SAW IT WAS QUITE SIMPLE. YOU WANTED A GOOD TIME; 'THEY', MEANING THE PARTY, WANTED TO STOP YOU HAVING IT.
ANY KIND OF ORGANISED REVOLT STRUCK HER AS STUPID.
THE CLEVER THING WAS TO BREAK THE RULES AND STAY ALIVE ALL THE SAME.
HE WONDERED VAGUELY HOW MANY OTHERS LIKE HER THERE MIGHT BE IN THE YOUNGER GENERATION.
PEOPLE WHO HAD GROWN UP IN THE WORLD OF THE REVOLUTION, KNOWING NOTHING ELSE, ACCEPTING THE PARTY AS SOMETHING UNALTERABLE, LIKE THE SKY.
NOT REBELLING AGAINST ITS AUTHORITY BUT SIMPLY EVADING IT, AS A RABBIT DODGES A DOG.

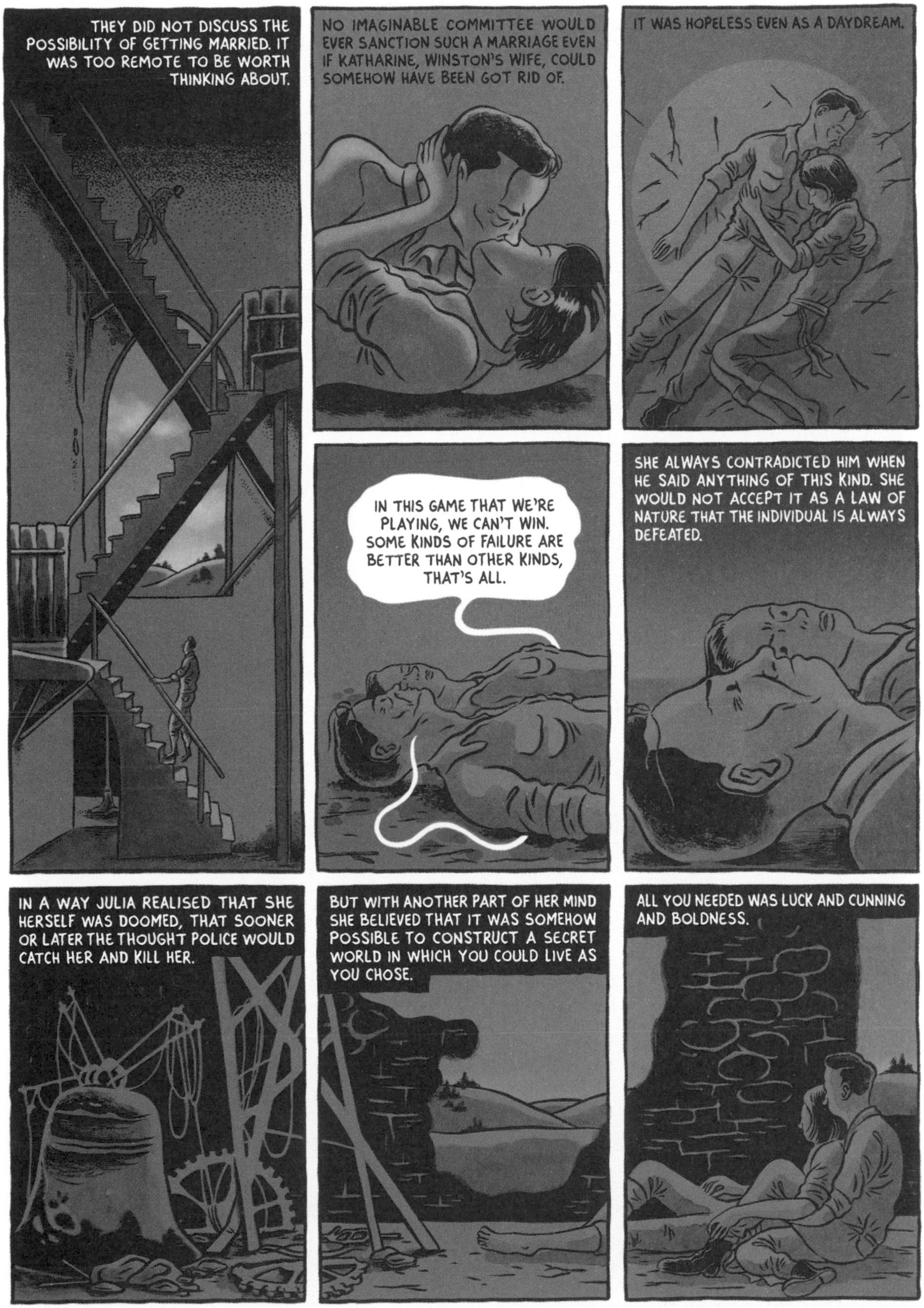

THEY DID NOT DISCUSS THE POSSIBILITY OF GETTING MARRIED. IT WAS TOO REMOTE TO BE WORTH THINKING ABOUT.
NO IMAGINABLE COMMITTEE WOULD EVER SANCTION SUCH A MARRIAGE EVEN IF KATHARINE, WINSTON'S WIFE, COULD SOMEHOW HAVE BEEN GOT RID OF.
IT WAS HOPELESS EVEN AS A DAYDREAM.
IN THIS GAME THAT WE'RE PLAYING, WE CAN'T WIN. SOME KINDS OF FAILURE ARE BETTER THAN OTHER KINDS, THAT'S ALL.
SHE ALWAYS CONTRADICTED HIM WHEN HE SAID ANYTHING OF THIS KIND. SHE WOULD NOT ACCEPT IT AS A LAW OF NATURE THAT THE INDIVIDUAL IS ALWAYS DEFEATED.
IN A WAY JULIA REALISED THAT SHE HERSELF WAS DOOMED, THAT SOONER OR LATER THE THOUGHT POLICE WOULD CATCH HER AND KILL HER.
BUT WITH ANOTHER PART OF HER MIND SHE BELIEVED THAT IT WAS SOMEHOW POSSIBLE TO CONSTRUCT A SECRET WORLD IN WHICH YOU COULD LIVE AS YOU CHOSE.
ALL YOU NEEDED WAS LUCK AND CUNNING AND BOLDNESS.

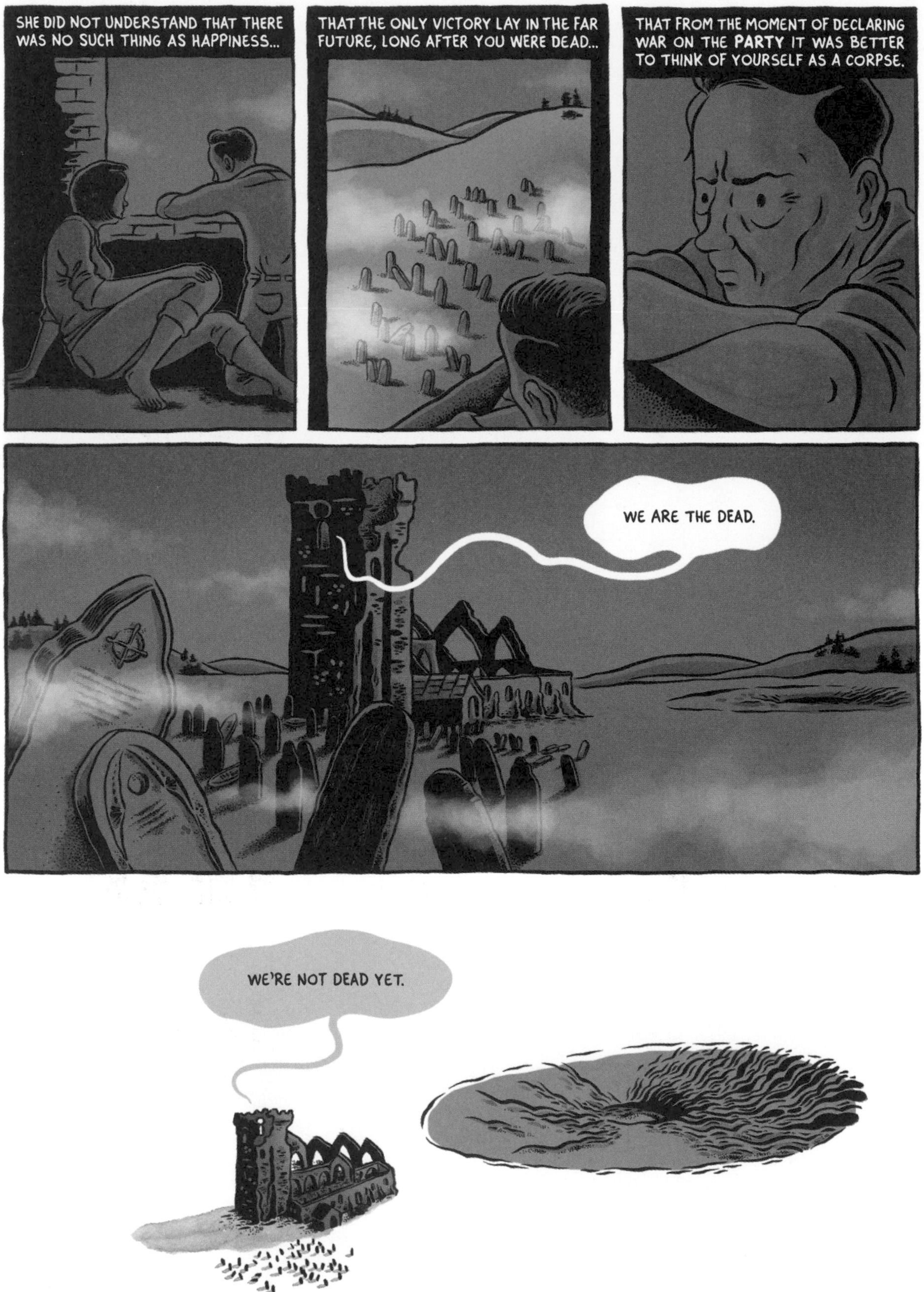
SHE DID NOT UNDERSTAND THAT THERE WAS NO SUCH THING AS HAPPINESS...
THAT THE ONLY VICTORY LAY IN THE FAR FUTURE, LONG AFTER YOU WERE DEAD...
THAT FROM THE MOMENT OF DECLARING WAR ON THE PARTY IT WAS BETTER TO THINK OF YOURSELF AS A CORPSE.
WE ARE THE DEAD.
WE'RE NOT DEAD YET.

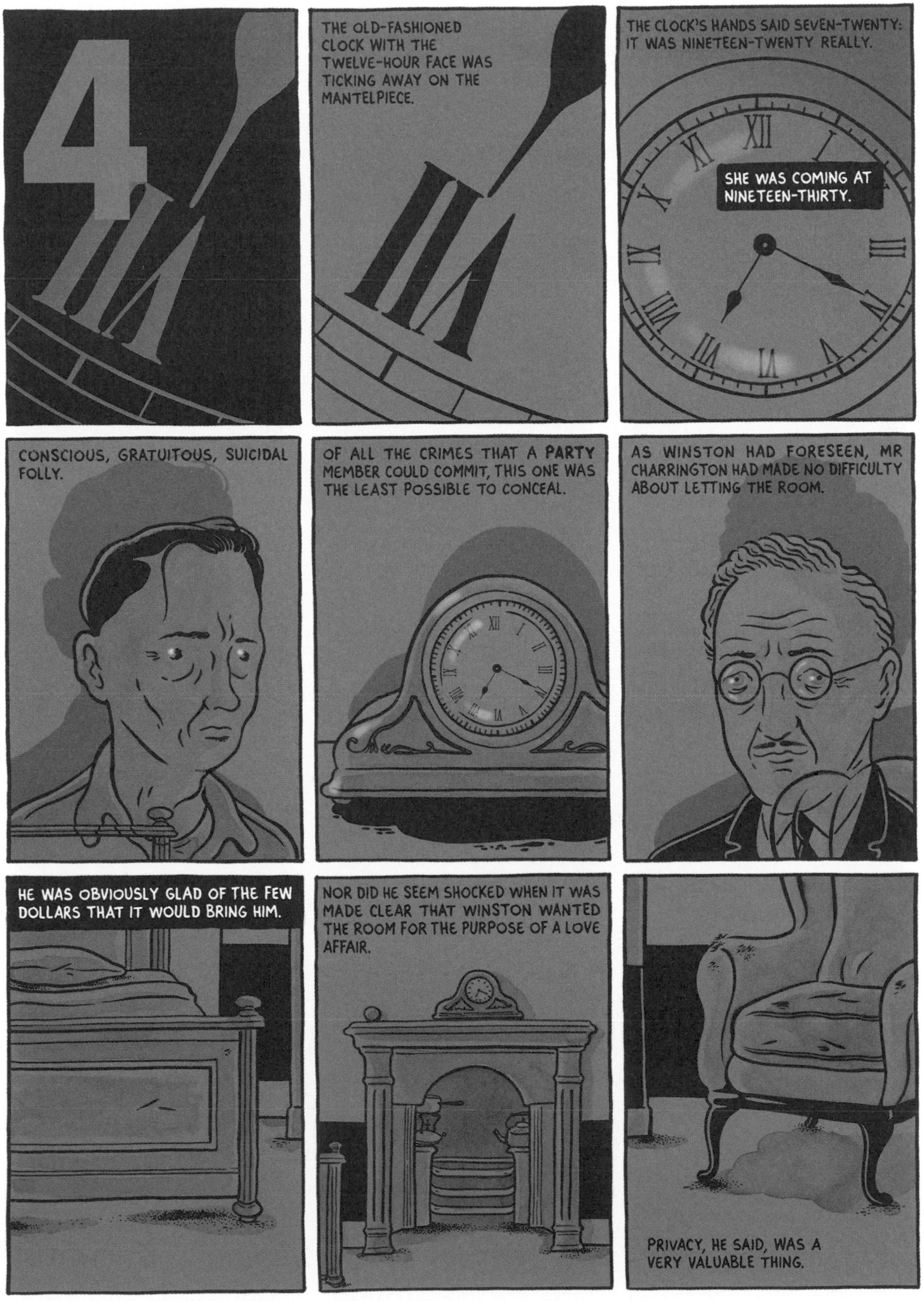

4
THE OLD-FASHIONED CLOCK WITH THE TWELVE-HOUR FACE WAS TICKING AWAY ON THE MANTELPIECE.
THE CLOCK'S HANDS SAID SEVEN-TWENTY: IT WAS NINETEEN-TWENTY REALLY.
SHE WAS COMING AT NINETEEN-THIRTY.
CONSCIOUS, GRATUITOUS, SUICIDAL FOLLY.
OF ALL THE CRIMES THAT A PARTY MEMBER COULD COMMIT, THIS ONE WAS THE LEAST POSSIBLE TO CONCEAL.
AS WINSTON HAD FORESEEN, MR CHARRINGTON HAD MADE NO DIFFICULTY ABOUT LETTING THE ROOM.
HE WAS OBVIOUSLY GLAD OF THE FEW DOLLARS THAT IT WOULD BRING HIM.
NOR DID HE SEEM SHOCKED WHEN IT WAS MADE CLEAR THAT WINSTON WANTED THE ROOM FOR THE PURPOSE OF A LOVE AFFAIR.
PRIVACY, HE SAID, WAS A VERY VALUABLE THING.

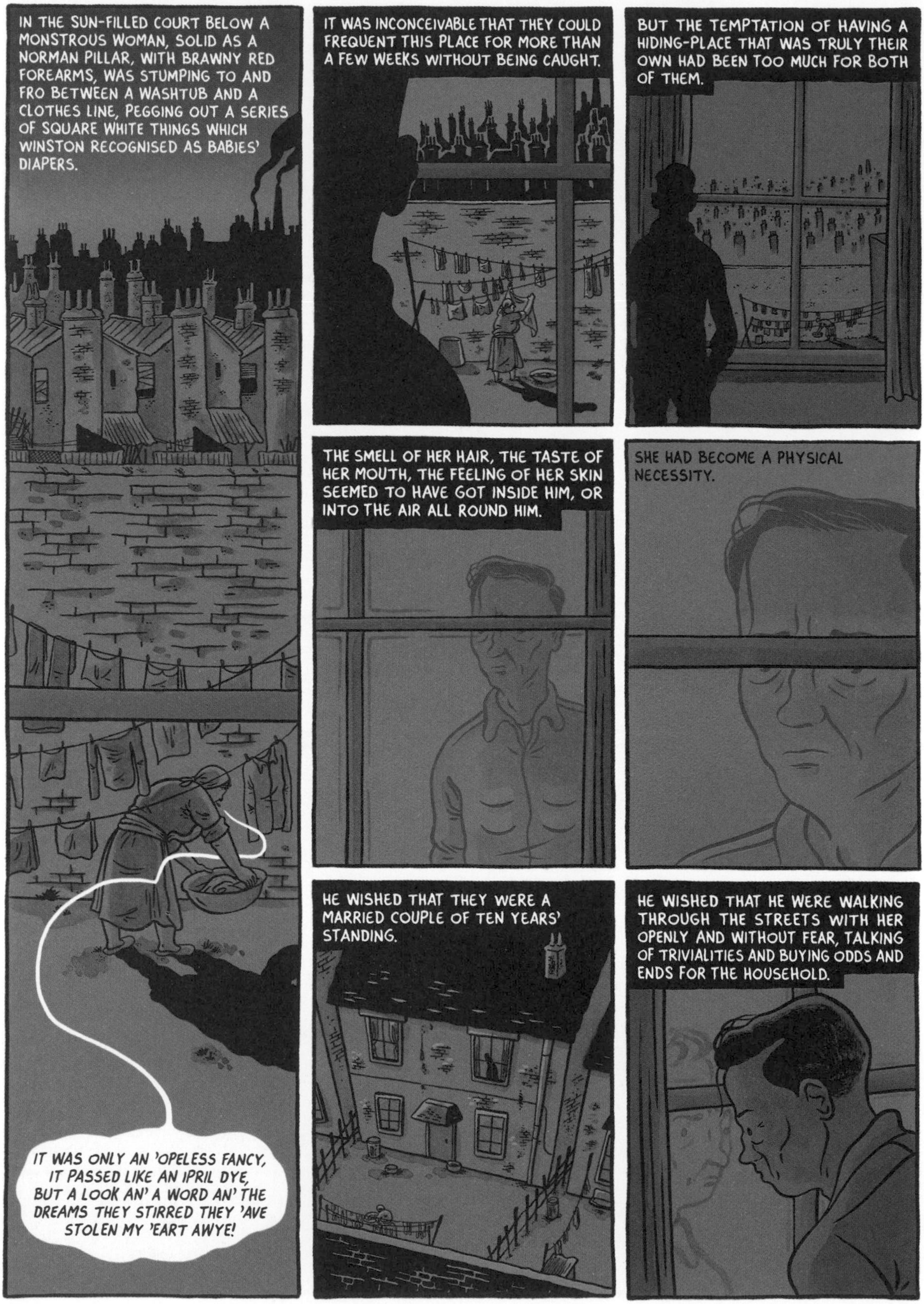
IN THE SUN-FILLED COURT BELOW A MONSTROUS WOMAN, SOLID AS A NORMAN PILLAR, WITH BRAWNY RED FOREARMS, WAS STUMPING TO AND FRO BETWEEN A WASHTUB AND A CLOTHES LINE, PEGGING OUT A SERIES OF SQUARE WHITE THINGS WHICH WINSTON RECOGNISED AS BABIES' DIAPERS.
IT WAS ONLY AN 'OPELESS FANCY, IT PASSED LIKE AN IPRIL DYE, BUT A LOOK AN' A WORD AN' THE DREAMS THEY STIRRED THEY 'AVE STOLEN MY 'EART AWYE!
IT WAS INCONCEIVABLE THAT THEY COULD FREQUENT THIS PLACE FOR MORE THAN A FEW WEEKS WITHOUT BEING CAUGHT.
BUT THE TEMPTATION OF HAVING A HIDING-PLACE THAT WAS TRULY THEIR OWN HAD BEEN TOO MUCH FOR BOTH OF THEM.
THE SMELL OF HER HAIR, THE TASTE OF HER MOUTH, THE FEELING OF HER SKIN SEEMED TO HAVE GOT INSIDE HIM, OR INTO THE AIR ALL ROUND HIM.
SHE HAD BECOME A PHYSICAL NECESSITY.
HE WISHED THAT THEY WERE A MARRIED COUPLE OF TEN YEARS' STANDING.
HE WISHED THAT HE WERE WALKING THROUGH THE STREETS WITH HER OPENLY AND WITHOUT FEAR, TALKING OF TRIVIALITIES AND BUYING ODDS AND ENDS FOR THE HOUSEHOLD.

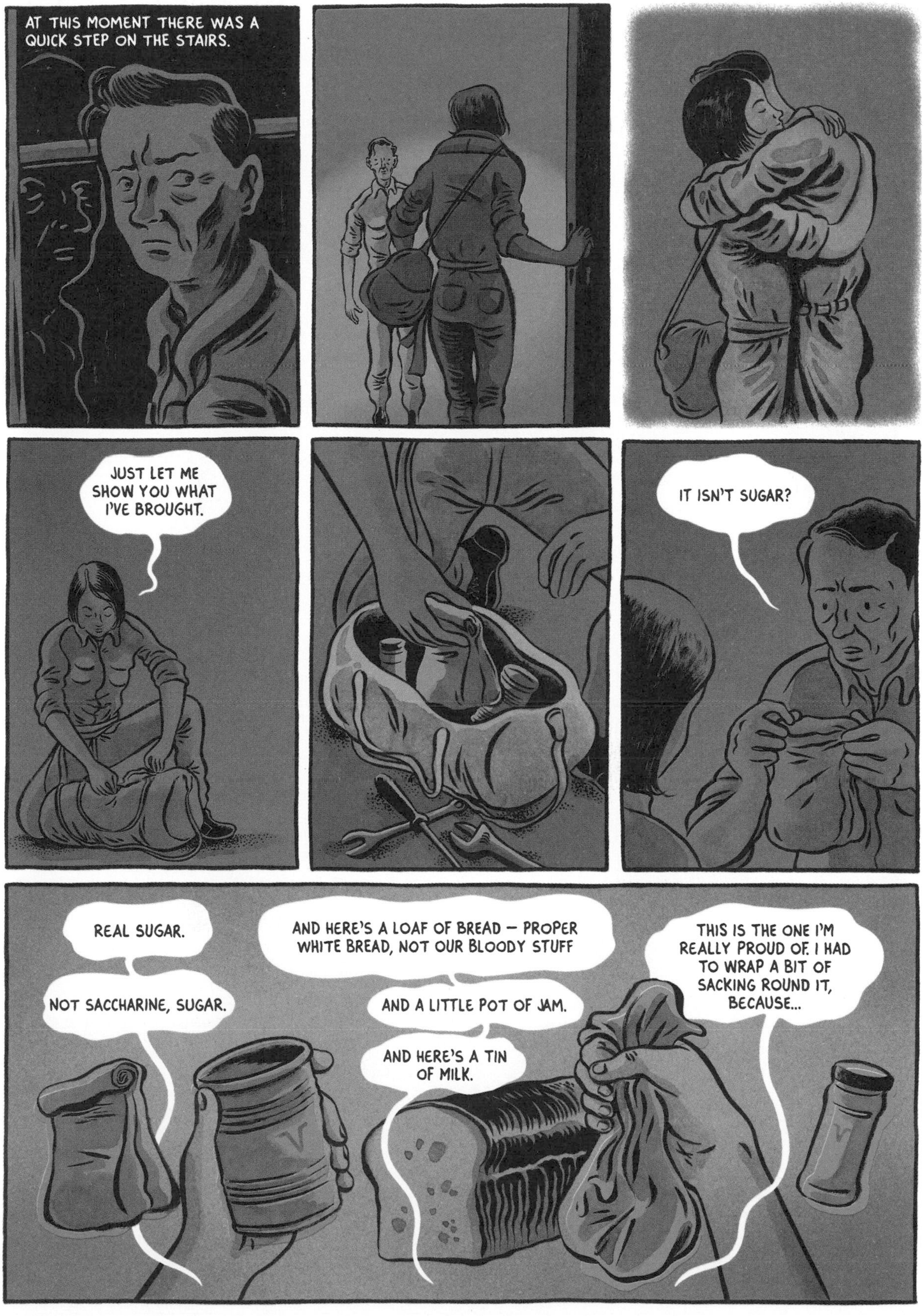

AT THIS MOMENT THERE WAS A QUICK STEP ON THE STAIRS.
JUST LET ME SHOW YOU WHAT I'VE BROUGHT.
IT ISN'T SUGAR?
REAL SUGAR.
NOT SACCHARINE, SUGAR.
AND HERE'S A LOAF OF BREAD — PROPER WHITE BREAD, NOT OUR BLOODY STUFF
AND A LITTLE POT OF JAM.
AND HERE'S A TIN OF MILK.
THIS IS THE ONE I'M REALLY PROUD OF. I HAD TO WRAP A BIT OF SACKING ROUND IT, BECAUSE...

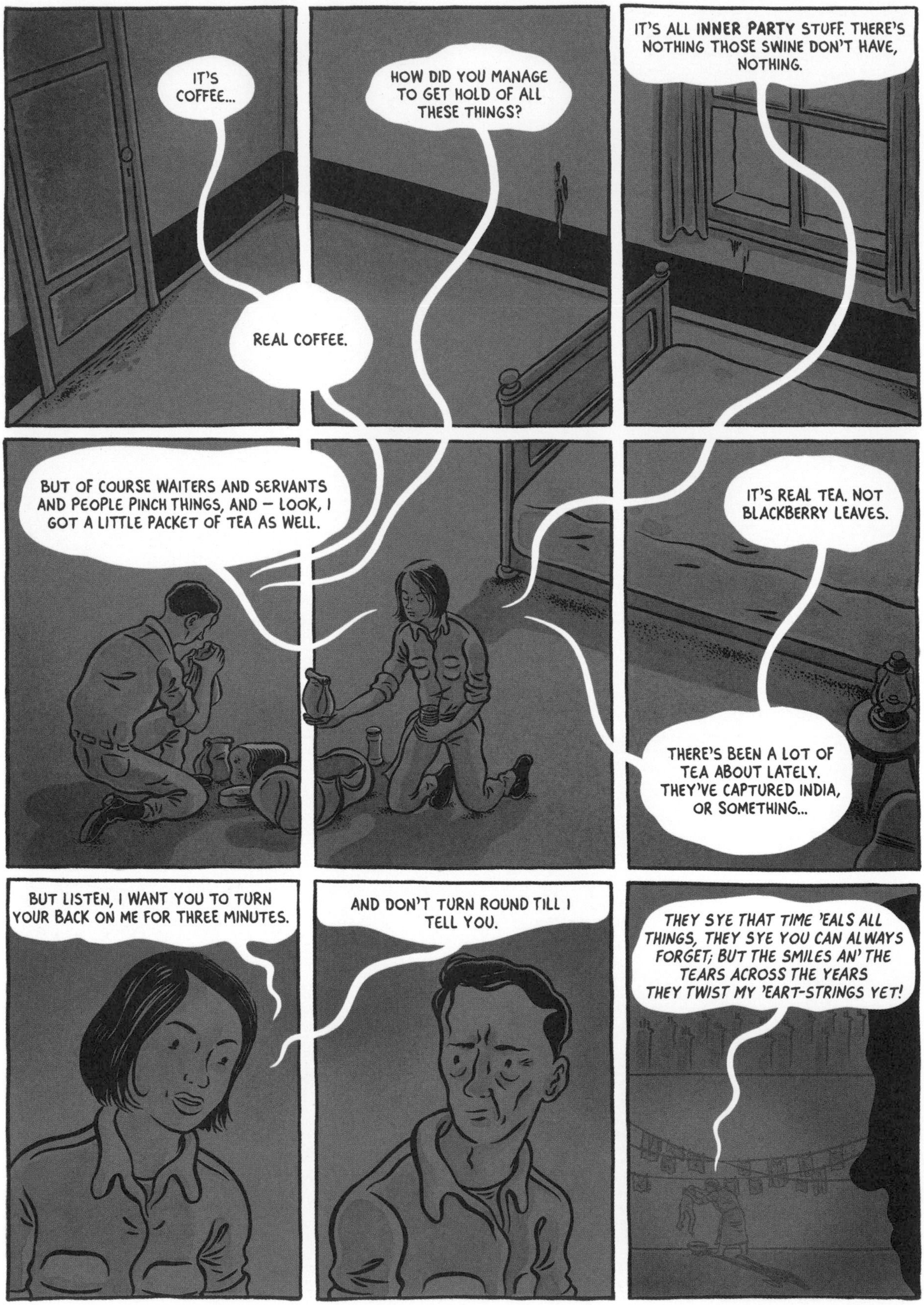
IT'S COFFEE...
HOW DID YOU MANAGE TO GET HOLD OF ALL THESE THINGS?
IT'S ALL **INNER PARTY** STUFF. THERE'S NOTHING THOSE SWINE DON'T HAVE, NOTHING.
REAL COFFEE.
BUT OF COURSE WAITERS AND SERVANTS AND PEOPLE PINCH THINGS, AND — LOOK, I GOT A LITTLE PACKET OF TEA AS WELL.
IT'S REAL TEA. NOT BLACKBERRY LEAVES.
THERE'S BEEN A LOT OF TEA ABOUT LATELY. THEY'VE CAPTURED INDIA, OR SOMETHING...
BUT LISTEN, I WANT YOU TO TURN YOUR BACK ON ME FOR THREE MINUTES.
AND DON'T TURN ROUND TILL I TELL YOU.
THEY SYE THAT TIME 'EALS ALL THINGS, THEY SYE YOU CAN ALWAYS FORGET; BUT THE SMILES AN' THE TEARS ACROSS THE YEARS THEY TWIST MY 'EART-STRINGS YET!

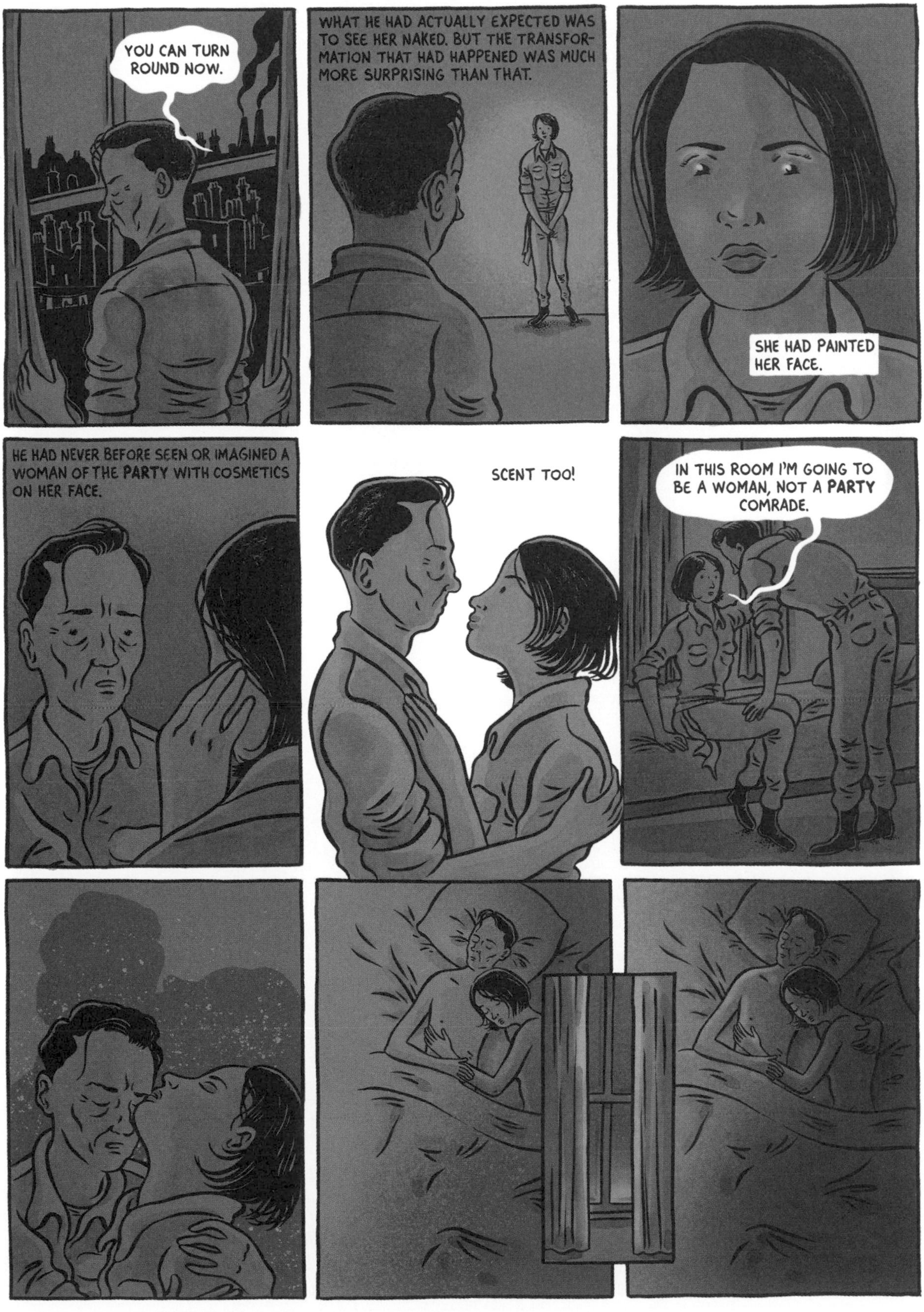
YOU CAN TURN ROUND NOW.
WHAT HE HAD ACTUALLY EXPECTED WAS TO SEE HER NAKED. BUT THE TRANSFORMATION THAT HAD HAPPENED WAS MUCH MORE SURPRISING THAN THAT.
SHE HAD PAINTED HER FACE.
HE HAD NEVER BEFORE SEEN OR IMAGINED A WOMAN OF THE PARTY WITH COSMETICS ON HER FACE.
SCENT TOO!
IN THIS ROOM I'M GOING TO BE A WOMAN, NOT A PARTY COMRADE.

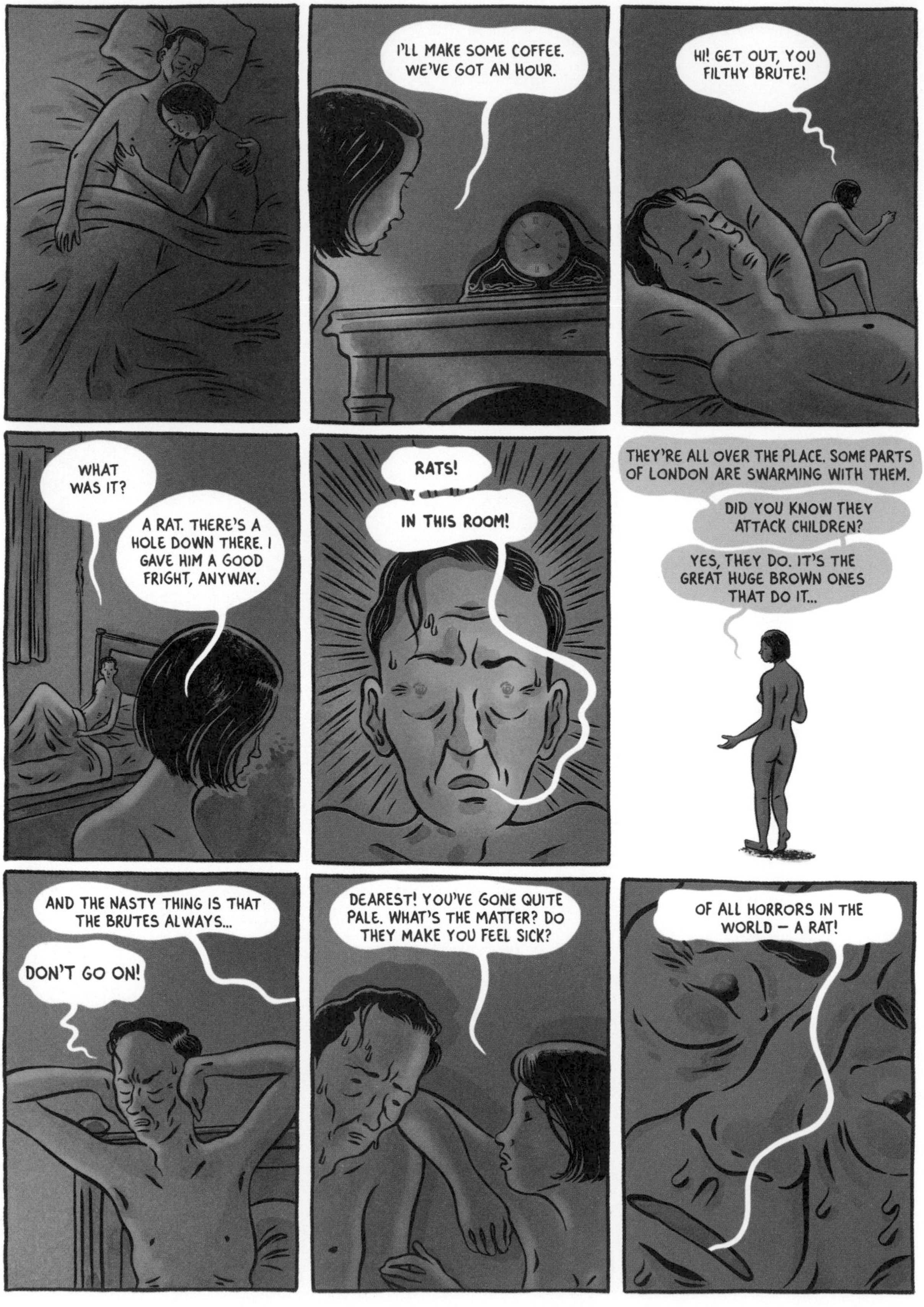

I'LL MAKE SOME COFFEE. WE'VE GOT AN HOUR.
HI! GET OUT, YOU FILTHY BRUTE!
WHAT WAS IT?
A RAT. THERE'S A HOLE DOWN THERE. I GAVE HIM A GOOD FRIGHT, ANYWAY.
RATS!
IN THIS ROOM!
THEY'RE ALL OVER THE PLACE. SOME PARTS OF LONDON ARE SWARMING WITH THEM.
DID YOU KNOW THEY ATTACK CHILDREN?
YES, THEY DO. IT'S THE GREAT HUGE BROWN ONES THAT DO IT...
AND THE NASTY THING IS THAT THE BRUTES ALWAYS...
DON'T GO ON!
DEAREST! YOU'VE GONE QUITE PALE. WHAT'S THE MATTER? DO THEY MAKE YOU FEEL SICK?
OF ALL HORRORS IN THE WORLD — A RAT!

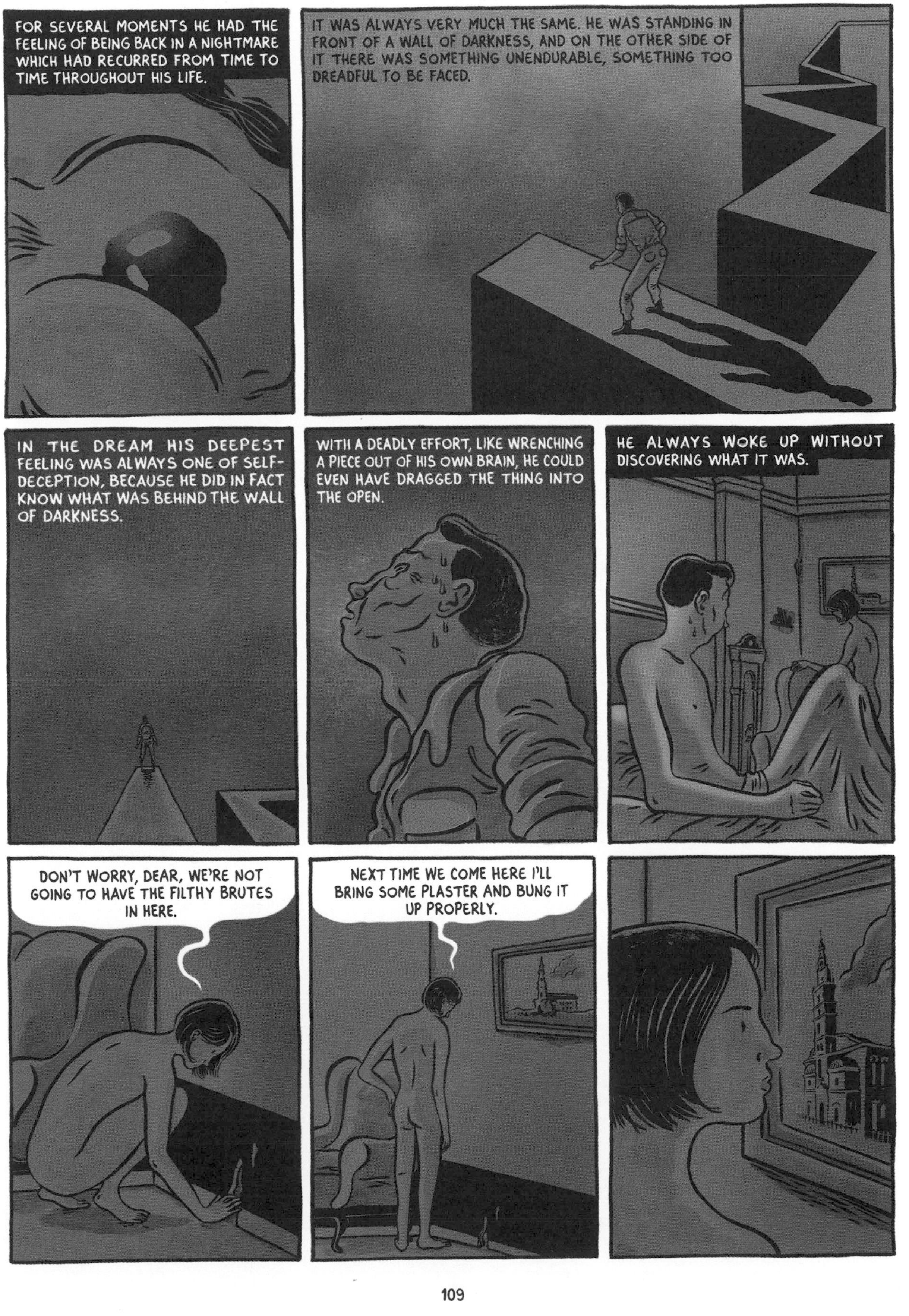
FOR SEVERAL MOMENTS HE HAD THE FEELING OF BEING BACK IN A NIGHTMARE WHICH HAD RECURRED FROM TIME TO TIME THROUGHOUT HIS LIFE.
IT WAS ALWAYS VERY MUCH THE SAME. HE WAS STANDING IN FRONT OF A WALL OF DARKNESS, AND ON THE OTHER SIDE OF IT THERE WAS SOMETHING UNENDURABLE, SOMETHING TOO DREADFUL TO BE FACED.
IN THE DREAM HIS DEEPEST FEELING WAS ALWAYS ONE OF SELF-DECEPTION, BECAUSE HE DID IN FACT KNOW WHAT WAS BEHIND THE WALL OF DARKNESS.
WITH A DEADLY EFFORT, LIKE WRENCHING A PIECE OUT OF HIS OWN BRAIN, HE COULD EVEN HAVE DRAGGED THE THING INTO THE OPEN.
HE ALWAYS WOKE UP WITHOUT DISCOVERING WHAT IT WAS.
DON'T WORRY, DEAR, WE'RE NOT GOING TO HAVE THE FILTHY BRUTES IN HERE.
NEXT TIME WE COME HERE I'LL BRING SOME PLASTER AND BUNG IT UP PROPERLY.

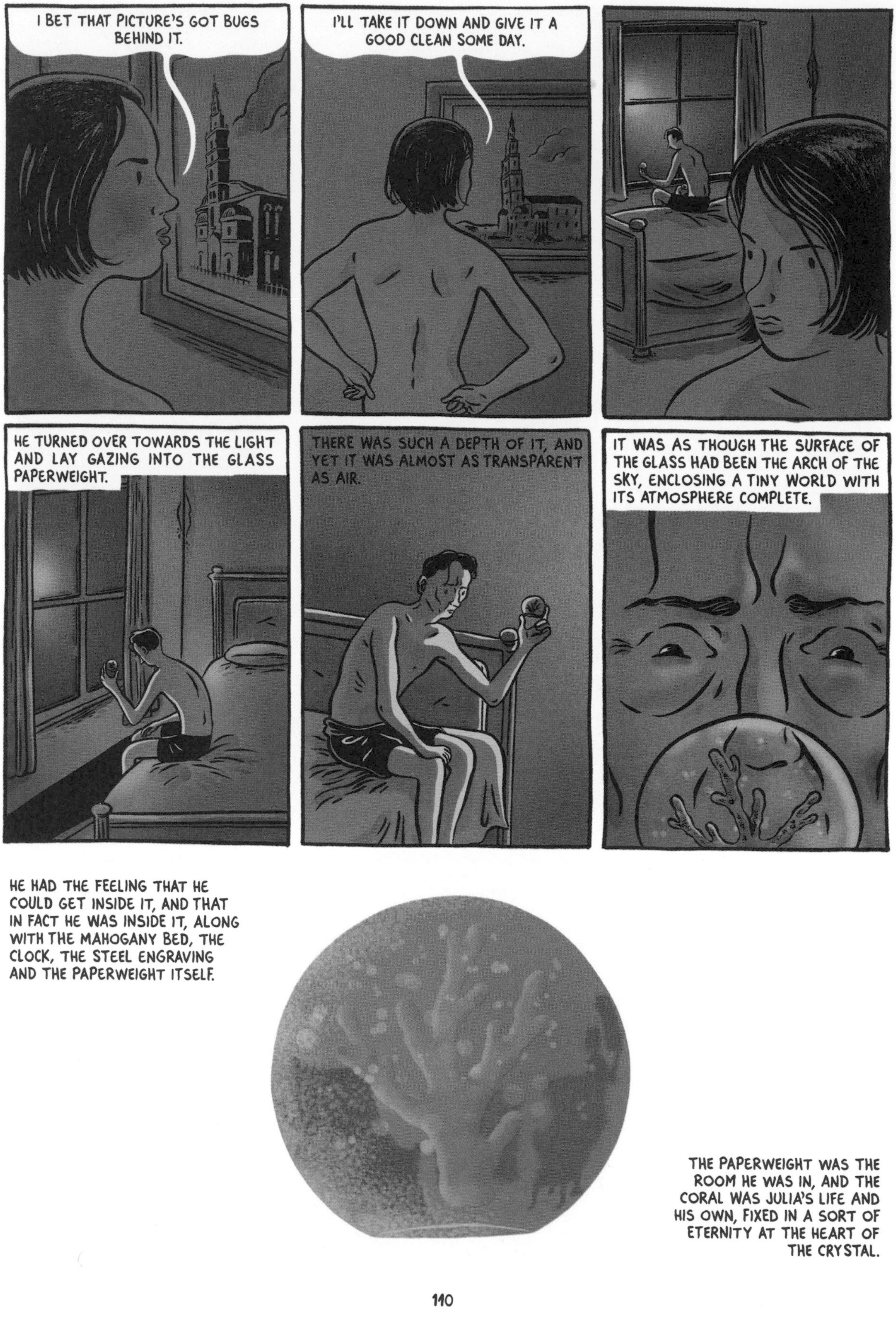
I BET THAT PICTURE'S GOT BUGS BEHIND IT.
I'LL TAKE IT DOWN AND GIVE IT A GOOD CLEAN SOME DAY.
HE TURNED OVER TOWARDS THE LIGHT AND LAY GAZING INTO THE GLASS PAPERWEIGHT.
THERE WAS SUCH A DEPTH OF IT, AND YET IT WAS ALMOST AS TRANSPARENT AS AIR.
IT WAS AS THOUGH THE SURFACE OF THE GLASS HAD BEEN THE ARCH OF THE SKY, ENCLOSING A TINY WORLD WITH ITS ATMOSPHERE COMPLETE.
HE HAD THE FEELING THAT HE COULD GET INSIDE IT, AND THAT IN FACT HE WAS INSIDE IT, ALONG WITH THE MAHOGANY BED, THE CLOCK, THE STEEL ENGRAVING AND THE PAPERWEIGHT ITSELF.
THE PAPERWEIGHT WAS THE ROOM HE WAS IN, AND THE CORAL WAS JULIA'S LIFE AND HIS OWN, FIXED IN A SORT OF ETERNITY AT THE HEART OF THE CRYSTAL.

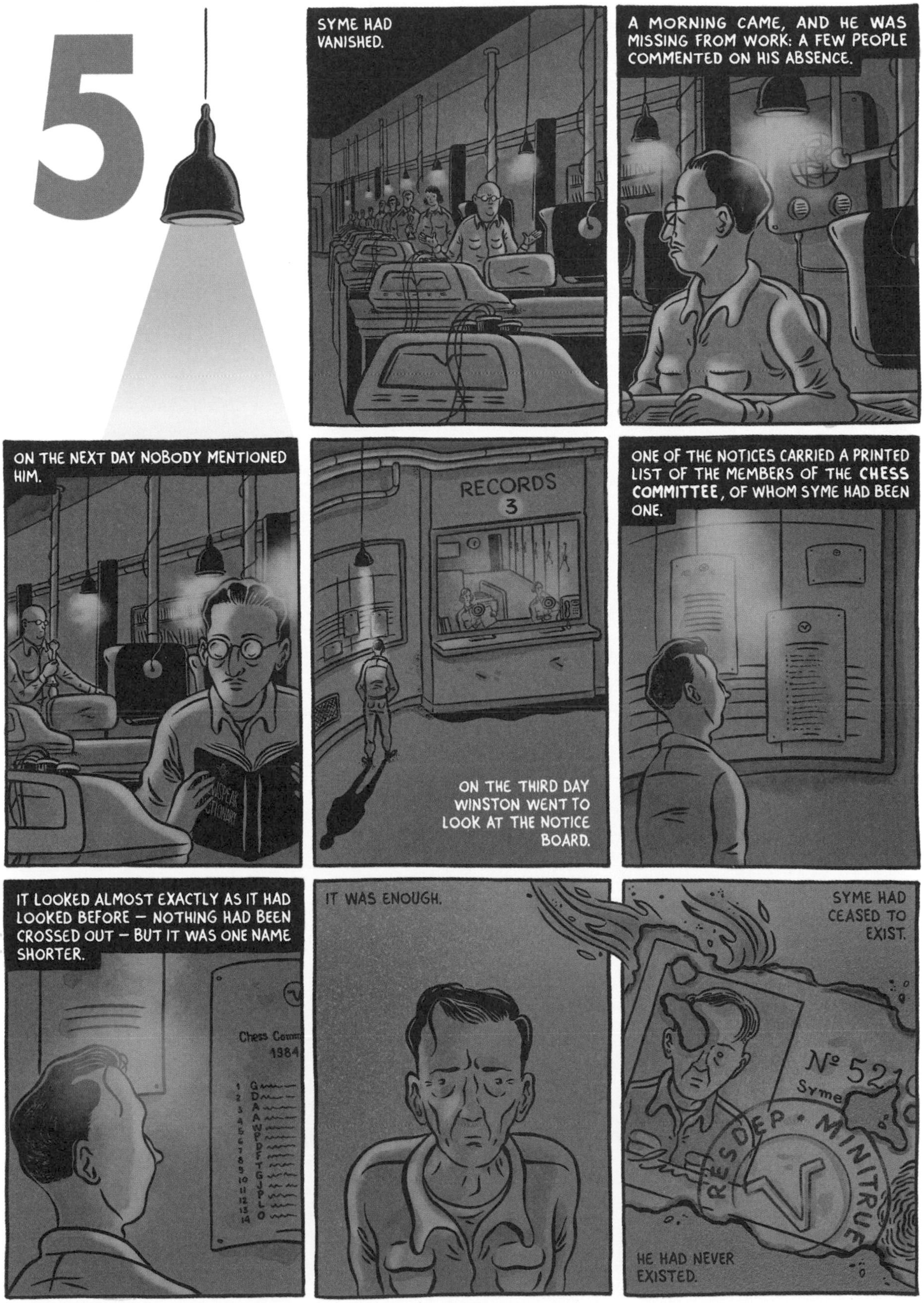
5
SYME HAD VANISHED.
A MORNING CAME, AND HE WAS MISSING FROM WORK: A FEW PEOPLE COMMENTED ON HIS ABSENCE.
ON THE NEXT DAY NOBODY MENTIONED HIM.
RECORDS
3
ON THE THIRD DAY WINSTON WENT TO LOOK AT THE NOTICE BOARD.
ONE OF THE NOTICES CARRIED A PRINTED LIST OF THE MEMBERS OF THE **CHESS COMMITTEE**, OF WHOM SYME HAD BEEN ONE.
IT LOOKED ALMOST EXACTLY AS IT HAD LOOKED BEFORE — NOTHING HAD BEEN CROSSED OUT — BUT IT WAS ONE NAME SHORTER.
Chess Comm
1984
IT WAS ENOUGH.
SYME HAD CEASED TO EXIST.
Nº 521
Syme
RESDEP • MINITRUE
HE HAD NEVER EXISTED.

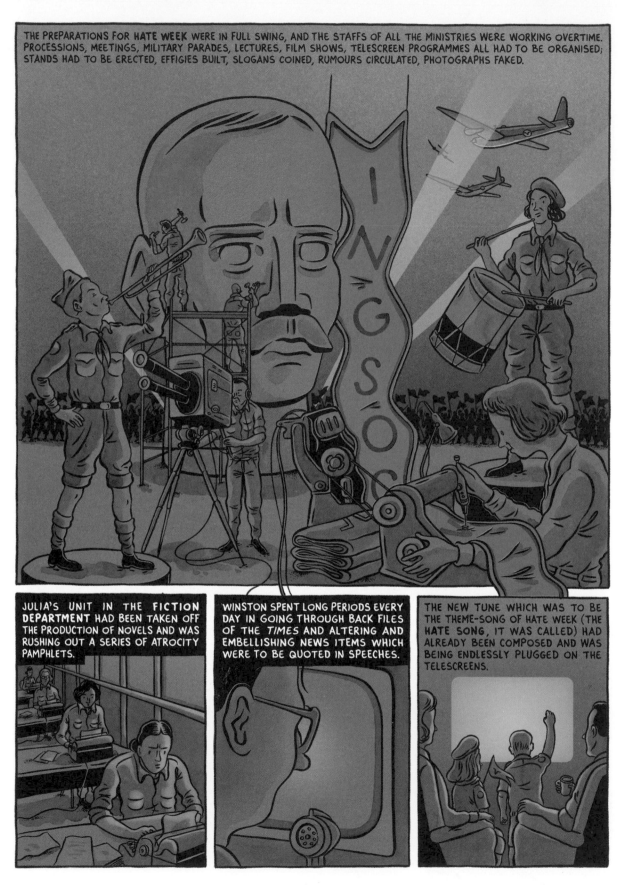

THE PREPARATIONS FOR **HATE WEEK** WERE IN FULL SWING, AND THE STAFFS OF ALL THE MINISTRIES WERE WORKING OVERTIME. PROCESSIONS, MEETINGS, MILITARY PARADES, LECTURES, FILM SHOWS, TELESCREEN PROGRAMMES ALL HAD TO BE ORGANISED; STANDS HAD TO BE ERECTED, EFFIGIES BUILT, SLOGANS COINED, RUMOURS CIRCULATED, PHOTOGRAPHS FAKED.

JULIA'S UNIT IN THE **FICTION DEPARTMENT** HAD BEEN TAKEN OFF THE PRODUCTION OF NOVELS AND WAS RUSHING OUT A SERIES OF ATROCITY PAMPHLETS.

WINSTON SPENT LONG PERIODS EVERY DAY IN GOING THROUGH BACK FILES OF THE *TIMES* AND ALTERING AND EMBELLISHING NEWS ITEMS WHICH WERE TO BE QUOTED IN SPEECHES.

THE NEW TUNE WHICH WAS TO BE THE THEME-SONG OF HATE WEEK (THE HATE SONG, IT WAS CALLED) HAD ALREADY BEEN COMPOSED AND WAS BEING ENDLESSLY PLUGGED ON THE TELESCREENS.

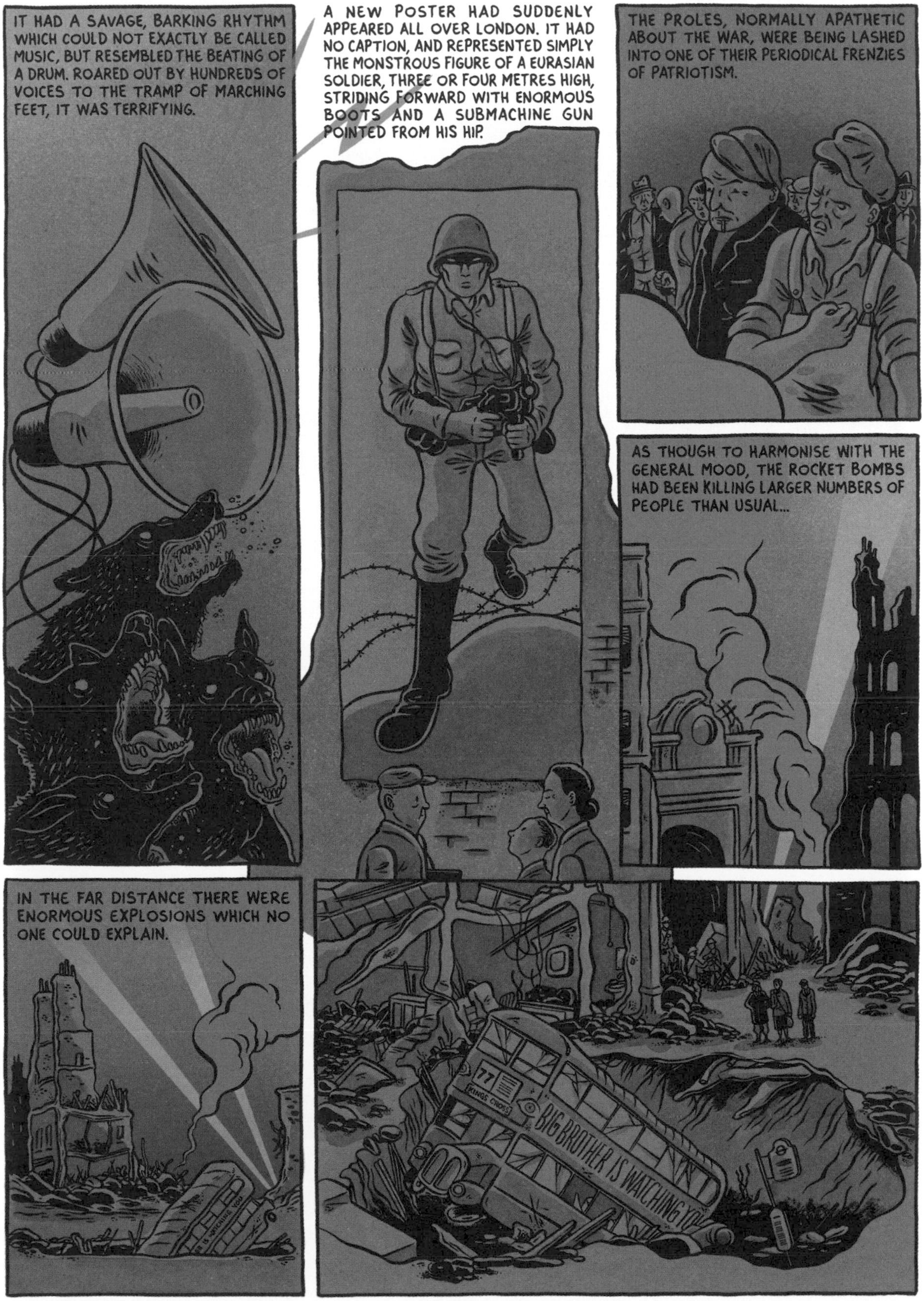
IT HAD A SAVAGE, BARKING RHYTHM WHICH COULD NOT EXACTLY BE CALLED MUSIC, BUT RESEMBLED THE BEATING OF A DRUM. ROARED OUT BY HUNDREDS OF VOICES TO THE TRAMP OF MARCHING FEET, IT WAS TERRIFYING.
A NEW POSTER HAD SUDDENLY APPEARED ALL OVER LONDON. IT HAD NO CAPTION, AND REPRESENTED SIMPLY THE MONSTROUS FIGURE OF A EURASIAN SOLDIER, THREE OR FOUR METRES HIGH, STRIDING FORWARD WITH ENORMOUS BOOTS AND A SUBMACHINE GUN POINTED FROM HIS HIP.
THE PROLES, NORMALLY APATHETIC ABOUT THE WAR, WERE BEING LASHED INTO ONE OF THEIR PERIODICAL FRENZIES OF PATRIOTISM.
AS THOUGH TO HARMONISE WITH THE GENERAL MOOD, THE ROCKET BOMBS HAD BEEN KILLING LARGER NUMBERS OF PEOPLE THAN USUAL...
IN THE FAR DISTANCE THERE WERE ENORMOUS EXPLOSIONS WHICH NO ONE COULD EXPLAIN.
77
KINGS CROSS
BIG BROTHER IS WATCHING YO

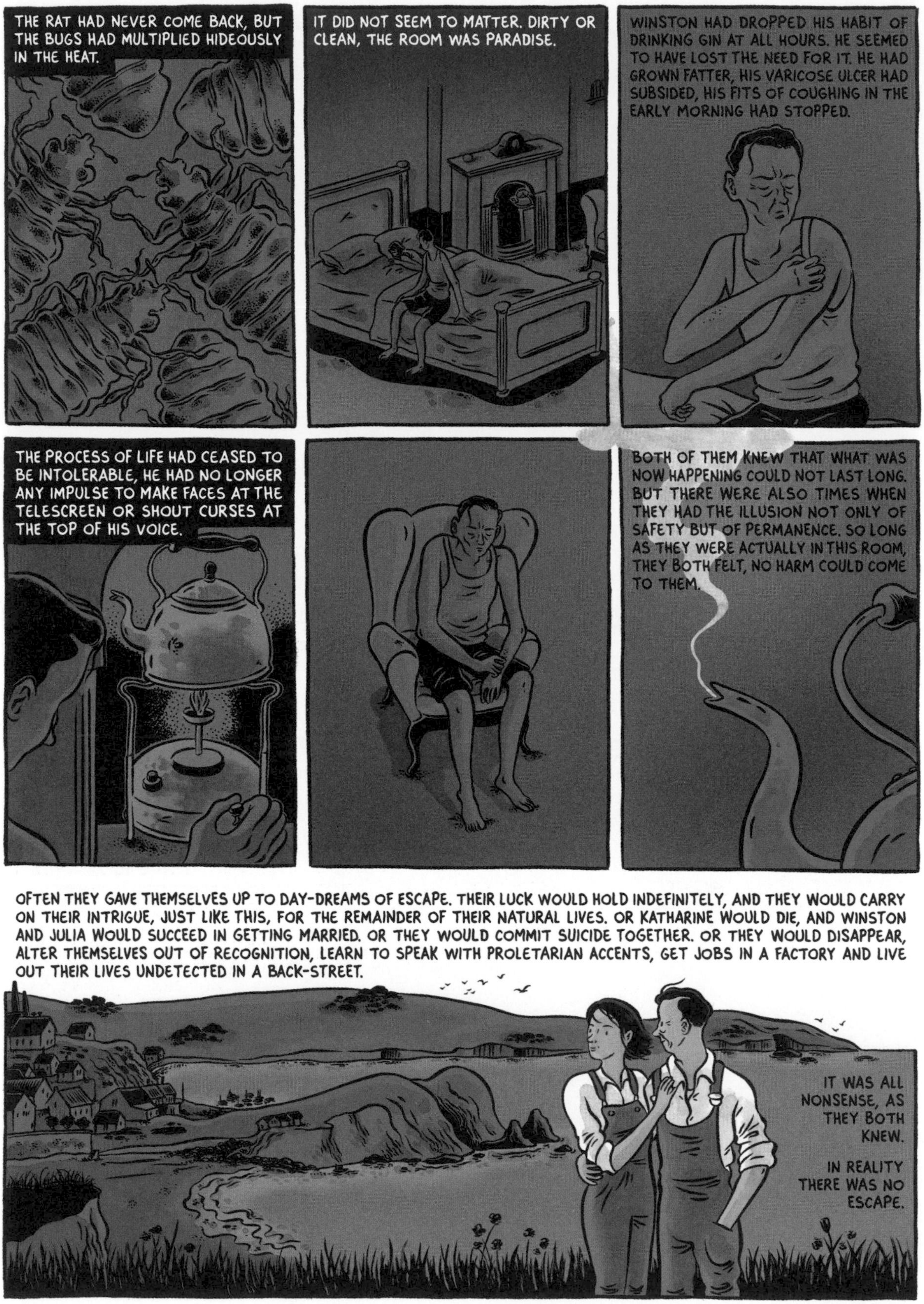
THE RAT HAD NEVER COME BACK, BUT THE BUGS HAD MULTIPLIED HIDEOUSLY IN THE HEAT.
IT DID NOT SEEM TO MATTER. DIRTY OR CLEAN, THE ROOM WAS PARADISE.
WINSTON HAD DROPPED HIS HABIT OF DRINKING GIN AT ALL HOURS. HE SEEMED TO HAVE LOST THE NEED FOR IT. HE HAD GROWN FATTER, HIS VARICOSE ULCER HAD SUBSIDED, HIS FITS OF COUGHING IN THE EARLY MORNING HAD STOPPED.
THE PROCESS OF LIFE HAD CEASED TO BE INTOLERABLE, HE HAD NO LONGER ANY IMPULSE TO MAKE FACES AT THE TELESCREEN OR SHOUT CURSES AT THE TOP OF HIS VOICE.
BOTH OF THEM KNEW THAT WHAT WAS NOW HAPPENING COULD NOT LAST LONG. BUT THERE WERE ALSO TIMES WHEN THEY HAD THE ILLUSION NOT ONLY OF SAFETY BUT OF PERMANENCE. SO LONG AS THEY WERE ACTUALLY IN THIS ROOM, THEY BOTH FELT, NO HARM COULD COME TO THEM.
OFTEN THEY GAVE THEMSELVES UP TO DAY-DREAMS OF ESCAPE. THEIR LUCK WOULD HOLD INDEFINITELY, AND THEY WOULD CARRY ON THEIR INTRIGUE, JUST LIKE THIS, FOR THE REMAINDER OF THEIR NATURAL LIVES. OR KATHARINE WOULD DIE, AND WINSTON AND JULIA WOULD SUCCEED IN GETTING MARRIED. OR THEY WOULD COMMIT SUICIDE TOGETHER. OR THEY WOULD DISAPPEAR, ALTER THEMSELVES OUT OF RECOGNITION, LEARN TO SPEAK WITH PROLETARIAN ACCENTS, GET JOBS IN A FACTORY AND LIVE OUT THEIR LIVES UNDETECTED IN A BACK-STREET.
IT WAS ALL NONSENSE, AS THEY BOTH KNEW.
IN REALITY THERE WAS NO ESCAPE.

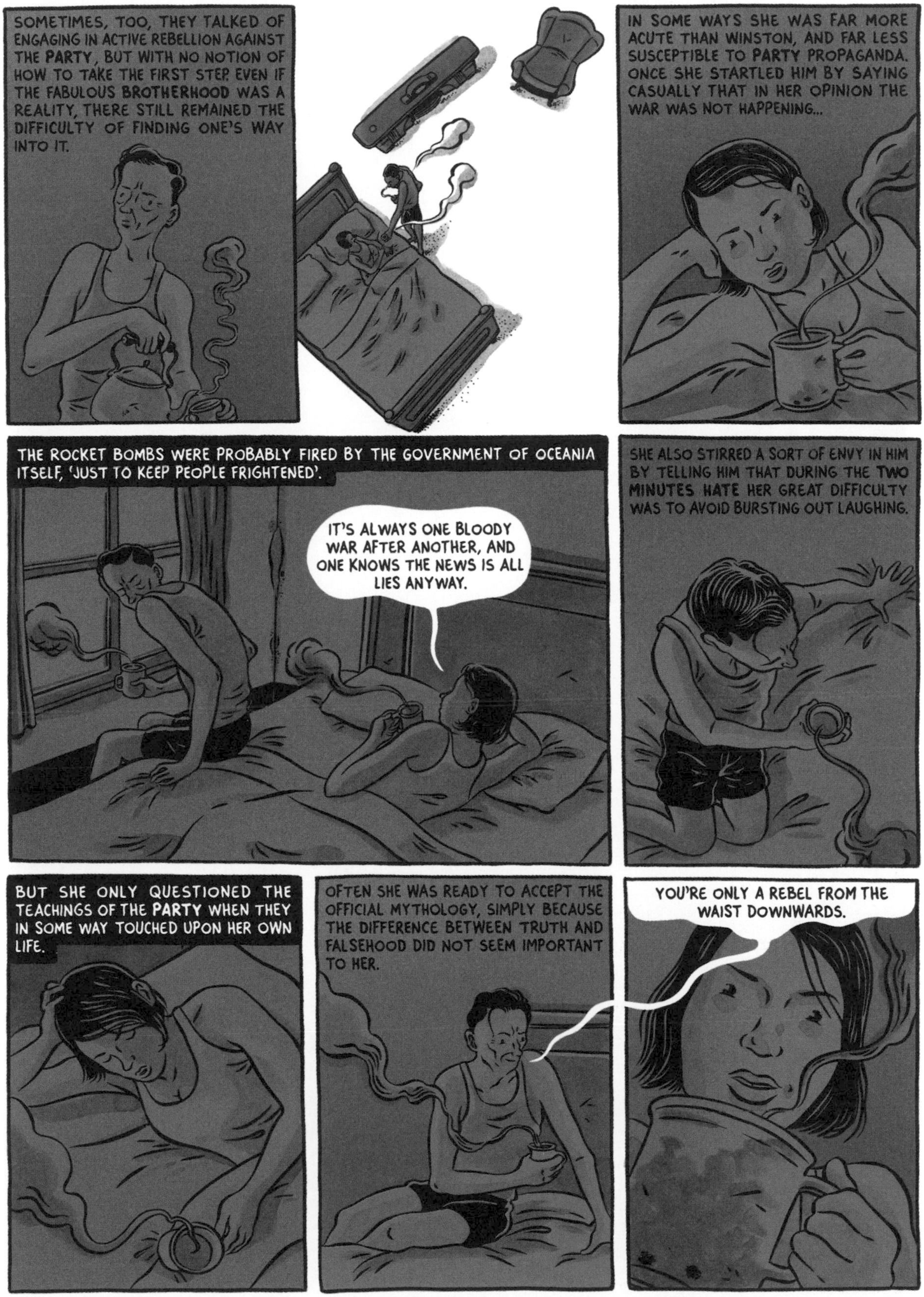
SOMETIMES, TOO, THEY TALKED OF ENGAGING IN ACTIVE REBELLION AGAINST THE PARTY, BUT WITH NO NOTION OF HOW TO TAKE THE FIRST STEP. EVEN IF THE FABULOUS BROTHERHOOD WAS A REALITY, THERE STILL REMAINED THE DIFFICULTY OF FINDING ONE'S WAY INTO IT.
IN SOME WAYS SHE WAS FAR MORE ACUTE THAN WINSTON, AND FAR LESS SUSCEPTIBLE TO PARTY PROPAGANDA. ONCE SHE STARTLED HIM BY SAYING CASUALLY THAT IN HER OPINION THE WAR WAS NOT HAPPENING...
THE ROCKET BOMBS WERE PROBABLY FIRED BY THE GOVERNMENT OF OCEANIA ITSELF, 'JUST TO KEEP PEOPLE FRIGHTENED'.
IT'S ALWAYS ONE BLOODY WAR AFTER ANOTHER, AND ONE KNOWS THE NEWS IS ALL LIES ANYWAY.
SHE ALSO STIRRED A SORT OF ENVY IN HIM BY TELLING HIM THAT DURING THE TWO MINUTES HATE HER GREAT DIFFICULTY WAS TO AVOID BURSTING OUT LAUGHING.
BUT SHE ONLY QUESTIONED THE TEACHINGS OF THE PARTY WHEN THEY IN SOME WAY TOUCHED UPON HER OWN LIFE.
OFTEN SHE WAS READY TO ACCEPT THE OFFICIAL MYTHOLOGY, SIMPLY BECAUSE THE DIFFERENCE BETWEEN TRUTH AND FALSEHOOD DID NOT SEEM IMPORTANT TO HER.
YOU'RE ONLY A REBEL FROM THE WAIST DOWNWARDS.

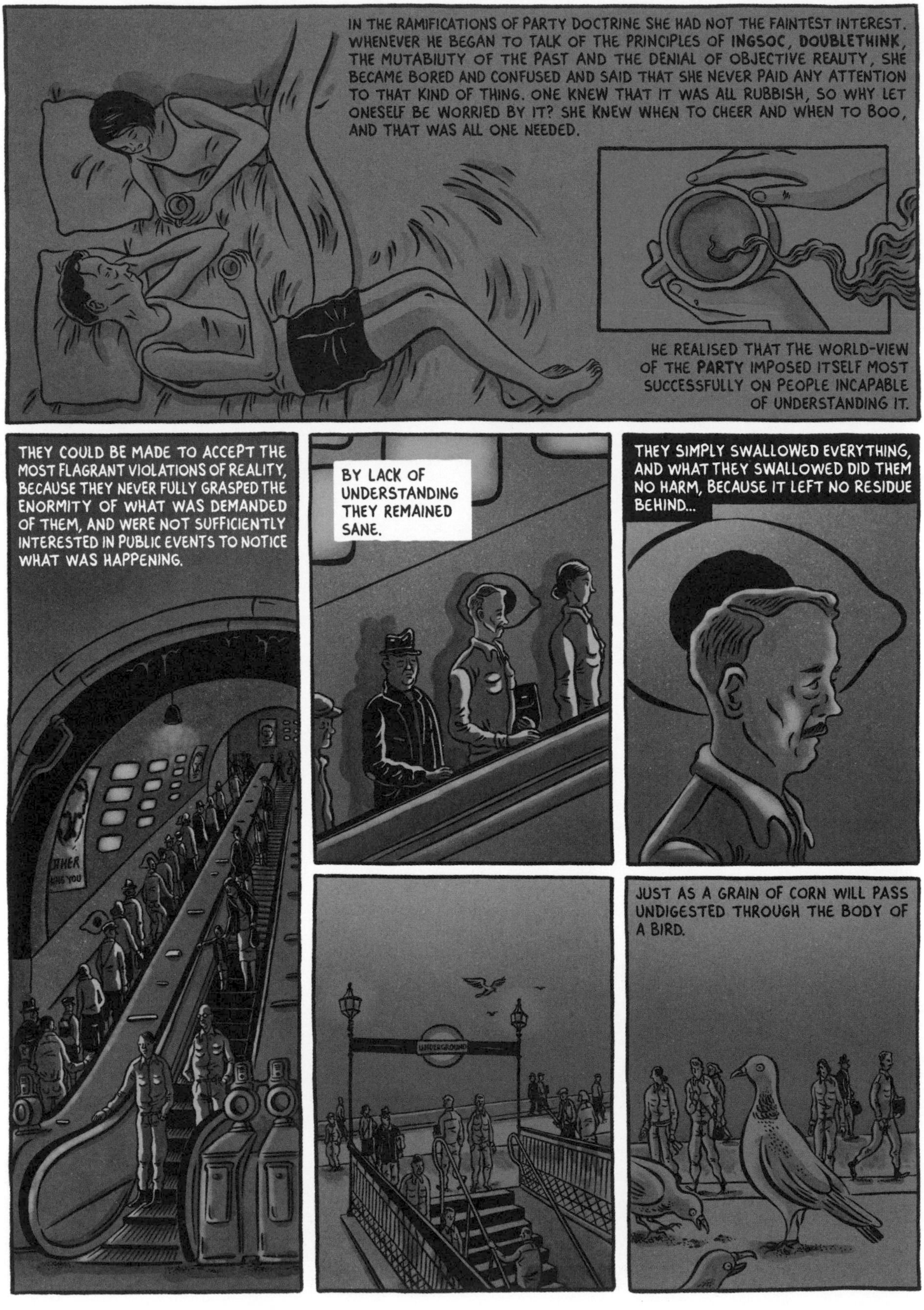
IN THE RAMIFICATIONS OF PARTY DOCTRINE SHE HAD NOT THE FAINTEST INTEREST. WHENEVER HE BEGAN TO TALK OF THE PRINCIPLES OF INGSOC, DOUBLETHINK, THE MUTABILITY OF THE PAST AND THE DENIAL OF OBJECTIVE REALITY, SHE BECAME BORED AND CONFUSED AND SAID THAT SHE NEVER PAID ANY ATTENTION TO THAT KIND OF THING. ONE KNEW THAT IT WAS ALL RUBBISH, SO WHY LET ONESELF BE WORRIED BY IT? SHE KNEW WHEN TO CHEER AND WHEN TO BOO, AND THAT WAS ALL ONE NEEDED.
HE REALISED THAT THE WORLD-VIEW OF THE PARTY IMPOSED ITSELF MOST SUCCESSFULLY ON PEOPLE INCAPABLE OF UNDERSTANDING IT.
THEY COULD BE MADE TO ACCEPT THE MOST FLAGRANT VIOLATIONS OF REALITY, BECAUSE THEY NEVER FULLY GRASPED THE ENORMITY OF WHAT WAS DEMANDED OF THEM, AND WERE NOT SUFFICIENTLY INTERESTED IN PUBLIC EVENTS TO NOTICE WHAT WAS HAPPENING.
BY LACK OF UNDERSTANDING THEY REMAINED SANE.
THEY SIMPLY SWALLOWED EVERYTHING, AND WHAT THEY SWALLOWED DID THEM NO HARM, BECAUSE IT LEFT NO RESIDUE BEHIND...
UNDERGROUND
JUST AS A GRAIN OF CORN WILL PASS UNDIGESTED THROUGH THE BODY OF A BIRD.

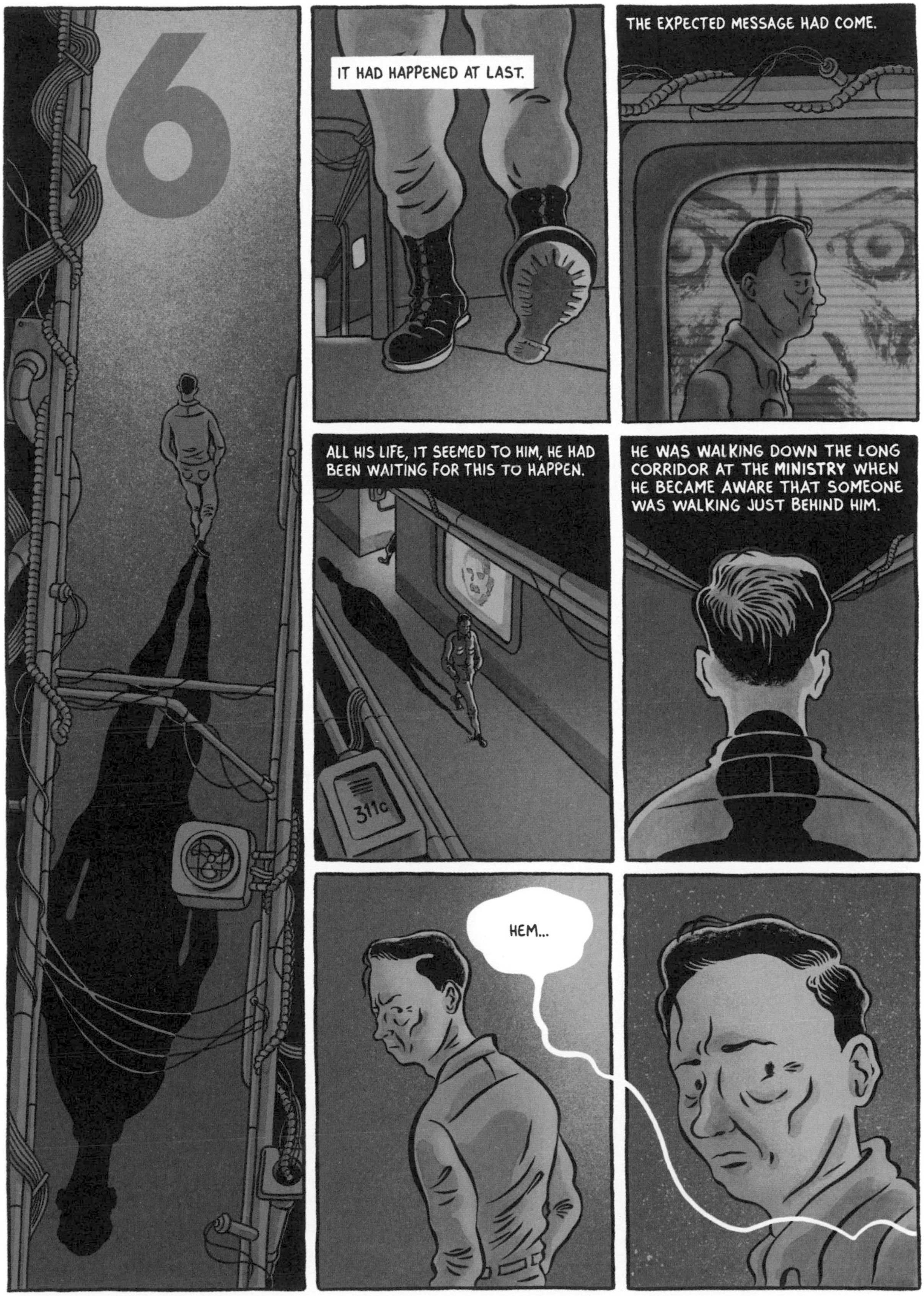
6
IT HAD HAPPENED AT LAST.
THE EXPECTED MESSAGE HAD COME.
ALL HIS LIFE, IT SEEMED TO HIM, HE HAD BEEN WAITING FOR THIS TO HAPPEN.
311c
HE WAS WALKING DOWN THE LONG CORRIDOR AT THE MINISTRY WHEN HE BECAME AWARE THAT SOMEONE WAS WALKING JUST BEHIND HIM.
HEM...

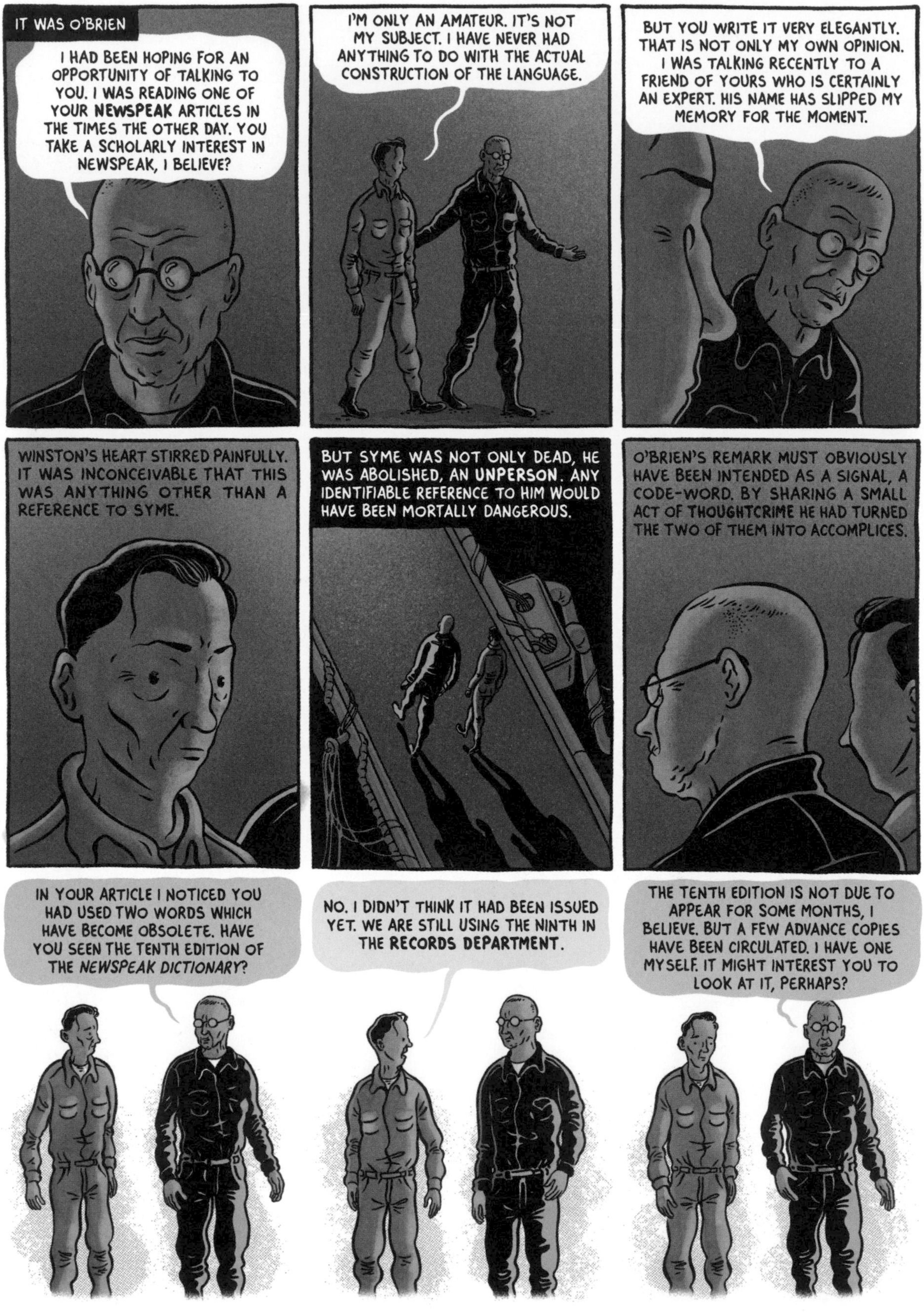
IT WAS O'BRIEN
I HAD BEEN HOPING FOR AN OPPORTUNITY OF TALKING TO YOU. I WAS READING ONE OF YOUR **NEWSPEAK** ARTICLES IN THE TIMES THE OTHER DAY. YOU TAKE A SCHOLARLY INTEREST IN NEWSPEAK, I BELIEVE?
I'M ONLY AN AMATEUR. IT'S NOT MY SUBJECT. I HAVE NEVER HAD ANYTHING TO DO WITH THE ACTUAL CONSTRUCTION OF THE LANGUAGE.
BUT YOU WRITE IT VERY ELEGANTLY. THAT IS NOT ONLY MY OWN OPINION. I WAS TALKING RECENTLY TO A FRIEND OF YOURS WHO IS CERTAINLY AN EXPERT. HIS NAME HAS SLIPPED MY MEMORY FOR THE MOMENT.
WINSTON'S HEART STIRRED PAINFULLY. IT WAS INCONCEIVABLE THAT THIS WAS ANYTHING OTHER THAN A REFERENCE TO SYME.
BUT SYME WAS NOT ONLY DEAD, HE WAS ABOLISHED, AN **UNPERSON**. ANY IDENTIFIABLE REFERENCE TO HIM WOULD HAVE BEEN MORTALLY DANGEROUS.
O'BRIEN'S REMARK MUST OBVIOUSLY HAVE BEEN INTENDED AS A SIGNAL, A CODE-WORD. BY SHARING A SMALL ACT OF **THOUGHTCRIME** HE HAD TURNED THE TWO OF THEM INTO ACCOMPLICES.
IN YOUR ARTICLE I NOTICED YOU HAD USED TWO WORDS WHICH HAVE BECOME OBSOLETE. HAVE YOU SEEN THE TENTH EDITION OF THE *NEWSPEAK DICTIONARY*?
NO. I DIDN'T THINK IT HAD BEEN ISSUED YET. WE ARE STILL USING THE NINTH IN THE **RECORDS DEPARTMENT**.
THE TENTH EDITION IS NOT DUE TO APPEAR FOR SOME MONTHS, I BELIEVE. BUT A FEW ADVANCE COPIES HAVE BEEN CIRCULATED. I HAVE ONE MYSELF. IT MIGHT INTEREST YOU TO LOOK AT IT, PERHAPS?

SOME OF THE NEW DEVELOPMENTS ARE MOST INGENIOUS. THE REDUCTION IN THE NUMBER OF VERBS — THAT IS THE POINT THAT WILL APPEAL TO YOU, I THINK.

PERHAPS YOU COULD PICK IT UP AT MY FLAT AT SOME TIME THAT SUITED YOU?

WAIT. LET ME GIVE YOU MY ADDRESS.

IMMEDIATELY BENEATH THE TELESCREEN, IN SUCH A POSITION THAT ANYONE WHO WAS WATCHING AT THE OTHER END OF THE INSTRUMENT COULD READ WHAT HE WAS WRITING, HE SCRIBBLED AN ADDRESS AND TORE OUT THE PAGE.

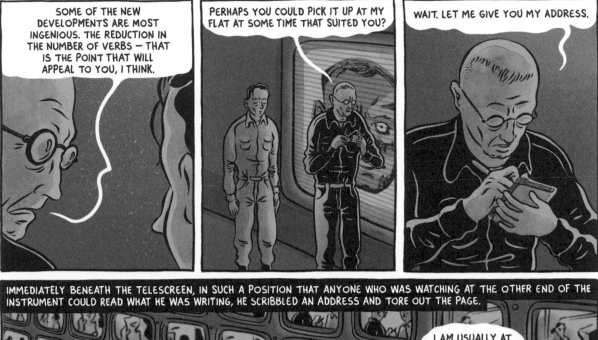

I AM USUALLY AT HOME IN THE EVENINGS.

HE WAS GONE, LEAVING WINSTON HOLDING THE SCRAP OF PAPER.

PERHAPS THERE WOULD EVEN BE A MESSAGE CONCEALED SOMEWHERE IN THE DICTIONARY.

THE CONSPIRACY THAT HE HAD DREAMED OF DID EXIST, AND HE HAD REACHED THE OUTER EDGES OF IT.

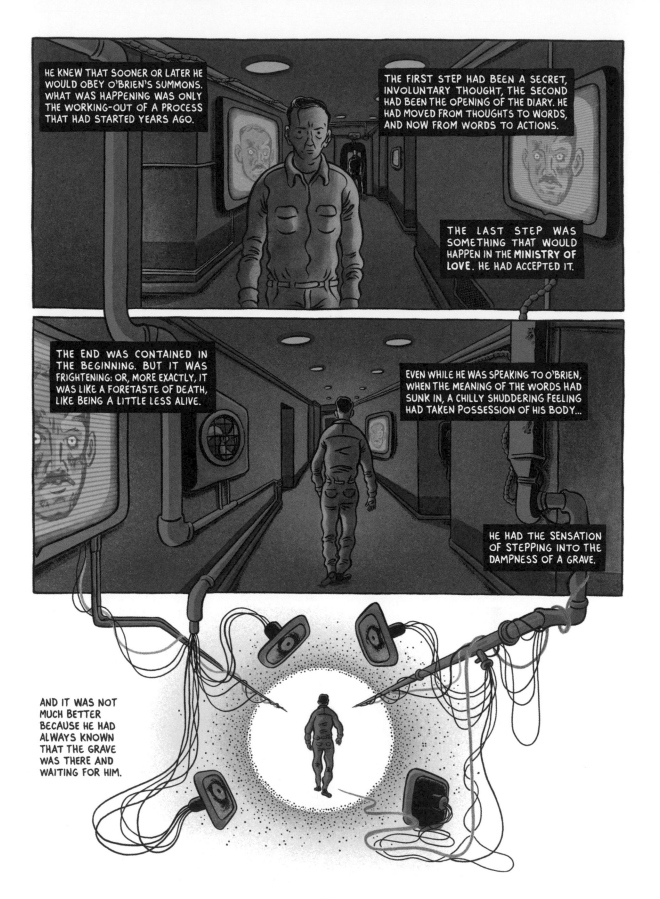

HE KNEW THAT SOONER OR LATER HE WOULD OBEY O'BRIEN'S SUMMONS. WHAT WAS HAPPENING WAS ONLY THE WORKING-OUT OF A PROCESS THAT HAD STARTED YEARS AGO.

THE FIRST STEP HAD BEEN A SECRET, INVOLUNTARY THOUGHT, THE SECOND HAD BEEN THE OPENING OF THE DIARY. HE HAD MOVED FROM THOUGHTS TO WORDS, AND NOW FROM WORDS TO ACTIONS.

THE LAST STEP WAS SOMETHING THAT WOULD HAPPEN IN THE **MINISTRY OF LOVE**. HE HAD ACCEPTED IT.

THE END WAS CONTAINED IN THE BEGINNING. BUT IT WAS FRIGHTENING: OR, MORE EXACTLY, IT WAS LIKE A FORETASTE OF DEATH, LIKE BEING A LITTLE LESS ALIVE.

EVEN WHILE HE WAS SPEAKING TO O'BRIEN, WHEN THE MEANING OF THE WORDS HAD SUNK IN, A CHILLY SHUDDERING FEELING HAD TAKEN POSSESSION OF HIS BODY...

HE HAD THE SENSATION OF STEPPING INTO THE DAMPNESS OF A GRAVE.

AND IT WAS NOT MUCH BETTER BECAUSE HE HAD ALWAYS KNOWN THAT THE GRAVE WAS THERE AND WAITING FOR HIM.

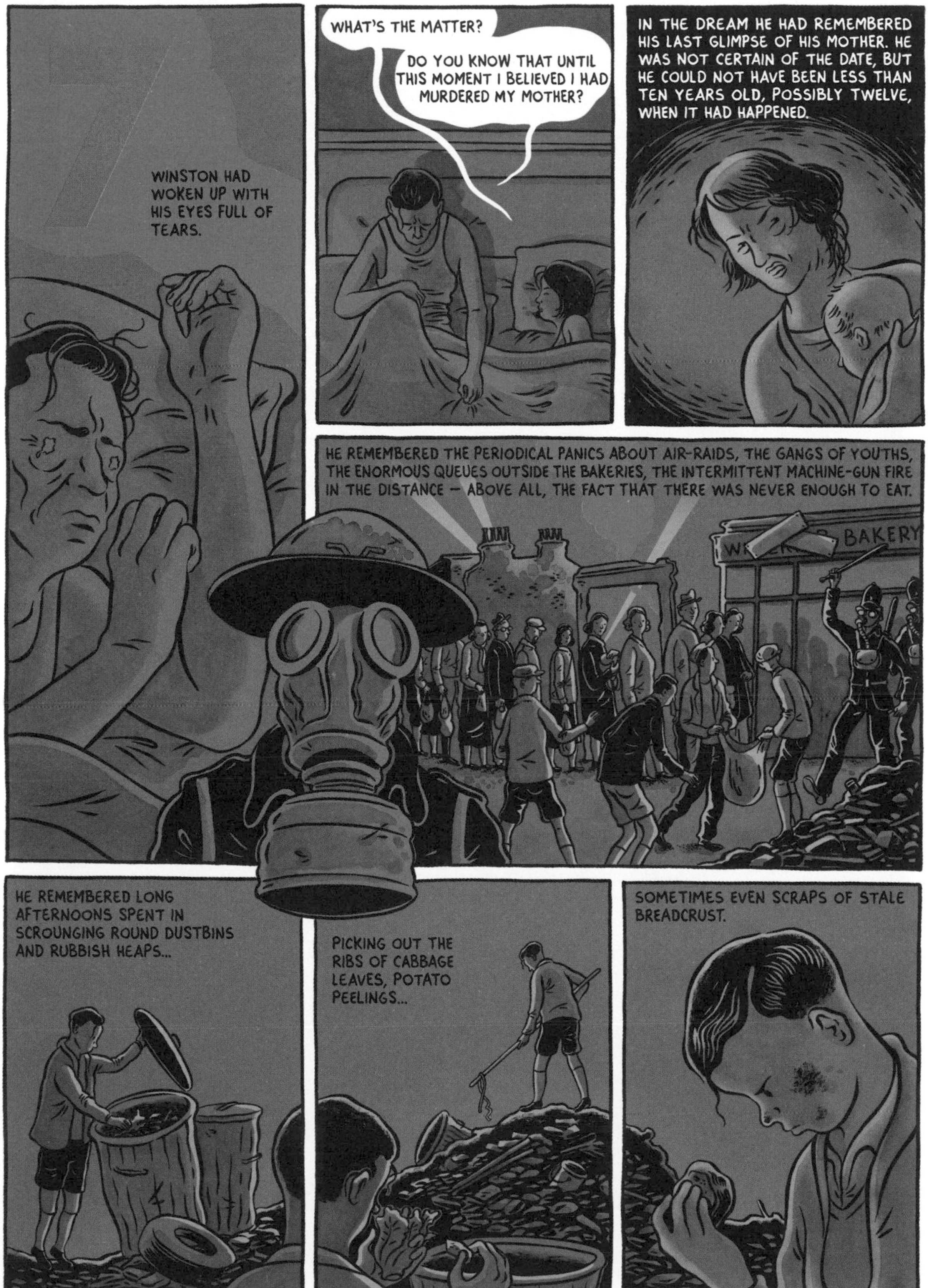
WINSTON HAD WOKEN UP WITH HIS EYES FULL OF TEARS.
WHAT'S THE MATTER?
DO YOU KNOW THAT UNTIL THIS MOMENT I BELIEVED I HAD MURDERED MY MOTHER?
IN THE DREAM HE HAD REMEMBERED HIS LAST GLIMPSE OF HIS MOTHER. HE WAS NOT CERTAIN OF THE DATE, BUT HE COULD NOT HAVE BEEN LESS THAN TEN YEARS OLD, POSSIBLY TWELVE, WHEN IT HAD HAPPENED.
HE REMEMBERED THE PERIODICAL PANICS ABOUT AIR-RAIDS, THE GANGS OF YOUTHS, THE ENORMOUS QUEUES OUTSIDE THE BAKERIES, THE INTERMITTENT MACHINE-GUN FIRE IN THE DISTANCE — ABOVE ALL, THE FACT THAT THERE WAS NEVER ENOUGH TO EAT.
BAKERY
HE REMEMBERED LONG AFTERNOONS SPENT IN SCROUNGING ROUND DUSTBINS AND RUBBISH HEAPS...
PICKING OUT THE RIBS OF CABBAGE LEAVES, POTATO PEELINGS...
SOMETIMES EVEN SCRAPS OF STALE BREADCRUST.

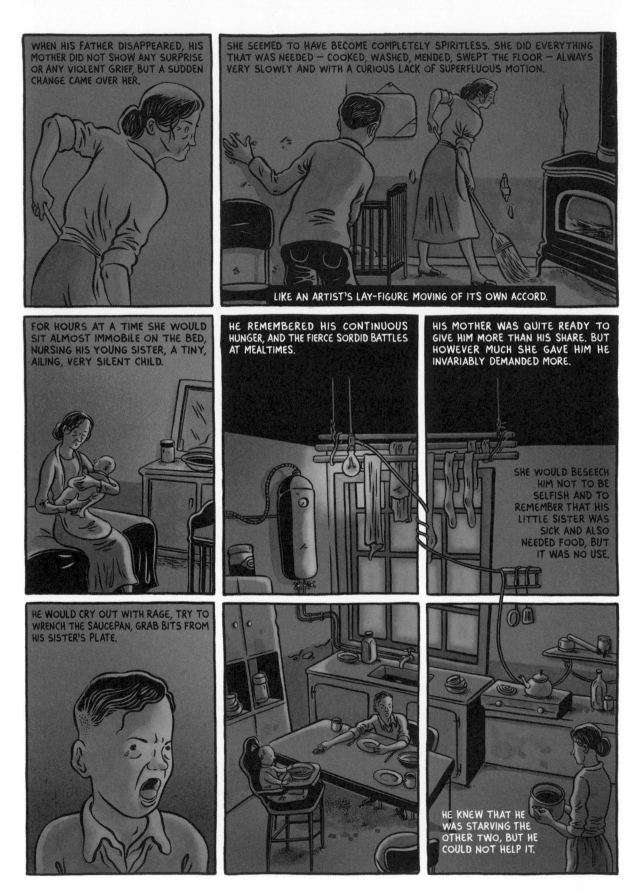

WHEN HIS FATHER DISAPPEARED, HIS MOTHER DID NOT SHOW ANY SURPRISE OR ANY VIOLENT GRIEF, BUT A SUDDEN CHANGE CAME OVER HER.

SHE SEEMED TO HAVE BECOME COMPLETELY SPIRITLESS. SHE DID EVERYTHING THAT WAS NEEDED — COOKED, WASHED, MENDED, SWEPT THE FLOOR — ALWAYS VERY SLOWLY AND WITH A CURIOUS LACK OF SUPERFLUOUS MOTION.

LIKE AN ARTIST'S LAY-FIGURE MOVING OF ITS OWN ACCORD.

FOR HOURS AT A TIME SHE WOULD SIT ALMOST IMMOBILE ON THE BED, NURSING HIS YOUNG SISTER, A TINY, AILING, VERY SILENT CHILD.

HE REMEMBERED HIS CONTINUOUS HUNGER, AND THE FIERCE SORDID BATTLES AT MEALTIMES.

HIS MOTHER WAS QUITE READY TO GIVE HIM MORE THAN HIS SHARE. BUT HOWEVER MUCH SHE GAVE HIM HE INVARIABLY DEMANDED MORE.

SHE WOULD BESEECH HIM NOT TO BE SELFISH AND TO REMEMBER THAT HIS LITTLE SISTER WAS SICK AND ALSO NEEDED FOOD, BUT IT WAS NO USE.

HE WOULD CRY OUT WITH RAGE, TRY TO WRENCH THE SAUCEPAN, GRAB BITS FROM HIS SISTER'S PLATE.

HE KNEW THAT HE WAS STARVING THE OTHER TWO, BUT HE COULD NOT HELP IT.

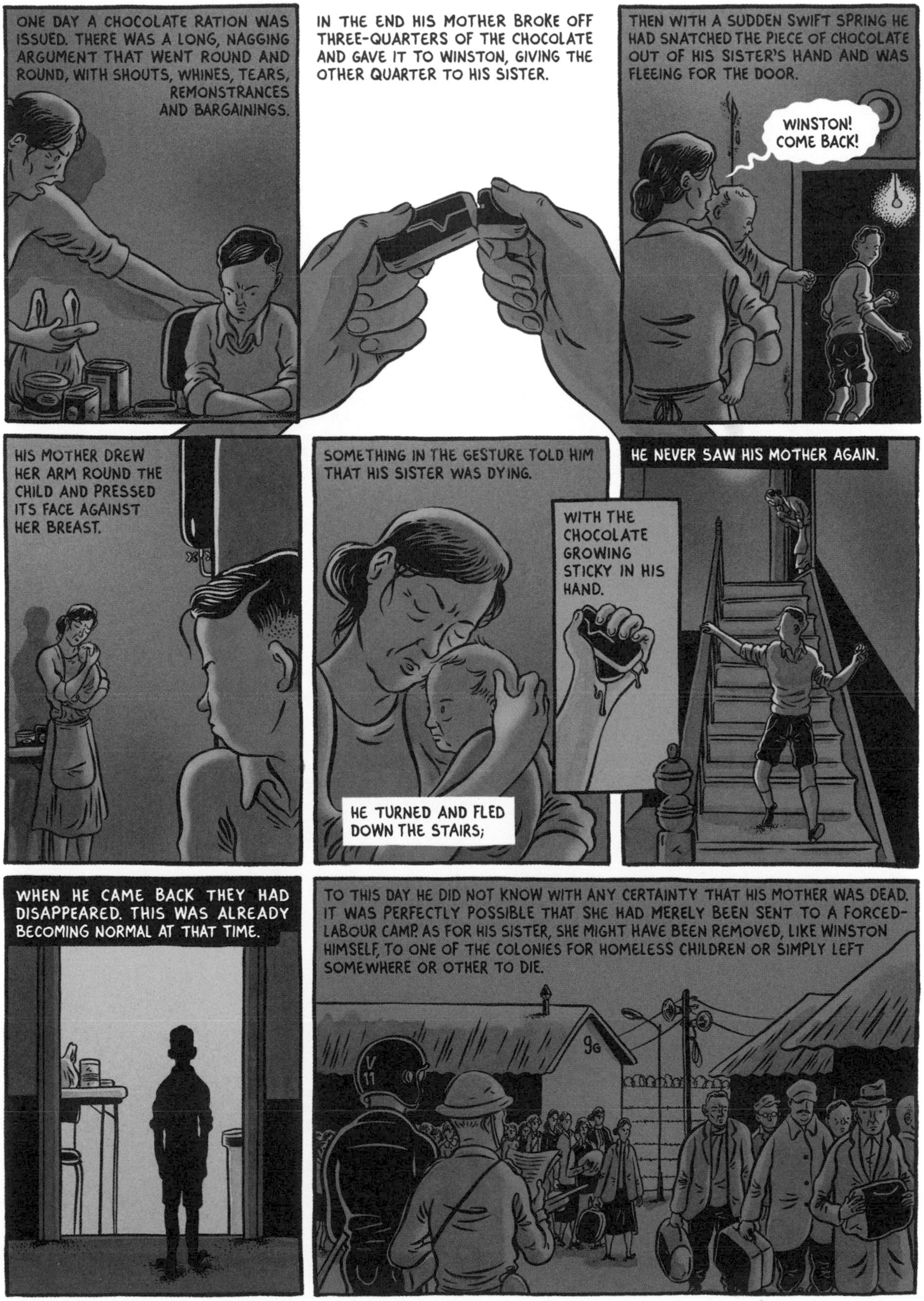
ONE DAY A CHOCOLATE RATION WAS ISSUED. THERE WAS A LONG, NAGGING ARGUMENT THAT WENT ROUND AND ROUND, WITH SHOUTS, WHINES, TEARS, REMONSTRANCES AND BARGAININGS.
IN THE END HIS MOTHER BROKE OFF THREE-QUARTERS OF THE CHOCOLATE AND GAVE IT TO WINSTON, GIVING THE OTHER QUARTER TO HIS SISTER.
THEN WITH A SUDDEN SWIFT SPRING HE HAD SNATCHED THE PIECE OF CHOCOLATE OUT OF HIS SISTER'S HAND AND WAS FLEEING FOR THE DOOR.
WINSTON! COME BACK!
HIS MOTHER DREW HER ARM ROUND THE CHILD AND PRESSED ITS FACE AGAINST HER BREAST.
SOMETHING IN THE GESTURE TOLD HIM THAT HIS SISTER WAS DYING.
WITH THE CHOCOLATE GROWING STICKY IN HIS HAND.
HE TURNED AND FLED DOWN THE STAIRS;
HE NEVER SAW HIS MOTHER AGAIN.
WHEN HE CAME BACK THEY HAD DISAPPEARED. THIS WAS ALREADY BECOMING NORMAL AT THAT TIME.
TO THIS DAY HE DID NOT KNOW WITH ANY CERTAINTY THAT HIS MOTHER WAS DEAD. IT WAS PERFECTLY POSSIBLE THAT SHE HAD MERELY BEEN SENT TO A FORCED-LABOUR CAMP. AS FOR HIS SISTER, SHE MIGHT HAVE BEEN REMOVED, LIKE WINSTON HIMSELF, TO ONE OF THE COLONIES FOR HOMELESS CHILDREN OR SIMPLY LEFT SOMEWHERE OR OTHER TO DIE.
9G
V 11

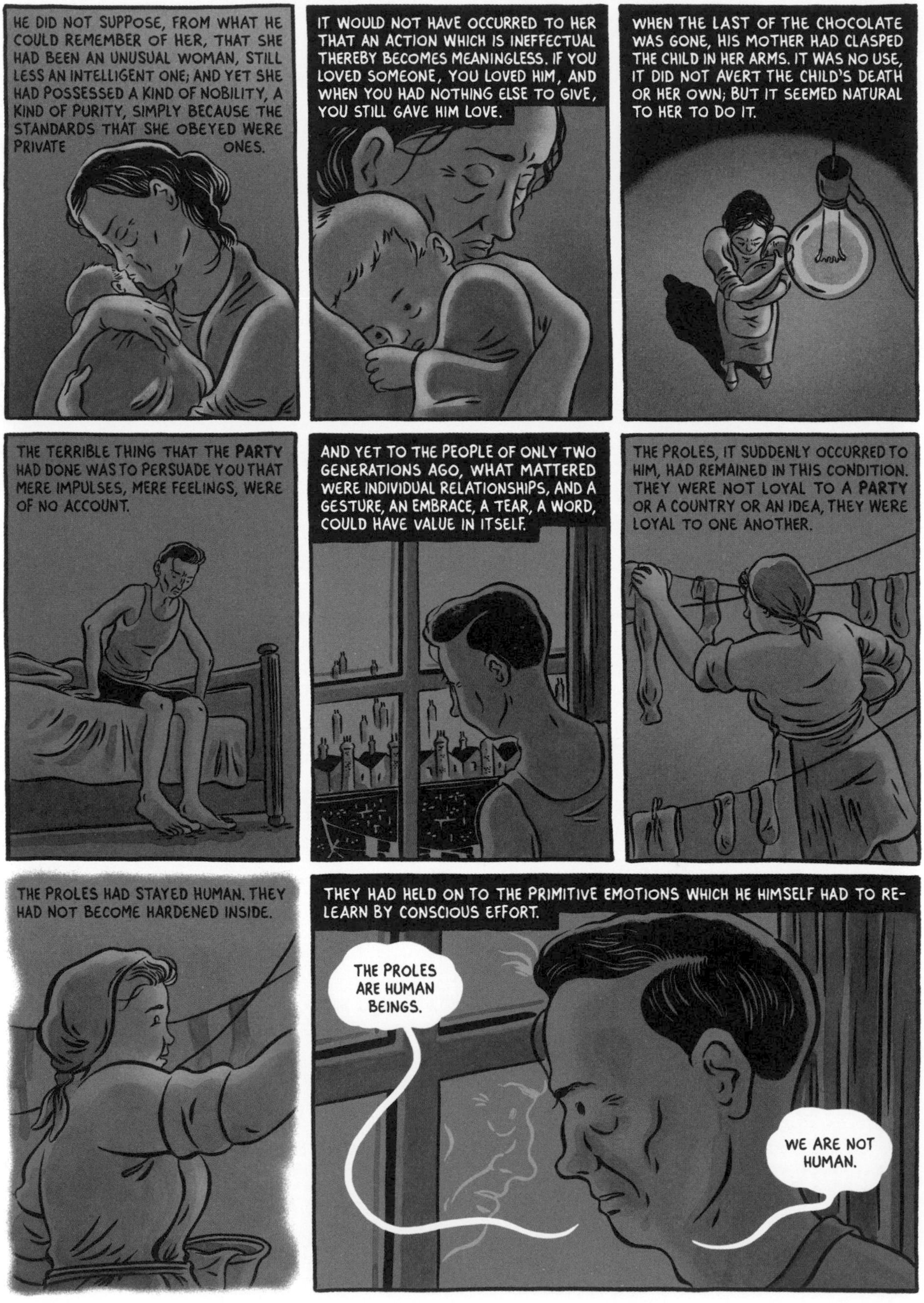
HE DID NOT SUPPOSE, FROM WHAT HE COULD REMEMBER OF HER, THAT SHE HAD BEEN AN UNUSUAL WOMAN, STILL LESS AN INTELLIGENT ONE; AND YET SHE HAD POSSESSED A KIND OF NOBILITY, A KIND OF PURITY, SIMPLY BECAUSE THE STANDARDS THAT SHE OBEYED WERE PRIVATE ONES.
IT WOULD NOT HAVE OCCURRED TO HER THAT AN ACTION WHICH IS INEFFECTUAL THEREBY BECOMES MEANINGLESS. IF YOU LOVED SOMEONE, YOU LOVED HIM, AND WHEN YOU HAD NOTHING ELSE TO GIVE, YOU STILL GAVE HIM LOVE.
WHEN THE LAST OF THE CHOCOLATE WAS GONE, HIS MOTHER HAD CLASPED THE CHILD IN HER ARMS. IT WAS NO USE, IT DID NOT AVERT THE CHILD'S DEATH OR HER OWN; BUT IT SEEMED NATURAL TO HER TO DO IT.
THE TERRIBLE THING THAT THE PARTY HAD DONE WAS TO PERSUADE YOU THAT MERE IMPULSES, MERE FEELINGS, WERE OF NO ACCOUNT.
AND YET TO THE PEOPLE OF ONLY TWO GENERATIONS AGO, WHAT MATTERED WERE INDIVIDUAL RELATIONSHIPS, AND A GESTURE, AN EMBRACE, A TEAR, A WORD, COULD HAVE VALUE IN ITSELF.
THE PROLES, IT SUDDENLY OCCURRED TO HIM, HAD REMAINED IN THIS CONDITION. THEY WERE NOT LOYAL TO A PARTY OR A COUNTRY OR AN IDEA, THEY WERE LOYAL TO ONE ANOTHER.
THE PROLES HAD STAYED HUMAN. THEY HAD NOT BECOME HARDENED INSIDE.
THEY HAD HELD ON TO THE PRIMITIVE EMOTIONS WHICH HE HIMSELF HAD TO RE-LEARN BY CONSCIOUS EFFORT.
THE PROLES ARE HUMAN BEINGS.
WE ARE NOT HUMAN.

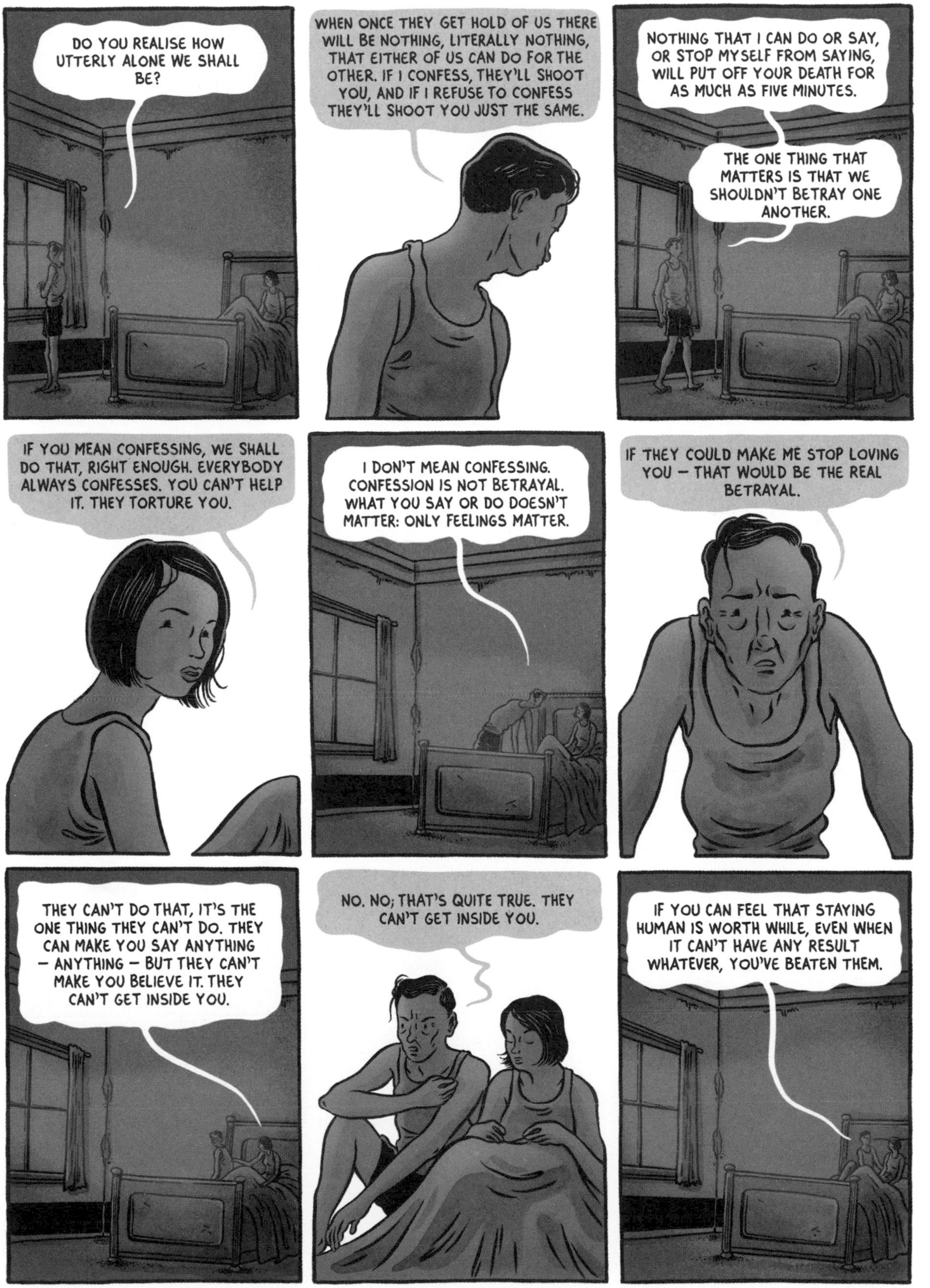
DO YOU REALISE HOW UTTERLY ALONE WE SHALL BE?
WHEN ONCE THEY GET HOLD OF US THERE WILL BE NOTHING, LITERALLY NOTHING, THAT EITHER OF US CAN DO FOR THE OTHER. IF I CONFESS, THEY'LL SHOOT YOU, AND IF I REFUSE TO CONFESS THEY'LL SHOOT YOU JUST THE SAME.
NOTHING THAT I CAN DO OR SAY, OR STOP MYSELF FROM SAYING, WILL PUT OFF YOUR DEATH FOR AS MUCH AS FIVE MINUTES.
THE ONE THING THAT MATTERS IS THAT WE SHOULDN'T BETRAY ONE ANOTHER.
IF YOU MEAN CONFESSING, WE SHALL DO THAT, RIGHT ENOUGH. EVERYBODY ALWAYS CONFESSES. YOU CAN'T HELP IT. THEY TORTURE YOU.
I DON'T MEAN CONFESSING. CONFESSION IS NOT BETRAYAL. WHAT YOU SAY OR DO DOESN'T MATTER: ONLY FEELINGS MATTER.
IF THEY COULD MAKE ME STOP LOVING YOU — THAT WOULD BE THE REAL BETRAYAL.
THEY CAN'T DO THAT, IT'S THE ONE THING THEY CAN'T DO. THEY CAN MAKE YOU SAY ANYTHING — ANYTHING — BUT THEY CAN'T MAKE YOU BELIEVE IT. THEY CAN'T GET INSIDE YOU.
NO. NO; THAT'S QUITE TRUE. THEY CAN'T GET INSIDE YOU.
IF YOU CAN FEEL THAT STAYING HUMAN IS WORTH WHILE, EVEN WHEN IT CAN'T HAVE ANY RESULT WHATEVER, YOU'VE BEATEN THEM.

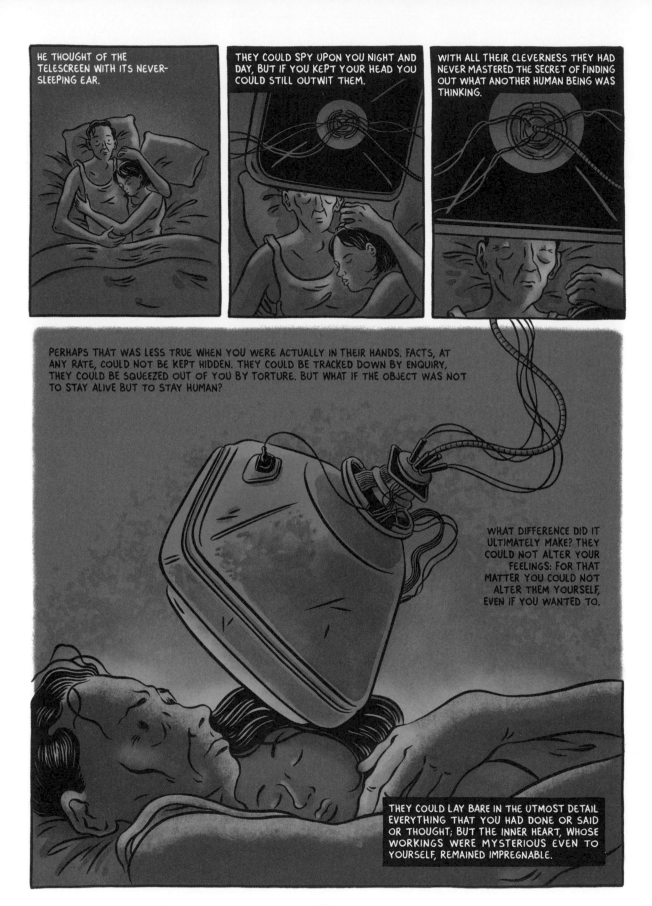

HE THOUGHT OF THE TELESCREEN WITH ITS NEVER-SLEEPING EAR.

THEY COULD SPY UPON YOU NIGHT AND DAY, BUT IF YOU KEPT YOUR HEAD YOU COULD STILL OUTWIT THEM.

WITH ALL THEIR CLEVERNESS THEY HAD NEVER MASTERED THE SECRET OF FINDING OUT WHAT ANOTHER HUMAN BEING WAS THINKING.

PERHAPS THAT WAS LESS TRUE WHEN YOU WERE ACTUALLY IN THEIR HANDS. FACTS, AT ANY RATE, COULD NOT BE KEPT HIDDEN. THEY COULD BE TRACKED DOWN BY ENQUIRY, THEY COULD BE SQUEEZED OUT OF YOU BY TORTURE. BUT WHAT IF THE OBJECT WAS NOT TO STAY ALIVE BUT TO STAY HUMAN?

WHAT DIFFERENCE DID IT ULTIMATELY MAKE? THEY COULD NOT ALTER YOUR FEELINGS: FOR THAT MATTER YOU COULD NOT ALTER THEM YOURSELF, EVEN IF YOU WANTED TO.

THEY COULD LAY BARE IN THE UTMOST DETAIL EVERYTHING THAT YOU HAD DONE OR SAID OR THOUGHT; BUT THE INNER HEART, WHOSE WORKINGS WERE MYSTERIOUS EVEN TO YOURSELF, REMAINED IMPREGNABLE.

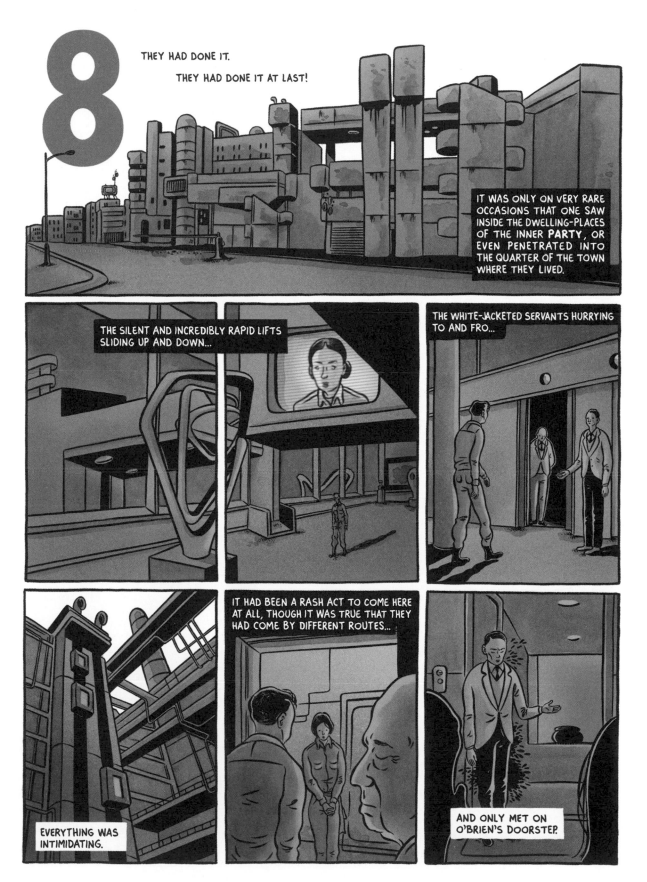

8

THEY HAD DONE IT.

THEY HAD DONE IT AT LAST!

IT WAS ONLY ON VERY RARE OCCASIONS THAT ONE SAW INSIDE THE DWELLING-PLACES OF THE INNER **PARTY**, OR EVEN PENETRATED INTO THE QUARTER OF THE TOWN WHERE THEY LIVED.

THE SILENT AND INCREDIBLY RAPID LIFTS SLIDING UP AND DOWN...

THE WHITE-JACKETED SERVANTS HURRYING TO AND FRO...

IT HAD BEEN A RASH ACT TO COME HERE AT ALL, THOUGH IT WAS TRUE THAT THEY HAD COME BY DIFFERENT ROUTES...

AND ONLY MET ON O'BRIEN'S DOORSTEP.

EVERYTHING WAS INTIMIDATING.

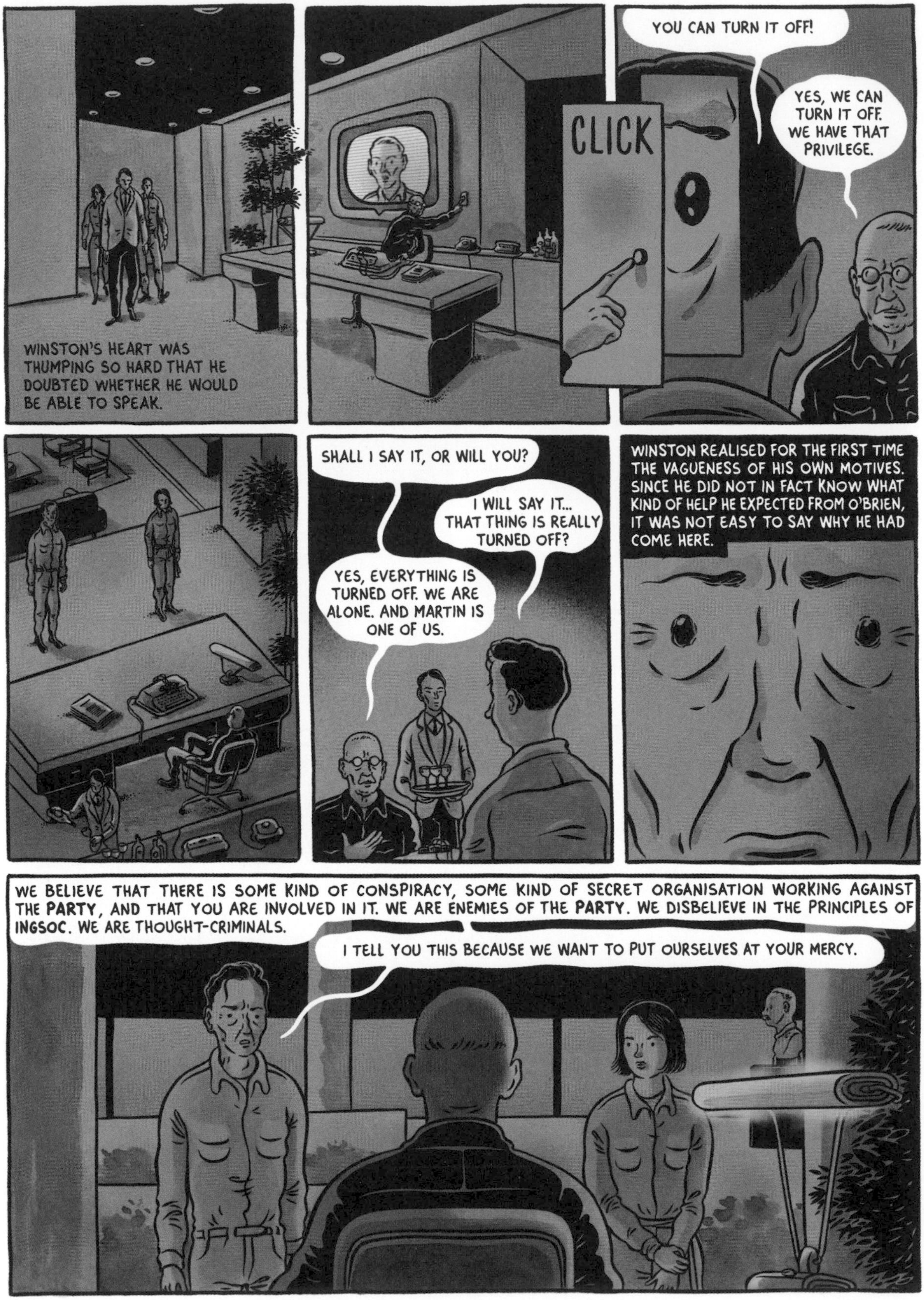
WINSTON'S HEART WAS THUMPING SO HARD THAT HE DOUBTED WHETHER HE WOULD BE ABLE TO SPEAK.
CLICK
YOU CAN TURN IT OFF!
YES, WE CAN TURN IT OFF. WE HAVE THAT PRIVILEGE.
SHALL I SAY IT, OR WILL YOU?
I WILL SAY IT... THAT THING IS REALLY TURNED OFF?
YES, EVERYTHING IS TURNED OFF. WE ARE ALONE. AND MARTIN IS ONE OF US.
WINSTON REALISED FOR THE FIRST TIME THE VAGUENESS OF HIS OWN MOTIVES. SINCE HE DID NOT IN FACT KNOW WHAT KIND OF HELP HE EXPECTED FROM O'BRIEN, IT WAS NOT EASY TO SAY WHY HE HAD COME HERE.
WE BELIEVE THAT THERE IS SOME KIND OF CONSPIRACY, SOME KIND OF SECRET ORGANISATION WORKING AGAINST THE PARTY, AND THAT YOU ARE INVOLVED IN IT. WE ARE ENEMIES OF THE PARTY. WE DISBELIEVE IN THE PRINCIPLES OF INGSOC. WE ARE THOUGHT-CRIMINALS.
I TELL YOU THIS BECAUSE WE WANT TO PUT OURSELVES AT YOUR MERCY.

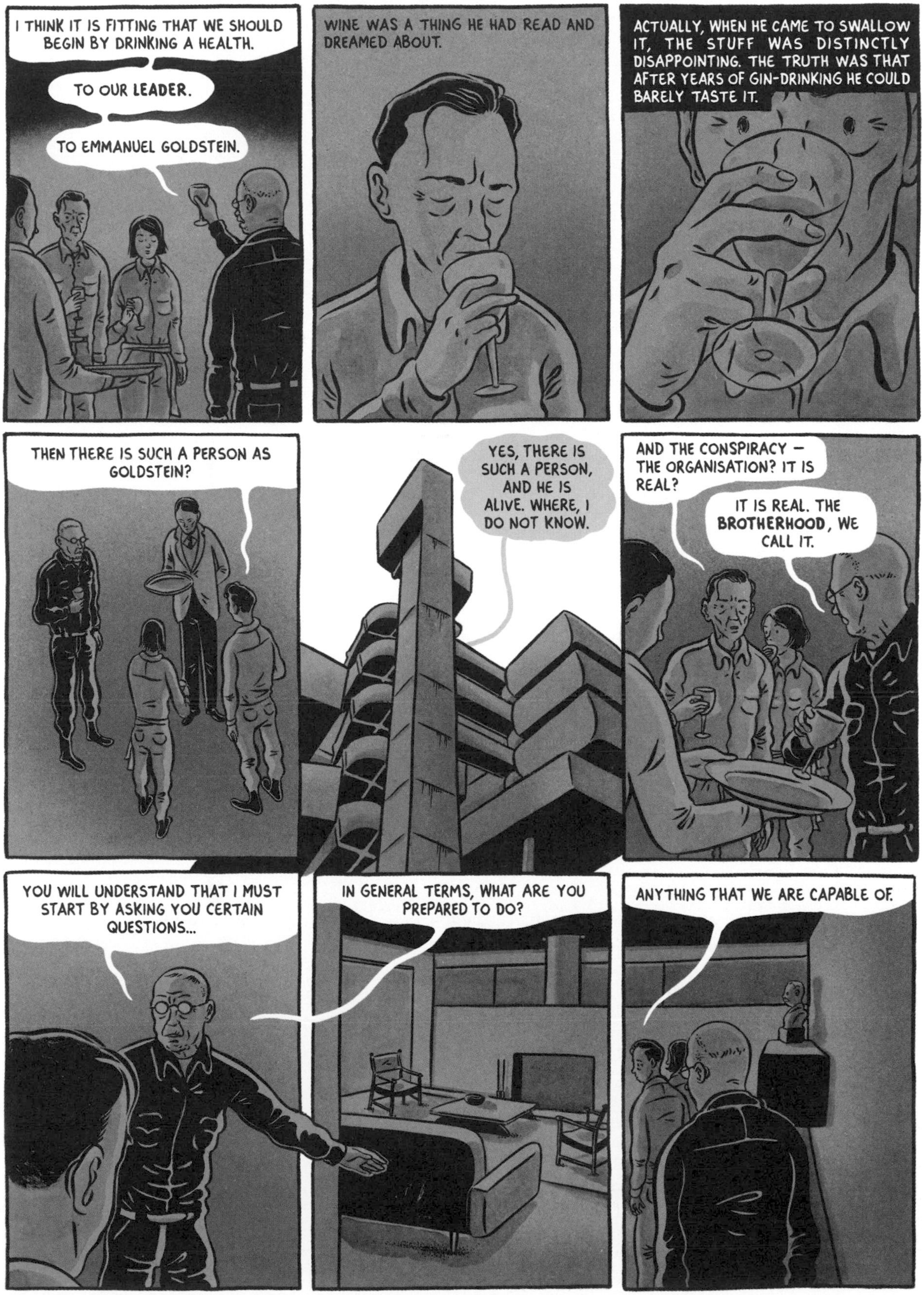
I THINK IT IS FITTING THAT WE SHOULD BEGIN BY DRINKING A HEALTH.
TO OUR LEADER.
TO EMMANUEL GOLDSTEIN.
WINE WAS A THING HE HAD READ AND DREAMED ABOUT.
ACTUALLY, WHEN HE CAME TO SWALLOW IT, THE STUFF WAS DISTINCTLY DISAPPOINTING. THE TRUTH WAS THAT AFTER YEARS OF GIN-DRINKING HE COULD BARELY TASTE IT.
THEN THERE IS SUCH A PERSON AS GOLDSTEIN?
YES, THERE IS SUCH A PERSON, AND HE IS ALIVE. WHERE, I DO NOT KNOW.
AND THE CONSPIRACY – THE ORGANISATION? IT IS REAL?
IT IS REAL. THE BROTHERHOOD, WE CALL IT.
YOU WILL UNDERSTAND THAT I MUST START BY ASKING YOU CERTAIN QUESTIONS...
IN GENERAL TERMS, WHAT ARE YOU PREPARED TO DO?
ANYTHING THAT WE ARE CAPABLE OF.

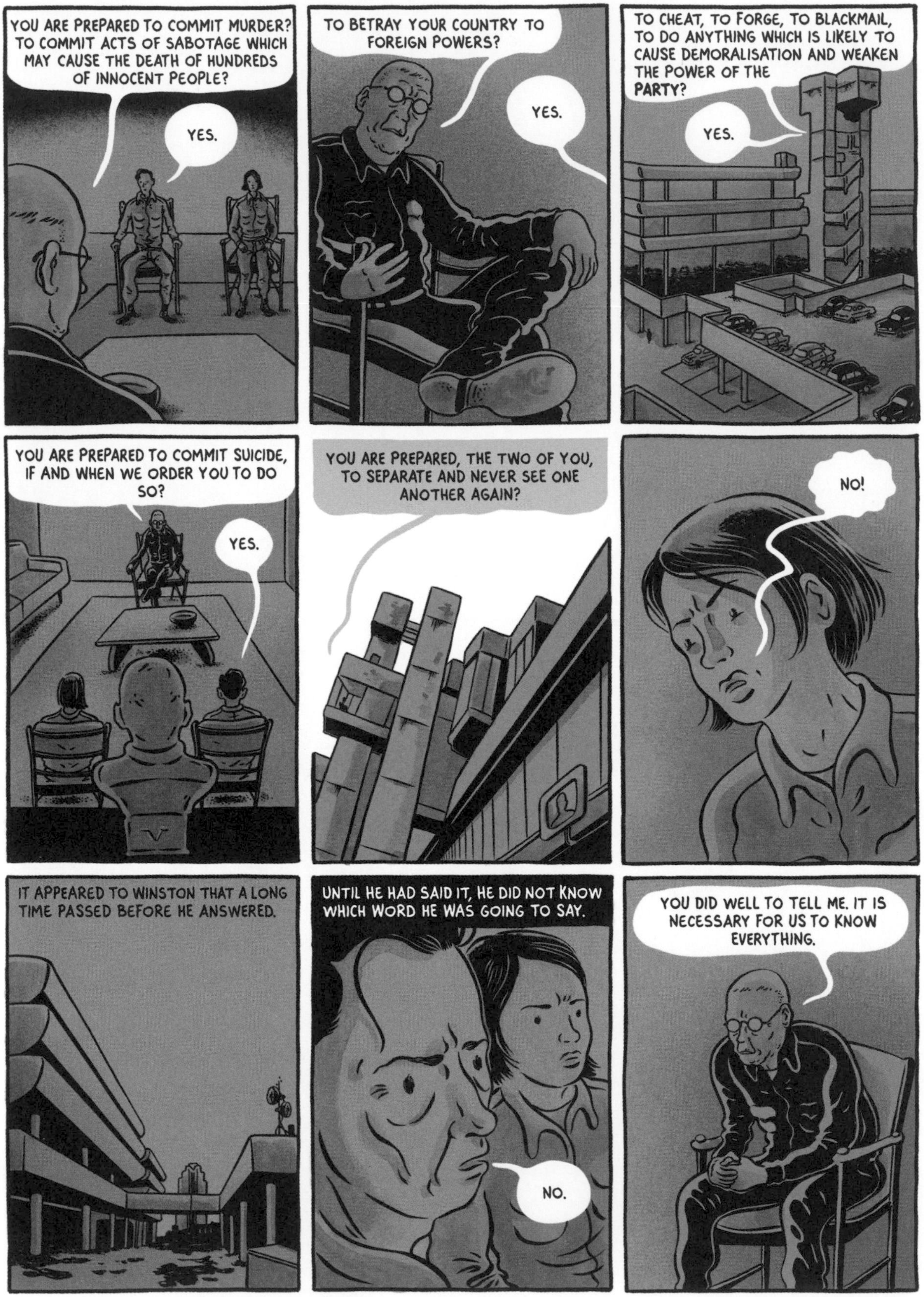
YOU ARE PREPARED TO COMMIT MURDER? TO COMMIT ACTS OF SABOTAGE WHICH MAY CAUSE THE DEATH OF HUNDREDS OF INNOCENT PEOPLE?
YES.
TO BETRAY YOUR COUNTRY TO FOREIGN POWERS?
YES.
TO CHEAT, TO FORGE, TO BLACKMAIL, TO DO ANYTHING WHICH IS LIKELY TO CAUSE DEMORALISATION AND WEAKEN THE POWER OF THE **PARTY**?
YES.
YOU ARE PREPARED TO COMMIT SUICIDE, IF AND WHEN WE ORDER YOU TO DO SO?
YES.
YOU ARE PREPARED, THE TWO OF YOU, TO SEPARATE AND NEVER SEE ONE ANOTHER AGAIN?
NO!
IT APPEARED TO WINSTON THAT A LONG TIME PASSED BEFORE HE ANSWERED.
UNTIL HE HAD SAID IT, HE DID NOT KNOW WHICH WORD HE WAS GOING TO SAY.
NO.
YOU DID WELL TO TELL ME. IT IS NECESSARY FOR US TO KNOW EVERYTHING.

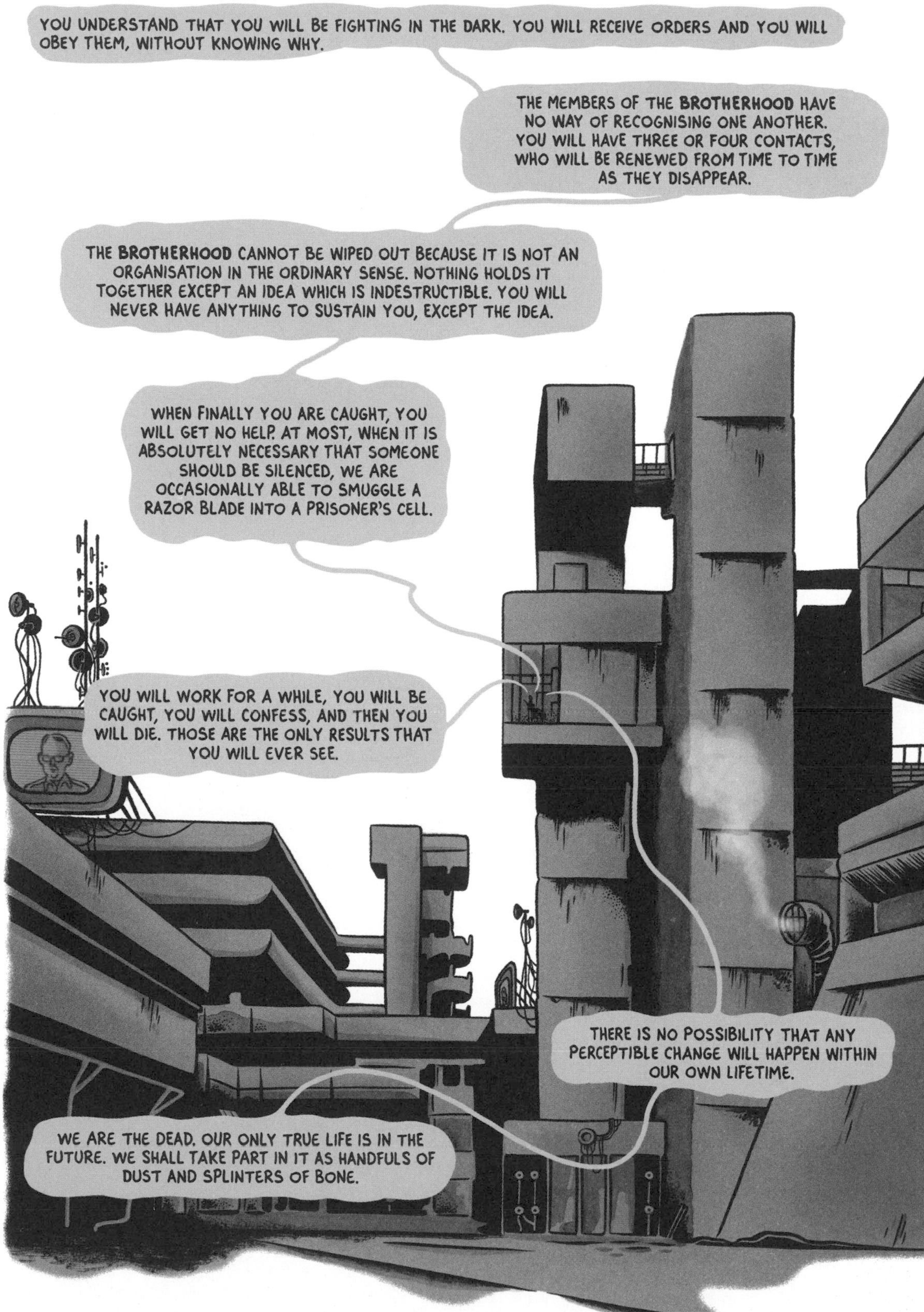
YOU UNDERSTAND THAT YOU WILL BE FIGHTING IN THE DARK. YOU WILL RECEIVE ORDERS AND YOU WILL OBEY THEM, WITHOUT KNOWING WHY.
THE MEMBERS OF THE **BROTHERHOOD** HAVE NO WAY OF RECOGNISING ONE ANOTHER. YOU WILL HAVE THREE OR FOUR CONTACTS, WHO WILL BE RENEWED FROM TIME TO TIME AS THEY DISAPPEAR.
THE **BROTHERHOOD** CANNOT BE WIPED OUT BECAUSE IT IS NOT AN ORGANISATION IN THE ORDINARY SENSE. NOTHING HOLDS IT TOGETHER EXCEPT AN IDEA WHICH IS INDESTRUCTIBLE. YOU WILL NEVER HAVE ANYTHING TO SUSTAIN YOU, EXCEPT THE IDEA.
WHEN FINALLY YOU ARE CAUGHT, YOU WILL GET NO HELP. AT MOST, WHEN IT IS ABSOLUTELY NECESSARY THAT SOMEONE SHOULD BE SILENCED, WE ARE OCCASIONALLY ABLE TO SMUGGLE A RAZOR BLADE INTO A PRISONER'S CELL.
YOU WILL WORK FOR A WHILE, YOU WILL BE CAUGHT, YOU WILL CONFESS, AND THEN YOU WILL DIE. THOSE ARE THE ONLY RESULTS THAT YOU WILL EVER SEE.
THERE IS NO POSSIBILITY THAT ANY PERCEPTIBLE CHANGE WILL HAPPEN WITHIN OUR OWN LIFETIME.
WE ARE THE DEAD. OUR ONLY TRUE LIFE IS IN THE FUTURE. WE SHALL TAKE PART IN IT AS HANDFULS OF DUST AND SPLINTERS OF BONE.

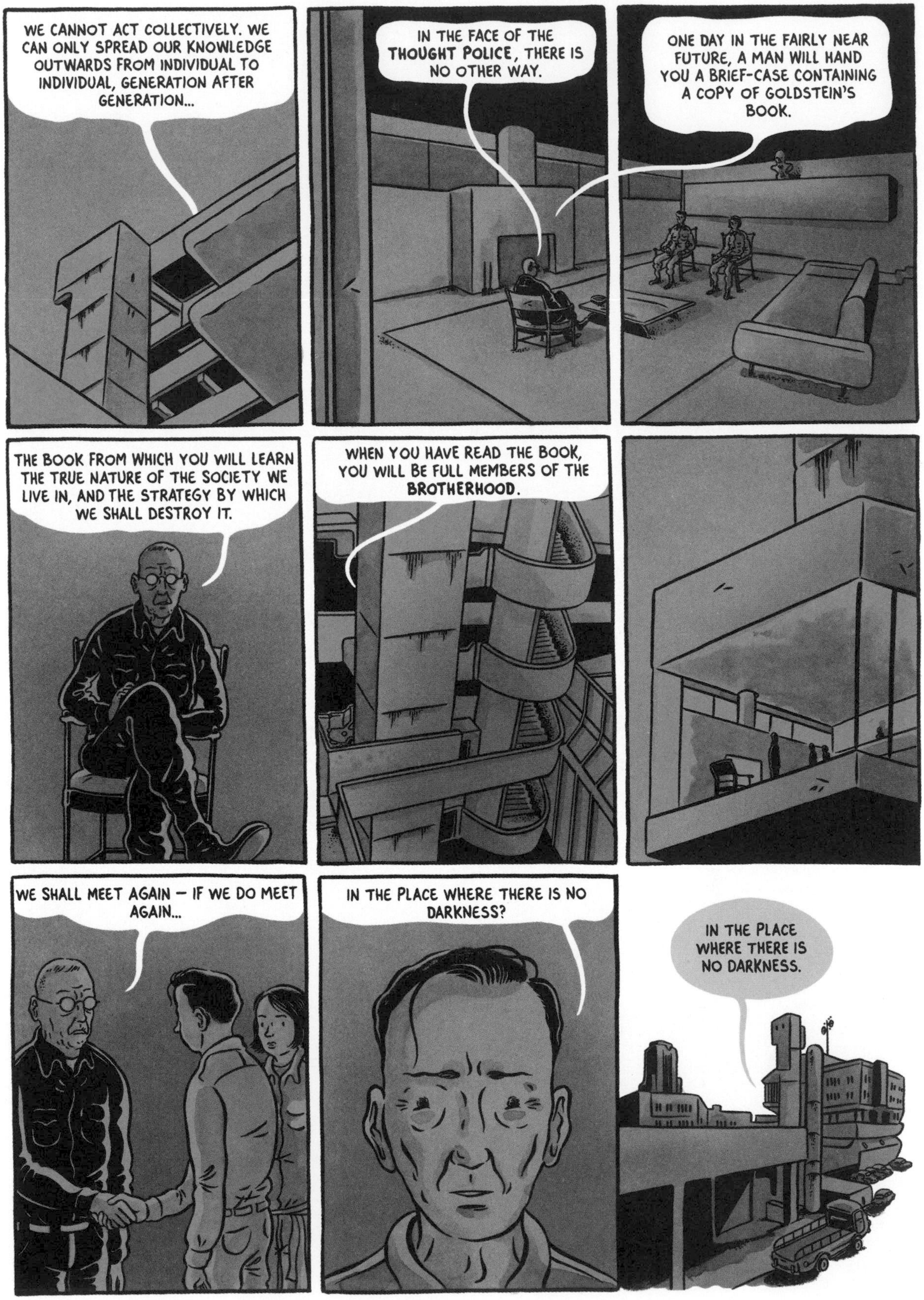
WE CANNOT ACT COLLECTIVELY. WE CAN ONLY SPREAD OUR KNOWLEDGE OUTWARDS FROM INDIVIDUAL TO INDIVIDUAL, GENERATION AFTER GENERATION...
IN THE FACE OF THE THOUGHT POLICE, THERE IS NO OTHER WAY.
ONE DAY IN THE FAIRLY NEAR FUTURE, A MAN WILL HAND YOU A BRIEF-CASE CONTAINING A COPY OF GOLDSTEIN'S BOOK.
THE BOOK FROM WHICH YOU WILL LEARN THE TRUE NATURE OF THE SOCIETY WE LIVE IN, AND THE STRATEGY BY WHICH WE SHALL DESTROY IT.
WHEN YOU HAVE READ THE BOOK, YOU WILL BE FULL MEMBERS OF THE BROTHERHOOD.
WE SHALL MEET AGAIN — IF WE DO MEET AGAIN...
IN THE PLACE WHERE THERE IS NO DARKNESS?
IN THE PLACE WHERE THERE IS NO DARKNESS.

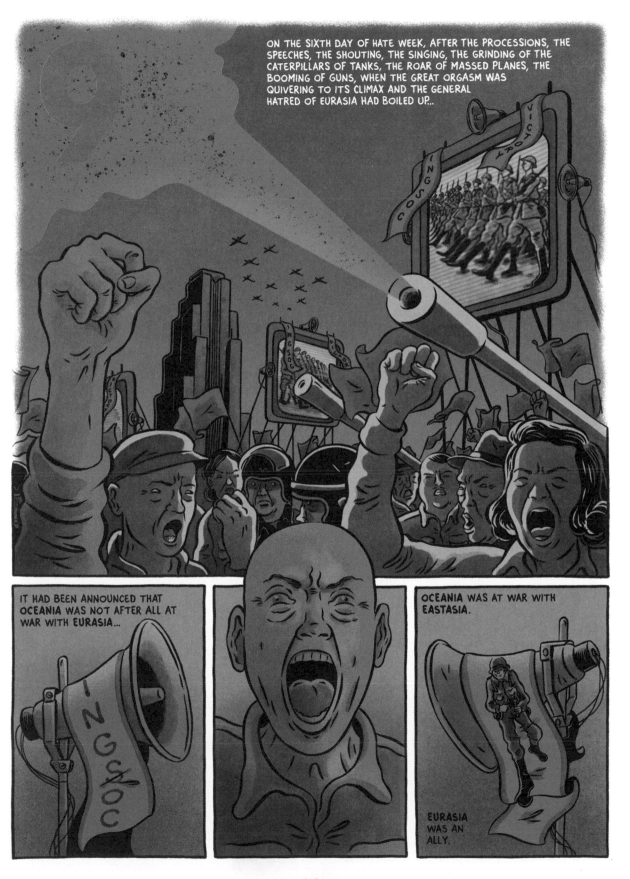

ON THE SIXTH DAY OF HATE WEEK, AFTER THE PROCESSIONS, THE SPEECHES, THE SHOUTING, THE SINGING, THE GRINDING OF THE CATERPILLARS OF TANKS, THE ROAR OF MASSED PLANES, THE BOOMING OF GUNS, WHEN THE GREAT ORGASM WAS QUIVERING TO ITS CLIMAX AND THE GENERAL HATRED OF EURASIA HAD BOILED UP...

IT HAD BEEN ANNOUNCED THAT OCEANIA WAS NOT AFTER ALL AT WAR WITH EURASIA...

OCEANIA WAS AT WAR WITH EASTASIA.

EURASIA WAS AN ALLY.

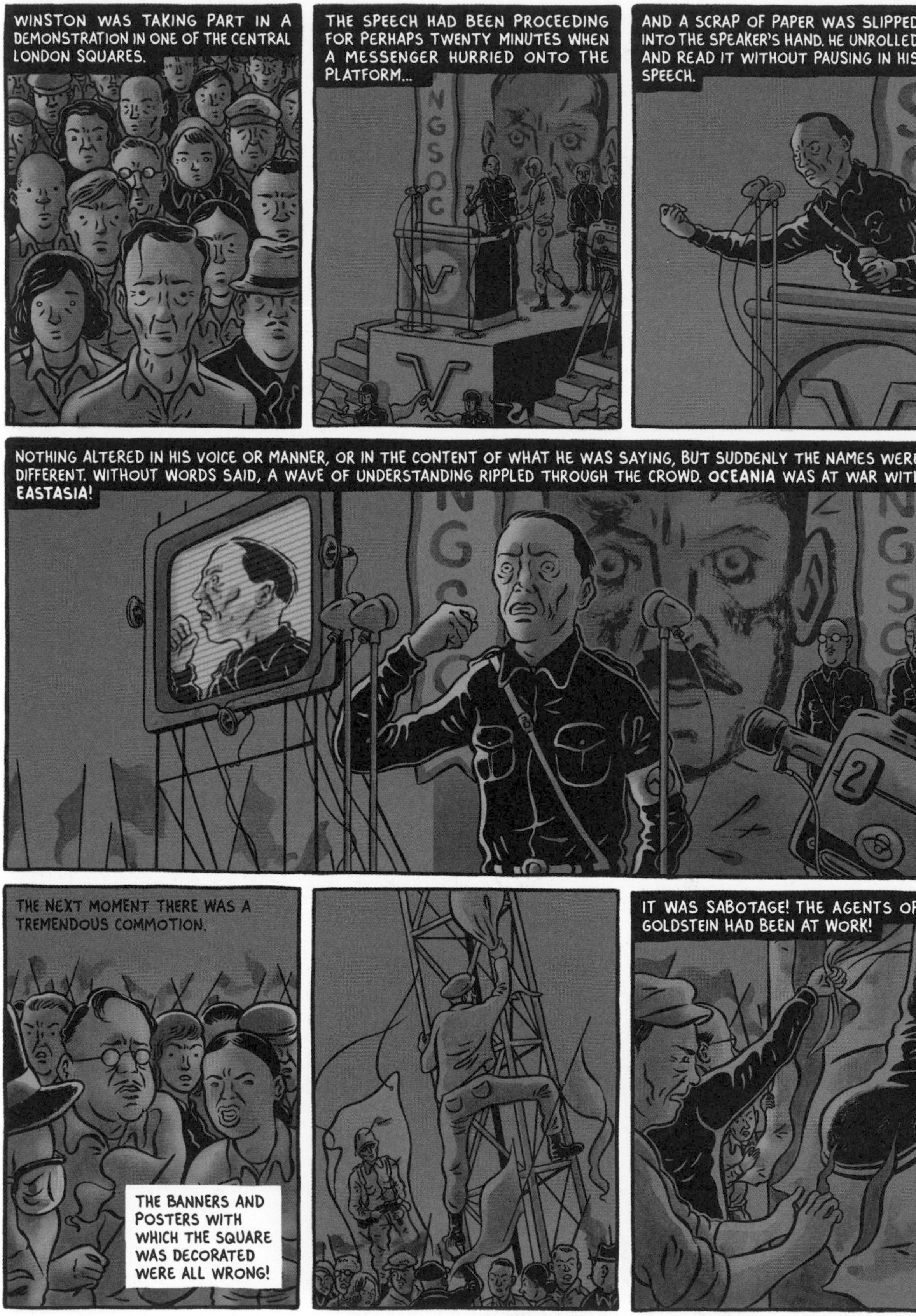
WINSTON WAS TAKING PART IN A DEMONSTRATION IN ONE OF THE CENTRAL LONDON SQUARES.
THE SPEECH HAD BEEN PROCEEDING FOR PERHAPS TWENTY MINUTES WHEN A MESSENGER HURRIED ONTO THE PLATFORM...
AND A SCRAP OF PAPER WAS SLIPPED INTO THE SPEAKER'S HAND. HE UNROLLED AND READ IT WITHOUT PAUSING IN HIS SPEECH.
NOTHING ALTERED IN HIS VOICE OR MANNER, OR IN THE CONTENT OF WHAT HE WAS SAYING, BUT SUDDENLY THE NAMES WERE DIFFERENT. WITHOUT WORDS SAID, A WAVE OF UNDERSTANDING RIPPLED THROUGH THE CROWD. OCEANIA WAS AT WAR WITH EASTASIA!
THE NEXT MOMENT THERE WAS A TREMENDOUS COMMOTION.
THE BANNERS AND POSTERS WITH WHICH THE SQUARE WAS DECORATED WERE ALL WRONG!
IT WAS SABOTAGE! THE AGENTS OF GOLDSTEIN HAD BEEN AT WORK!

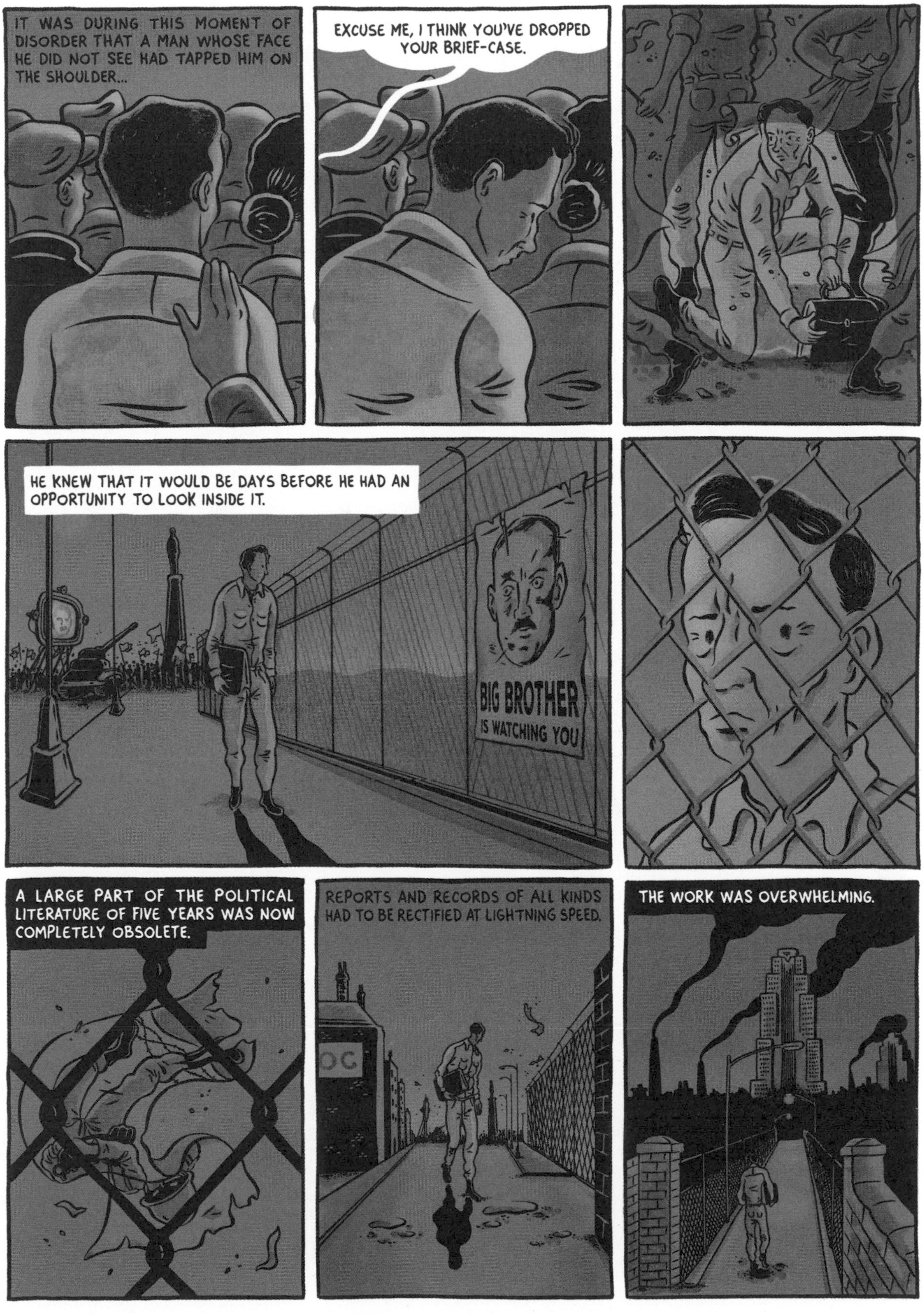
IT WAS DURING THIS MOMENT OF DISORDER THAT A MAN WHOSE FACE HE DID NOT SEE HAD TAPPED HIM ON THE SHOULDER...
EXCUSE ME, I THINK YOU'VE DROPPED YOUR BRIEF-CASE.
HE KNEW THAT IT WOULD BE DAYS BEFORE HE HAD AN OPPORTUNITY TO LOOK INSIDE IT.
BIG BROTHER IS WATCHING YOU
A LARGE PART OF THE POLITICAL LITERATURE OF FIVE YEARS WAS NOW COMPLETELY OBSOLETE.
REPORTS AND RECORDS OF ALL KINDS HAD TO BE RECTIFIED AT LIGHTNING SPEED.
THE WORK WAS OVERWHELMING.

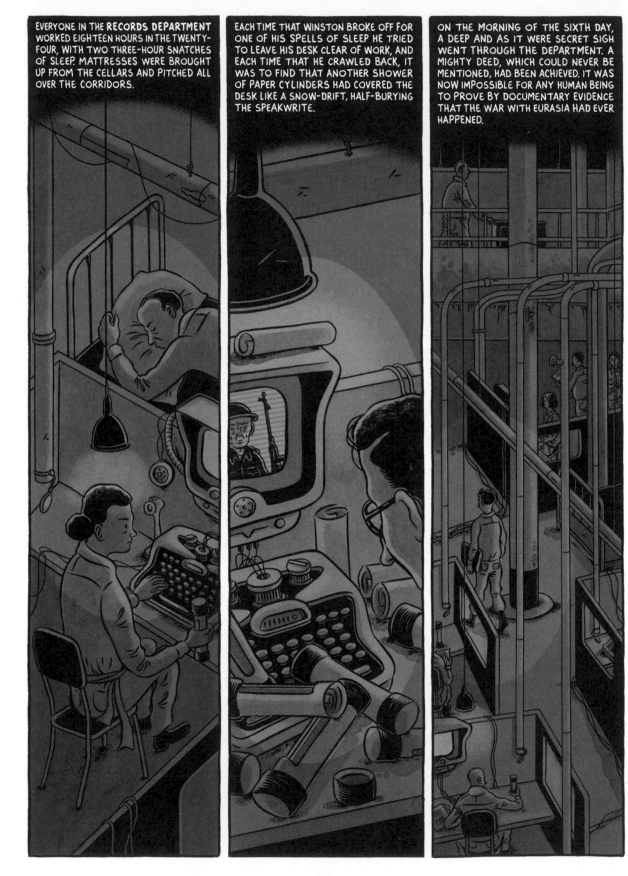

EVERYONE IN THE **RECORDS DEPARTMENT** WORKED EIGHTEEN HOURS IN THE TWENTY-FOUR, WITH TWO THREE-HOUR SNATCHES OF SLEEP. MATTRESSES WERE BROUGHT UP FROM THE CELLARS AND PITCHED ALL OVER THE CORRIDORS.

EACH TIME THAT WINSTON BROKE OFF FOR ONE OF HIS SPELLS OF SLEEP HE TRIED TO LEAVE HIS DESK CLEAR OF WORK, AND EACH TIME THAT HE CRAWLED BACK, IT WAS TO FIND THAT ANOTHER SHOWER OF PAPER CYLINDERS HAD COVERED THE DESK LIKE A SNOW-DRIFT, HALF-BURYING THE SPEAKWRITE.

ON THE MORNING OF THE SIXTH DAY, A DEEP AND AS IT WERE SECRET SIGH WENT THROUGH THE DEPARTMENT. A MIGHTY DEED, WHICH COULD NEVER BE MENTIONED, HAD BEEN ACHIEVED. IT WAS NOW IMPOSSIBLE FOR ANY HUMAN BEING TO PROVE BY DOCUMENTARY EVIDENCE THAT THE WAR WITH EURASIA HAD EVER HAPPENED.

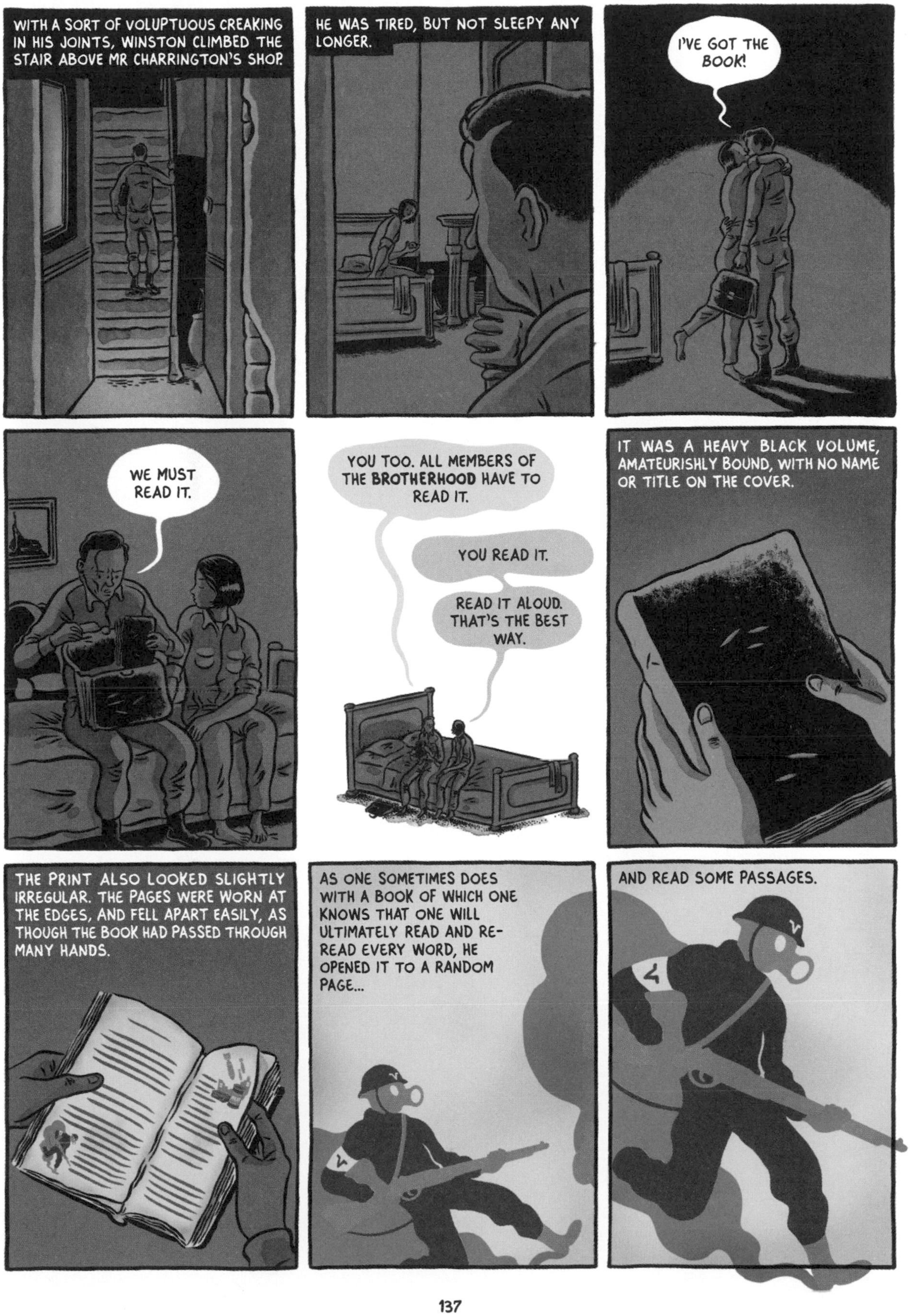
WITH A SORT OF VOLUPTUOUS CREAKING IN HIS JOINTS, WINSTON CLIMBED THE STAIR ABOVE MR CHARRINGTON'S SHOP.
HE WAS TIRED, BUT NOT SLEEPY ANY LONGER.
I'VE GOT THE BOOK!
WE MUST READ IT.
YOU TOO. ALL MEMBERS OF THE **BROTHERHOOD** HAVE TO READ IT.
YOU READ IT.
READ IT ALOUD. THAT'S THE BEST WAY.
IT WAS A HEAVY BLACK VOLUME, AMATEURISHLY BOUND, WITH NO NAME OR TITLE ON THE COVER.
THE PRINT ALSO LOOKED SLIGHTLY IRREGULAR. THE PAGES WERE WORN AT THE EDGES, AND FELL APART EASILY, AS THOUGH THE BOOK HAD PASSED THROUGH MANY HANDS.
AS ONE SOMETIMES DOES WITH A BOOK OF WHICH ONE KNOWS THAT ONE WILL ULTIMATELY READ AND RE-READ EVERY WORD, HE OPENED IT TO A RANDOM PAGE...
AND READ SOME PASSAGES.

Chapter III
War is Peace

The splitting-up of the world into three great super-states was an event which could be and indeed was foreseen before the middle of the twentieth century. With the absorption of Europe by Russia and of the British Empire by the United States, two of the three existing powers, Eurasia and Oceania, were already effectively in being. The third, Eastasia, only emerged as a distinct unit after another decade of confused fighting. The frontiers between the three super-states are in some places arbitrary, and in others they fluctuate according to the fortunes of war, but in general they follow geographical lines. Eurasia comprises the whole of the northern part of the European and Asiatic land-mass, from Portugal to the Bering Strait. Oceania comprises the Americas, the Atlantic islands including the British Isles, Australasia and the southern portion of Africa. Eastasia, smaller than the others and with a less definite western frontier, comprises China and the countries to the south of it, the Japanese islands and a large but fluctuating portion of Manchuria, Mongolia and Tibet.

In one combination or another, these three super-states are permanently at war, and have been so for the past twenty-five years. War, however, is no longer the desperate, annihilating struggle that it was in the early decades of the twentieth century. It is a warfare of limited aims between combatants who are unable to destroy one another, have no material cause for fighting and are not divided by any genuine

ideological difference. This is not to say that either the conduct of war, or the prevailing attitude towards it, has become less bloodthirsty or more chivalrous. On the contrary, war hysteria is continuous and universal in all countries, and such acts as raping, looting, the slaughter of children, the reduction of whole populations to slavery, are looked upon as normal.

The fighting, when there is any, takes place on the vague frontiers whose whereabouts the average man can only guess at, or round the Floating Fortresses which guard strategic spots on the sea lanes. In the centres of civilisation war means no more than a continuous shortage of consumption goods, and the occasional crash of a rocket bomb which may cause a few scores of deaths.

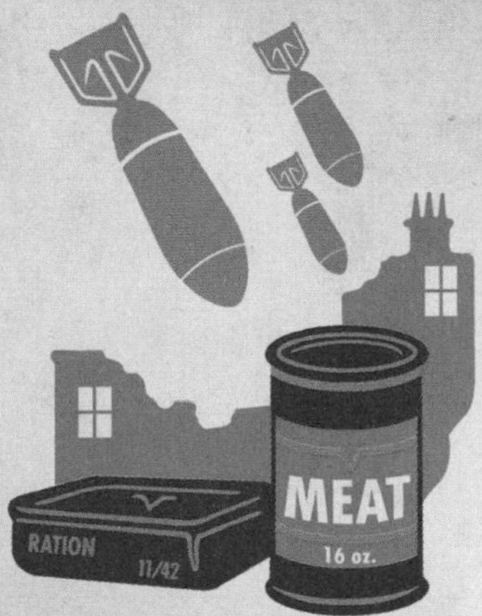
MEAT
16 oz.
RATION
11/42

War has in fact changed its character. More exactly, the reasons for which war is waged have changed in their order of importance. Motives which were already present to some small extent in the great wars of the early twentieth century have now become dominant and are consciously recognised and acted upon.

To understand the nature of the present war – for in spite of the re-grouping which occurs every few years, it is always the same war – one must realise in the first place that it is impossible for it to be decisive. None of the three super-states could be definitively conquered even by the other two in combination. They are too evenly matched, and their natural defences are too formidable. Eurasia is protected by its vast land spaces, Oceania by the width of the Atlantic and the Pacific, Eastasia by the fecundity and industriousness of its inhabitants.

The primary aim of modern warfare is to use up the products of the machine without raising the general standard of living. The world of today is a bare, hungry, dilapidated place compared with the world that existed before 1914, and still more so if compared with the imaginary future to which the people of that period looked forward.

In the early twentieth century, the vision of a future society unbelievably rich, leisured, orderly and efficient – a glittering antiseptic world of glass and steel and snow-white concrete – was part of the consciousness of nearly every literate person. Science and technology were developing at a prodigious speed, and it seemed natural to assume that they would go on developing. This failed to happen, partly because of the impoverishment caused by a long series of wars and revolutions, partly because scientific and technical progress depended on the empirical habit of thought, which could not survive in a strictly regimented society.

As a whole the world is more primitive today than it was fifty years ago. The machine did raise the living standards of the average human being very greatly over a period of about fifty years at the end of the

nineteenth and the beginning of the twentieth centuries. But it was also clear that an all-round increase in wealth threatened the destruction — indeed, in some sense was the destruction — of a hierarchical society. In a world in which everyone worked short hours, had enough to eat, lived in a house with a bathroom and a refrigerator, and possessed a motor-car or even an aeroplane, the most obvious and perhaps the most important form of inequality would already have disappeared.

But in practice such a society could not long remain stable. For if leisure and security were enjoyed by all alike, the great mass of human beings who are normally stupefied by poverty would become literate and would learn to think for themselves; and when once they had done this, they would sooner or later realise that the privileged minority had no function, and they would sweep it away. In the long run, a hierarchical society was only possible on a basis of poverty and ignorance.

To return to the agricultural past, as some thinkers about the beginning of the twentieth century dreamed of doing, was not a practicable solution: any country which remained industrially backward was helpless and was bound to be dominated by its more advanced rivals.

Nor was it a satisfactory solution to keep the masses in poverty by restricting the output of goods. This, too, entailed military weakness.

The problem was how to keep the wheels of industry turning without increasing the real wealth of the world. Goods must be produced, but they must not be distributed. And in practice the only way of achieving this was by continuous warfare. It is deliberate policy to keep even the favoured groups somewhere near the brink of hardship, because a general state of scarcity increases the importance of small privileges and thus magnifies the distinction between one group and another. By the standards of the early twentieth century, even a member of the Inner Party lives an austere, laborious kind of life. Nevertheless, the few luxuries that he does enjoy — his large well-appointed flat, the better texture of his clothes, the better quality of his food and drink and tobacco, his two or three servants, his private motor-car or helicopter — set him in a different world from a member of the Outer Party, and the members of the Outer Party have a similar advantage in comparison with the submerged masses whom we call 'the proles'.

The social atmosphere is that of a besieged city, where the possession of a lump of horseflesh makes the difference between wealth and poverty. And at the same time the consciousness of being at war, and therefore in danger, makes the handing-over of all power to a small caste seem the natural, unavoidable condition of survival.

War, it will be seen, not only accomplishes the necessary destruction, but accomplishes it in a psychologically acceptable way.

What is concerned here is not the morale of the masses, whose attitude is unimportant so long as they are kept steadily at work, but the morale of the Party itself. Even the humblest Party member is expected to be competent, industrious and even intelligent within narrow limits, but it is also necessary that he should be a credulous and ignorant fanatic whose prevailing moods are fear, hatred, adulation and orgiastic triumph. In other words it is necessary that he should have the mentality appropriate to a state of war. It does not matter whether the war is actually happening, and, since no decisive victory is possible, it does not matter whether the war is going well or badly. All that is needed is that a state of war should exist.

The two aims of the Party are to conquer the whole surface of the earth and to extinguish once and for all the possibility of independent thought. There are therefore two great problems which the Party is concerned to solve. One is how to discover, against his will, what another human being is thinking, and the other is how to kill several hundred million people in a few seconds without giving warning beforehand. In so far as scientific research still continues, this is its subject matter. The scientist of today is either a mixture of psychologist and inquisitor, studying with extraordinary minuteness the meaning of facial expressions, gestures and tones of voice, and testing the truth-producing effects of drugs, shock therapy, hypnosis and physical torture; or he is chemist, physicist or biologist concerned only with such branches of his special subject as are relevant to the taking of life. In the vast laboratories

of the Ministry of Peace, and in the experimental stations hidden in the Brazilian forests, or in the Australian desert, or on lost islands of the Antarctic, the teams of experts are indefatigably at work. Some are concerned simply with planning the logistics of future wars; others devise larger and larger rocket bombs, more and more powerful explosives, and more and more impenetrable armour-plating; others search for new and deadlier gases, or for soluble poisons capable of being produced in such quantities as to destroy the vegetation of whole continents, or for breeds of disease germs immunised against all possible antibodies.

All three powers already possess, in the atomic bomb, a weapon far more powerful than any that their present researches are likely to discover, but are convinced that a few more atomic bombs would mean the end of organised society, and hence of their own power. Thereafter all three powers merely continue to produce atomic bombs and store them up against the decisive opportunity which they all believe will come sooner or later.

It is absolutely necessary to their structure that there should be no contact with foreigners. Except with war prisoners, the average citizen of Oceania never sets eyes on a citizen of either Eurasia or Eastasia, and he is forbidden the knowledge of foreign languages. If he were allowed contact with foreigners he would discover that they are creatures similar to himself and that most of what he has been told about them is lies. The sealed world in which he lives would be broken, and the fear, hatred and self-righteousness on which his morale depends might evaporate.

Under this lies a fact never mentioned aloud, but tacitly understood and acted upon: namely, that the conditions of life in all three super-states are very much the same. In Oceania the prevailing philosophy is called Ingsoc, in Eurasia it is called Neo-Bolshevism, and in Eastasia it is called by a Chinese name usually translated as Death-Worship, but perhaps better rendered as Obliteration of the Self. The citizen of Oceania is not allowed to know anything of the tenets of the other two

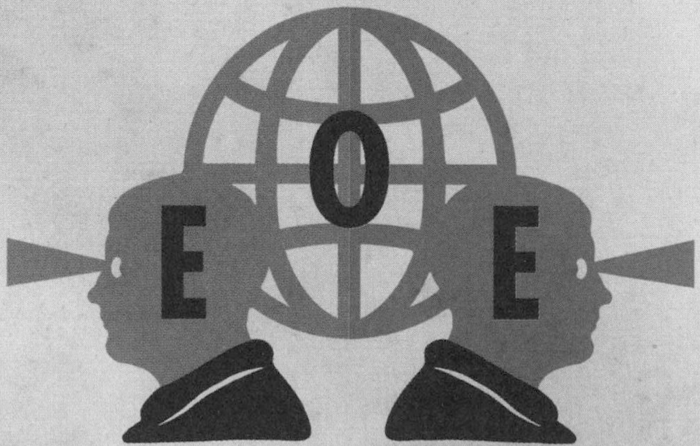
E
O
E

philosophies, but he is taught to execrate them as barbarous outrages upon morality and common sense. Actually the three philosophies are barely distinguishable, and the social systems which they support are not distinguishable at all. Everywhere there is the same pyramidal structure, the same worship of a semi-divine leader, the same economy existing by and for continuous warfare.

The three super-states are dedicated to world conquest, but they also know that it is necessary that the war should continue everlastingly and without victory. Meanwhile the fact that there is no danger of conquest makes possible the denial of reality which is the special feature of Ingsoc and its rival systems of thought. By becoming continuous war has fundamentally changed its character. Efficiency, even military efficiency, is no longer needed. Nothing is efficient in Oceania except the Thought Police.

Since each of the three super-states is unconquerable, each is in effect a separate universe within which almost any perversion of thought can be safely practised. The rulers of such a state are absolute, as the Pharaohs or the Caesars could not be. They can twist reality into whatever shape they choose.

The war is waged by each ruling group against its own subjects, and the object of the war is not to make or prevent conquests of territory, but to keep the structure of society intact. The very word 'war', therefore, has become misleading. It would probably be accurate to say that by becoming continuous war has ceased to exist. The peculiar pressure that it exerted on human beings has disappeared and been replaced by something quite different.

The effect would be much the same if the three super-states, instead of fighting one another, should agree to live in perpetual peace, each inviolate within its own boundaries. For in that case each would still be a self-contained universe, freed for ever from the sobering influence of external danger. A peace that was truly permanent would be the same as a permanent war. This — although the vast majority of Party members understand it only in a shallower sense — is the inner meaning of the Party slogan: War is Peace.

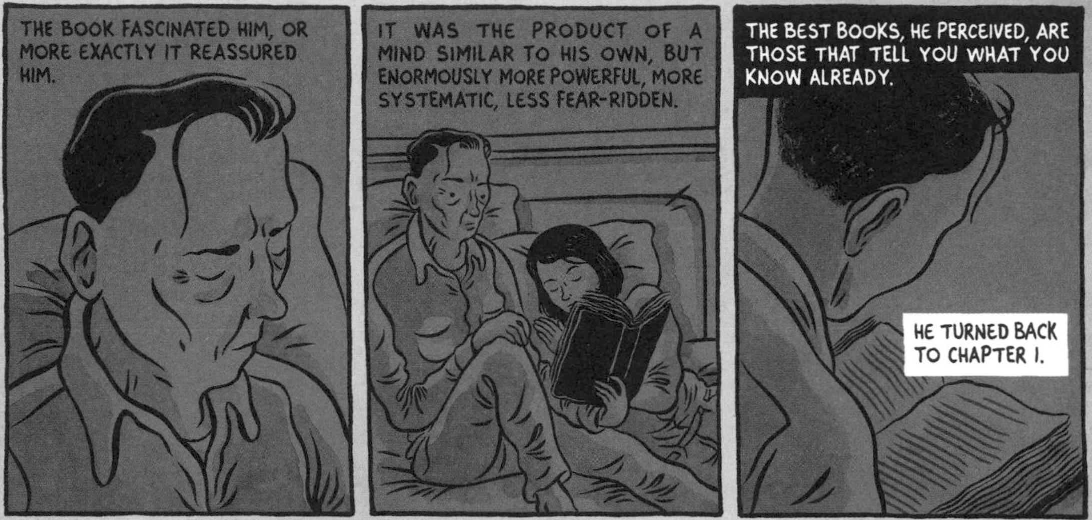
THE BOOK FASCINATED HIM, OR MORE EXACTLY IT REASSURED HIM.
IT WAS THE PRODUCT OF A MIND SIMILAR TO HIS OWN, BUT ENORMOUSLY MORE POWERFUL, MORE SYSTEMATIC, LESS FEAR-RIDDEN.
THE BEST BOOKS, HE PERCEIVED, ARE THOSE THAT TELL YOU WHAT YOU KNOW ALREADY.
HE TURNED BACK TO CHAPTER I.

Chapter I
Ignorance is Strength

Throughout recorded time, and probably since the end of the Neolithic Age, there have been three kinds of people in the world, the High, the Middle and the Low. They have been subdivided in many ways, they have borne countless different names, and their relative numbers, as well as their attitude towards one another, have varied from age to age: but the essential structure of society has never altered. Even after enormous upheavals and seemingly irrevocable changes, the same pattern has always reasserted itself.

The aims of these three groups are entirely irreconcilable. The aim of the High is to remain where they are. The aim of the Middle is to change places with the High. The aim of the Low, when they have an aim – for it is an abiding characteristic of the Low that they are too much crushed by drudgery to be more than intermittently conscious of anything outside their daily lives – is to abolish all distinctions and create a society in which all men shall be equal. Thus throughout history a struggle which is the same in its main outlines recurs over and over again. For long periods the High seem to be securely in power, but sooner or later there always comes a moment when they lose either their belief in themselves or their capacity to govern efficiently, or both. They are then overthrown by the Middle, who enlist the Low on their side by pretending to them that they are fighting for liberty and justice. As soon as they have reached their objective, the Middle thrust the Low back into their old position of servitude, and themselves become the High. Presently a new Middle group splits off from one of the other groups, or from both of them, and the struggle begins over again. Of the three groups, only the Low are never even temporarily successful in achieving their aims. No progress of a material kind, no advance in wealth, no softening of manners, no reform or revolution has ever brought human equality a millimetre nearer. From the point of view of the Low, no historic change has ever meant much more than a change in the name of their masters.

By the late nineteenth century the recurrence of this pattern had become obvious to many observers. There then arose schools of thinkers who interpreted history as a cyclical process and claimed to show that inequality was the unalterable law of human life. This doctrine, of course, had always had its adherents, but in the manner in which it was now put forward there was a significant change. In the past the need for a hierarchical form of society had been the doctrine specifically of the High. It had been preached by kings and aristocrats and by the priests, lawyers and the like who were parasitical upon them, and it had generally been softened by promises of compensation in an imaginary world beyond the grave. The Middle, so long as it was struggling for power, had always made use of such terms as freedom, justice and fraternity. Now, however, the concept of human brotherhood began to be assailed by people who were not yet in positions of command, but merely hoped to be so before long.

Socialism, a theory which appeared in the early nineteenth century and was the last link in a chain of thought stretching back to the slave rebellions of antiquity, was still deeply infected by the Utopianism of past ages. But in each variant of Socialism that appeared from about 1900 onwards the aim of establishing liberty and equality was more and more openly abandoned. The new movements had the conscious aim of perpetuating unfreedom and inequality. These new movements, of course, grew out of the old ones and tended to keep their names and pay lip-service to their ideology. But the purpose of all of

them was to arrest progress and freeze history at a chosen moment.

As early as the beginning of the twentieth century, human equality had become technically possible. With the development of machine production, even if it was still necessary for human beings to do different kinds of work, it was no longer necessary for them to live at different social or economic levels. Therefore, from the point of view of the new groups who were on the point of seizing power, human equality was no longer an ideal to be striven after, but a danger to be averted. The idea of an earthly paradise in which men should live together in a state of brotherhood, without laws and without brute labour, had haunted the human imagination for thousands of years. The heirs of the French, English and American revolutions had partly believed in their own phrases about the rights of man, freedom of speech, equality before the law, and the like, and had even allowed their conduct to be influenced by them to some extent. But by the fourth decade of the twentieth century all the main currents of political thought were authoritarian. The earthly paradise had been discredited at exactly the moment when it became realisable.

It was only after a decade of national wars, civil wars, revolutions and counter-revolutions in all parts of the world that Ingsoc and its rivals emerged as fully worked-out political theories. As compared with their opposite number in past ages, the people who would control this world were less avaricious, less tempted by luxury, hungrier for pure power, and, above all, more conscious of what they were doing and more intent on crushing opposition. This last difference was cardinal. By comparison with that existing today, all the tyrannies of the past were half-hearted and inefficient. In the past no government had the power to keep its citizens under constant surveillance. The invention of print, however, made it easier to manipulate public opinion, and the film and the radio carried the process further. With the development of television, and the technical advance which made it possible to receive and transmit simultaneously on the same instrument, private life came to an end. Every citizen, or at least every citizen important enough to be worth watching, could be kept for twenty-four hours a day under the eyes of the police and in the sound of official propaganda, with all other channels of communication closed. The possibility of enforcing not only complete obedience to the will of the State, but complete uniformity of opinion on all subjects, now existed for the first time.

In the general structure of Oceanic society, at the apex of the pyramid comes Big Brother. Big Brother is infallible and all-powerful. Every success, every achievement, every victory, every scientific discovery, all knowledge, all wisdom, all happiness, all virtue, are held to issue directly from his leadership and inspiration. Nobody has ever seen Big Brother. He is a face on the hoardings, a voice on the telescreen. We may be reasonably sure that he will never die, and there is already considerable uncertainty as to when he was born. Big Brother is the guise in which the Party chooses to exhibit itself to the world. His function is to act as a focusing point for love, fear and reverence, emotions which are more easily felt towards an individual than towards an organisation. Below Big Brother comes the Inner Party, its numbers limited to six millions, or something less than two per cent of the population of Oceania. Below the Inner Party comes the Outer Party, which, if the Inner Party is described as the brain of the State, may be justly likened to the hands. Below that come the dumb masses whom we habitually refer to as 'the proles', numbering perhaps eighty-five per cent of the population.

The older kind of Socialist, who had been trained to fight against something called 'class privilege', assumed that what is not hereditary cannot be permanent. He did not see that the continuity of an oli

garchy need not be physical, nor did he pause to reflect that hereditary aristocracies have always been shortlived, whereas adoptive organisations such as the Catholic Church have sometimes lasted for hundreds or thousands of years. The essence of oligarchical rule is not father-to-son inheritance, but the persistence of a certain world-view and a certain way of life, imposed by the dead upon the living. A ruling group is a ruling group so long as it can nominate its successors. The Party is not concerned with perpetuating its blood but with perpetuating itself. *Who*

wields power is not important, provided that the hierarchical structure remains always the same.

All the beliefs, habits, tastes, emotions, mental attitudes that characterise our time are really designed to sustain the mystique of the Party and prevent the true nature of present-day society from being perceived. Physical rebellion, or any preliminary move towards rebellion, is at present not possible. From the proletarians nothing is to be feared. Left to themselves, they will continue from generation to generation and from century to century, working, breeding and dying, not only without any impulse to rebel, but without the power of grasping that the world could be other than it is. They could only become dangerous if the advance of industrial technique made it necessary to educate them more highly; but, since military and commercial rivalry are no longer important, the level of popular education is actually declining. What opinions the masses hold, or do not hold, is looked on as a matter of indifference. They can be granted intellectual liberty because they have no intellect. In a Party member, on the other hand, not even the smallest deviation of opinion on the most unimportant subject can be tolerated.

A Party member lives from birth to death under the eye of the Thought Police. Even when he is alone he can never be sure that he is alone. Wherever he may be, asleep or awake, working or resting, in his bath or in bed, he can be inspected without warning and without knowing that he is being inspected. Nothing that he does is indifferent. His friendships, his relaxations, his behaviour towards his wife and children, the expression of his face when he is alone, the words he mutters in sleep, even the characteristic movements of his body, are all jealously scrutinised. Not only any actual misdemeanour, but any eccentricity, however small, any change of habits, any nervous mannerism that could possibly be the symptom of an inner struggle, is certain to be detected. He has no freedom of choice in any direction whatever. On the other hand his actions are not regulated by law or by any clearly formulated code of behaviour. In Oceania there is no law. Thoughts and actions which, when detected, mean certain death are not formally forbidden, and the endless purges, arrests, tortures, imprisonments and vaporisations are not inflicted as punishment for crimes which have actually been committed, but are merely the wiping-out of persons who might perhaps commit a crime at some time in the future. A Party member is required to have not only the right opinions, but the right instincts. Many of the beliefs and attitudes demanded of him are never plainly stated, and could not be stated without laying bare the contradictions inherent in Ingsoc. If he is a person naturally orthodox (in Newspeak a goodthinker), he will in all circumstances know, without taking thought, what is the true belief or the desirable emotion. But in any case an elaborate mental training, undergone in childhood and grouping itself round the Newspeak words crimestop, blackwhite and doublethink, makes him unwilling and unable to think too deeply on any subject whatever.

A Party member is expected to have no private emotions and no respites from enthusiasm. He is supposed to live in a continuous frenzy of hatred of foreign enemies and internal traitors, triumph over victories, and self-abasement before the power and wisdom of the Party. The discontents produced by his bare, unsatisfying life are deliberately turned outwards and dissipated by such devices as the Two Minutes Hate, and the speculations which might possibly induce a sceptical or rebellious attitude are killed in advance by his early-acquired inner discipline. The first and simplest stage in the discipline, which can be taught even to young children, is called, in Newspeak, crimestop. Crimestop means the faculty of stopping short, as though by instinct, at the threshold of any dangerous thought. It includes the power of not grasping analogies, of failing to perceive logical errors, of misunderstanding the simplest arguments if they are inimical to Ingsoc, and of being bored or repelled by any train of thought which is capable of leading in a heretical direction. Crimestop, in short, means protective stupidity.

But stupidity is not enough. On the contrary, orthodoxy in the full sense demands a control over one's own mental processes as complete as that of a contortionist over his body. Oceanic society rests ultimately on the belief that Big Brother is omnipotent and that the Party is infallible. But since in reality Big Brother is not omnipotent and the Party is not infallible, there is need for an unwearying, moment-to-moment flexibility in the treatment of facts. The key-word here is blackwhite. Like so many Newspeak words, this word has two mutually contradictory meanings. Applied to an opponent,

it means the habit of impudently claiming that black is white, in contradiction of the plain facts. Applied to a Party member, it means a loyal willingness to say that black is white when Party discipline demands this. But it means also the ability to *believe* that black is white, and more, to *know* that black is white, and to forget that one has ever believed the contrary. This demands a continuous alteration of the past, made possible by the system of thought which really embraces all the rest, and which is known in Newspeak as doublethink.

Doublethink means the power of holding two contradictory beliefs in one's mind simultaneously, and accepting both of them. The Party intellectual knows in which direction his memories must be altered; he therefore knows that he is playing tricks with reality; but by the exercise of doublethink he also satisfies himself that reality is not violated.

The process has to be conscious, or it would not be carried out with sufficient precision, but it also has to be unconscious, or it would bring with it a feeling of falsity and hence of guilt. Doublethink lies at the very heart of Ingsoc, since the essential act of the Party is to use conscious deception while retaining the firmness of purpose that goes with complete honesty. Even in using the word doublethink it is necessary to exercise doublethink. For by using the word one admits that one is tampering with reality; by a fresh act of doublethink one erases this knowledge; and so on indefinitely, with the lie always one leap ahead of the truth. Ultimately it is by means of doublethink that the Party has been able — and may, for all we know, continue to be able for thousands of years — to arrest the course of history.

All past oligarchies have fallen from power either because they ossified or because they grew soft. Either they became stupid and arrogant, failed to adjust themselves to changing circumstances, and were overthrown; or they became liberal and cowardly, made concessions when they should have used force, and once again were overthrown. They fell, that is to say, either through consciousness or through unconsciousness. It is the achievement of the Party to have produced a system of thought in which both conditions can exist simultaneously. And upon no other intellectual basis could the dominion of the Party be made permanent. If one is to rule, and to continue ruling, one must be able to dislocate the sense of reality. For the secret of rulership is to combine a belief in one's own infallibility with the power to learn from past mistakes.

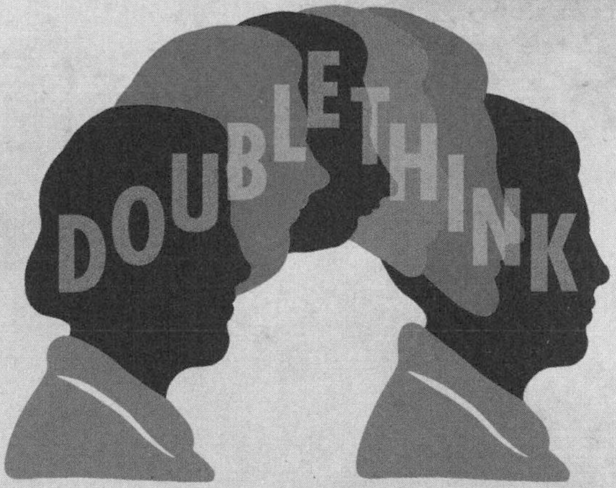
DOUBLETHINK

The official ideology abounds with contradictions even where there is no practical reason for them. It preaches a contempt for the working class unexampled for centuries past, and it dresses its members in a uniform which was at one time peculiar to manual workers and was adopted for that reason. It systematically undermines the solidarity of the family, and it calls its leader by a name which is a direct appeal to the sentiment of family loyalty. Even the names of the four Ministries by which we are governed exhibit a sort of impudence in their deliberate reversal of the facts. The Ministry of Peace concerns itself with war, the Ministry of Truth with lies, the Ministry of Love with torture and the Ministry of Plenty with starvation. These contradictions are not accidental, nor do they result from ordinary hypocrisy: they are deliberate exercises in doublethink. For it is only by reconciling contradictions that power can be retained indefinitely. In no other way could the ancient cycle be broken. If human equality is to be for ever averted – if the High, as we have called them, are to keep their places permanently – then the prevailing mental condition must be controlled insanity.

But there is one question which until this moment we have almost ignored. It is: *why* should human equality be averted? What is the motive for this huge, accurately planned effort to freeze history at a particular moment of time? What is the original motive, the never-questioned instinct that first led to the seizure of power and brought doublethink, the Thought Police, continuous warfare and all the other necessary paraphernalia into existence afterwards?

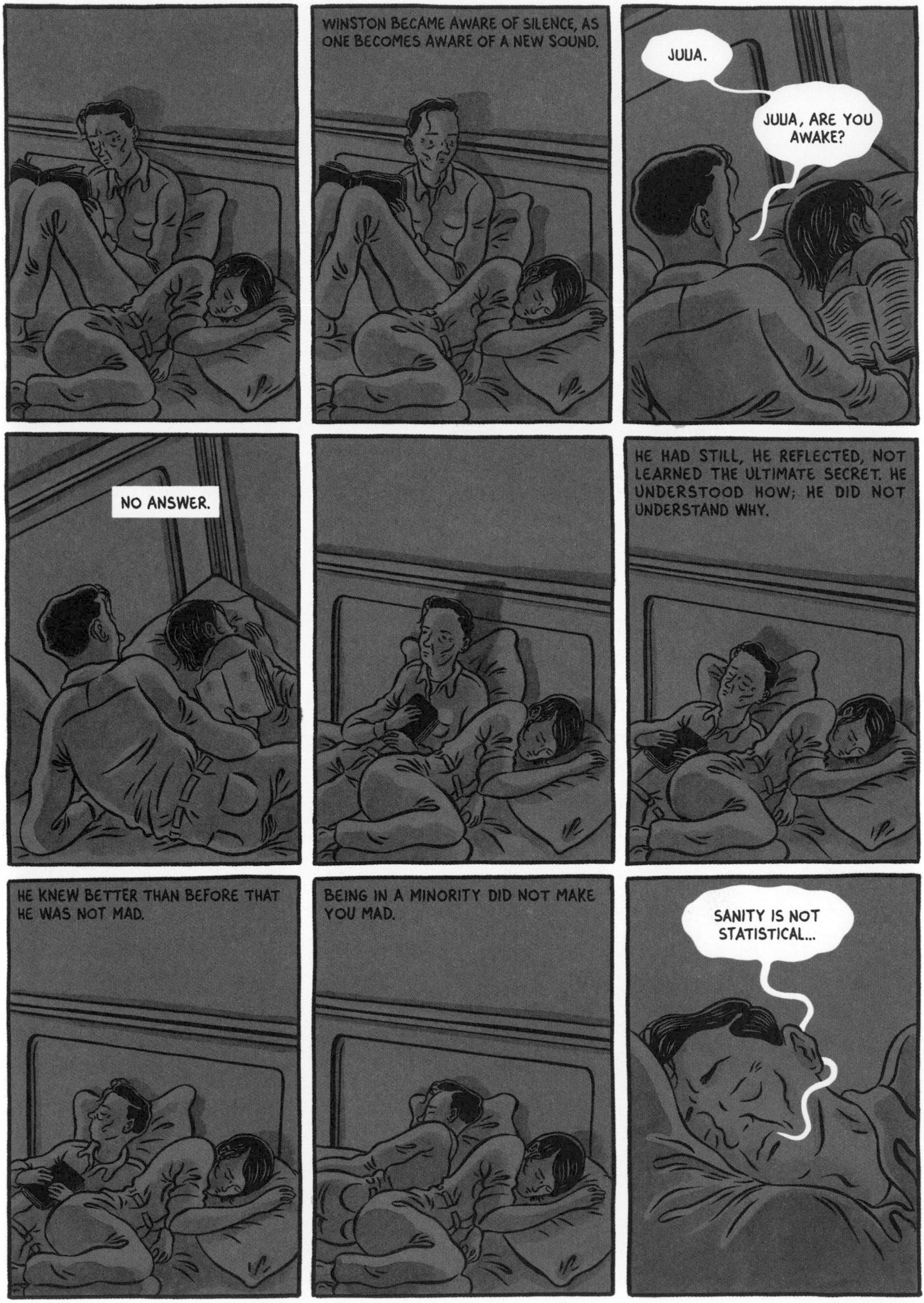
WINSTON BECAME AWARE OF SILENCE, AS ONE BECOMES AWARE OF A NEW SOUND.
JULIA.
JULIA, ARE YOU AWAKE?
NO ANSWER.
HE HAD STILL, HE REFLECTED, NOT LEARNED THE ULTIMATE SECRET. HE UNDERSTOOD HOW; HE DID NOT UNDERSTAND WHY.
HE KNEW BETTER THAN BEFORE THAT HE WAS NOT MAD.
BEING IN A MINORITY DID NOT MAKE YOU MAD.
SANITY IS NOT STATISTICAL...

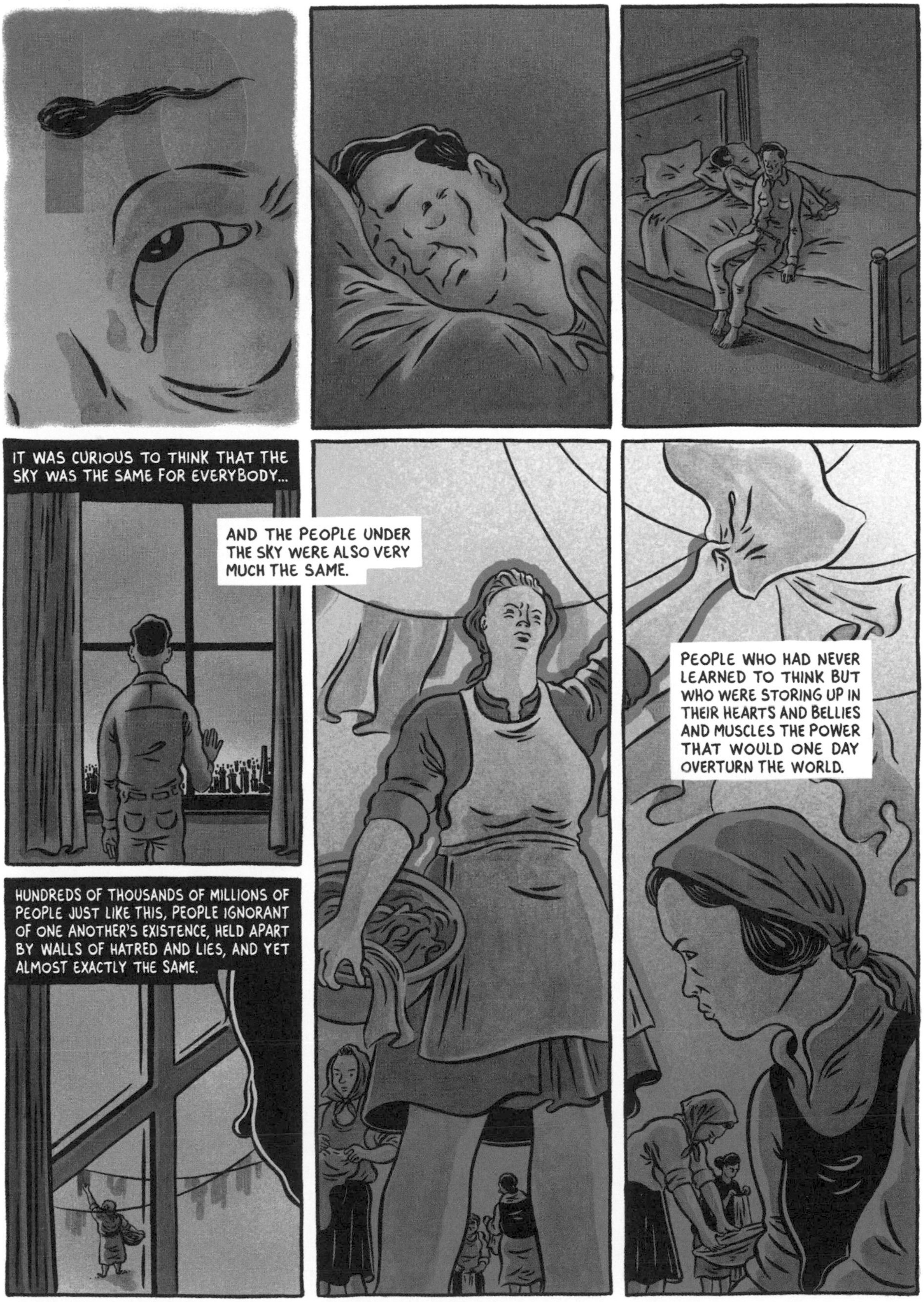
IT WAS CURIOUS TO THINK THAT THE SKY WAS THE SAME FOR EVERYBODY...
AND THE PEOPLE UNDER THE SKY WERE ALSO VERY MUCH THE SAME.
PEOPLE WHO HAD NEVER LEARNED TO THINK BUT WHO WERE STORING UP IN THEIR HEARTS AND BELLIES AND MUSCLES THE POWER THAT WOULD ONE DAY OVERTURN THE WORLD.
HUNDREDS OF THOUSANDS OF MILLIONS OF PEOPLE JUST LIKE THIS, PEOPLE IGNORANT OF ONE ANOTHER'S EXISTENCE, HELD APART BY WALLS OF HATRED AND LIES, AND YET ALMOST EXACTLY THE SAME.

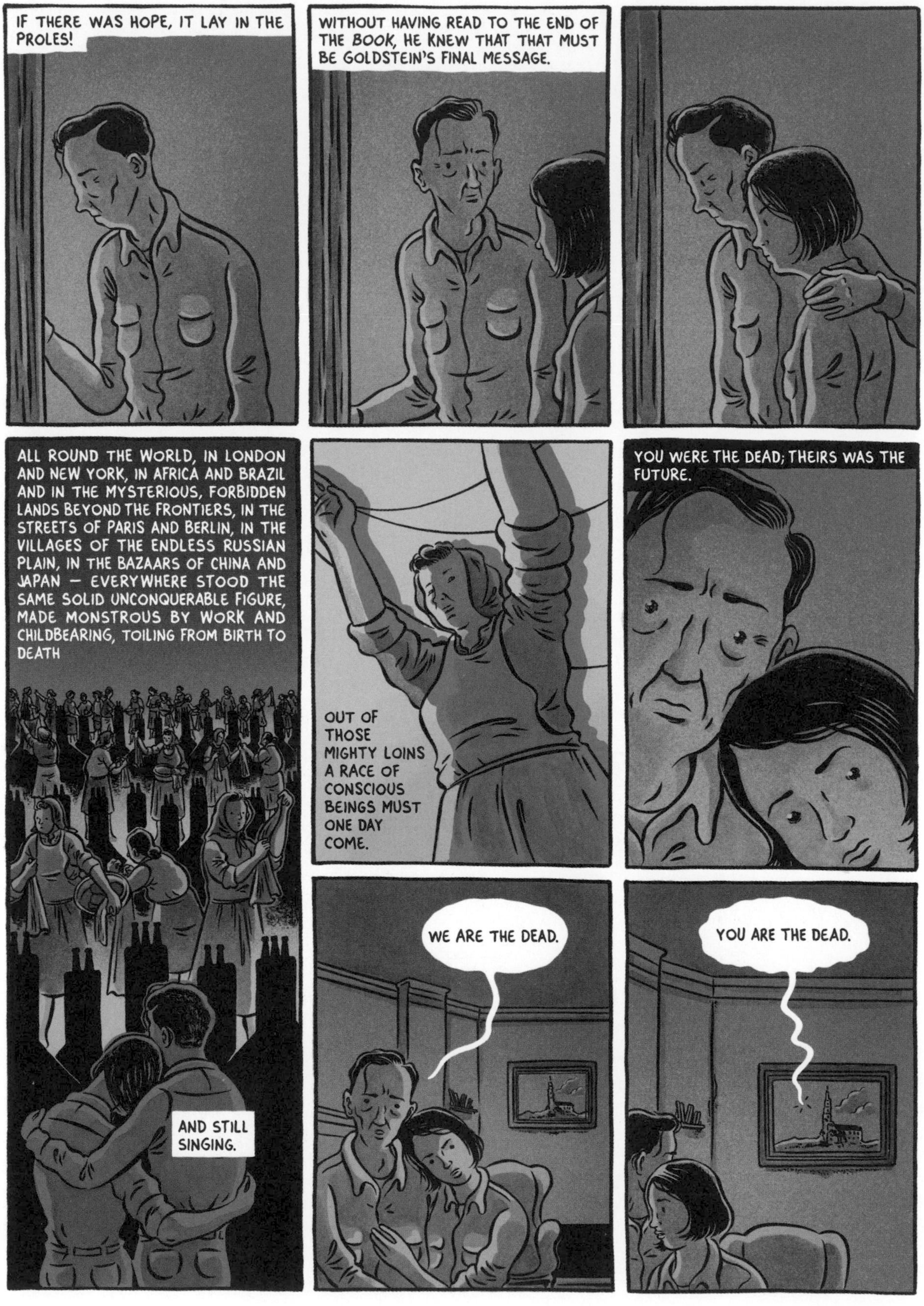
IF THERE WAS HOPE, IT LAY IN THE PROLES!
WITHOUT HAVING READ TO THE END OF THE *BOOK*, HE KNEW THAT THAT MUST BE GOLDSTEIN'S FINAL MESSAGE.
ALL ROUND THE WORLD, IN LONDON AND NEW YORK, IN AFRICA AND BRAZIL AND IN THE MYSTERIOUS, FORBIDDEN LANDS BEYOND THE FRONTIERS, IN THE STREETS OF PARIS AND BERLIN, IN THE VILLAGES OF THE ENDLESS RUSSIAN PLAIN, IN THE BAZAARS OF CHINA AND JAPAN — EVERYWHERE STOOD THE SAME SOLID UNCONQUERABLE FIGURE, MADE MONSTROUS BY WORK AND CHILDBEARING, TOILING FROM BIRTH TO DEATH
AND STILL SINGING.
OUT OF THOSE MIGHTY LOINS A RACE OF CONSCIOUS BEINGS MUST ONE DAY COME.
YOU WERE THE DEAD; THEIRS WAS THE FUTURE.
WE ARE THE DEAD.
YOU ARE THE DEAD.

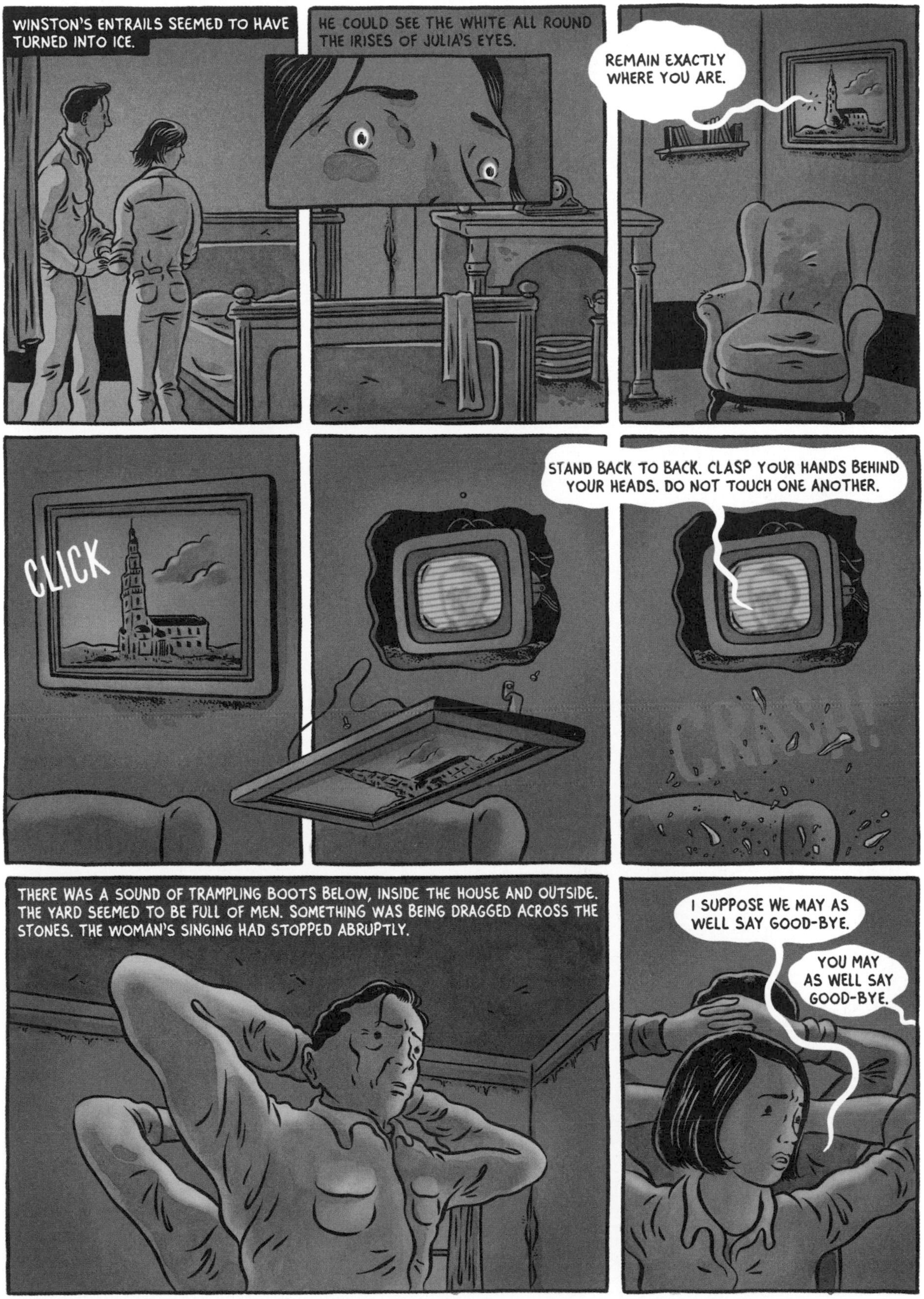
WINSTON'S ENTRAILS SEEMED TO HAVE TURNED INTO ICE.
HE COULD SEE THE WHITE ALL ROUND THE IRISES OF JULIA'S EYES.
REMAIN EXACTLY WHERE YOU ARE.
CLICK
STAND BACK TO BACK. CLASP YOUR HANDS BEHIND YOUR HEADS. DO NOT TOUCH ONE ANOTHER.
CRASH!
THERE WAS A SOUND OF TRAMPLING BOOTS BELOW, INSIDE THE HOUSE AND OUTSIDE. THE YARD SEEMED TO BE FULL OF MEN. SOMETHING WAS BEING DRAGGED ACROSS THE STONES. THE WOMAN'S SINGING HAD STOPPED ABRUPTLY.
I SUPPOSE WE MAY AS WELL SAY GOOD-BYE.
YOU MAY AS WELL SAY GOOD-BYE.

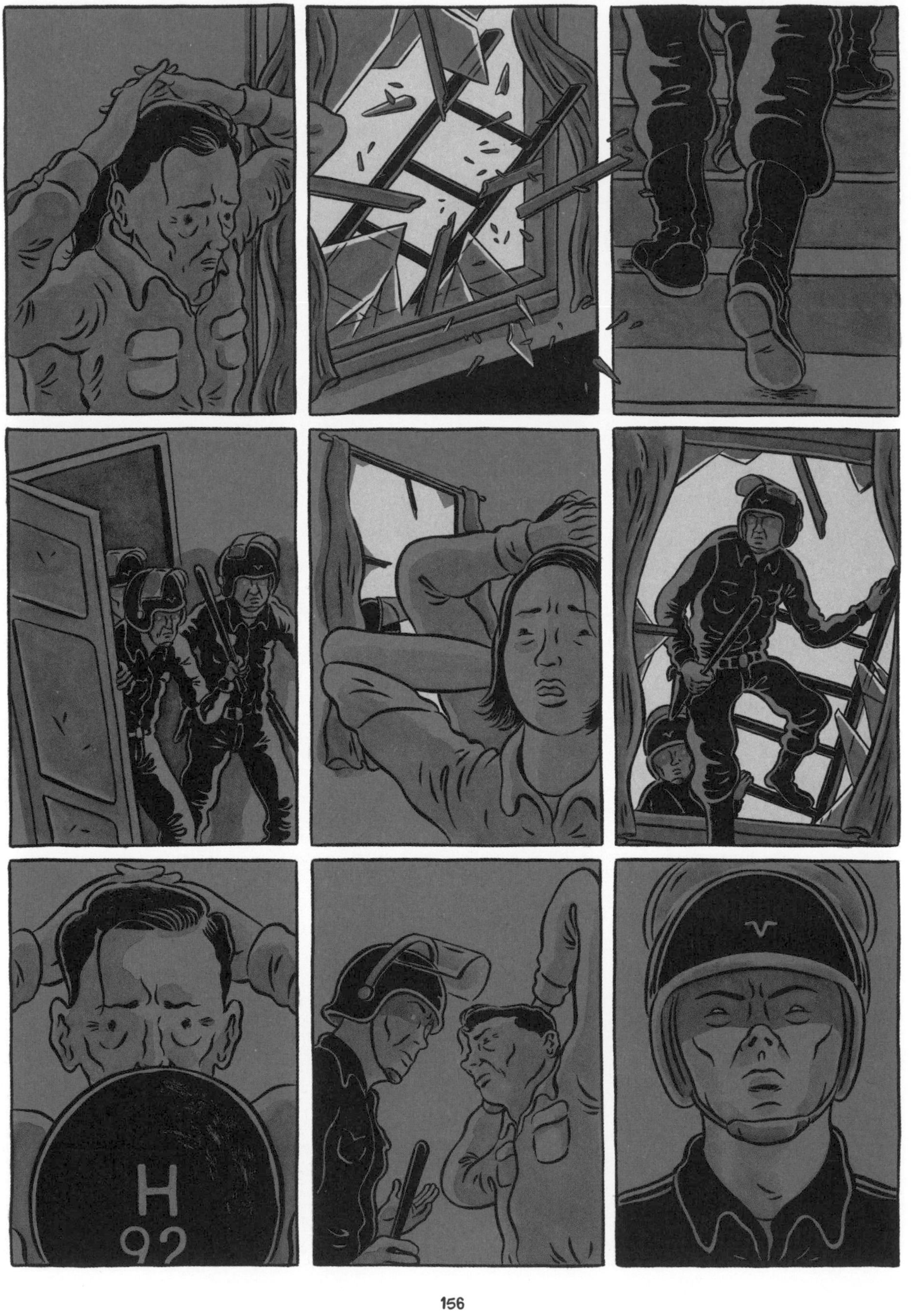
H
92

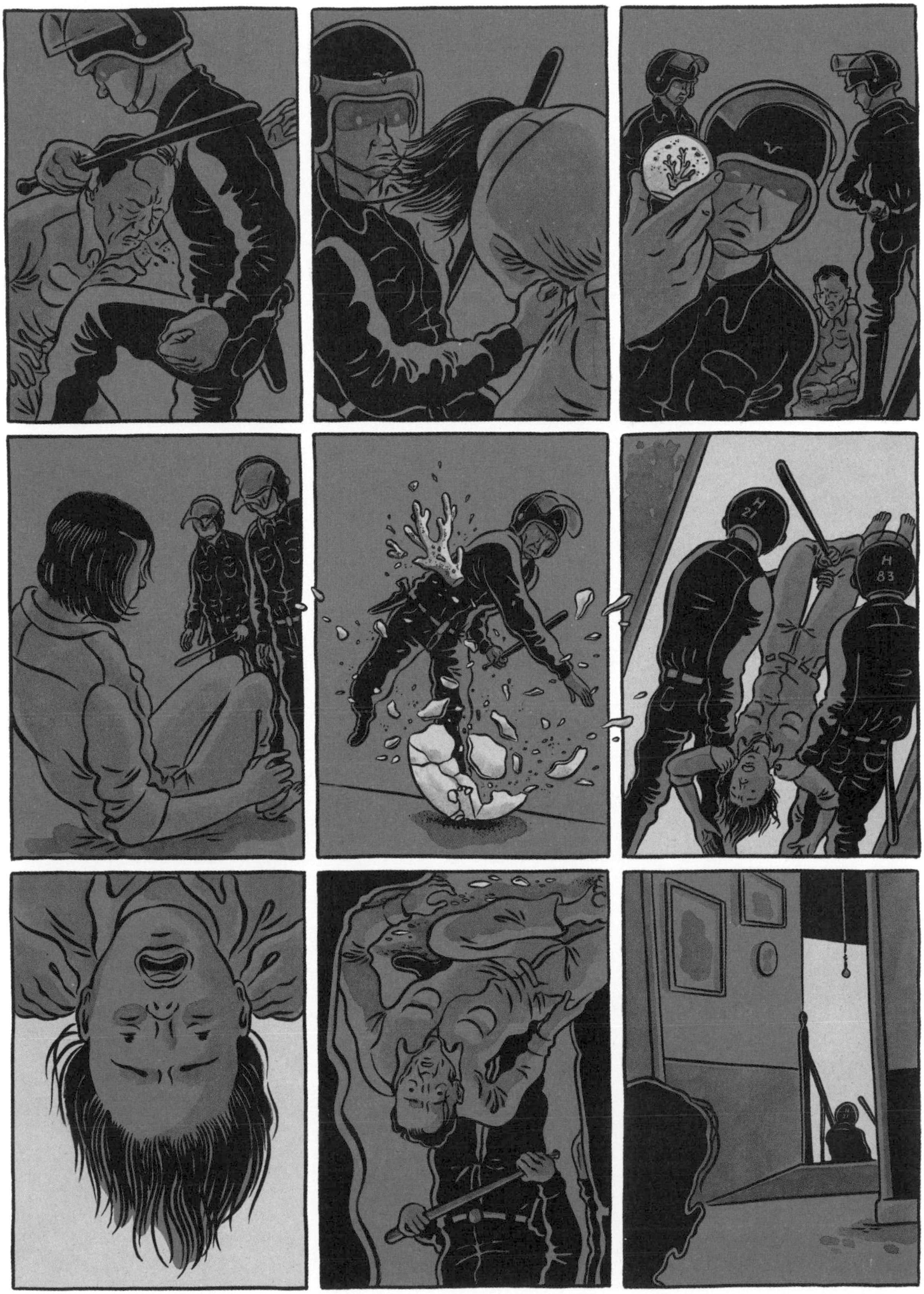
H 21
H 83

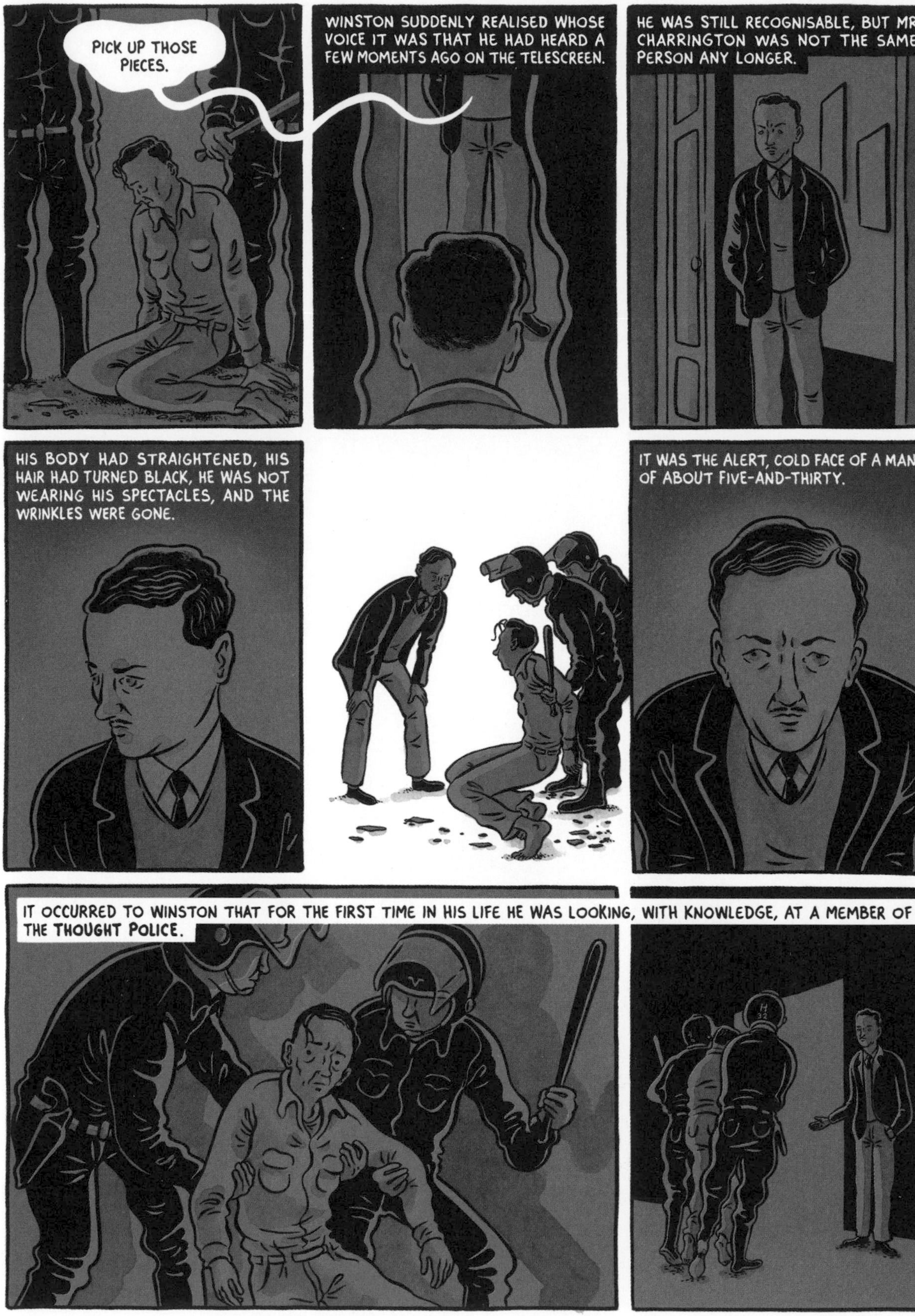
PICK UP THOSE PIECES.
WINSTON SUDDENLY REALISED WHOSE VOICE IT WAS THAT HE HAD HEARD A FEW MOMENTS AGO ON THE TELESCREEN.
HE WAS STILL RECOGNISABLE, BUT MR CHARRINGTON WAS NOT THE SAME PERSON ANY LONGER.
HIS BODY HAD STRAIGHTENED, HIS HAIR HAD TURNED BLACK, HE WAS NOT WEARING HIS SPECTACLES, AND THE WRINKLES WERE GONE.
IT WAS THE ALERT, COLD FACE OF A MAN OF ABOUT FIVE-AND-THIRTY.
IT OCCURRED TO WINSTON THAT FOR THE FIRST TIME IN HIS LIFE HE WAS LOOKING, WITH KNOWLEDGE, AT A MEMBER OF THE THOUGHT POLICE.

PART 3

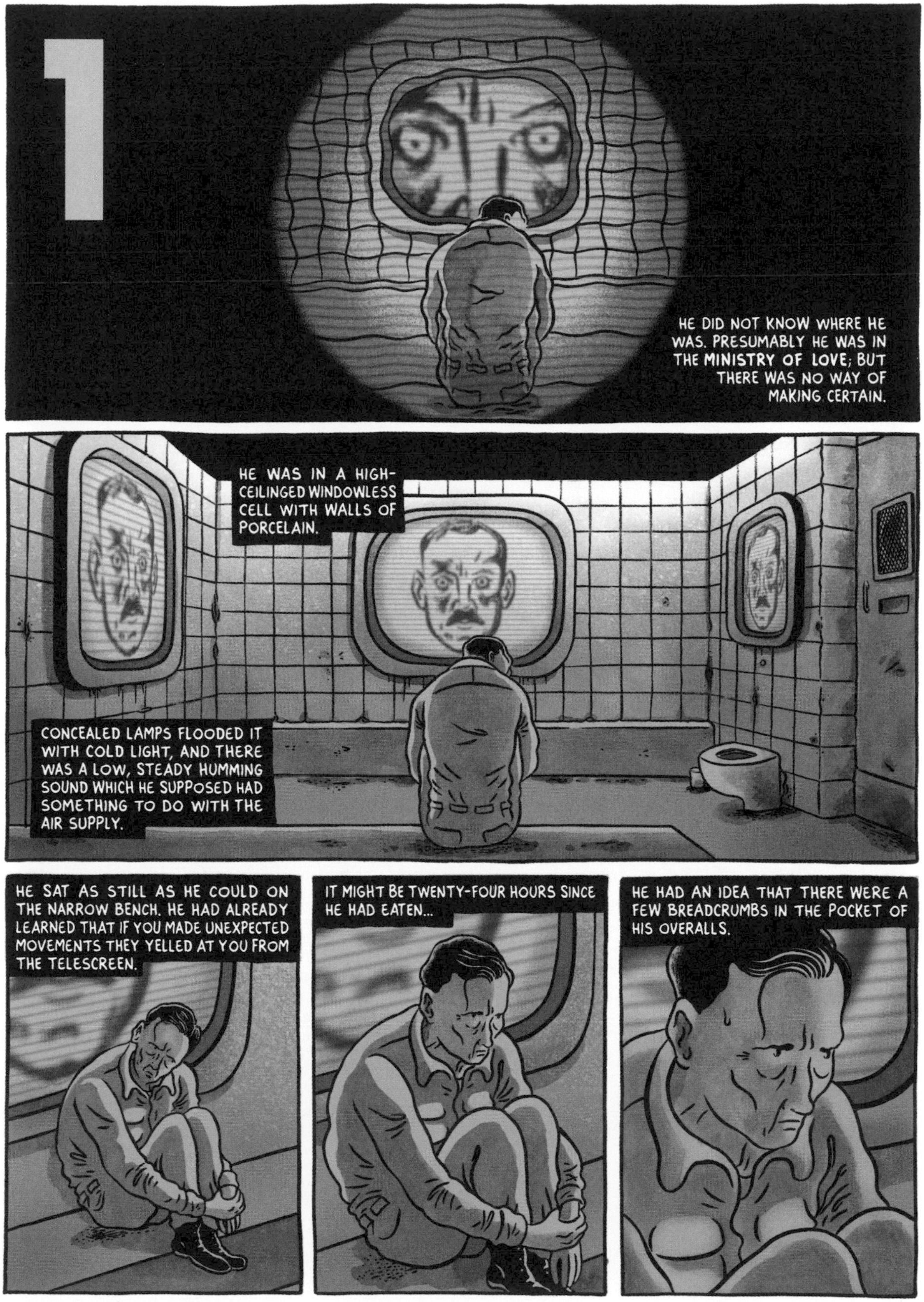
1
HE DID NOT KNOW WHERE HE WAS. PRESUMABLY HE WAS IN THE MINISTRY OF LOVE; BUT THERE WAS NO WAY OF MAKING CERTAIN.
HE WAS IN A HIGH-CEILINGED WINDOWLESS CELL WITH WALLS OF PORCELAIN.
CONCEALED LAMPS FLOODED IT WITH COLD LIGHT, AND THERE WAS A LOW, STEADY HUMMING SOUND WHICH HE SUPPOSED HAD SOMETHING TO DO WITH THE AIR SUPPLY.
HE SAT AS STILL AS HE COULD ON THE NARROW BENCH. HE HAD ALREADY LEARNED THAT IF YOU MADE UNEXPECTED MOVEMENTS THEY YELLED AT YOU FROM THE TELESCREEN.
IT MIGHT BE TWENTY-FOUR HOURS SINCE HE HAD EATEN...
HE HAD AN IDEA THAT THERE WERE A FEW BREADCRUMBS IN THE POCKET OF HIS OVERALLS.

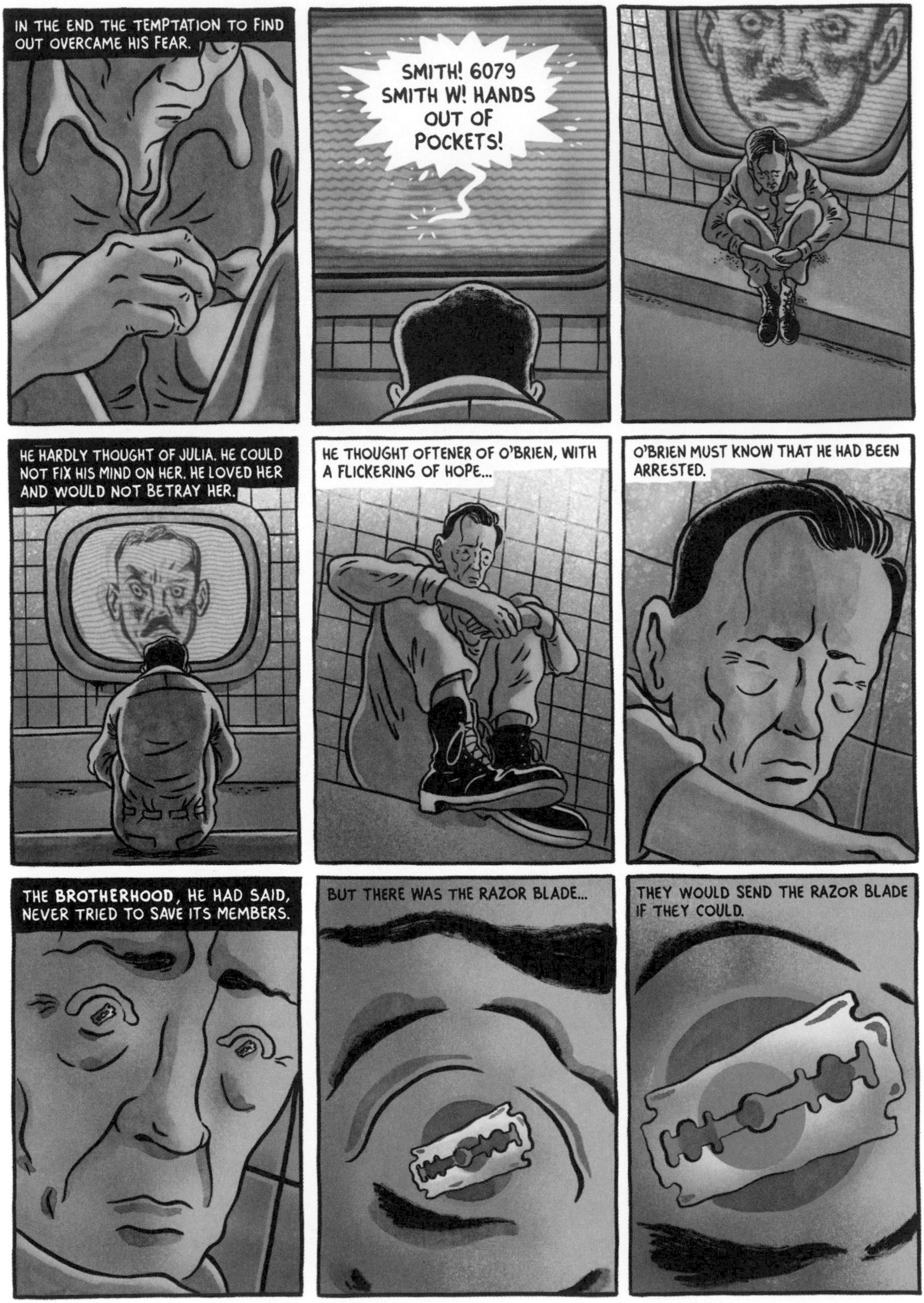
IN THE END THE TEMPTATION TO FIND OUT OVERCAME HIS FEAR.
SMITH! 6079 SMITH W! HANDS OUT OF POCKETS!
HE HARDLY THOUGHT OF JULIA. HE COULD NOT FIX HIS MIND ON HER. HE LOVED HER AND WOULD NOT BETRAY HER.
HE THOUGHT OFTENER OF O'BRIEN, WITH A FLICKERING OF HOPE...
O'BRIEN MUST KNOW THAT HE HAD BEEN ARRESTED.
THE BROTHERHOOD, HE HAD SAID, NEVER TRIED TO SAVE ITS MEMBERS.
BUT THERE WAS THE RAZOR BLADE...
THEY WOULD SEND THE RAZOR BLADE IF THEY COULD.

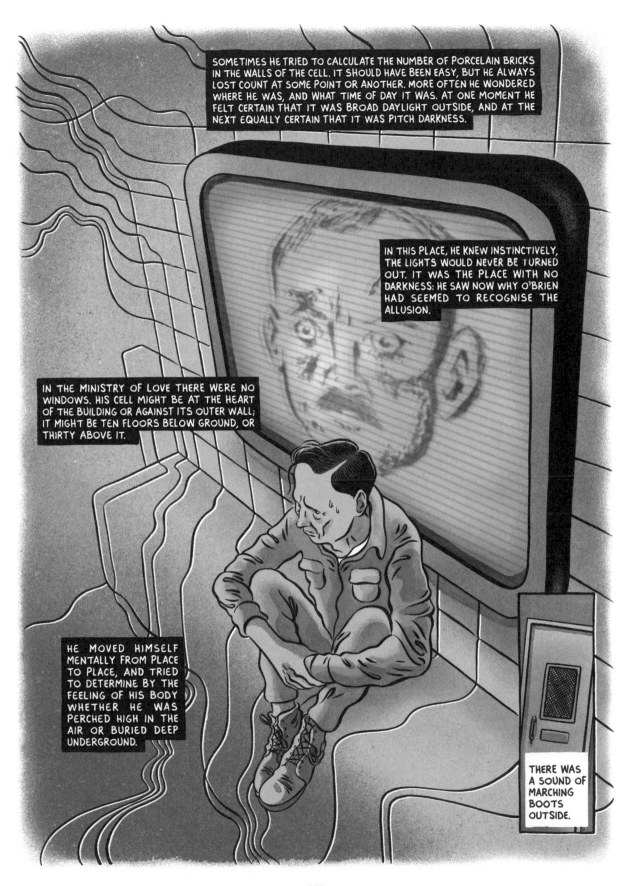

SOMETIMES HE TRIED TO CALCULATE THE NUMBER OF PORCELAIN BRICKS IN THE WALLS OF THE CELL. IT SHOULD HAVE BEEN EASY, BUT HE ALWAYS LOST COUNT AT SOME POINT OR ANOTHER. MORE OFTEN HE WONDERED WHERE HE WAS, AND WHAT TIME OF DAY IT WAS. AT ONE MOMENT HE FELT CERTAIN THAT IT WAS BROAD DAYLIGHT OUTSIDE, AND AT THE NEXT EQUALLY CERTAIN THAT IT WAS PITCH DARKNESS.

IN THIS PLACE, HE KNEW INSTINCTIVELY, THE LIGHTS WOULD NEVER BE TURNED OUT. IT WAS THE PLACE WITH NO DARKNESS: HE SAW NOW WHY O'BRIEN HAD SEEMED TO RECOGNISE THE ALLUSION.

IN THE MINISTRY OF LOVE THERE WERE NO WINDOWS. HIS CELL MIGHT BE AT THE HEART OF THE BUILDING OR AGAINST ITS OUTER WALL; IT MIGHT BE TEN FLOORS BELOW GROUND, OR THIRTY ABOVE IT.

HE MOVED HIMSELF MENTALLY FROM PLACE TO PLACE, AND TRIED TO DETERMINE BY THE FEELING OF HIS BODY WHETHER HE WAS PERCHED HIGH IN THE AIR OR BURIED DEEP UNDERGROUND.

THERE WAS A SOUND OF MARCHING BOOTS OUTSIDE.

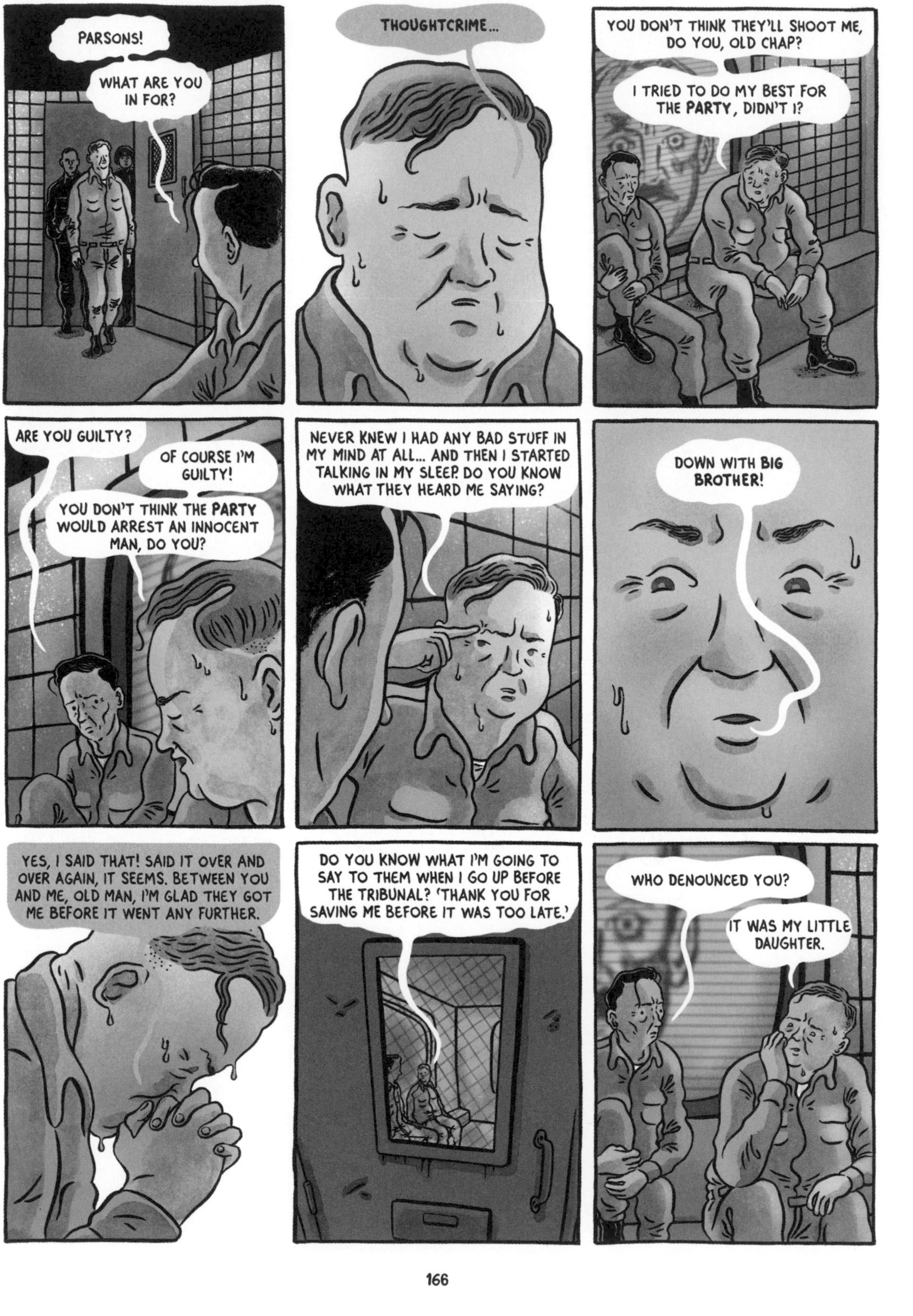
PARSONS!
WHAT ARE YOU IN FOR?
THOUGHTCRIME...
YOU DON'T THINK THEY'LL SHOOT ME, DO YOU, OLD CHAP?
I TRIED TO DO MY BEST FOR THE PARTY, DIDN'T I?
ARE YOU GUILTY?
OF COURSE I'M GUILTY!
YOU DON'T THINK THE PARTY WOULD ARREST AN INNOCENT MAN, DO YOU?
NEVER KNEW I HAD ANY BAD STUFF IN MY MIND AT ALL... AND THEN I STARTED TALKING IN MY SLEEP. DO YOU KNOW WHAT THEY HEARD ME SAYING?
DOWN WITH BIG BROTHER!
YES, I SAID THAT! SAID IT OVER AND OVER AGAIN, IT SEEMS. BETWEEN YOU AND ME, OLD MAN, I'M GLAD THEY GOT ME BEFORE IT WENT ANY FURTHER.
DO YOU KNOW WHAT I'M GOING TO SAY TO THEM WHEN I GO UP BEFORE THE TRIBUNAL? 'THANK YOU FOR SAVING ME BEFORE IT WAS TOO LATE.'
WHO DENOUNCED YOU?
IT WAS MY LITTLE DAUGHTER.

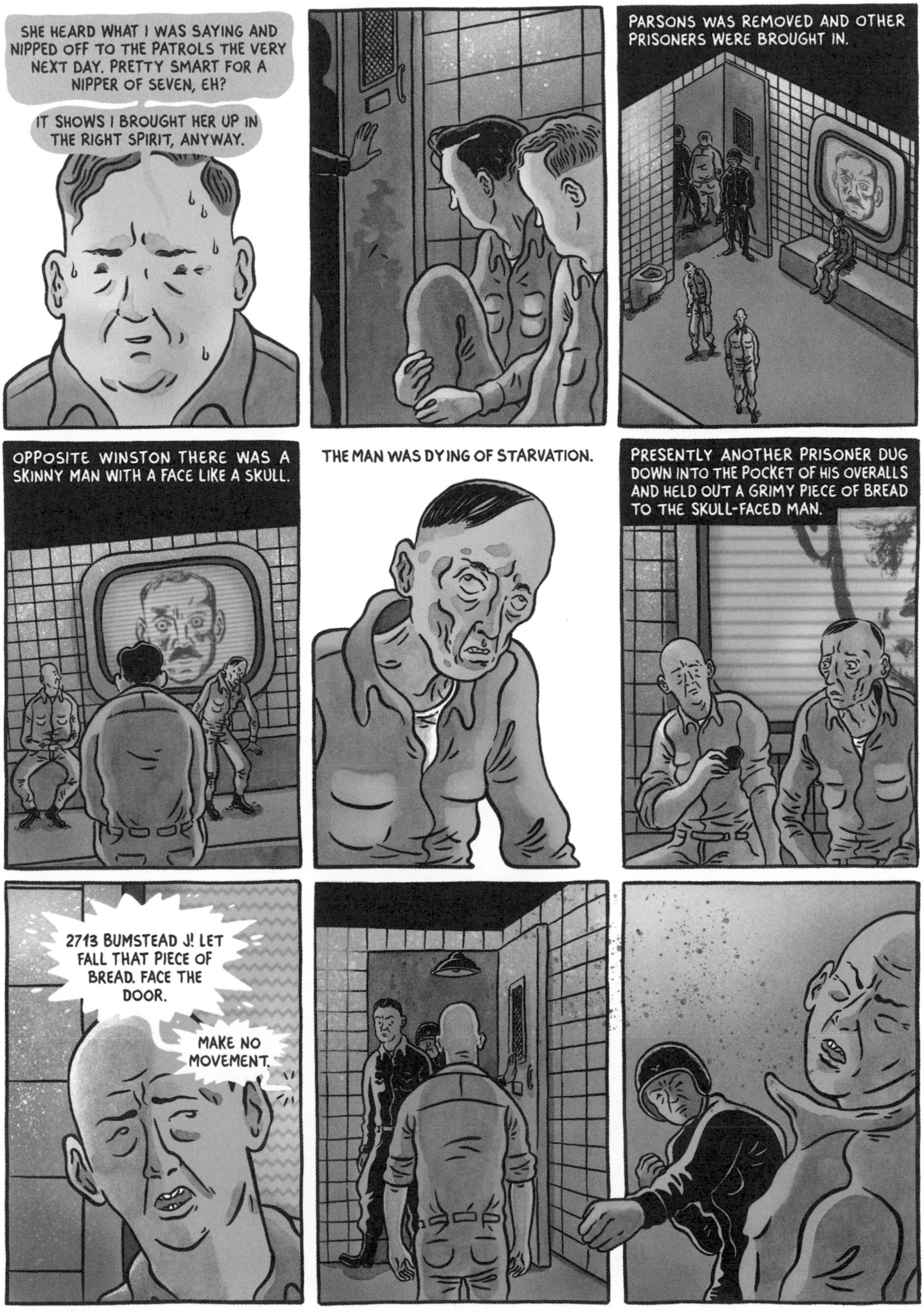
SHE HEARD WHAT I WAS SAYING AND NIPPED OFF TO THE PATROLS THE VERY NEXT DAY. PRETTY SMART FOR A NIPPER OF SEVEN, EH?
IT SHOWS I BROUGHT HER UP IN THE RIGHT SPIRIT, ANYWAY.
PARSONS WAS REMOVED AND OTHER PRISONERS WERE BROUGHT IN.
OPPOSITE WINSTON THERE WAS A SKINNY MAN WITH A FACE LIKE A SKULL.
THE MAN WAS DYING OF STARVATION.
PRESENTLY ANOTHER PRISONER DUG DOWN INTO THE POCKET OF HIS OVERALLS AND HELD OUT A GRIMY PIECE OF BREAD TO THE SKULL-FACED MAN.
2713 BUMSTEAD J! LET FALL THAT PIECE OF BREAD. FACE THE DOOR.
MAKE NO MOVEMENT.

ROOM 101.

COMRADE! OFFICER! YOU DON'T HAVE TO TAKE ME TO THAT PLACE!

ROOM 101.

YOU'VE BEEN STARVING ME FOR WEEKS. FINISH IT OFF AND LET ME DIE.

SHOOT ME. HANG ME. ANYTHING! BUT NOT ROOM 101!

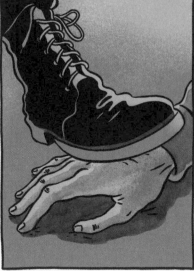

ROOM 101.

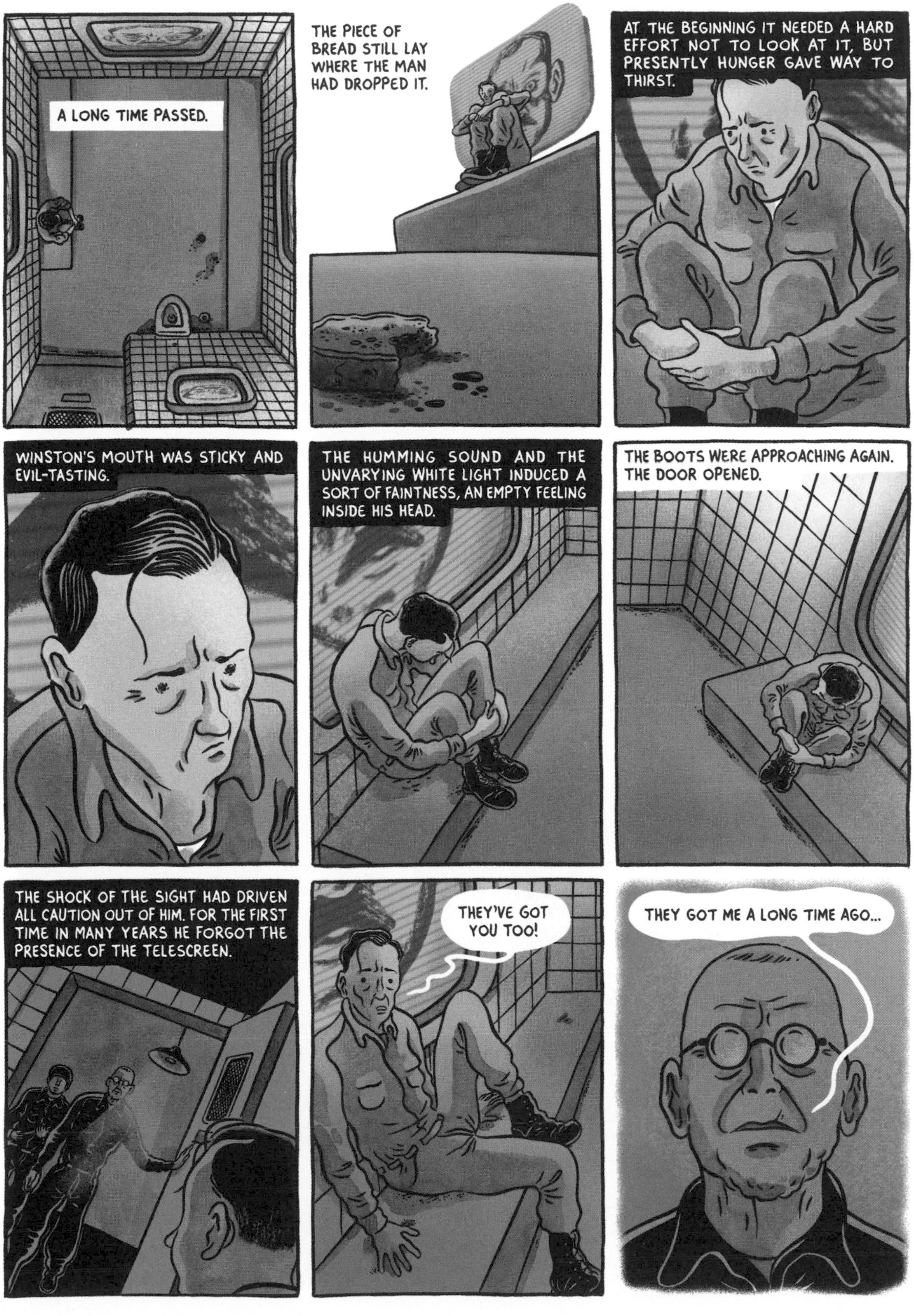
A LONG TIME PASSED.
THE PIECE OF BREAD STILL LAY WHERE THE MAN HAD DROPPED IT.
AT THE BEGINNING IT NEEDED A HARD EFFORT NOT TO LOOK AT IT, BUT PRESENTLY HUNGER GAVE WAY TO THIRST.
WINSTON'S MOUTH WAS STICKY AND EVIL-TASTING.
THE HUMMING SOUND AND THE UNVARYING WHITE LIGHT INDUCED A SORT OF FAINTNESS, AN EMPTY FEELING INSIDE HIS HEAD.
THE BOOTS WERE APPROACHING AGAIN. THE DOOR OPENED.
THE SHOCK OF THE SIGHT HAD DRIVEN ALL CAUTION OUT OF HIM. FOR THE FIRST TIME IN MANY YEARS HE FORGOT THE PRESENCE OF THE TELESCREEN.
THEY'VE GOT YOU TOO!
THEY GOT ME A LONG TIME AGO...

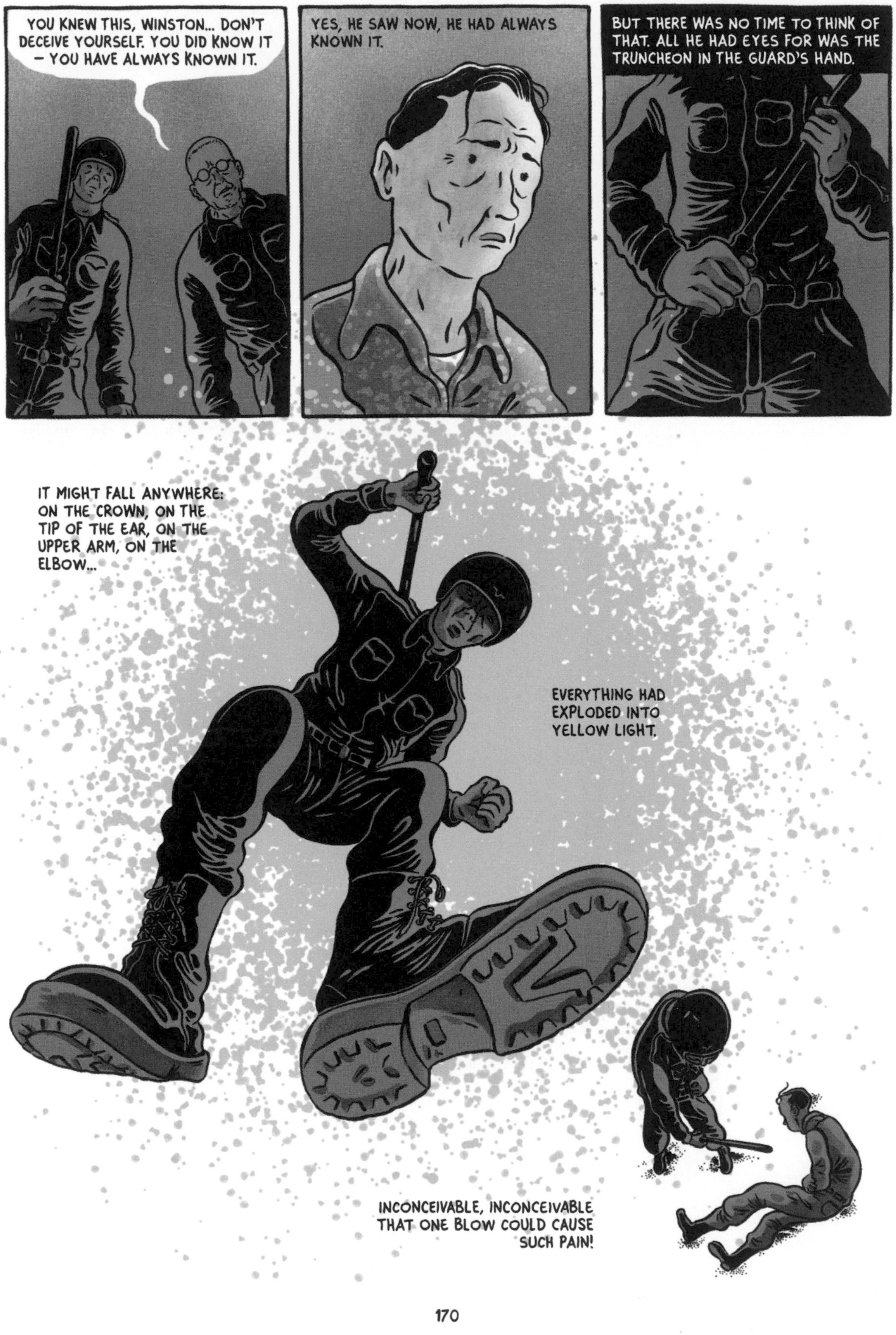
YOU KNEW THIS, WINSTON... DON'T DECEIVE YOURSELF. YOU DID KNOW IT – YOU HAVE ALWAYS KNOWN IT.
YES, HE SAW NOW, HE HAD ALWAYS KNOWN IT.
BUT THERE WAS NO TIME TO THINK OF THAT. ALL HE HAD EYES FOR WAS THE TRUNCHEON IN THE GUARD'S HAND.
IT MIGHT FALL ANYWHERE: ON THE CROWN, ON THE TIP OF THE EAR, ON THE UPPER ARM, ON THE ELBOW...
EVERYTHING HAD EXPLODED INTO YELLOW LIGHT.
INCONCEIVABLE, INCONCEIVABLE THAT ONE BLOW COULD CAUSE SUCH PAIN!

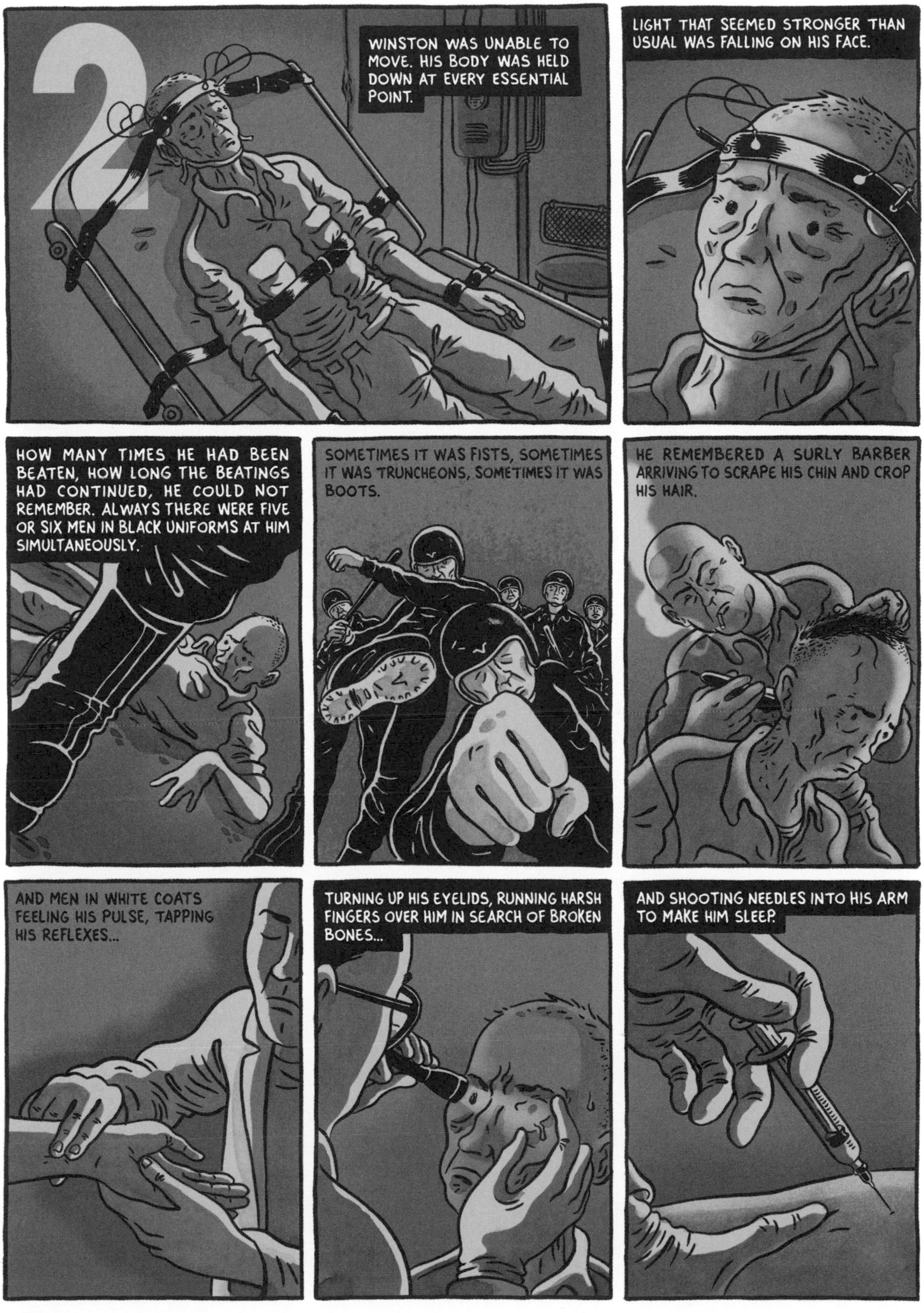
2
WINSTON WAS UNABLE TO MOVE. HIS BODY WAS HELD DOWN AT EVERY ESSENTIAL POINT.
LIGHT THAT SEEMED STRONGER THAN USUAL WAS FALLING ON HIS FACE.
HOW MANY TIMES HE HAD BEEN BEATEN, HOW LONG THE BEATINGS HAD CONTINUED, HE COULD NOT REMEMBER. ALWAYS THERE WERE FIVE OR SIX MEN IN BLACK UNIFORMS AT HIM SIMULTANEOUSLY.
SOMETIMES IT WAS FISTS, SOMETIMES IT WAS TRUNCHEONS, SOMETIMES IT WAS BOOTS.
HE REMEMBERED A SURLY BARBER ARRIVING TO SCRAPE HIS CHIN AND CROP HIS HAIR.
AND MEN IN WHITE COATS FEELING HIS PULSE, TAPPING HIS REFLEXES...
TURNING UP HIS EYELIDS, RUNNING HARSH FINGERS OVER HIM IN SEARCH OF BROKEN BONES...
AND SHOOTING NEEDLES INTO HIS ARM TO MAKE HIM SLEEP.

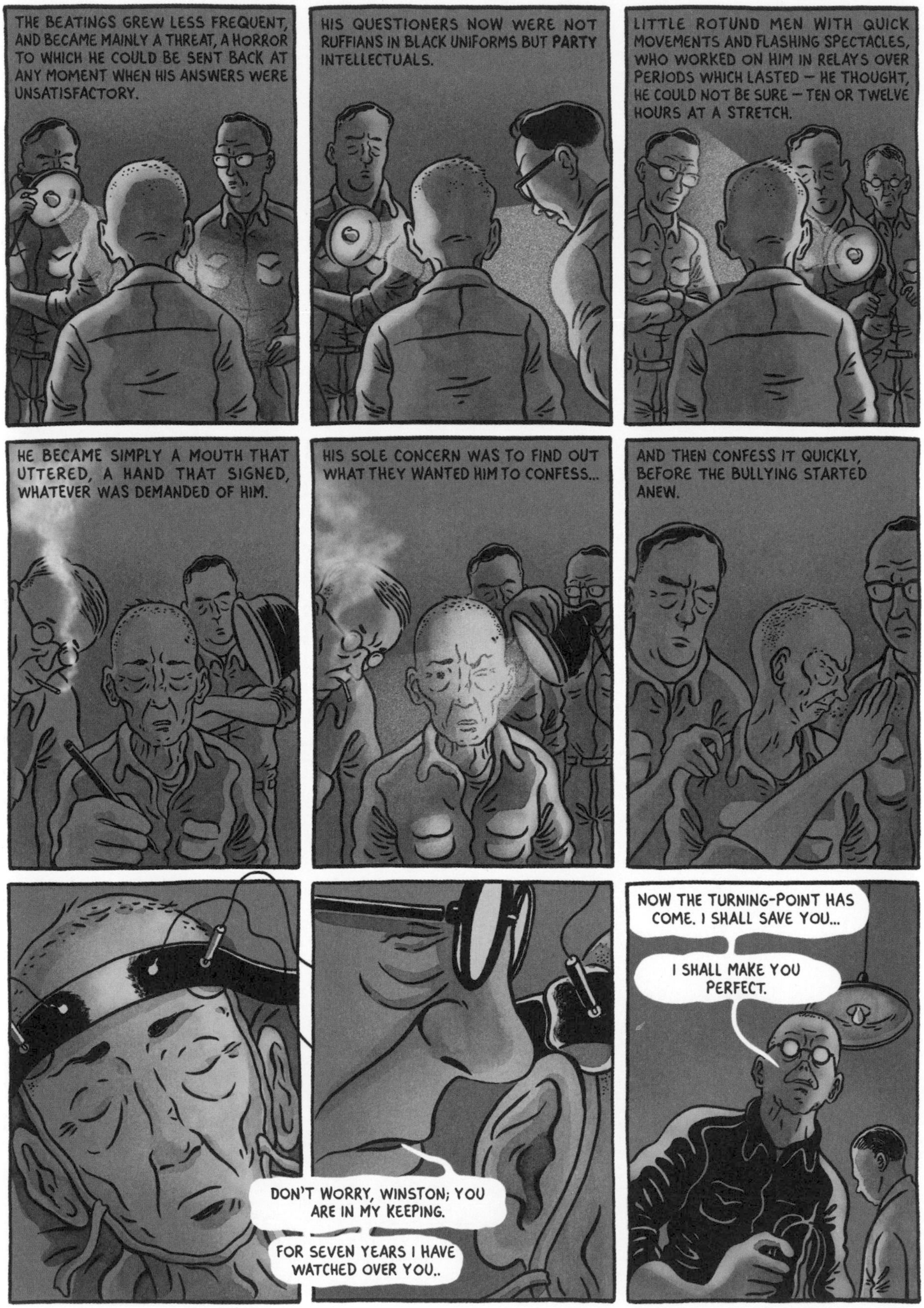
THE BEATINGS GREW LESS FREQUENT, AND BECAME MAINLY A THREAT, A HORROR TO WHICH HE COULD BE SENT BACK AT ANY MOMENT WHEN HIS ANSWERS WERE UNSATISFACTORY.
HIS QUESTIONERS NOW WERE NOT RUFFIANS IN BLACK UNIFORMS BUT PARTY INTELLECTUALS.
LITTLE ROTUND MEN WITH QUICK MOVEMENTS AND FLASHING SPECTACLES, WHO WORKED ON HIM IN RELAYS OVER PERIODS WHICH LASTED — HE THOUGHT, HE COULD NOT BE SURE — TEN OR TWELVE HOURS AT A STRETCH.
HE BECAME SIMPLY A MOUTH THAT UTTERED, A HAND THAT SIGNED, WHATEVER WAS DEMANDED OF HIM.
HIS SOLE CONCERN WAS TO FIND OUT WHAT THEY WANTED HIM TO CONFESS...
AND THEN CONFESS IT QUICKLY, BEFORE THE BULLYING STARTED ANEW.
DON'T WORRY, WINSTON; YOU ARE IN MY KEEPING.
FOR SEVEN YEARS I HAVE WATCHED OVER YOU..
NOW THE TURNING-POINT HAS COME. I SHALL SAVE YOU...
I SHALL MAKE YOU PERFECT.

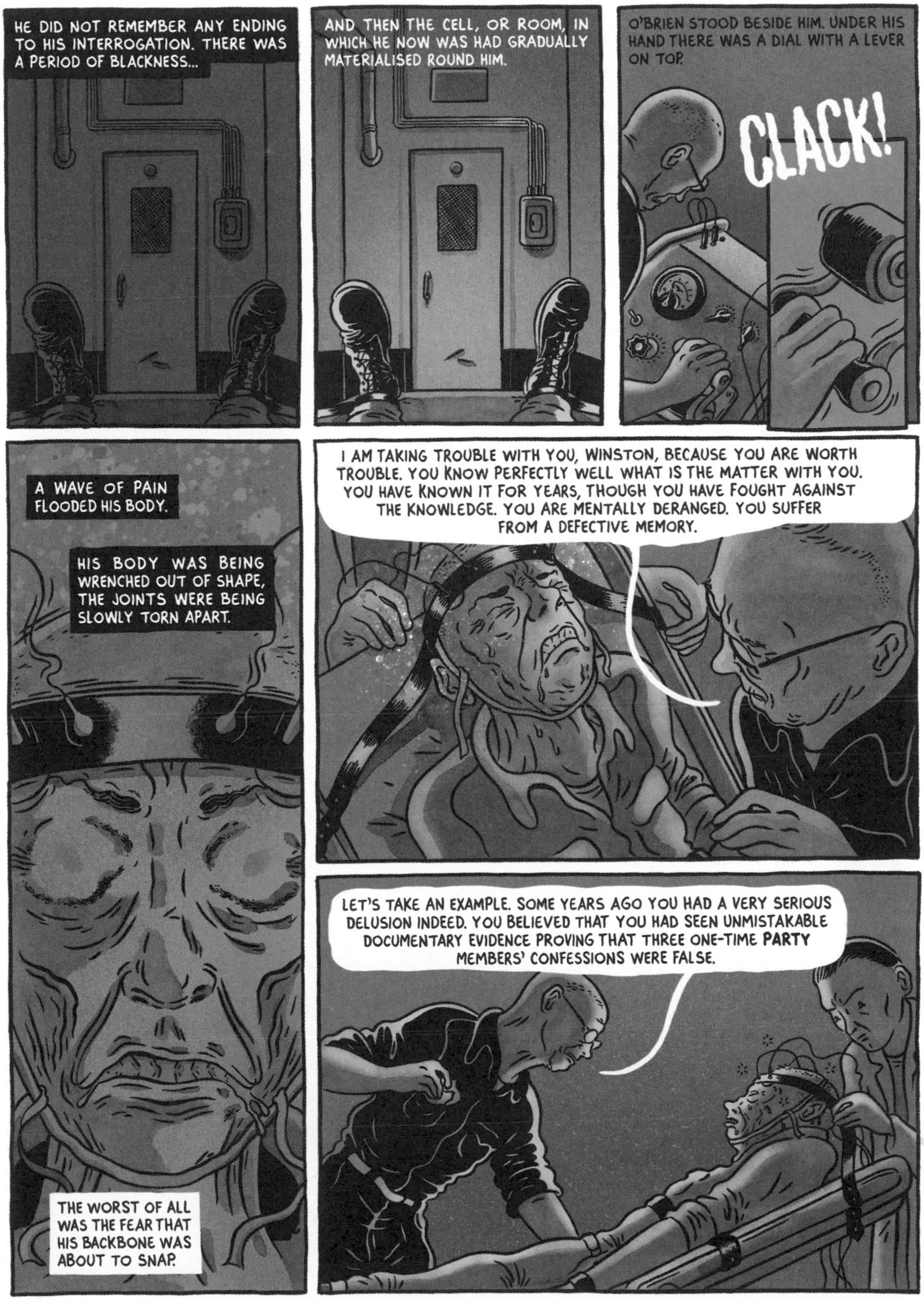
HE DID NOT REMEMBER ANY ENDING TO HIS INTERROGATION. THERE WAS A PERIOD OF BLACKNESS...
AND THEN THE CELL, OR ROOM, IN WHICH HE NOW WAS HAD GRADUALLY MATERIALISED ROUND HIM.
O'BRIEN STOOD BESIDE HIM. UNDER HIS HAND THERE WAS A DIAL WITH A LEVER ON TOP.
CLACK!
A WAVE OF PAIN FLOODED HIS BODY.
HIS BODY WAS BEING WRENCHED OUT OF SHAPE, THE JOINTS WERE BEING SLOWLY TORN APART.
THE WORST OF ALL WAS THE FEAR THAT HIS BACKBONE WAS ABOUT TO SNAP.
I AM TAKING TROUBLE WITH YOU, WINSTON, BECAUSE YOU ARE WORTH TROUBLE. YOU KNOW PERFECTLY WELL WHAT IS THE MATTER WITH YOU. YOU HAVE KNOWN IT FOR YEARS, THOUGH YOU HAVE FOUGHT AGAINST THE KNOWLEDGE. YOU ARE MENTALLY DERANGED. YOU SUFFER FROM A DEFECTIVE MEMORY.
LET'S TAKE AN EXAMPLE. SOME YEARS AGO YOU HAD A VERY SERIOUS DELUSION INDEED. YOU BELIEVED THAT YOU HAD SEEN UNMISTAKABLE DOCUMENTARY EVIDENCE PROVING THAT THREE ONE-TIME **PARTY** MEMBERS' CONFESSIONS WERE FALSE.

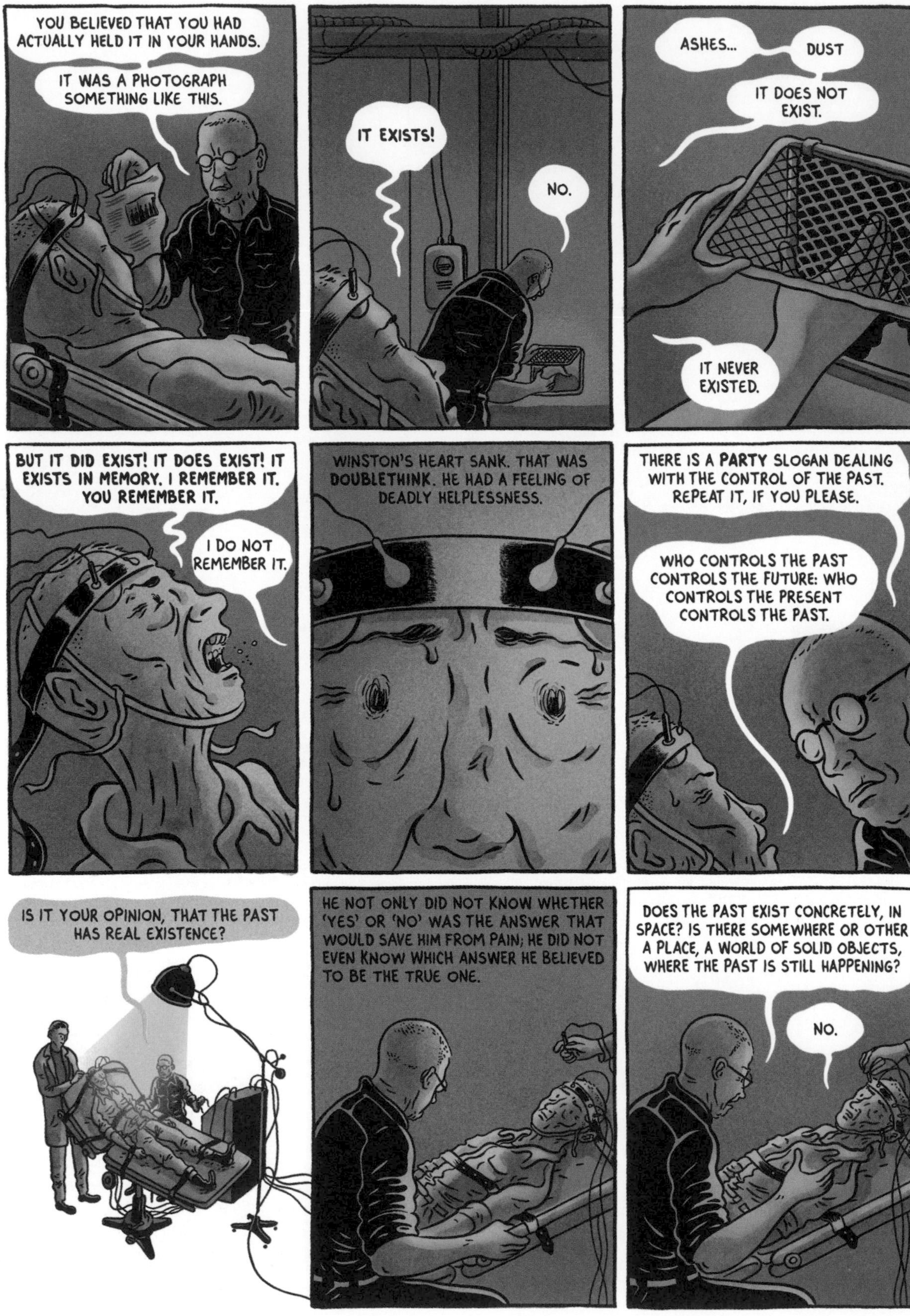
YOU BELIEVED THAT YOU HAD ACTUALLY HELD IT IN YOUR HANDS.
IT WAS A PHOTOGRAPH SOMETHING LIKE THIS.
IT EXISTS!
NO.
ASHES...
DUST
IT DOES NOT EXIST.
IT NEVER EXISTED.
BUT IT DID EXIST! IT DOES EXIST! IT EXISTS IN MEMORY. I REMEMBER IT. YOU REMEMBER IT.
I DO NOT REMEMBER IT.
WINSTON'S HEART SANK. THAT WAS DOUBLETHINK. HE HAD A FEELING OF DEADLY HELPLESSNESS.
THERE IS A PARTY SLOGAN DEALING WITH THE CONTROL OF THE PAST. REPEAT IT, IF YOU PLEASE.
WHO CONTROLS THE PAST CONTROLS THE FUTURE: WHO CONTROLS THE PRESENT CONTROLS THE PAST.
IS IT YOUR OPINION, THAT THE PAST HAS REAL EXISTENCE?
HE NOT ONLY DID NOT KNOW WHETHER 'YES' OR 'NO' WAS THE ANSWER THAT WOULD SAVE HIM FROM PAIN; HE DID NOT EVEN KNOW WHICH ANSWER HE BELIEVED TO BE THE TRUE ONE.
DOES THE PAST EXIST CONCRETELY, IN SPACE? IS THERE SOMEWHERE OR OTHER A PLACE, A WORLD OF SOLID OBJECTS, WHERE THE PAST IS STILL HAPPENING?
NO.

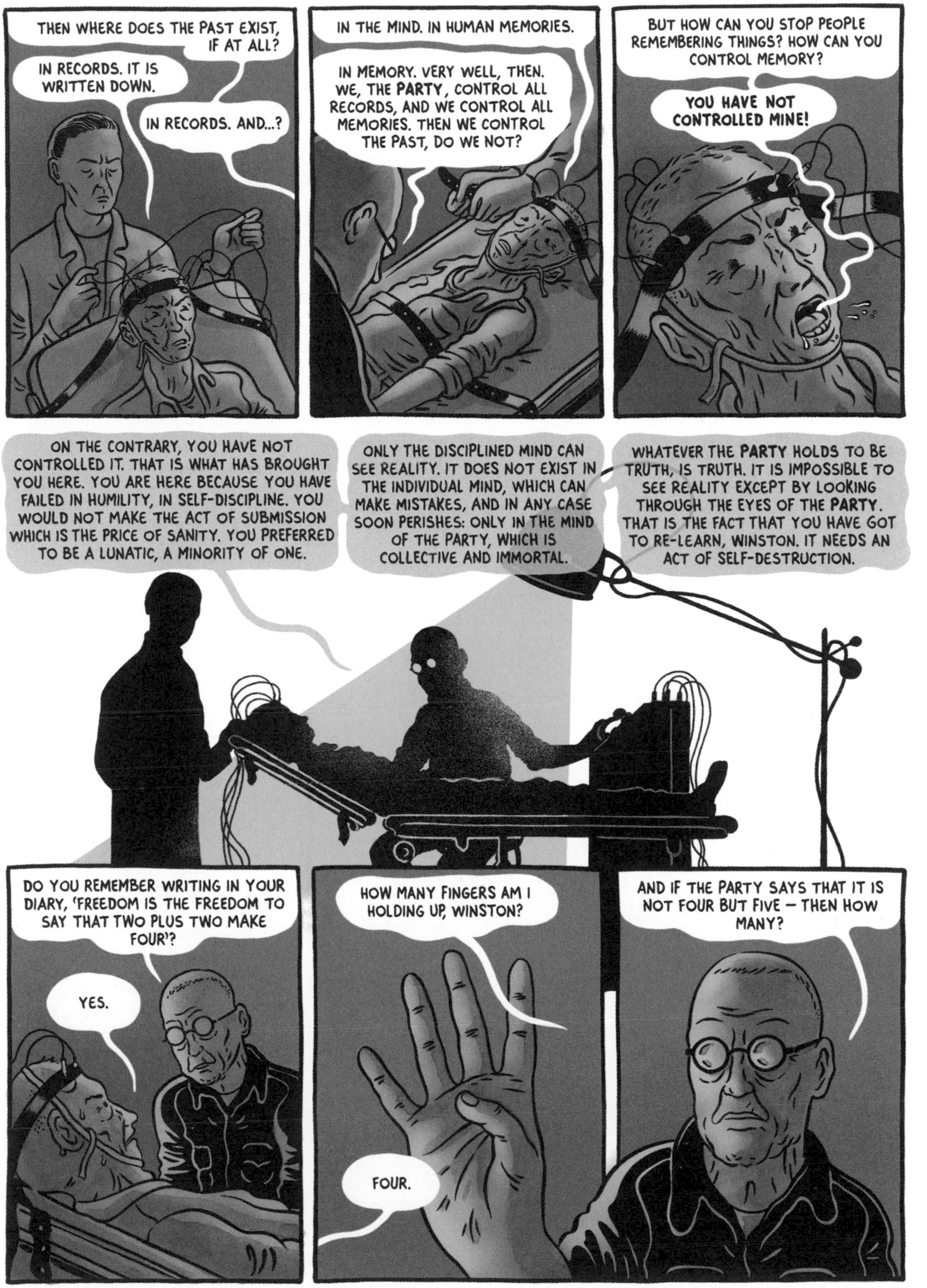
THEN WHERE DOES THE PAST EXIST, IF AT ALL?
IN RECORDS. IT IS WRITTEN DOWN.
IN RECORDS. AND...?
IN THE MIND. IN HUMAN MEMORIES.
IN MEMORY. VERY WELL, THEN. WE, THE PARTY, CONTROL ALL RECORDS, AND WE CONTROL ALL MEMORIES. THEN WE CONTROL THE PAST, DO WE NOT?
BUT HOW CAN YOU STOP PEOPLE REMEMBERING THINGS? HOW CAN YOU CONTROL MEMORY?
YOU HAVE NOT CONTROLLED MINE!
ON THE CONTRARY, YOU HAVE NOT CONTROLLED IT. THAT IS WHAT HAS BROUGHT YOU HERE. YOU ARE HERE BECAUSE YOU HAVE FAILED IN HUMILITY, IN SELF-DISCIPLINE. YOU WOULD NOT MAKE THE ACT OF SUBMISSION WHICH IS THE PRICE OF SANITY. YOU PREFERRED TO BE A LUNATIC, A MINORITY OF ONE.
ONLY THE DISCIPLINED MIND CAN SEE REALITY. IT DOES NOT EXIST IN THE INDIVIDUAL MIND, WHICH CAN MAKE MISTAKES, AND IN ANY CASE SOON PERISHES: ONLY IN THE MIND OF THE PARTY, WHICH IS COLLECTIVE AND IMMORTAL.
WHATEVER THE PARTY HOLDS TO BE TRUTH, IS TRUTH. IT IS IMPOSSIBLE TO SEE REALITY EXCEPT BY LOOKING THROUGH THE EYES OF THE PARTY. THAT IS THE FACT THAT YOU HAVE GOT TO RE-LEARN, WINSTON. IT NEEDS AN ACT OF SELF-DESTRUCTION.
DO YOU REMEMBER WRITING IN YOUR DIARY, 'FREEDOM IS THE FREEDOM TO SAY THAT TWO PLUS TWO MAKE FOUR'?
YES.
HOW MANY FINGERS AM I HOLDING UP, WINSTON?
FOUR.
AND IF THE PARTY SAYS THAT IT IS NOT FOUR BUT FIVE — THEN HOW MANY?

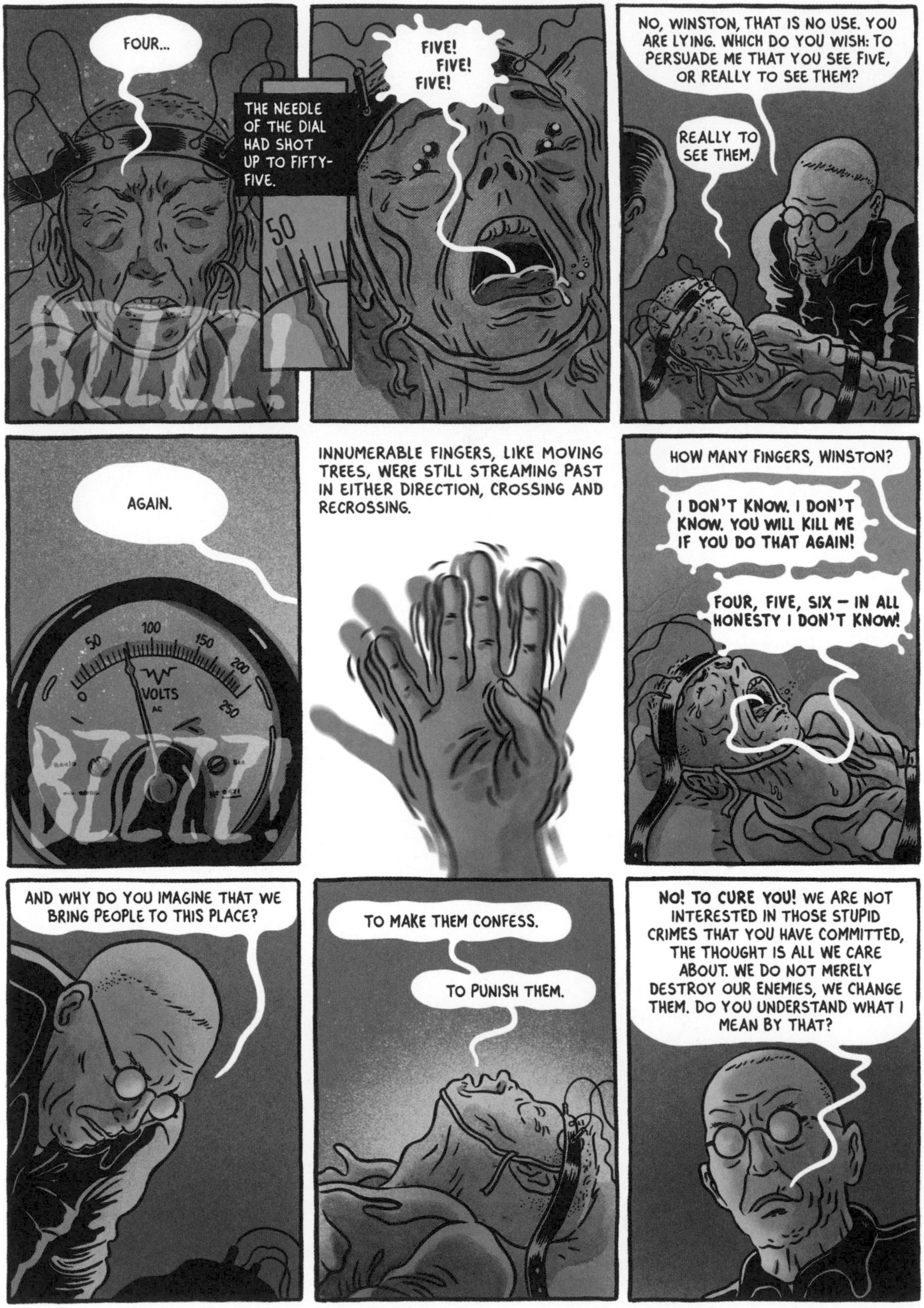
FOUR...
BZZZZ!
THE NEEDLE OF THE DIAL HAD SHOT UP TO FIFTY-FIVE.
50
FIVE! FIVE! FIVE!
NO, WINSTON, THAT IS NO USE. YOU ARE LYING. WHICH DO YOU WISH: TO PERSUADE ME THAT YOU SEE FIVE, OR REALLY TO SEE THEM?
REALLY TO SEE THEM.
AGAIN.
50 100 150 200 0 250
VOLTS
AC
BZZZZ!
INNUMERABLE FINGERS, LIKE MOVING TREES, WERE STILL STREAMING PAST IN EITHER DIRECTION, CROSSING AND RECROSSING.
HOW MANY FINGERS, WINSTON?
I DON'T KNOW. I DON'T KNOW. YOU WILL KILL ME IF YOU DO THAT AGAIN!
FOUR, FIVE, SIX – IN ALL HONESTY I DON'T KNOW!
AND WHY DO YOU IMAGINE THAT WE BRING PEOPLE TO THIS PLACE?
TO MAKE THEM CONFESS.
TO PUNISH THEM.
NO! TO CURE YOU! WE ARE NOT INTERESTED IN THOSE STUPID CRIMES THAT YOU HAVE COMMITTED, THE THOUGHT IS ALL WE CARE ABOUT. WE DO NOT MERELY DESTROY OUR ENEMIES, WE CHANGE THEM. DO YOU UNDERSTAND WHAT I MEAN BY THAT?

IN THIS PLACE THERE ARE NO MARTYRDOMS. IN THE MIDDLE AGES THERE WAS THE INQUISITION. IT WAS A FAILURE. FOR EVERY HERETIC IT BURNED AT THE STAKE, THOUSANDS OF OTHERS ROSE UP. WHY WAS THAT? BECAUSE IT KILLED THEM WHILE THEY WERE STILL UNREPENTANT: IN FACT, IT KILLED THEM BECAUSE THEY WERE UNREPENTANT. MEN WERE DYING BECAUSE THEY WOULD NOT ABANDON THEIR TRUE BELIEFS. NATURALLY ALL THE GLORY BELONGED TO THE VICTIM AND ALL THE SHAME TO THE INQUISITOR. WE DO NOT MAKE MISTAKES OF THAT KIND. ALL THE CONFESSIONS THAT ARE UTTERED HERE ARE TRUE.

GERMAN NAZIS AND THE RUSSIAN COMMUNISTS PERSECUTED HERESY MORE CRUELLY THAN THE INQUISITION HAD DONE. AND THEY IMAGINED THAT THEY HAD LEARNED FROM THE MISTAKES OF THE PAST; THEY KNEW, AT ANY RATE, THAT ONE MUST NOT MAKE MARTYRS. AND YET AFTER ONLY A FEW YEARS THE SAME THING HAD HAPPENED OVER AGAIN. THE DEAD MEN HAD BECOME MARTYRS. WE DO NOT ALLOW THE DEAD TO RISE UP AGAINST US.

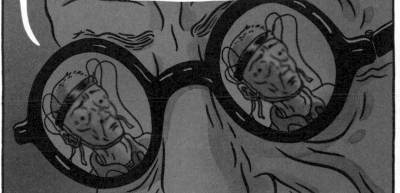

POSTERITY WILL NEVER HEAR OF YOU, WINSTON. WE SHALL TURN YOU INTO GAS AND POUR YOU INTO THE STRATOSPHERE. NOTHING WILL REMAIN OF YOU; NOT A NAME IN A REGISTER, NOT A MEMORY IN A LIVING BRAIN. YOU WILL BE ANNIHILATED IN THE PAST AS WELL AS IN THE FUTURE. YOU WILL NEVER HAVE EXISTED.

YOU ARE A FLAW IN THE PATTERN. IT IS INTOLERABLE TO US THAT AN ERRONEOUS THOUGHT SHOULD EXIST ANYWHERE IN THE WORLD, HOWEVER SECRET AND POWERLESS IT MAY BE.

EVEN IN THE INSTANT OF DEATH WE CANNOT PERMIT ANY DEVIATION. IN THE OLD DAYS THE HERETIC WALKED TO THE STAKE STILL A HERETIC, PROCLAIMING HIS HERESY.

EVEN THE VICTIM OF THE RUSSIAN PURGES COULD CARRY REBELLION LOCKED UP IN HIS SKULL AS HE WALKED DOWN THE PASSAGE WAITING FOR THE BULLET.

BUT WE MAKE THE BRAIN PERFECT BEFORE WE BLOW IT OUT.

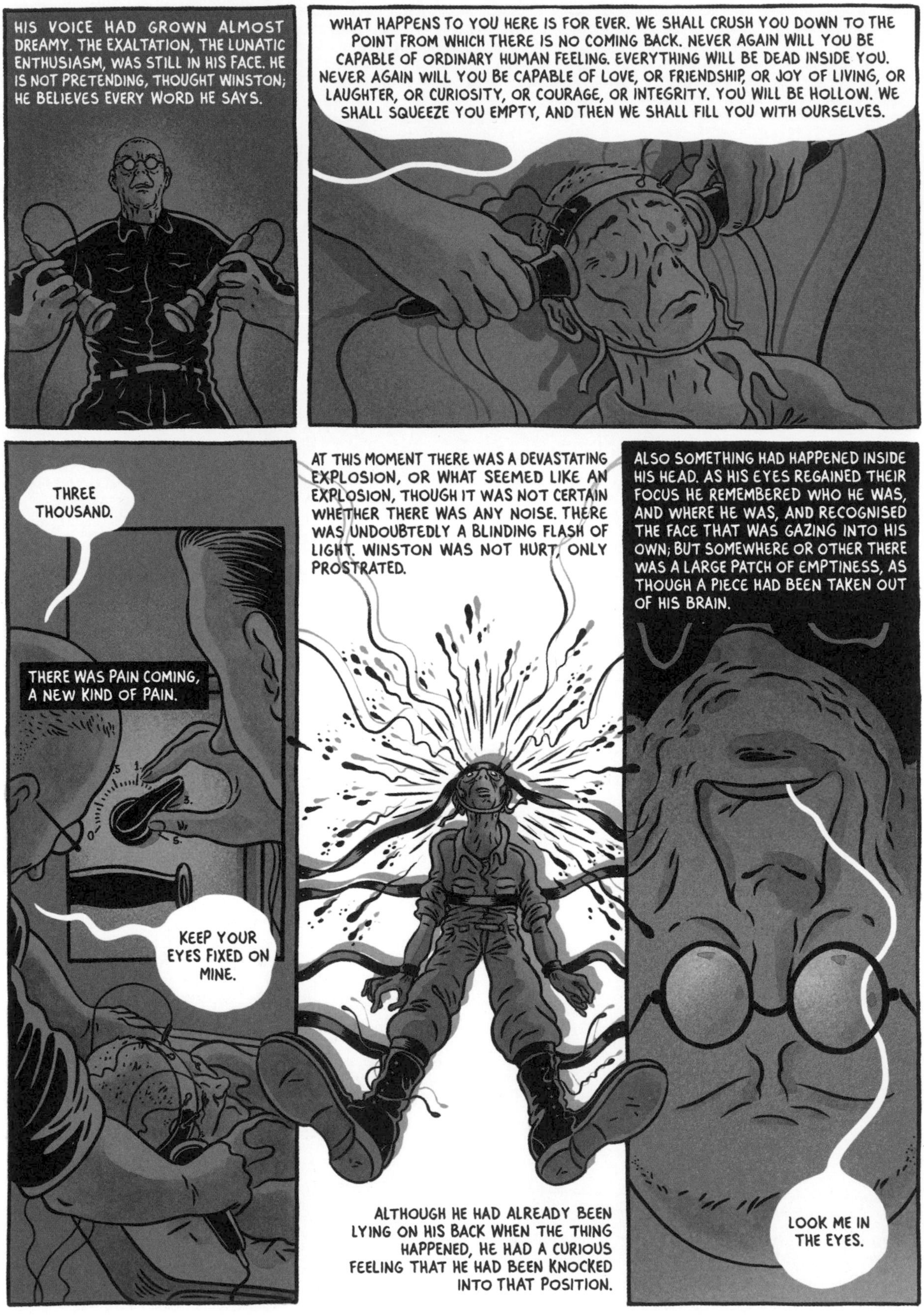
HIS VOICE HAD GROWN ALMOST DREAMY. THE EXALTATION, THE LUNATIC ENTHUSIASM, WAS STILL IN HIS FACE. HE IS NOT PRETENDING, THOUGHT WINSTON; HE BELIEVES EVERY WORD HE SAYS.
WHAT HAPPENS TO YOU HERE IS FOR EVER. WE SHALL CRUSH YOU DOWN TO THE POINT FROM WHICH THERE IS NO COMING BACK. NEVER AGAIN WILL YOU BE CAPABLE OF ORDINARY HUMAN FEELING. EVERYTHING WILL BE DEAD INSIDE YOU. NEVER AGAIN WILL YOU BE CAPABLE OF LOVE, OR FRIENDSHIP, OR JOY OF LIVING, OR LAUGHTER, OR CURIOSITY, OR COURAGE, OR INTEGRITY. YOU WILL BE HOLLOW. WE SHALL SQUEEZE YOU EMPTY, AND THEN WE SHALL FILL YOU WITH OURSELVES.
THREE THOUSAND.
THERE WAS PAIN COMING, A NEW KIND OF PAIN.
KEEP YOUR EYES FIXED ON MINE.
AT THIS MOMENT THERE WAS A DEVASTATING EXPLOSION, OR WHAT SEEMED LIKE AN EXPLOSION, THOUGH IT WAS NOT CERTAIN WHETHER THERE WAS ANY NOISE. THERE WAS UNDOUBTEDLY A BLINDING FLASH OF LIGHT. WINSTON WAS NOT HURT, ONLY PROSTRATED.
ALTHOUGH HE HAD ALREADY BEEN LYING ON HIS BACK WHEN THE THING HAPPENED, HE HAD A CURIOUS FEELING THAT HE HAD BEEN KNOCKED INTO THAT POSITION.
ALSO SOMETHING HAD HAPPENED INSIDE HIS HEAD. AS HIS EYES REGAINED THEIR FOCUS HE REMEMBERED WHO HE WAS, AND WHERE HE WAS, AND RECOGNISED THE FACE THAT WAS GAZING INTO HIS OWN; BUT SOMEWHERE OR OTHER THERE WAS A LARGE PATCH OF EMPTINESS, AS THOUGH A PIECE HAD BEEN TAKEN OUT OF HIS BRAIN.
LOOK ME IN THE EYES.

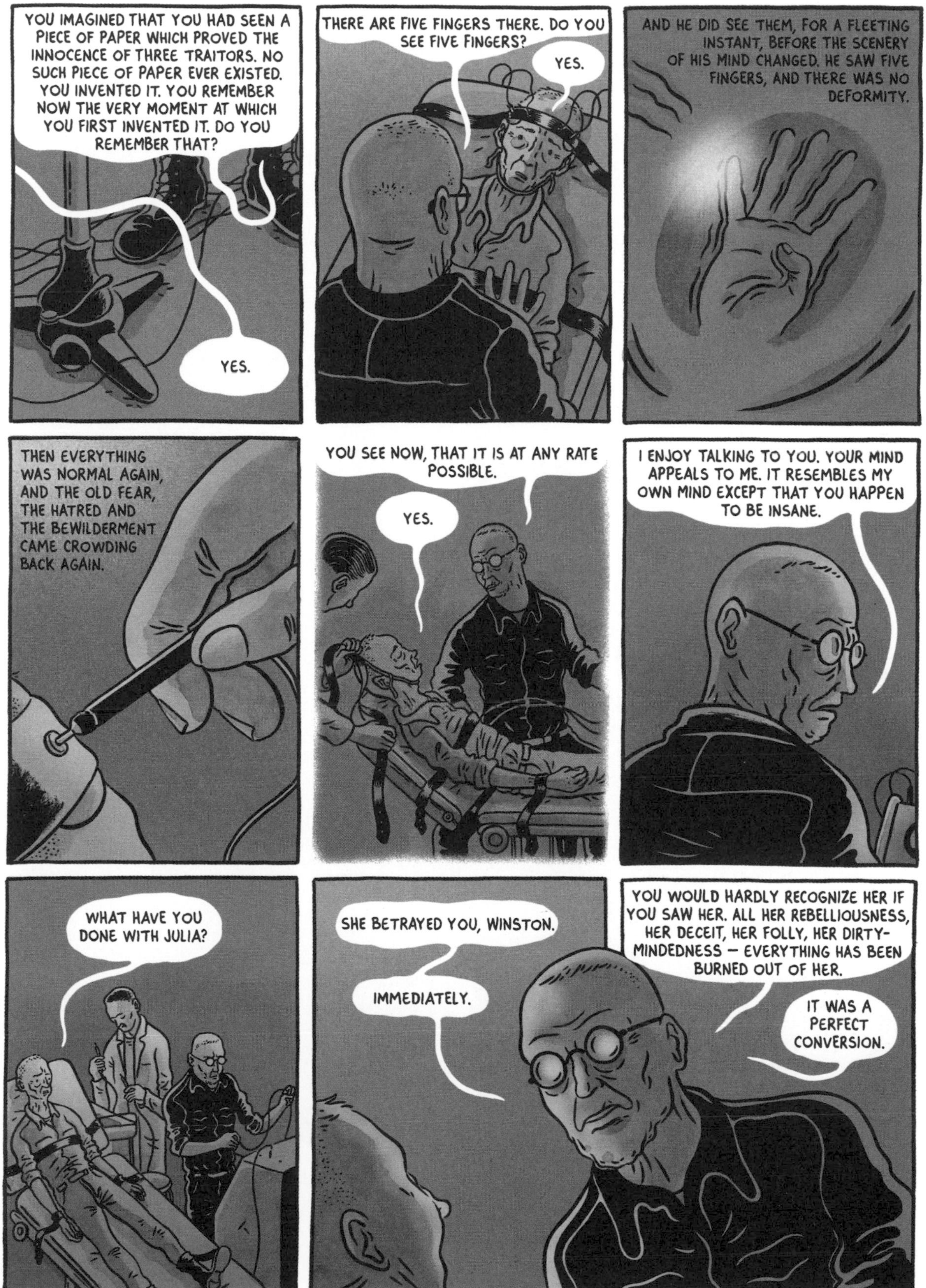
YOU IMAGINED THAT YOU HAD SEEN A PIECE OF PAPER WHICH PROVED THE INNOCENCE OF THREE TRAITORS. NO SUCH PIECE OF PAPER EVER EXISTED. YOU INVENTED IT. YOU REMEMBER NOW THE VERY MOMENT AT WHICH YOU FIRST INVENTED IT. DO YOU REMEMBER THAT?
YES.
THERE ARE FIVE FINGERS THERE. DO YOU SEE FIVE FINGERS?
YES.
AND HE DID SEE THEM, FOR A FLEETING INSTANT, BEFORE THE SCENERY OF HIS MIND CHANGED. HE SAW FIVE FINGERS, AND THERE WAS NO DEFORMITY.
THEN EVERYTHING WAS NORMAL AGAIN, AND THE OLD FEAR, THE HATRED AND THE BEWILDERMENT CAME CROWDING BACK AGAIN.
YOU SEE NOW, THAT IT IS AT ANY RATE POSSIBLE.
YES.
I ENJOY TALKING TO YOU. YOUR MIND APPEALS TO ME. IT RESEMBLES MY OWN MIND EXCEPT THAT YOU HAPPEN TO BE INSANE.
WHAT HAVE YOU DONE WITH JULIA?
SHE BETRAYED YOU, WINSTON.
IMMEDIATELY.
YOU WOULD HARDLY RECOGNIZE HER IF YOU SAW HER. ALL HER REBELLIOUSNESS, HER DECEIT, HER FOLLY, HER DIRTY-MINDEDNESS — EVERYTHING HAS BEEN BURNED OUT OF HER.
IT WAS A PERFECT CONVERSION.

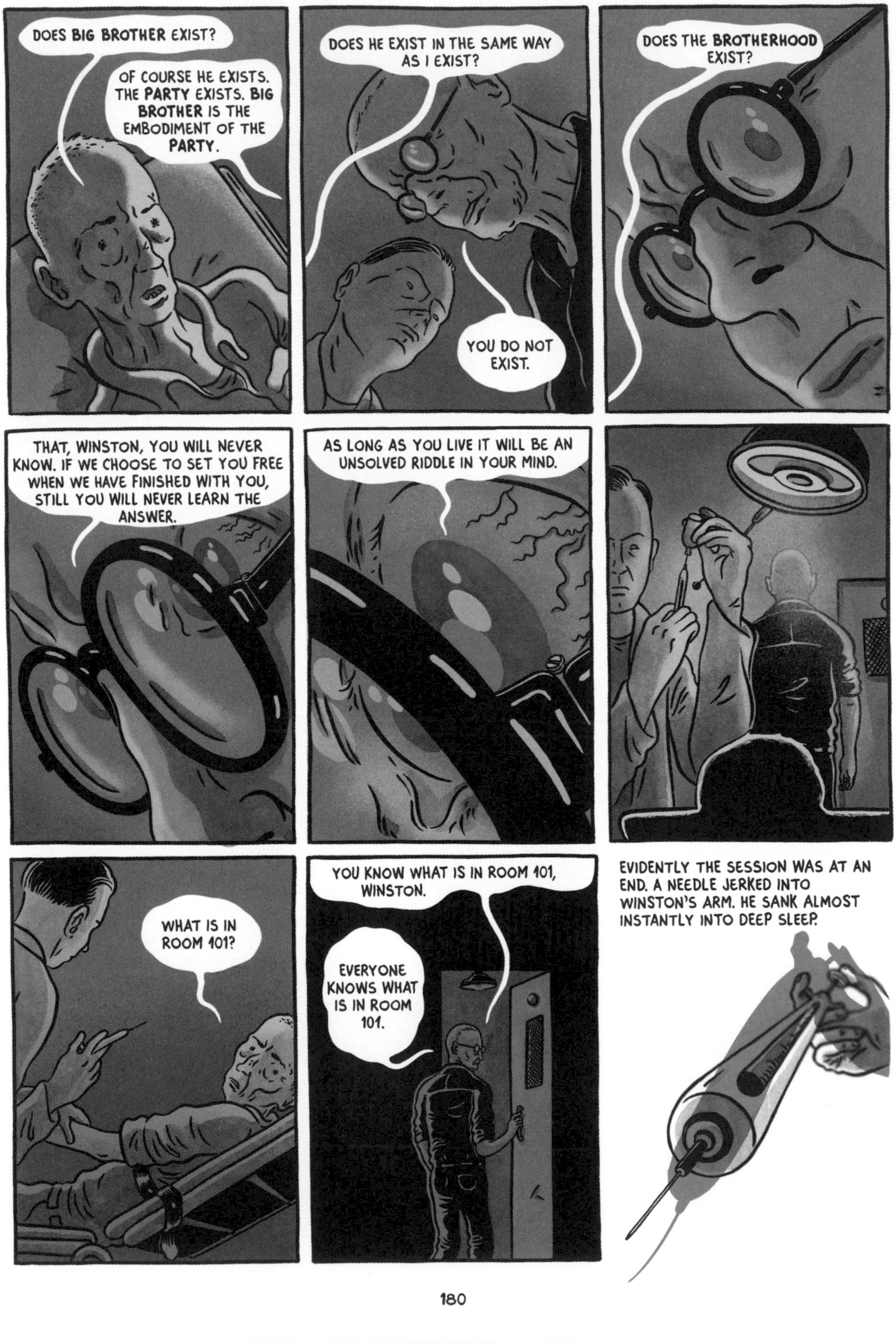
DOES BIG BROTHER EXIST?
OF COURSE HE EXISTS. THE PARTY EXISTS. BIG BROTHER IS THE EMBODIMENT OF THE PARTY.
DOES HE EXIST IN THE SAME WAY AS I EXIST?
YOU DO NOT EXIST.
DOES THE BROTHERHOOD EXIST?
THAT, WINSTON, YOU WILL NEVER KNOW. IF WE CHOOSE TO SET YOU FREE WHEN WE HAVE FINISHED WITH YOU, STILL YOU WILL NEVER LEARN THE ANSWER.
AS LONG AS YOU LIVE IT WILL BE AN UNSOLVED RIDDLE IN YOUR MIND.
WHAT IS IN ROOM 101?
YOU KNOW WHAT IS IN ROOM 101, WINSTON.
EVERYONE KNOWS WHAT IS IN ROOM 101.
EVIDENTLY THE SESSION WAS AT AN END. A NEEDLE JERKED INTO WINSTON'S ARM. HE SANK ALMOST INSTANTLY INTO DEEP SLEEP.

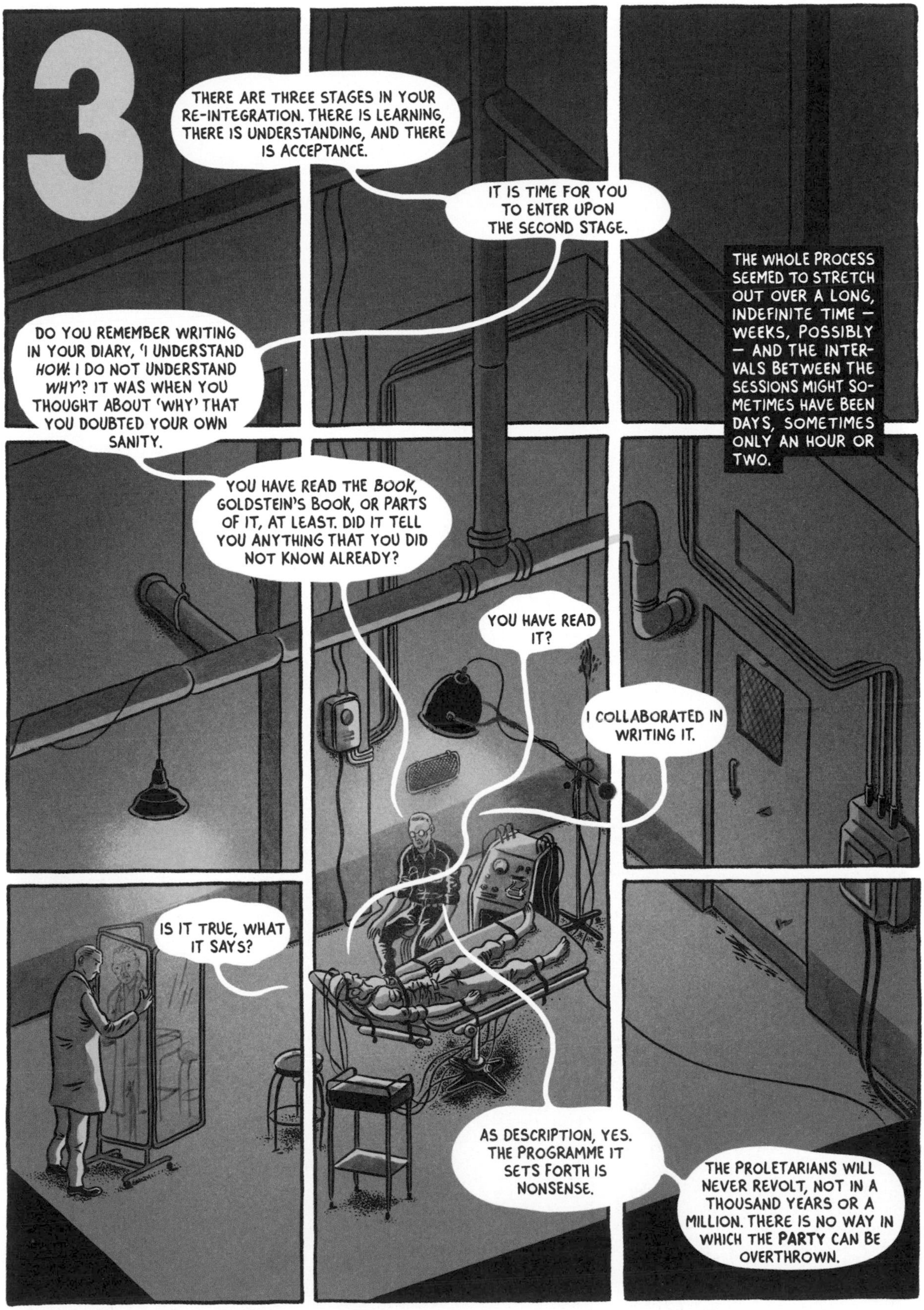
3
THERE ARE THREE STAGES IN YOUR RE-INTEGRATION. THERE IS LEARNING, THERE IS UNDERSTANDING, AND THERE IS ACCEPTANCE.
IT IS TIME FOR YOU TO ENTER UPON THE SECOND STAGE.
THE WHOLE PROCESS SEEMED TO STRETCH OUT OVER A LONG, INDEFINITE TIME — WEEKS, POSSIBLY — AND THE INTERVALS BETWEEN THE SESSIONS MIGHT SOMETIMES HAVE BEEN DAYS, SOMETIMES ONLY AN HOUR OR TWO.
DO YOU REMEMBER WRITING IN YOUR DIARY, 'I UNDERSTAND *HOW*: I DO NOT UNDERSTAND *WHY*'? IT WAS WHEN YOU THOUGHT ABOUT 'WHY' THAT YOU DOUBTED YOUR OWN SANITY.
YOU HAVE READ THE *BOOK*, GOLDSTEIN'S BOOK, OR PARTS OF IT, AT LEAST. DID IT TELL YOU ANYTHING THAT YOU DID NOT KNOW ALREADY?
YOU HAVE READ IT?
I COLLABORATED IN WRITING IT.
IS IT TRUE, WHAT IT SAYS?
AS DESCRIPTION, YES. THE PROGRAMME IT SETS FORTH IS NONSENSE.
THE PROLETARIANS WILL NEVER REVOLT, NOT IN A THOUSAND YEARS OR A MILLION. THERE IS NO WAY IN WHICH THE **PARTY** CAN BE OVERTHROWN.

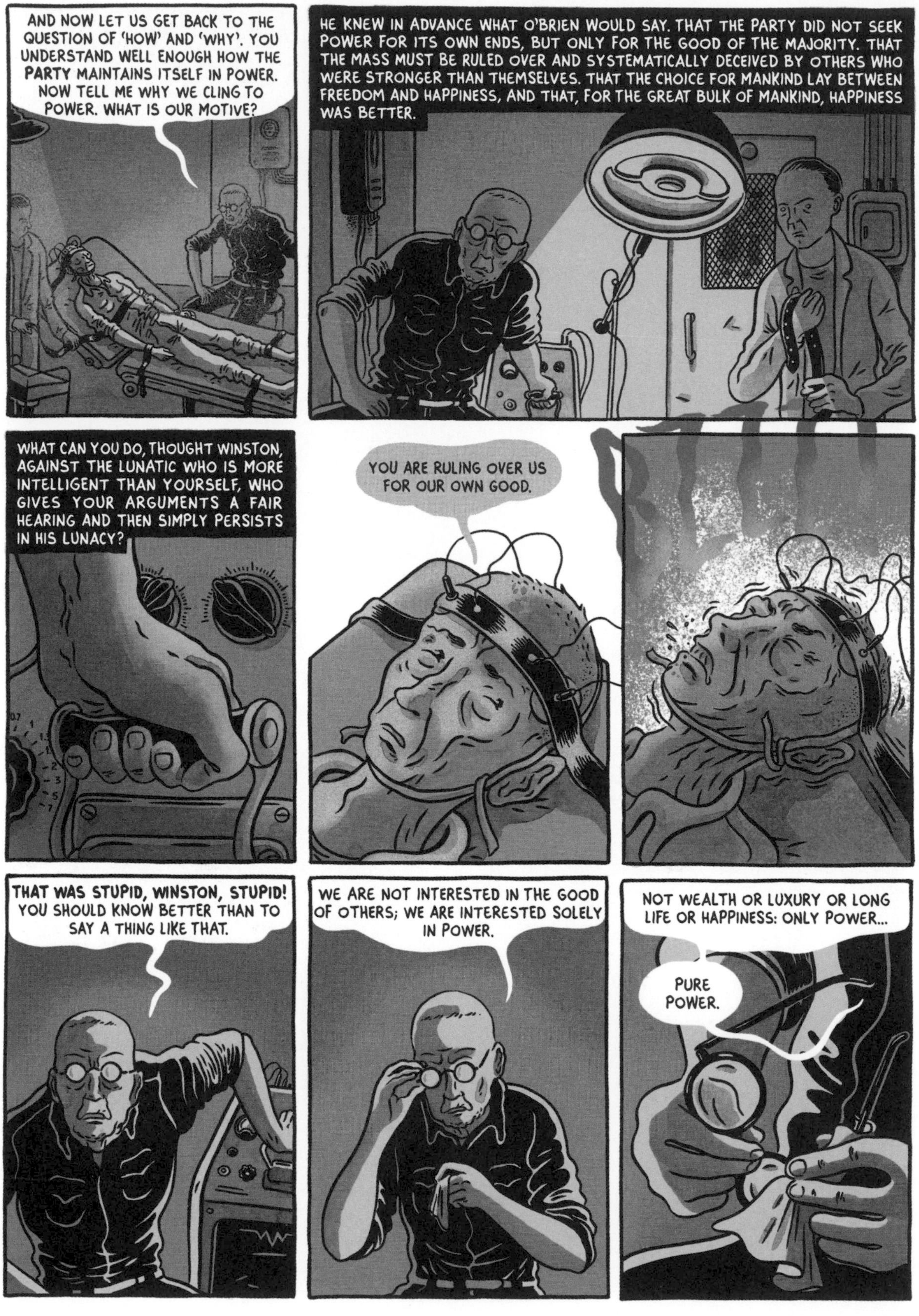
AND NOW LET US GET BACK TO THE QUESTION OF 'HOW' AND 'WHY'. YOU UNDERSTAND WELL ENOUGH HOW THE PARTY MAINTAINS ITSELF IN POWER. NOW TELL ME WHY WE CLING TO POWER. WHAT IS OUR MOTIVE?
HE KNEW IN ADVANCE WHAT O'BRIEN WOULD SAY. THAT THE PARTY DID NOT SEEK POWER FOR ITS OWN ENDS, BUT ONLY FOR THE GOOD OF THE MAJORITY. THAT THE MASS MUST BE RULED OVER AND SYSTEMATICALLY DECEIVED BY OTHERS WHO WERE STRONGER THAN THEMSELVES. THAT THE CHOICE FOR MANKIND LAY BETWEEN FREEDOM AND HAPPINESS, AND THAT, FOR THE GREAT BULK OF MANKIND, HAPPINESS WAS BETTER.
WHAT CAN YOU DO, THOUGHT WINSTON, AGAINST THE LUNATIC WHO IS MORE INTELLIGENT THAN YOURSELF, WHO GIVES YOUR ARGUMENTS A FAIR HEARING AND THEN SIMPLY PERSISTS IN HIS LUNACY?
YOU ARE RULING OVER US FOR OUR OWN GOOD.
THAT WAS STUPID, WINSTON, STUPID! YOU SHOULD KNOW BETTER THAN TO SAY A THING LIKE THAT.
WE ARE NOT INTERESTED IN THE GOOD OF OTHERS; WE ARE INTERESTED SOLELY IN POWER.
NOT WEALTH OR LUXURY OR LONG LIFE OR HAPPINESS: ONLY POWER...
PURE POWER.

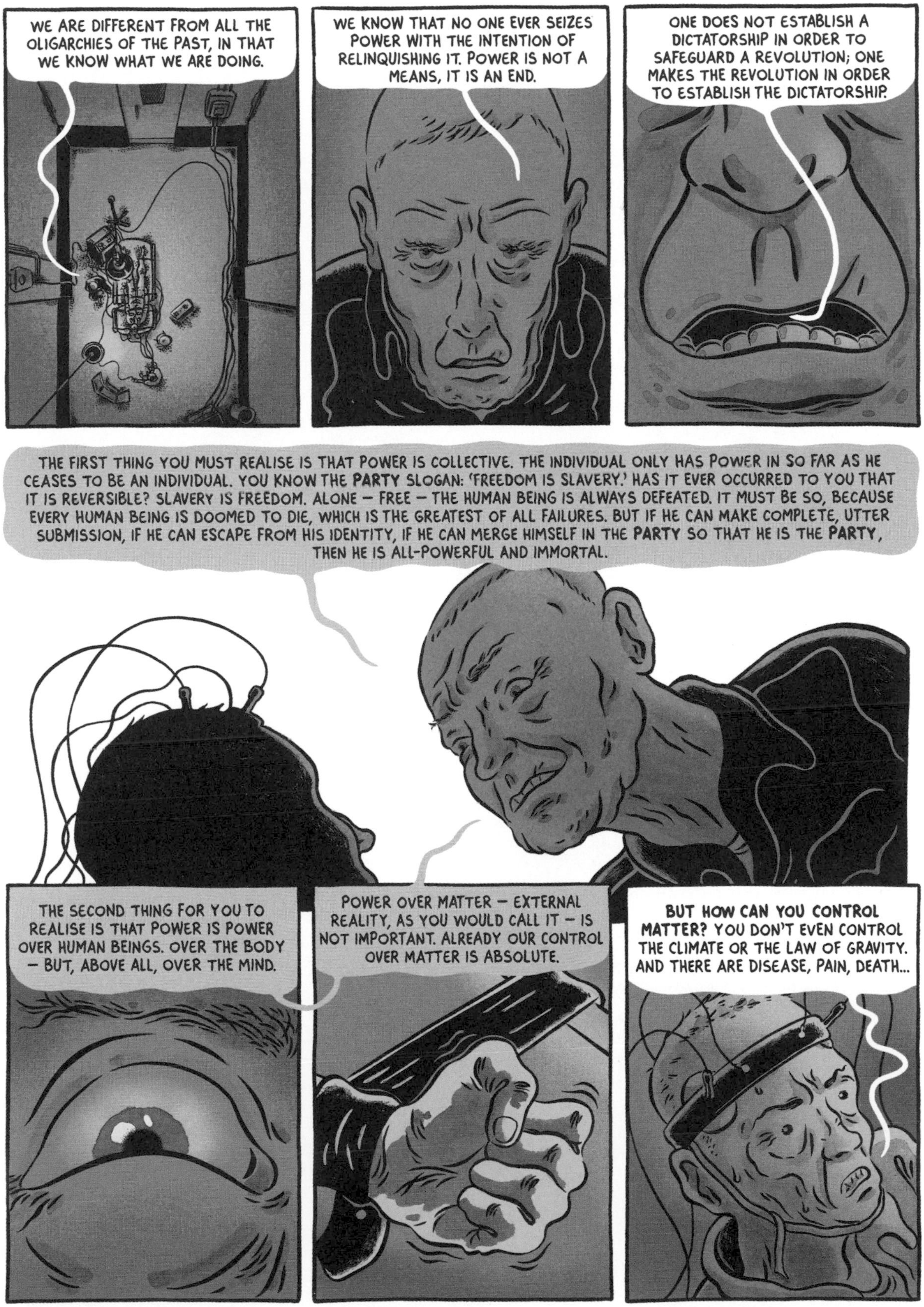
WE ARE DIFFERENT FROM ALL THE OLIGARCHIES OF THE PAST, IN THAT WE KNOW WHAT WE ARE DOING.
WE KNOW THAT NO ONE EVER SEIZES POWER WITH THE INTENTION OF RELINQUISHING IT. POWER IS NOT A MEANS, IT IS AN END.
ONE DOES NOT ESTABLISH A DICTATORSHIP IN ORDER TO SAFEGUARD A REVOLUTION; ONE MAKES THE REVOLUTION IN ORDER TO ESTABLISH THE DICTATORSHIP.
THE FIRST THING YOU MUST REALISE IS THAT POWER IS COLLECTIVE. THE INDIVIDUAL ONLY HAS POWER IN SO FAR AS HE CEASES TO BE AN INDIVIDUAL. YOU KNOW THE **PARTY** SLOGAN: 'FREEDOM IS SLAVERY.' HAS IT EVER OCCURRED TO YOU THAT IT IS REVERSIBLE? SLAVERY IS FREEDOM. ALONE – FREE – THE HUMAN BEING IS ALWAYS DEFEATED. IT MUST BE SO, BECAUSE EVERY HUMAN BEING IS DOOMED TO DIE, WHICH IS THE GREATEST OF ALL FAILURES. BUT IF HE CAN MAKE COMPLETE, UTTER SUBMISSION, IF HE CAN ESCAPE FROM HIS IDENTITY, IF HE CAN MERGE HIMSELF IN THE **PARTY** SO THAT HE IS THE **PARTY**, THEN HE IS ALL-POWERFUL AND IMMORTAL.
THE SECOND THING FOR YOU TO REALISE IS THAT POWER IS POWER OVER HUMAN BEINGS. OVER THE BODY – BUT, ABOVE ALL, OVER THE MIND.
POWER OVER MATTER – EXTERNAL REALITY, AS YOU WOULD CALL IT – IS NOT IMPORTANT. ALREADY OUR CONTROL OVER MATTER IS ABSOLUTE.
BUT HOW CAN YOU CONTROL MATTER? YOU DON'T EVEN CONTROL THE CLIMATE OR THE LAW OF GRAVITY. AND THERE ARE DISEASE, PAIN, DEATH...

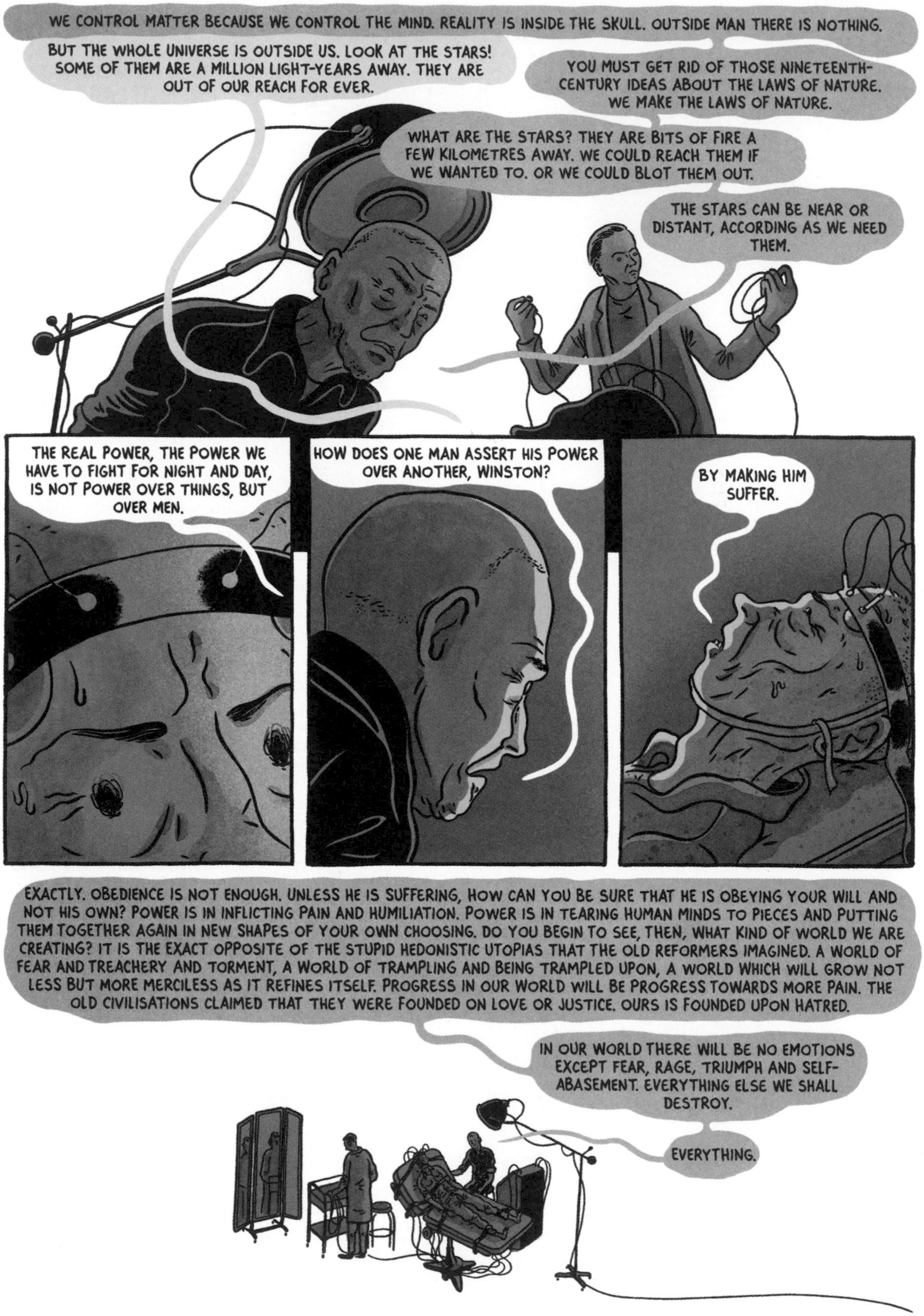
WE CONTROL MATTER BECAUSE WE CONTROL THE MIND. REALITY IS INSIDE THE SKULL. OUTSIDE MAN THERE IS NOTHING.
BUT THE WHOLE UNIVERSE IS OUTSIDE US. LOOK AT THE STARS! SOME OF THEM ARE A MILLION LIGHT-YEARS AWAY. THEY ARE OUT OF OUR REACH FOR EVER.
YOU MUST GET RID OF THOSE NINETEENTH-CENTURY IDEAS ABOUT THE LAWS OF NATURE. WE MAKE THE LAWS OF NATURE.
WHAT ARE THE STARS? THEY ARE BITS OF FIRE A FEW KILOMETRES AWAY. WE COULD REACH THEM IF WE WANTED TO. OR WE COULD BLOT THEM OUT.
THE STARS CAN BE NEAR OR DISTANT, ACCORDING AS WE NEED THEM.
THE REAL POWER, THE POWER WE HAVE TO FIGHT FOR NIGHT AND DAY, IS NOT POWER OVER THINGS, BUT OVER MEN.
HOW DOES ONE MAN ASSERT HIS POWER OVER ANOTHER, WINSTON?
BY MAKING HIM SUFFER.
EXACTLY. OBEDIENCE IS NOT ENOUGH. UNLESS HE IS SUFFERING, HOW CAN YOU BE SURE THAT HE IS OBEYING YOUR WILL AND NOT HIS OWN? POWER IS IN INFLICTING PAIN AND HUMILIATION. POWER IS IN TEARING HUMAN MINDS TO PIECES AND PUTTING THEM TOGETHER AGAIN IN NEW SHAPES OF YOUR OWN CHOOSING. DO YOU BEGIN TO SEE, THEN, WHAT KIND OF WORLD WE ARE CREATING? IT IS THE EXACT OPPOSITE OF THE STUPID HEDONISTIC UTOPIAS THAT THE OLD REFORMERS IMAGINED. A WORLD OF FEAR AND TREACHERY AND TORMENT, A WORLD OF TRAMPLING AND BEING TRAMPLED UPON, A WORLD WHICH WILL GROW NOT LESS BUT MORE MERCILESS AS IT REFINES ITSELF. PROGRESS IN OUR WORLD WILL BE PROGRESS TOWARDS MORE PAIN. THE OLD CIVILISATIONS CLAIMED THAT THEY WERE FOUNDED ON LOVE OR JUSTICE. OURS IS FOUNDED UPON HATRED.
IN OUR WORLD THERE WILL BE NO EMOTIONS EXCEPT FEAR, RAGE, TRIUMPH AND SELF-ABASEMENT. EVERYTHING ELSE WE SHALL DESTROY.
EVERYTHING.

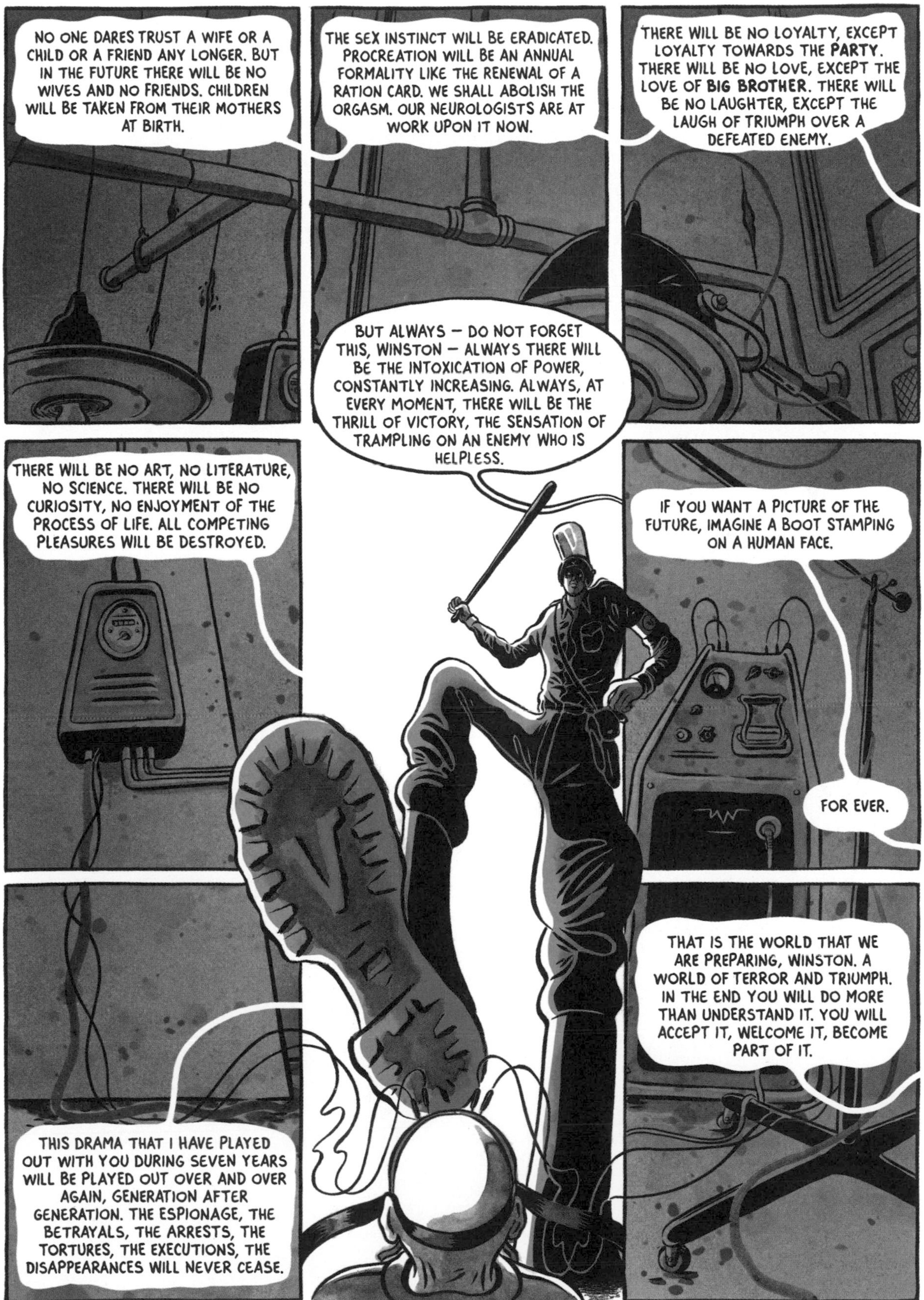
NO ONE DARES TRUST A WIFE OR A CHILD OR A FRIEND ANY LONGER. BUT IN THE FUTURE THERE WILL BE NO WIVES AND NO FRIENDS. CHILDREN WILL BE TAKEN FROM THEIR MOTHERS AT BIRTH.
THE SEX INSTINCT WILL BE ERADICATED. PROCREATION WILL BE AN ANNUAL FORMALITY LIKE THE RENEWAL OF A RATION CARD. WE SHALL ABOLISH THE ORGASM. OUR NEUROLOGISTS ARE AT WORK UPON IT NOW.
THERE WILL BE NO LOYALTY, EXCEPT LOYALTY TOWARDS THE **PARTY**. THERE WILL BE NO LOVE, EXCEPT THE LOVE OF **BIG BROTHER**. THERE WILL BE NO LAUGHTER, EXCEPT THE LAUGH OF TRIUMPH OVER A DEFEATED ENEMY.
THERE WILL BE NO ART, NO LITERATURE, NO SCIENCE. THERE WILL BE NO CURIOSITY, NO ENJOYMENT OF THE PROCESS OF LIFE. ALL COMPETING PLEASURES WILL BE DESTROYED.
BUT ALWAYS — DO NOT FORGET THIS, WINSTON — ALWAYS THERE WILL BE THE INTOXICATION OF POWER, CONSTANTLY INCREASING. ALWAYS, AT EVERY MOMENT, THERE WILL BE THE THRILL OF VICTORY, THE SENSATION OF TRAMPLING ON AN ENEMY WHO IS HELPLESS.
IF YOU WANT A PICTURE OF THE FUTURE, IMAGINE A BOOT STAMPING ON A HUMAN FACE.
FOR EVER.
THIS DRAMA THAT I HAVE PLAYED OUT WITH YOU DURING SEVEN YEARS WILL BE PLAYED OUT OVER AND OVER AGAIN, GENERATION AFTER GENERATION. THE ESPIONAGE, THE BETRAYALS, THE ARRESTS, THE TORTURES, THE EXECUTIONS, THE DISAPPEARANCES WILL NEVER CEASE.
THAT IS THE WORLD THAT WE ARE PREPARING, WINSTON. A WORLD OF TERROR AND TRIUMPH. IN THE END YOU WILL DO MORE THAN UNDERSTAND IT. YOU WILL ACCEPT IT, WELCOME IT, BECOME PART OF IT.

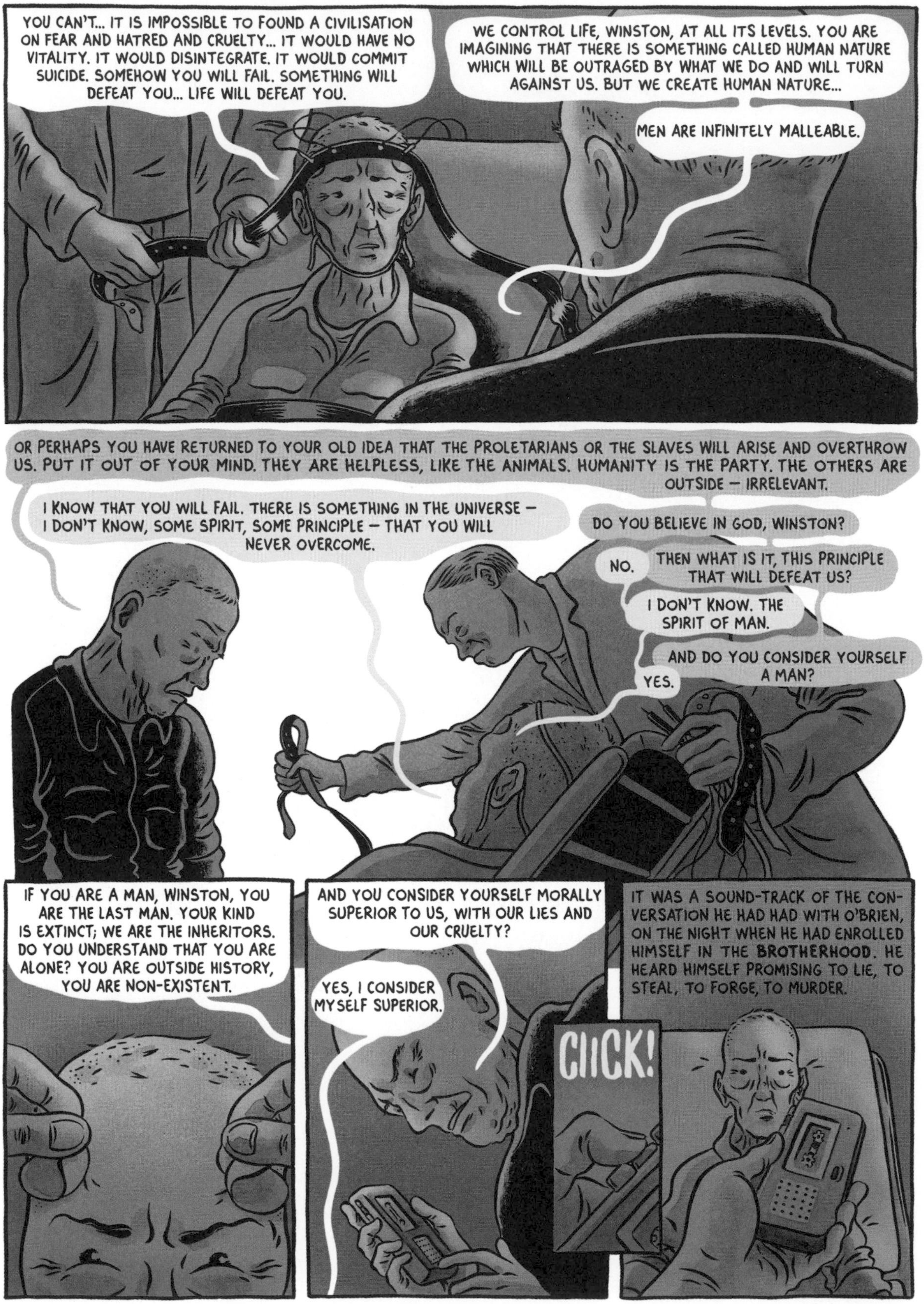
YOU CAN'T... IT IS IMPOSSIBLE TO FOUND A CIVILISATION ON FEAR AND HATRED AND CRUELTY... IT WOULD HAVE NO VITALITY. IT WOULD DISINTEGRATE. IT WOULD COMMIT SUICIDE. SOMEHOW YOU WILL FAIL. SOMETHING WILL DEFEAT YOU... LIFE WILL DEFEAT YOU.
WE CONTROL LIFE, WINSTON, AT ALL ITS LEVELS. YOU ARE IMAGINING THAT THERE IS SOMETHING CALLED HUMAN NATURE WHICH WILL BE OUTRAGED BY WHAT WE DO AND WILL TURN AGAINST US. BUT WE CREATE HUMAN NATURE...
MEN ARE INFINITELY MALLEABLE.
OR PERHAPS YOU HAVE RETURNED TO YOUR OLD IDEA THAT THE PROLETARIANS OR THE SLAVES WILL ARISE AND OVERTHROW US. PUT IT OUT OF YOUR MIND. THEY ARE HELPLESS, LIKE THE ANIMALS. HUMANITY IS THE PARTY. THE OTHERS ARE OUTSIDE – IRRELEVANT.
I KNOW THAT YOU WILL FAIL. THERE IS SOMETHING IN THE UNIVERSE – I DON'T KNOW, SOME SPIRIT, SOME PRINCIPLE – THAT YOU WILL NEVER OVERCOME.
DO YOU BELIEVE IN GOD, WINSTON?
NO.
THEN WHAT IS IT, THIS PRINCIPLE THAT WILL DEFEAT US?
I DON'T KNOW. THE SPIRIT OF MAN.
AND DO YOU CONSIDER YOURSELF A MAN?
YES.
IF YOU ARE A MAN, WINSTON, YOU ARE THE LAST MAN. YOUR KIND IS EXTINCT; WE ARE THE INHERITORS. DO YOU UNDERSTAND THAT YOU ARE ALONE? YOU ARE OUTSIDE HISTORY, YOU ARE NON-EXISTENT.
AND YOU CONSIDER YOURSELF MORALLY SUPERIOR TO US, WITH OUR LIES AND OUR CRUELTY?
YES, I CONSIDER MYSELF SUPERIOR.
CLICK!
IT WAS A SOUND-TRACK OF THE CONVERSATION HE HAD HAD WITH O'BRIEN, ON THE NIGHT WHEN HE HAD ENROLLED HIMSELF IN THE BROTHERHOOD. HE HEARD HIMSELF PROMISING TO LIE, TO STEAL, TO FORGE, TO MURDER.

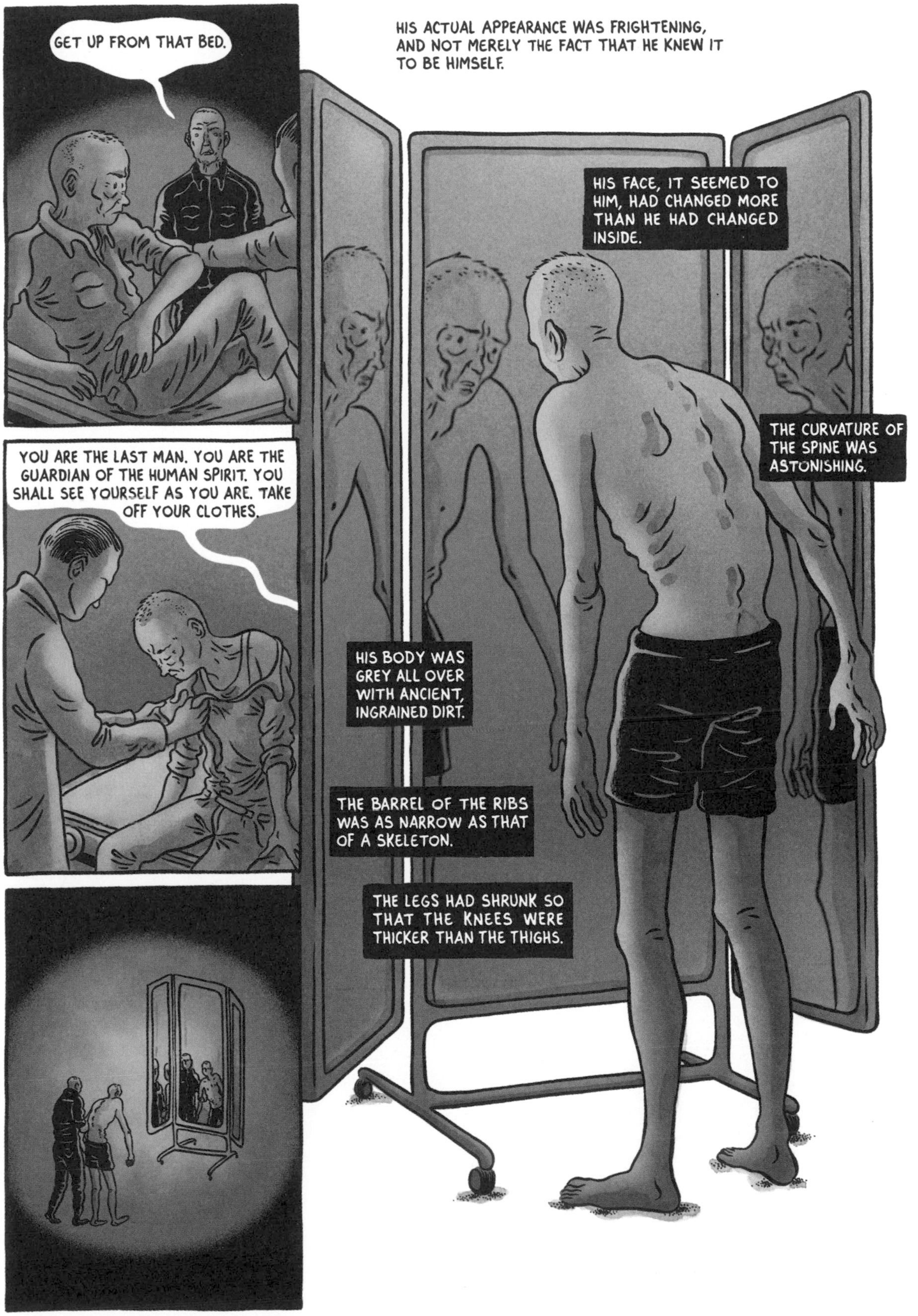
GET UP FROM THAT BED.
YOU ARE THE LAST MAN. YOU ARE THE GUARDIAN OF THE HUMAN SPIRIT. YOU SHALL SEE YOURSELF AS YOU ARE. TAKE OFF YOUR CLOTHES.
HIS ACTUAL APPEARANCE WAS FRIGHTENING, AND NOT MERELY THE FACT THAT HE KNEW IT TO BE HIMSELF.
HIS FACE, IT SEEMED TO HIM, HAD CHANGED MORE THAN HE HAD CHANGED INSIDE.
THE CURVATURE OF THE SPINE WAS ASTONISHING.
HIS BODY WAS GREY ALL OVER WITH ANCIENT, INGRAINED DIRT.
THE BARREL OF THE RIBS WAS AS NARROW AS THAT OF A SKELETON.
THE LEGS HAD SHRUNK SO THAT THE KNEES WERE THICKER THAN THE THIGHS.

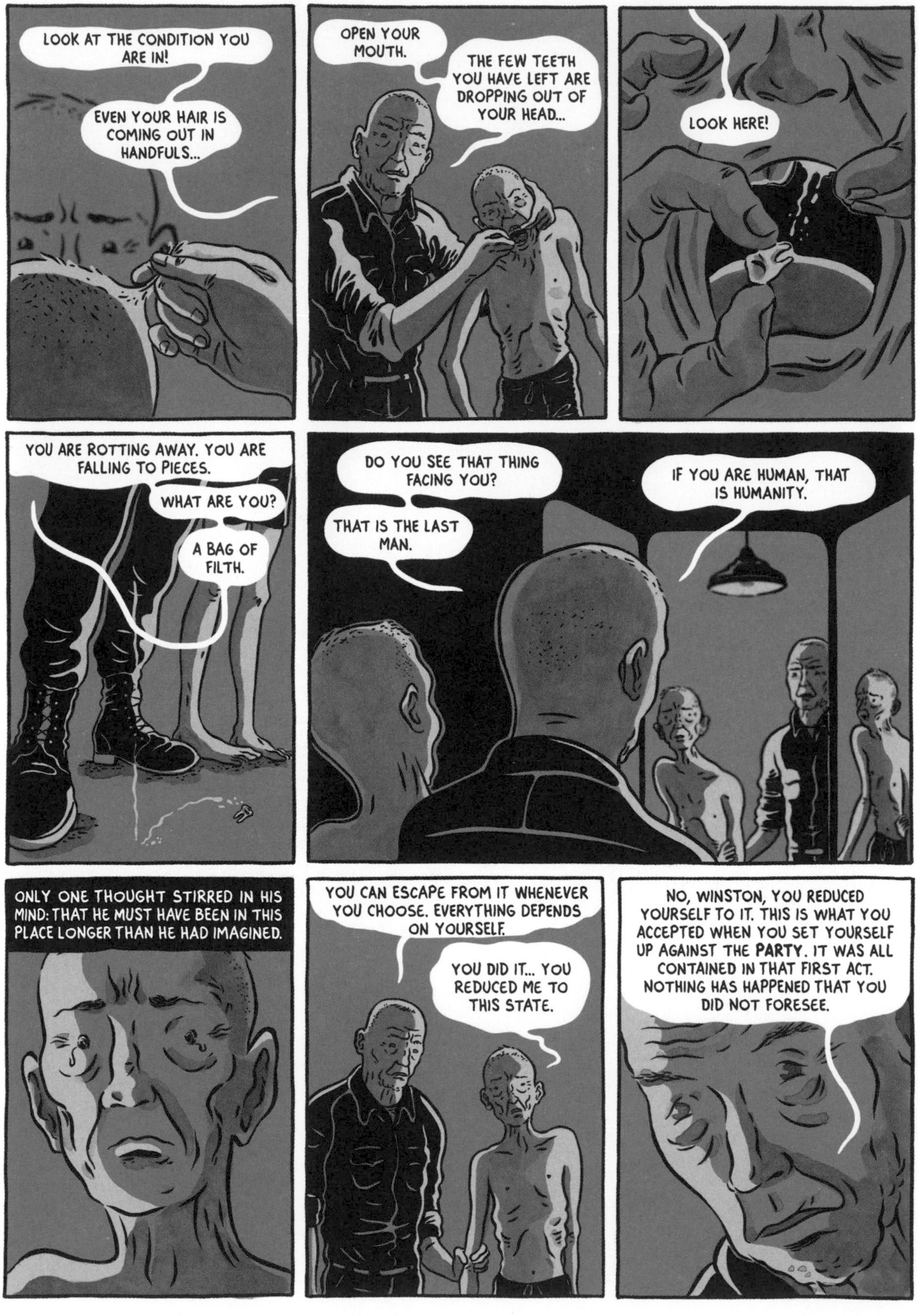

LOOK AT THE CONDITION YOU ARE IN!
EVEN YOUR HAIR IS COMING OUT IN HANDFULS...
OPEN YOUR MOUTH.
THE FEW TEETH YOU HAVE LEFT ARE DROPPING OUT OF YOUR HEAD...
LOOK HERE!
YOU ARE ROTTING AWAY. YOU ARE FALLING TO PIECES.
WHAT ARE YOU?
A BAG OF FILTH.
DO YOU SEE THAT THING FACING YOU?
THAT IS THE LAST MAN.
IF YOU ARE HUMAN, THAT IS HUMANITY.
ONLY ONE THOUGHT STIRRED IN HIS MIND: THAT HE MUST HAVE BEEN IN THIS PLACE LONGER THAN HE HAD IMAGINED.
YOU CAN ESCAPE FROM IT WHENEVER YOU CHOOSE. EVERYTHING DEPENDS ON YOURSELF.
YOU DID IT... YOU REDUCED ME TO THIS STATE.
NO, WINSTON, YOU REDUCED YOURSELF TO IT. THIS IS WHAT YOU ACCEPTED WHEN YOU SET YOURSELF UP AGAINST THE PARTY. IT WAS ALL CONTAINED IN THAT FIRST ACT. NOTHING HAS HAPPENED THAT YOU DID NOT FORESEE.

WE HAVE BEATEN YOU, WINSTON. WE HAVE BROKEN YOU UP. I DO NOT THINK THERE CAN BE MUCH PRIDE LEFT IN YOU. YOU HAVE BEEN KICKED AND FLOGGED AND INSULTED, YOU HAVE SCREAMED WITH PAIN, YOU HAVE ROLLED ON THE FLOOR IN YOUR OWN BLOOD AND VOMIT. YOU HAVE WHIMPERED FOR MERCY, YOU HAVE BETRAYED EVERYBODY AND EVERYTHING.

CAN YOU THINK OF A SINGLE DEGRADATION THAT HAS NOT HAPPENED TO YOU?

I HAVE NOT BETRAYED JULIA.

NO; THAT IS PERFECTLY TRUE.

YOU HAVE NOT BETRAYED JULIA.

NEVER DID O'BRIEN FAIL TO UNDERSTAND WHAT WAS SAID TO HIM. ANYONE ELSE ON EARTH WOULD HAVE ANSWERED PROMPTLY THAT HE HAD BETRAYED JULIA.

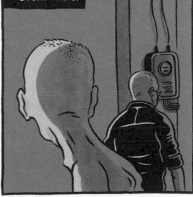

FOR WHAT WAS THERE THAT THEY HAD NOT SCREWED OUT OF HIM UNDER THE TORTURE? HE HAD TOLD THEM EVERYTHING HE KNEW ABOUT HER, HER HABITS, HER CHARACTER, THEIR MEETINGS, THEIR VAGUE PLOTTINGS AGAINST THE **PARTY** — EVERYTHING.

AND YET, IN THE SENSE IN WHICH HE INTENDED THE WORD, HE HAD NOT BETRAYED HER.

HIS FEELING TOWARDS HER HAD REMAINED THE SAME.

O'BRIEN HAD SEEN WHAT HE MEANT WITHOUT THE NEED FOR EXPLANATION.

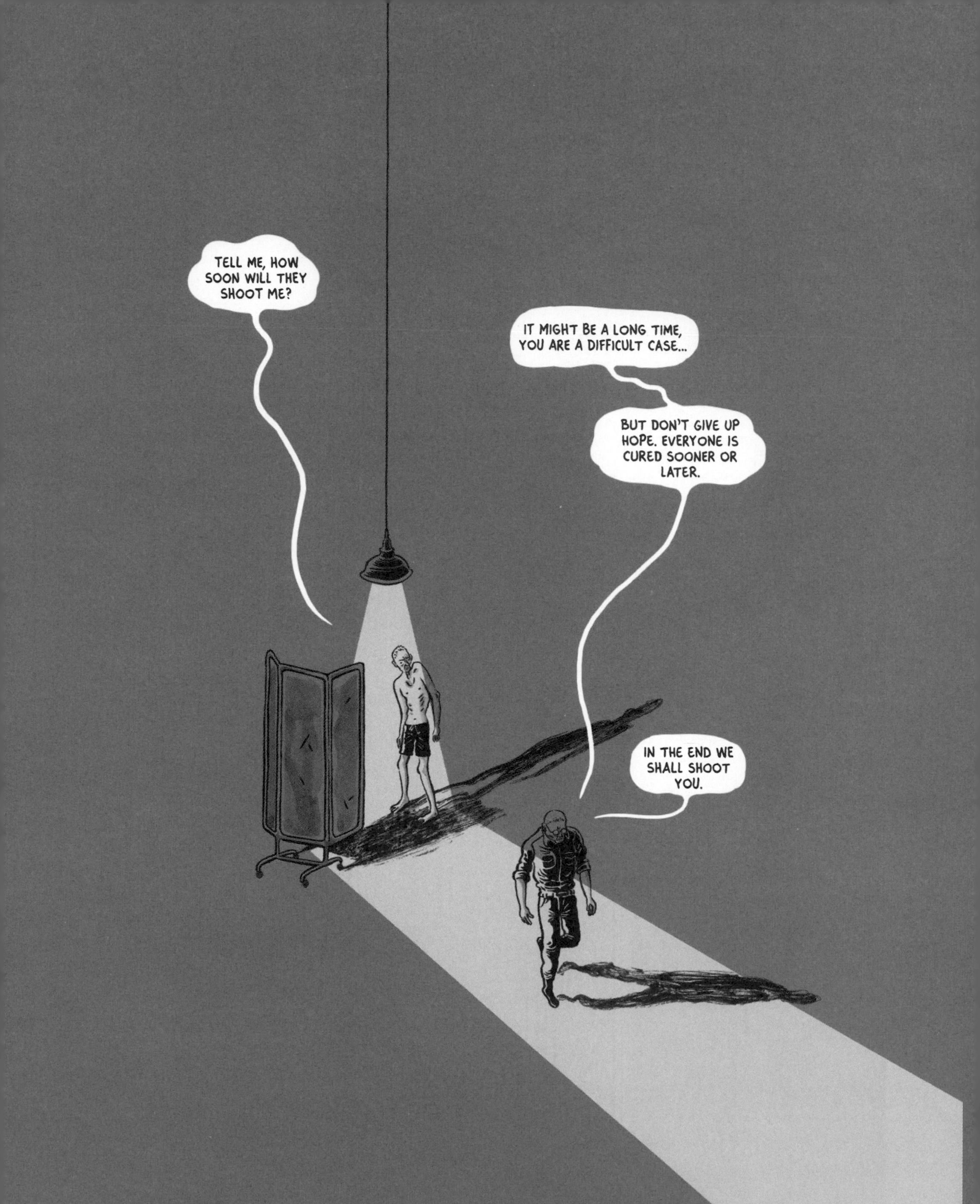
TELL ME, HOW SOON WILL THEY SHOOT ME?
IT MIGHT BE A LONG TIME, YOU ARE A DIFFICULT CASE...
BUT DON'T GIVE UP HOPE. EVERYONE IS CURED SOONER OR LATER.
IN THE END WE SHALL SHOOT YOU.

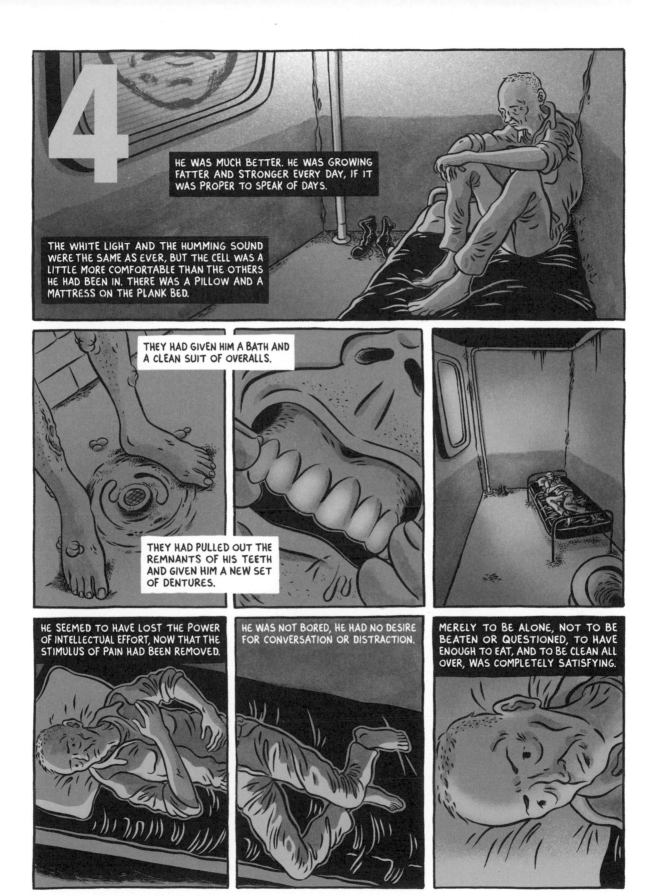

4

HE WAS MUCH BETTER. HE WAS GROWING FATTER AND STRONGER EVERY DAY, IF IT WAS PROPER TO SPEAK OF DAYS.

THE WHITE LIGHT AND THE HUMMING SOUND WERE THE SAME AS EVER, BUT THE CELL WAS A LITTLE MORE COMFORTABLE THAN THE OTHERS HE HAD BEEN IN. THERE WAS A PILLOW AND A MATTRESS ON THE PLANK BED.

THEY HAD GIVEN HIM A BATH AND A CLEAN SUIT OF OVERALLS.

THEY HAD PULLED OUT THE REMNANTS OF HIS TEETH AND GIVEN HIM A NEW SET OF DENTURES.

HE SEEMED TO HAVE LOST THE POWER OF INTELLECTUAL EFFORT, NOW THAT THE STIMULUS OF PAIN HAD BEEN REMOVED.

HE WAS NOT BORED, HE HAD NO DESIRE FOR CONVERSATION OR DISTRACTION.

MERELY TO BE ALONE, NOT TO BE BEATEN OR QUESTIONED, TO HAVE ENOUGH TO EAT, AND TO BE CLEAN ALL OVER, WAS COMPLETELY SATISFYING.

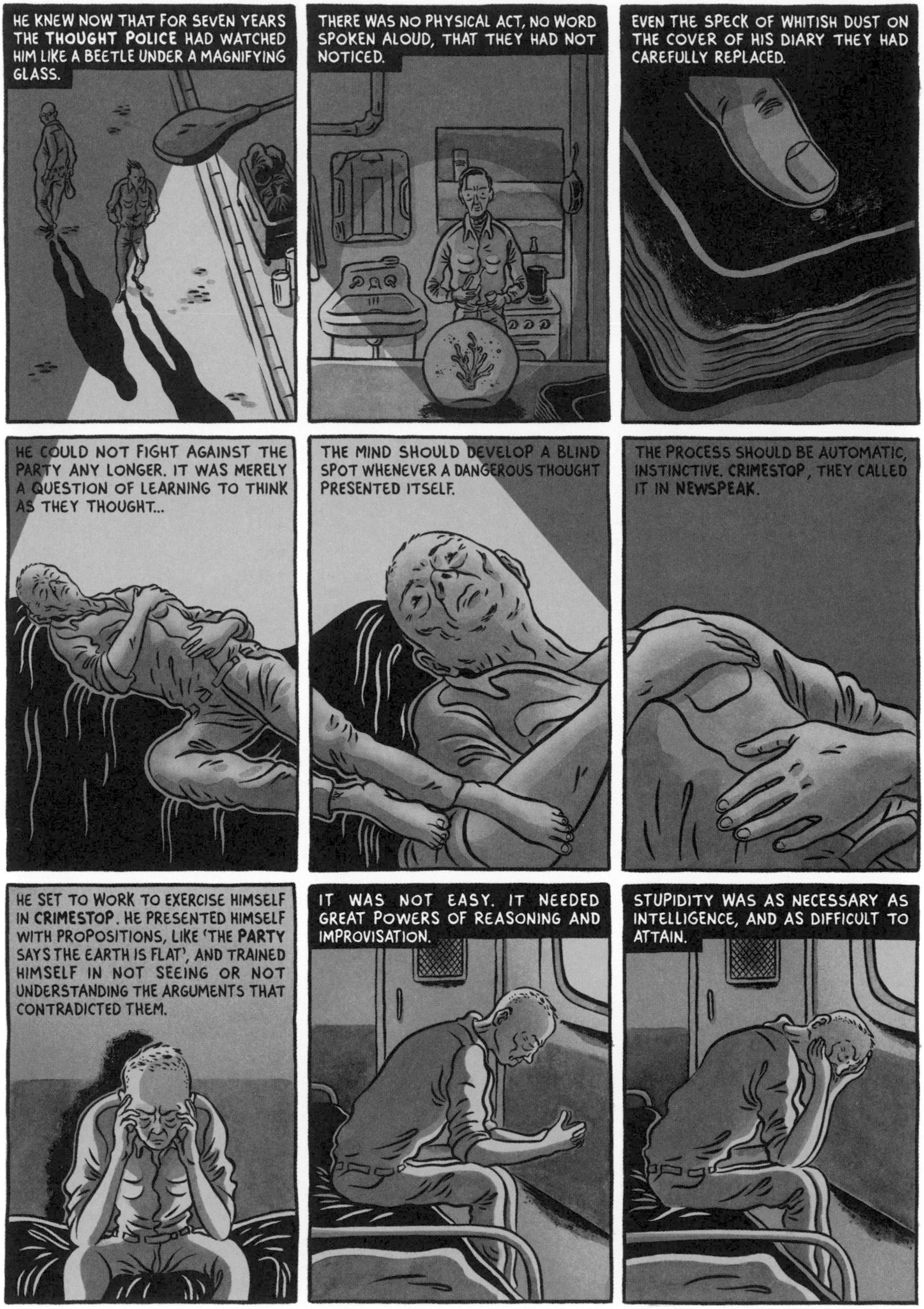
HE KNEW NOW THAT FOR SEVEN YEARS THE THOUGHT POLICE HAD WATCHED HIM LIKE A BEETLE UNDER A MAGNIFYING GLASS.
THERE WAS NO PHYSICAL ACT, NO WORD SPOKEN ALOUD, THAT THEY HAD NOT NOTICED.
EVEN THE SPECK OF WHITISH DUST ON THE COVER OF HIS DIARY THEY HAD CAREFULLY REPLACED.
HE COULD NOT FIGHT AGAINST THE PARTY ANY LONGER. IT WAS MERELY A QUESTION OF LEARNING TO THINK AS THEY THOUGHT...
THE MIND SHOULD DEVELOP A BLIND SPOT WHENEVER A DANGEROUS THOUGHT PRESENTED ITSELF.
THE PROCESS SHOULD BE AUTOMATIC, INSTINCTIVE. CRIMESTOP, THEY CALLED IT IN NEWSPEAK.
HE SET TO WORK TO EXERCISE HIMSELF IN CRIMESTOP. HE PRESENTED HIMSELF WITH PROPOSITIONS, LIKE 'THE PARTY SAYS THE EARTH IS FLAT', AND TRAINED HIMSELF IN NOT SEEING OR NOT UNDERSTANDING THE ARGUMENTS THAT CONTRADICTED THEM.
IT WAS NOT EASY. IT NEEDED GREAT POWERS OF REASONING AND IMPROVISATION.
STUPIDITY WAS AS NECESSARY AS INTELLIGENCE, AND AS DIFFICULT TO ATTAIN.

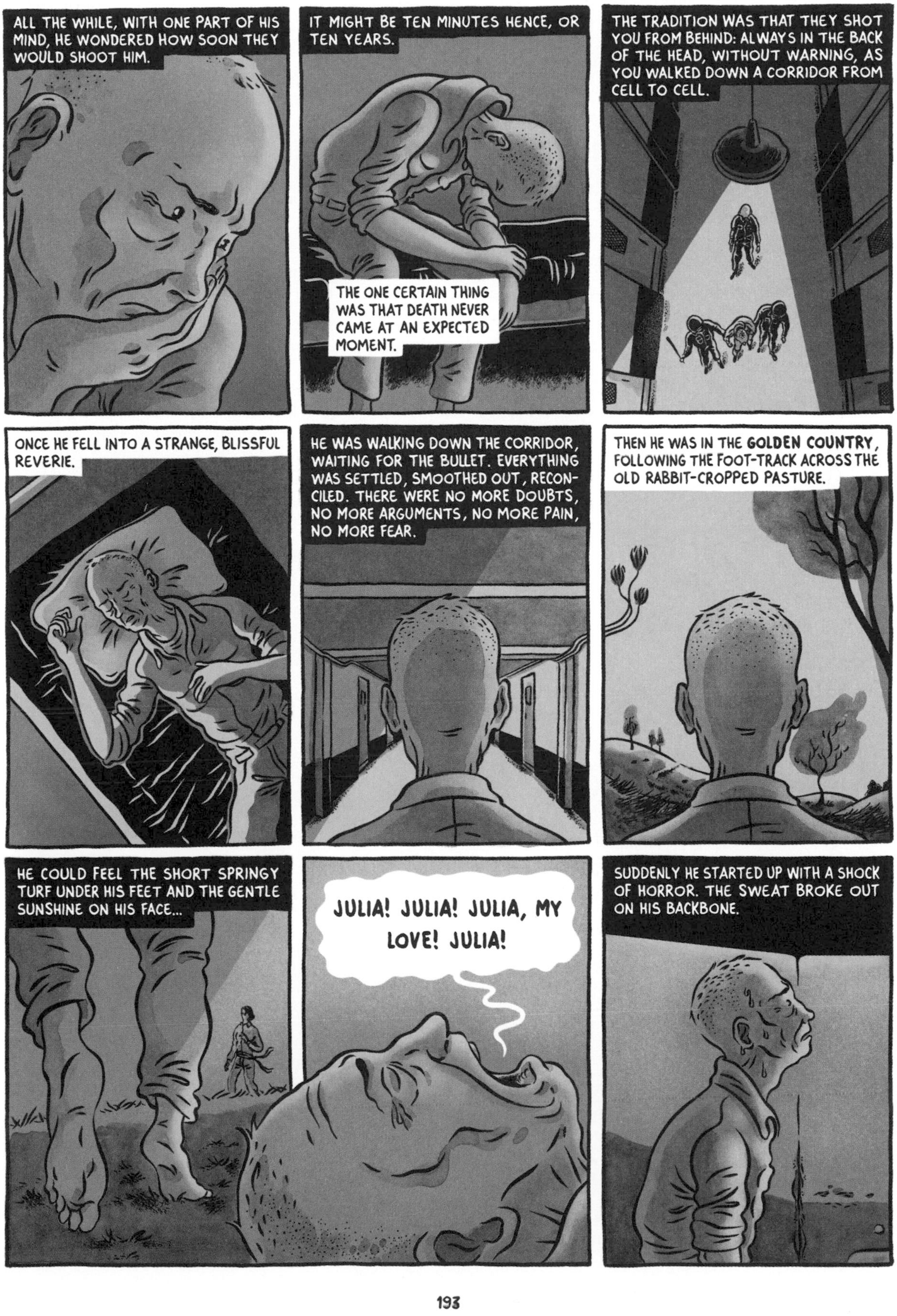
ALL THE WHILE, WITH ONE PART OF HIS MIND, HE WONDERED HOW SOON THEY WOULD SHOOT HIM.
IT MIGHT BE TEN MINUTES HENCE, OR TEN YEARS.
THE ONE CERTAIN THING WAS THAT DEATH NEVER CAME AT AN EXPECTED MOMENT.
THE TRADITION WAS THAT THEY SHOT YOU FROM BEHIND: ALWAYS IN THE BACK OF THE HEAD, WITHOUT WARNING, AS YOU WALKED DOWN A CORRIDOR FROM CELL TO CELL.
ONCE HE FELL INTO A STRANGE, BLISSFUL REVERIE.
HE WAS WALKING DOWN THE CORRIDOR, WAITING FOR THE BULLET. EVERYTHING WAS SETTLED, SMOOTHED OUT, RECONCILED. THERE WERE NO MORE DOUBTS, NO MORE ARGUMENTS, NO MORE PAIN, NO MORE FEAR.
THEN HE WAS IN THE GOLDEN COUNTRY, FOLLOWING THE FOOT-TRACK ACROSS THE OLD RABBIT-CROPPED PASTURE.
HE COULD FEEL THE SHORT SPRINGY TURF UNDER HIS FEET AND THE GENTLE SUNSHINE ON HIS FACE...
JULIA! JULIA! JULIA, MY LOVE! JULIA!
SUDDENLY HE STARTED UP WITH A SHOCK OF HORROR. THE SWEAT BROKE OUT ON HIS BACKBONE.

FOR A MOMENT HE HAD HAD AN OVERWHELMING HALLUCINATION OF HER PRESENCE. SHE HAD SEEMED TO BE NOT MERELY WITH HIM, BUT INSIDE HIM. IN THAT MOMENT HE HAD LOVED HER FAR MORE THAN HE HAD EVER DONE WHEN THEY WERE TOGETHER AND FREE.

ALSO HE KNEW THAT SOMEWHERE OR OTHER SHE WAS STILL ALIVE AND NEEDED HIS HELP.

HE TRIED TO COMPOSE HIMSELF. WHAT HAD HE DONE? HOW MANY YEARS HAD HE ADDED TO HIS SERVITUDE BY THAT MOMENT OF WEAKNESS?

THEY WOULD KNOW NOW THAT HE WAS BREAKING THE AGREEMENT HE HAD MADE WITH THEM. HE OBEYED THE **PARTY**, BUT HE STILL HATED THE **PARTY**.

IN THE OLD DAYS HE HAD HIDDEN A HERETICAL MIND BENEATH AN APPEARANCE OF CONFORMITY. NOW HE HAD RETREATED A STEP FURTHER: IN THE MIND HE HAD SURRENDERED, BUT HE HAD HOPED TO KEEP THE INNER HEART INVIOLATE.

THEY WOULD UNDERSTAND THAT — O'BRIEN WOULD UNDERSTAND IT. IT WAS ALL CONFESSED IN THAT SINGLE FOOLISH CRY.

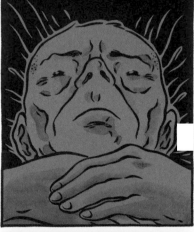

FOR THE FIRST TIME HE PERCEIVED THAT IF YOU WANT TO KEEP A SECRET YOU MUST ALSO HIDE IT FROM YOURSELF.

FROM NOW ONWARDS HE MUST NOT ONLY THINK RIGHT; HE MUST FEEL RIGHT, DREAM RIGHT.

AND ALL THE WHILE HE MUST KEEP HIS HATRED LOCKED UP INSIDE HIM.

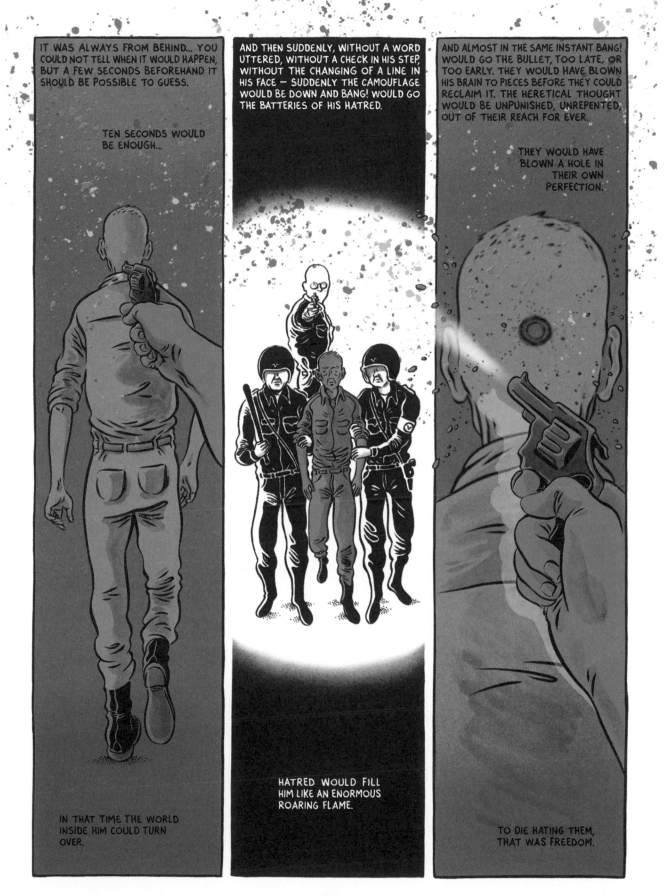

IT WAS ALWAYS FROM BEHIND... YOU COULD NOT TELL WHEN IT WOULD HAPPEN, BUT A FEW SECONDS BEFOREHAND IT SHOULD BE POSSIBLE TO GUESS.

TEN SECONDS WOULD BE ENOUGH...

IN THAT TIME THE WORLD INSIDE HIM COULD TURN OVER.

AND THEN SUDDENLY, WITHOUT A WORD UTTERED, WITHOUT A CHECK IN HIS STEP, WITHOUT THE CHANGING OF A LINE IN HIS FACE — SUDDENLY THE CAMOUFLAGE WOULD BE DOWN AND BANG! WOULD GO THE BATTERIES OF HIS HATRED.

HATRED WOULD FILL HIM LIKE AN ENORMOUS ROARING FLAME.

AND ALMOST IN THE SAME INSTANT BANG! WOULD GO THE BULLET, TOO LATE, OR TOO EARLY. THEY WOULD HAVE BLOWN HIS BRAIN TO PIECES BEFORE THEY COULD RECLAIM IT. THE HERETICAL THOUGHT WOULD BE UNPUNISHED, UNREPENTED, OUT OF THEIR REACH FOR EVER.

THEY WOULD HAVE BLOWN A HOLE IN THEIR OWN PERFECTION.

TO DIE HATING THEM, THAT WAS FREEDOM.

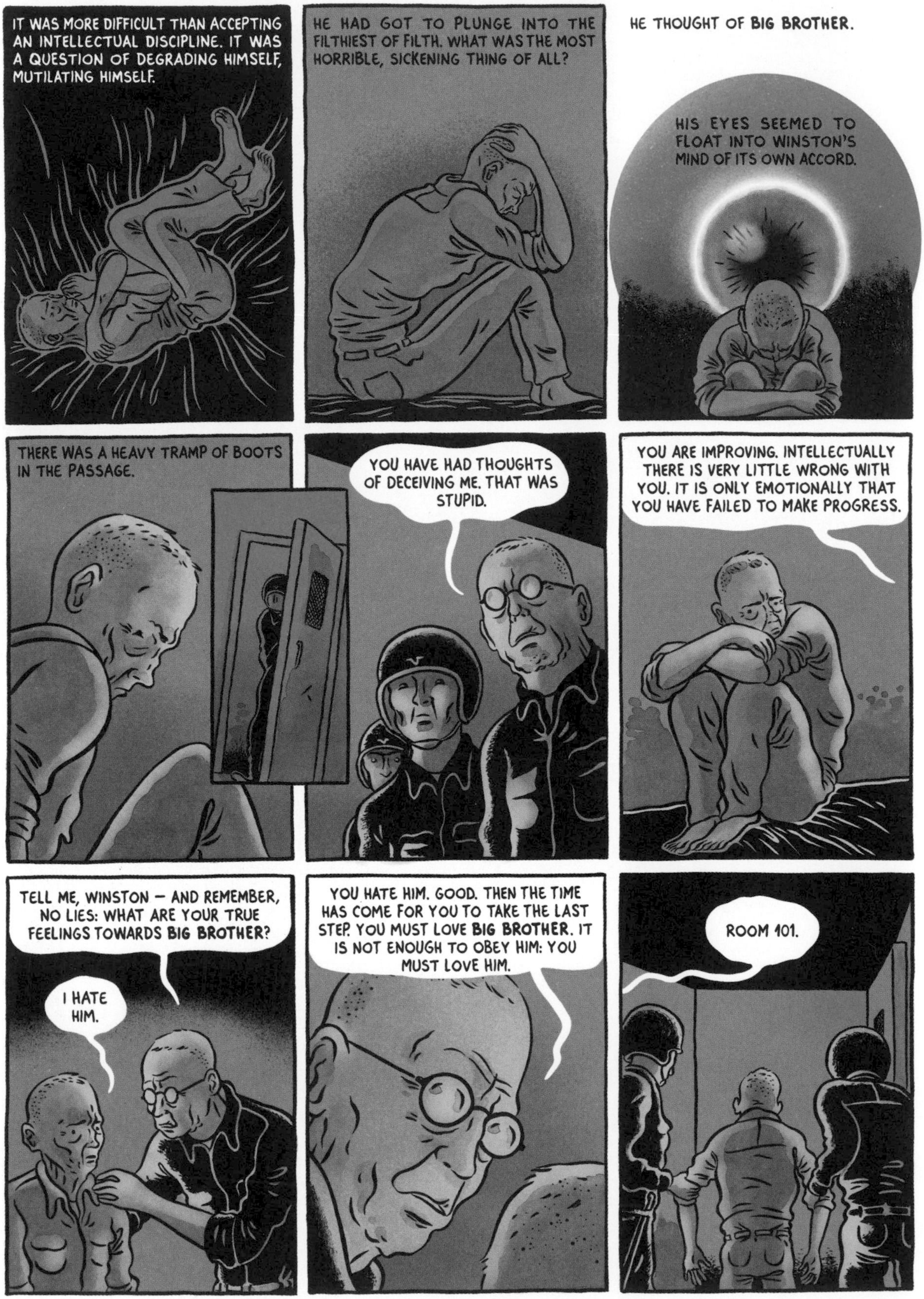
IT WAS MORE DIFFICULT THAN ACCEPTING AN INTELLECTUAL DISCIPLINE. IT WAS A QUESTION OF DEGRADING HIMSELF, MUTILATING HIMSELF.
HE HAD GOT TO PLUNGE INTO THE FILTHIEST OF FILTH. WHAT WAS THE MOST HORRIBLE, SICKENING THING OF ALL?
HE THOUGHT OF BIG BROTHER.
HIS EYES SEEMED TO FLOAT INTO WINSTON'S MIND OF ITS OWN ACCORD.
THERE WAS A HEAVY TRAMP OF BOOTS IN THE PASSAGE.
YOU HAVE HAD THOUGHTS OF DECEIVING ME. THAT WAS STUPID.
YOU ARE IMPROVING. INTELLECTUALLY THERE IS VERY LITTLE WRONG WITH YOU. IT IS ONLY EMOTIONALLY THAT YOU HAVE FAILED TO MAKE PROGRESS.
TELL ME, WINSTON — AND REMEMBER, NO LIES: WHAT ARE YOUR TRUE FEELINGS TOWARDS BIG BROTHER?
I HATE HIM.
YOU HATE HIM. GOOD. THEN THE TIME HAS COME FOR YOU TO TAKE THE LAST STEP. YOU MUST LOVE BIG BROTHER. IT IS NOT ENOUGH TO OBEY HIM: YOU MUST LOVE HIM.
ROOM 101.

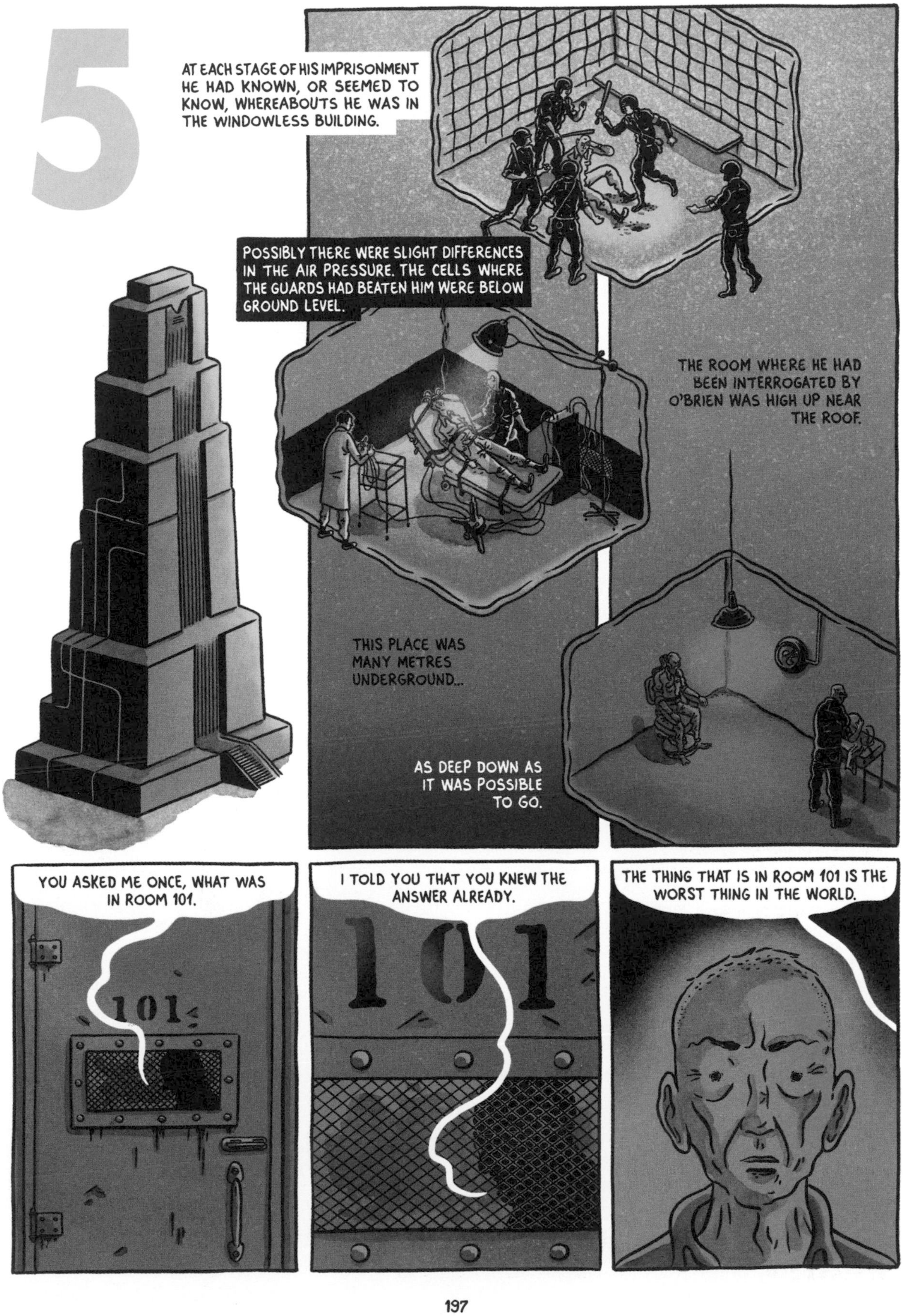
5
AT EACH STAGE OF HIS IMPRISONMENT HE HAD KNOWN, OR SEEMED TO KNOW, WHEREABOUTS HE WAS IN THE WINDOWLESS BUILDING.
POSSIBLY THERE WERE SLIGHT DIFFERENCES IN THE AIR PRESSURE. THE CELLS WHERE THE GUARDS HAD BEATEN HIM WERE BELOW GROUND LEVEL.
THE ROOM WHERE HE HAD BEEN INTERROGATED BY O'BRIEN WAS HIGH UP NEAR THE ROOF.
THIS PLACE WAS MANY METRES UNDERGROUND...
AS DEEP DOWN AS IT WAS POSSIBLE TO GO.
YOU ASKED ME ONCE, WHAT WAS IN ROOM 101.
101
I TOLD YOU THAT YOU KNEW THE ANSWER ALREADY.
101
THE THING THAT IS IN ROOM 101 IS THE WORST THING IN THE WORLD.

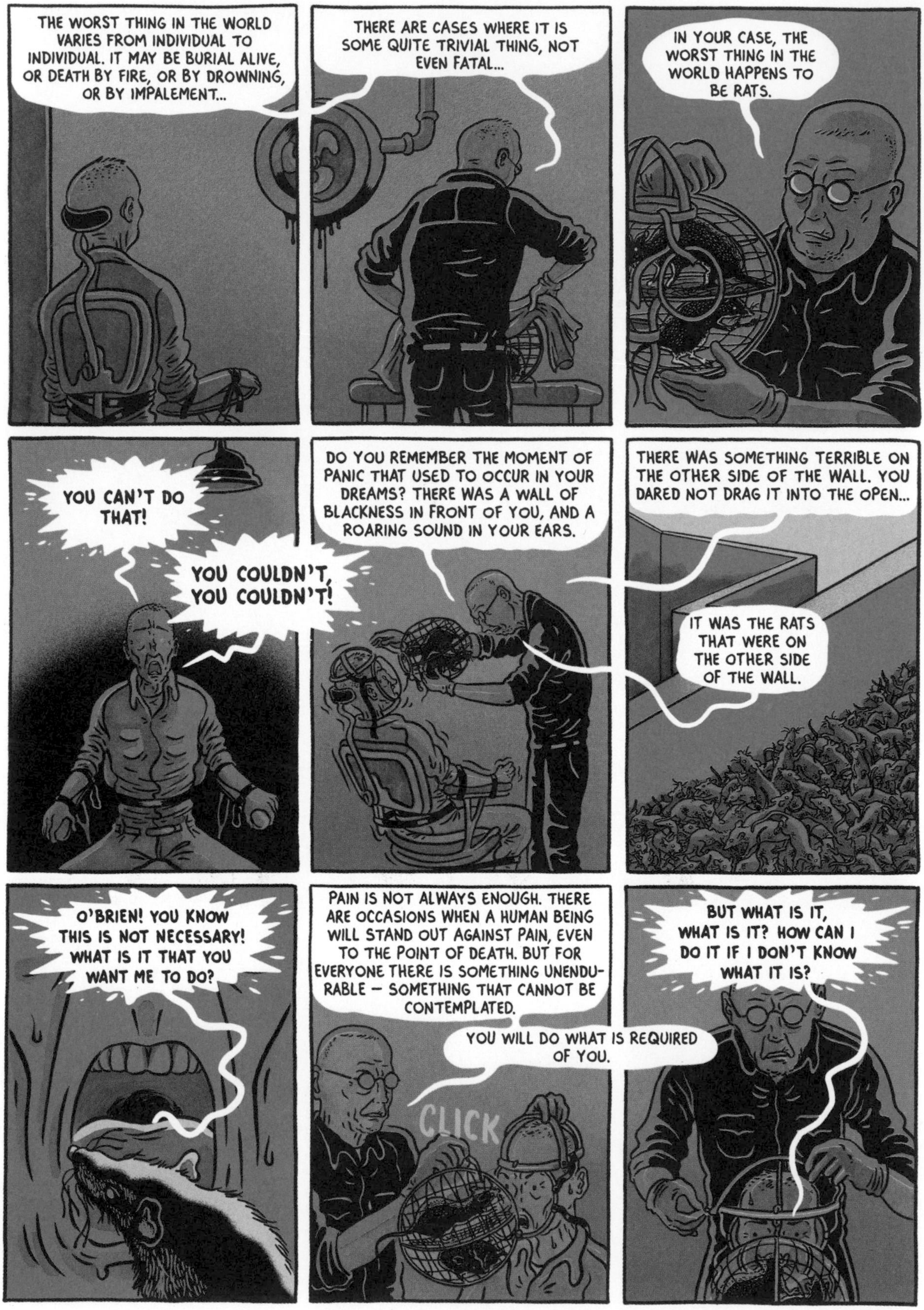
THE WORST THING IN THE WORLD VARIES FROM INDIVIDUAL TO INDIVIDUAL. IT MAY BE BURIAL ALIVE, OR DEATH BY FIRE, OR BY DROWNING, OR BY IMPALEMENT...
THERE ARE CASES WHERE IT IS SOME QUITE TRIVIAL THING, NOT EVEN FATAL...
IN YOUR CASE, THE WORST THING IN THE WORLD HAPPENS TO BE RATS.
YOU CAN'T DO THAT!
YOU COULDN'T, YOU COULDN'T!
DO YOU REMEMBER THE MOMENT OF PANIC THAT USED TO OCCUR IN YOUR DREAMS? THERE WAS A WALL OF BLACKNESS IN FRONT OF YOU, AND A ROARING SOUND IN YOUR EARS.
THERE WAS SOMETHING TERRIBLE ON THE OTHER SIDE OF THE WALL. YOU DARED NOT DRAG IT INTO THE OPEN...
IT WAS THE RATS THAT WERE ON THE OTHER SIDE OF THE WALL.
O'BRIEN! YOU KNOW THIS IS NOT NECESSARY! WHAT IS IT THAT YOU WANT ME TO DO?
PAIN IS NOT ALWAYS ENOUGH. THERE ARE OCCASIONS WHEN A HUMAN BEING WILL STAND OUT AGAINST PAIN, EVEN TO THE POINT OF DEATH. BUT FOR EVERYONE THERE IS SOMETHING UNENDURABLE — SOMETHING THAT CANNOT BE CONTEMPLATED.
YOU WILL DO WHAT IS REQUIRED OF YOU.
CLICK
BUT WHAT IS IT, WHAT IS IT? HOW CAN I DO IT IF I DON'T KNOW WHAT IT IS?

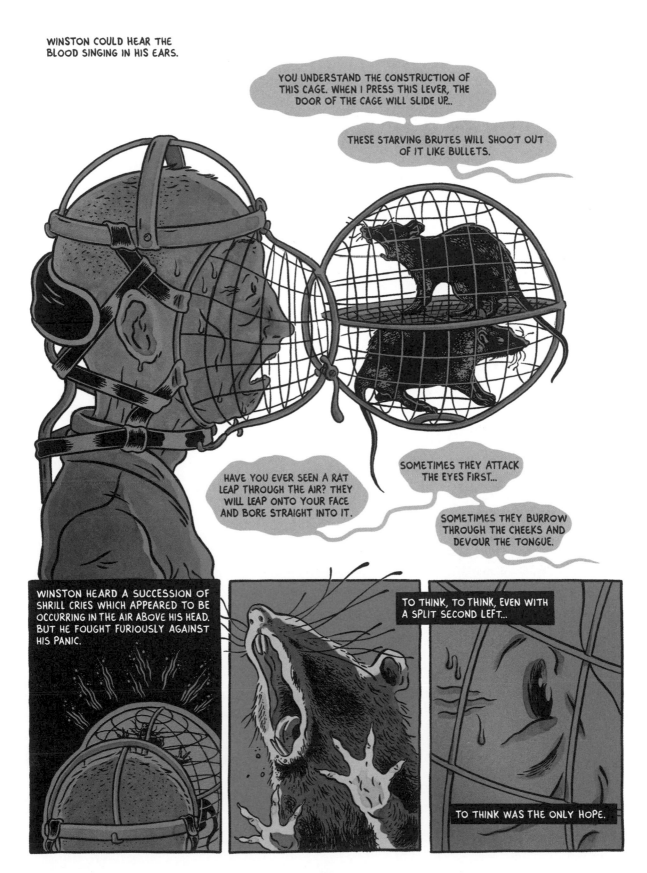

WINSTON COULD HEAR THE
BLOOD SINGING IN HIS EARS.

YOU UNDERSTAND THE CONSTRUCTION OF
THIS CAGE. WHEN I PRESS THIS LEVER, THE
DOOR OF THE CAGE WILL SLIDE UP...

THESE STARVING BRUTES WILL SHOOT OUT
OF IT LIKE BULLETS.

HAVE YOU EVER SEEN A RAT
LEAP THROUGH THE AIR? THEY
WILL LEAP ONTO YOUR FACE
AND BORE STRAIGHT INTO IT.

SOMETIMES THEY ATTACK
THE EYES FIRST...

SOMETIMES THEY BURROW
THROUGH THE CHEEKS AND
DEVOUR THE TONGUE.

WINSTON HEARD A SUCCESSION OF
SHRILL CRIES WHICH APPEARED TO BE
OCCURRING IN THE AIR ABOVE HIS HEAD.
BUT HE FOUGHT FURIOUSLY AGAINST
HIS PANIC.

TO THINK, TO THINK, EVEN WITH
A SPLIT SECOND LEFT...

TO THINK WAS THE ONLY HOPE.

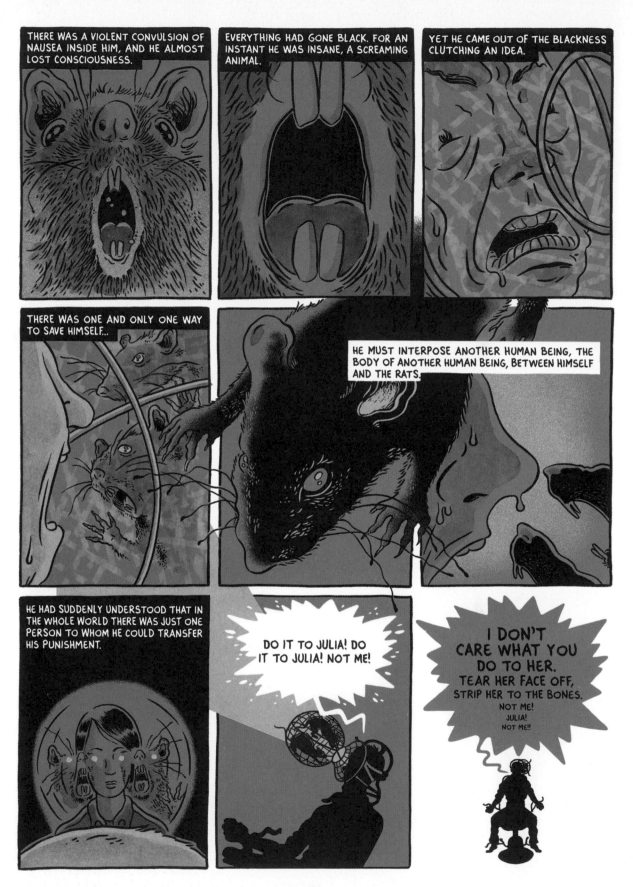

THERE WAS A VIOLENT CONVULSION OF NAUSEA INSIDE HIM, AND HE ALMOST LOST CONSCIOUSNESS.

EVERYTHING HAD GONE BLACK. FOR AN INSTANT HE WAS INSANE, A SCREAMING ANIMAL.

YET HE CAME OUT OF THE BLACKNESS CLUTCHING AN IDEA.

THERE WAS ONE AND ONLY ONE WAY TO SAVE HIMSELF...

HE MUST INTERPOSE ANOTHER HUMAN BEING, THE BODY OF ANOTHER HUMAN BEING, BETWEEN HIMSELF AND THE RATS.

HE HAD SUDDENLY UNDERSTOOD THAT IN THE WHOLE WORLD THERE WAS JUST ONE PERSON TO WHOM HE COULD TRANSFER HIS PUNISHMENT.

DO IT TO JULIA! DO IT TO JULIA! NOT ME!

I DON'T CARE WHAT YOU DO TO HER. TEAR HER FACE OFF, STRIP HER TO THE BONES. NOT ME! JULIA! NOT ME!!

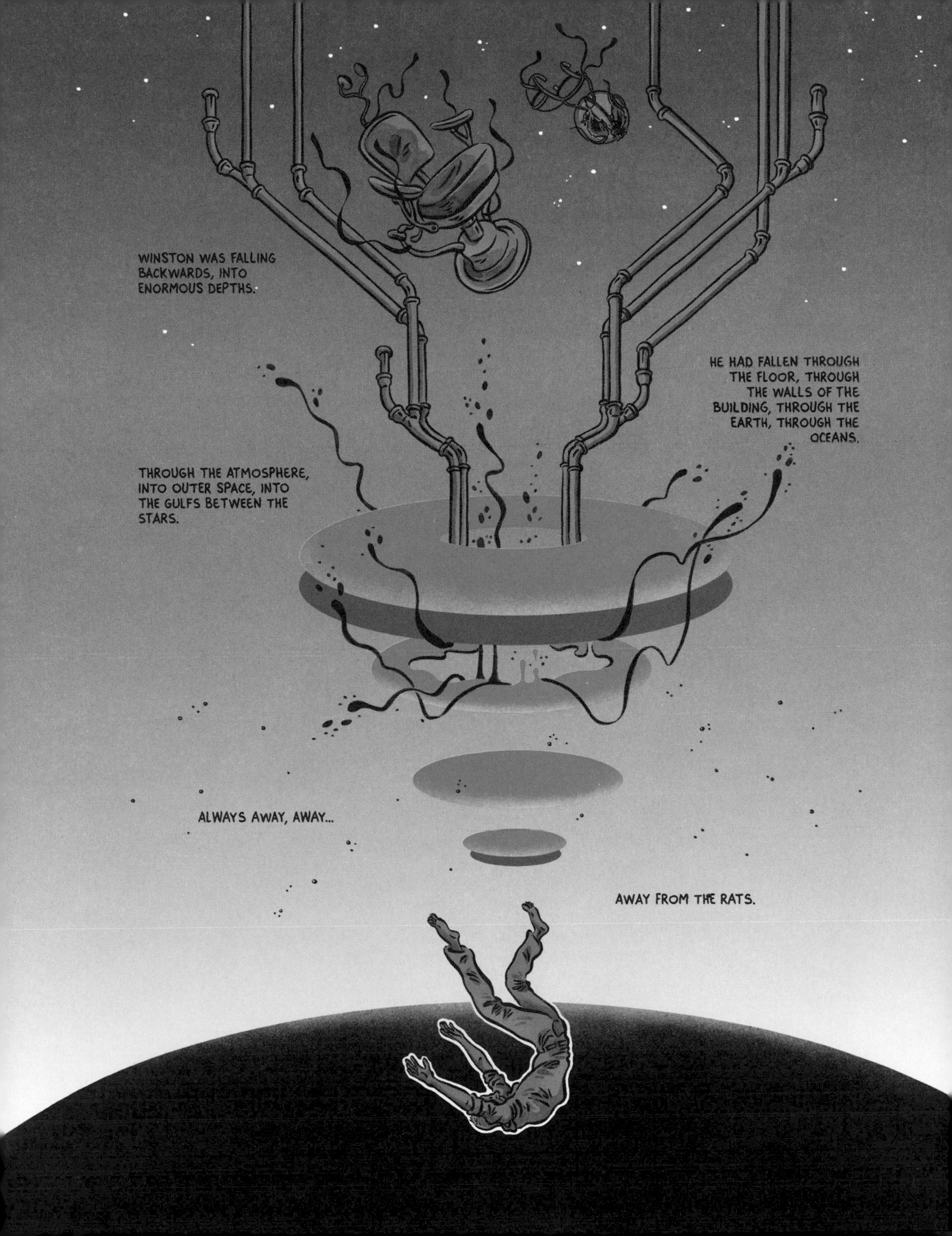
WINSTON WAS FALLING BACKWARDS, INTO ENORMOUS DEPTHS.
HE HAD FALLEN THROUGH THE FLOOR, THROUGH THE WALLS OF THE BUILDING, THROUGH THE EARTH, THROUGH THE OCEANS.
THROUGH THE ATMOSPHERE, INTO OUTER SPACE, INTO THE GULFS BETWEEN THE STARS.
ALWAYS AWAY, AWAY...
AWAY FROM THE RATS.

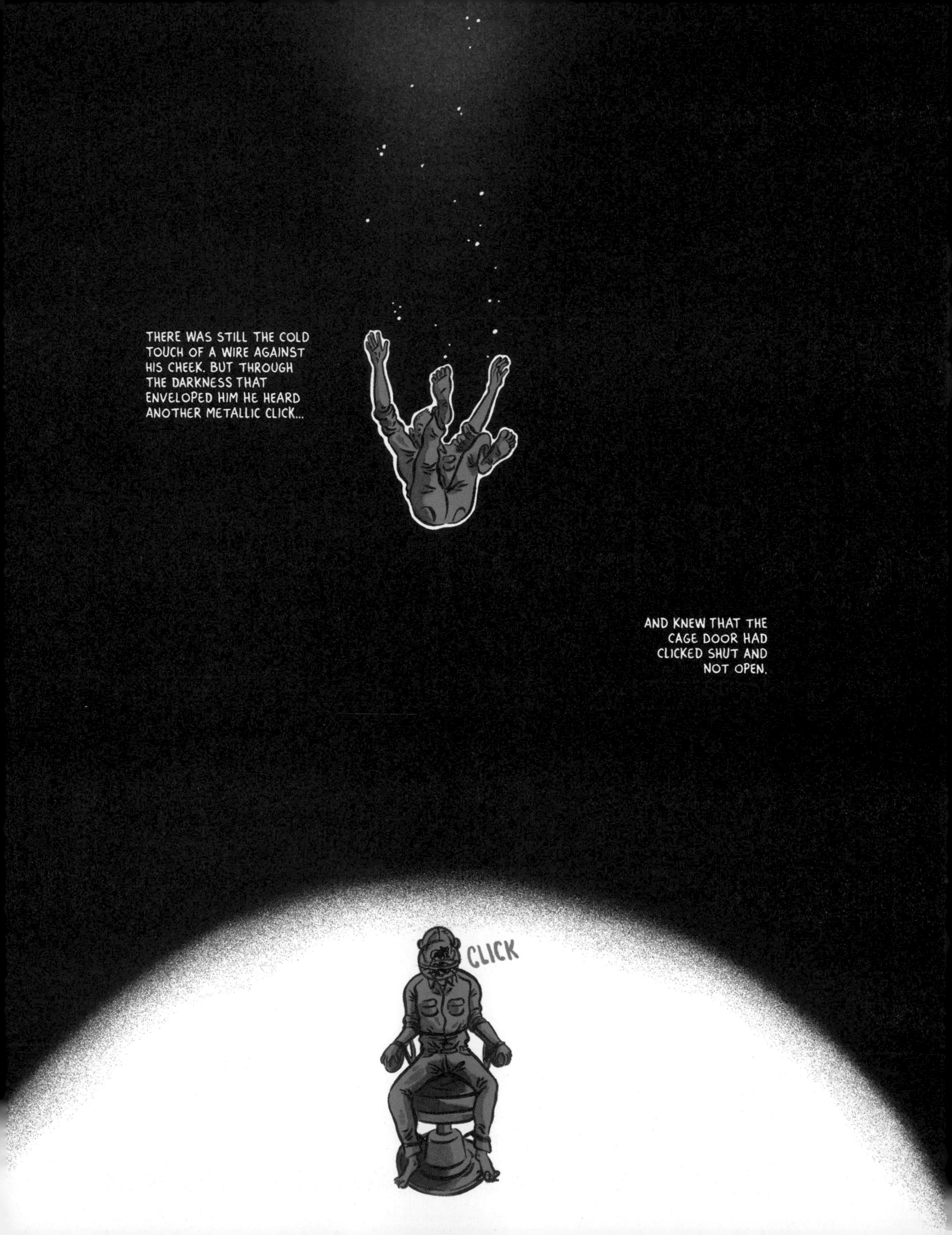
THERE WAS STILL THE COLD TOUCH OF A WIRE AGAINST HIS CHEEK. BUT THROUGH THE DARKNESS THAT ENVELOPED HIM HE HEARD ANOTHER METALLIC CLICK...
AND KNEW THAT THE CAGE DOOR HAD CLICKED SHUT AND NOT OPEN.
CLICK

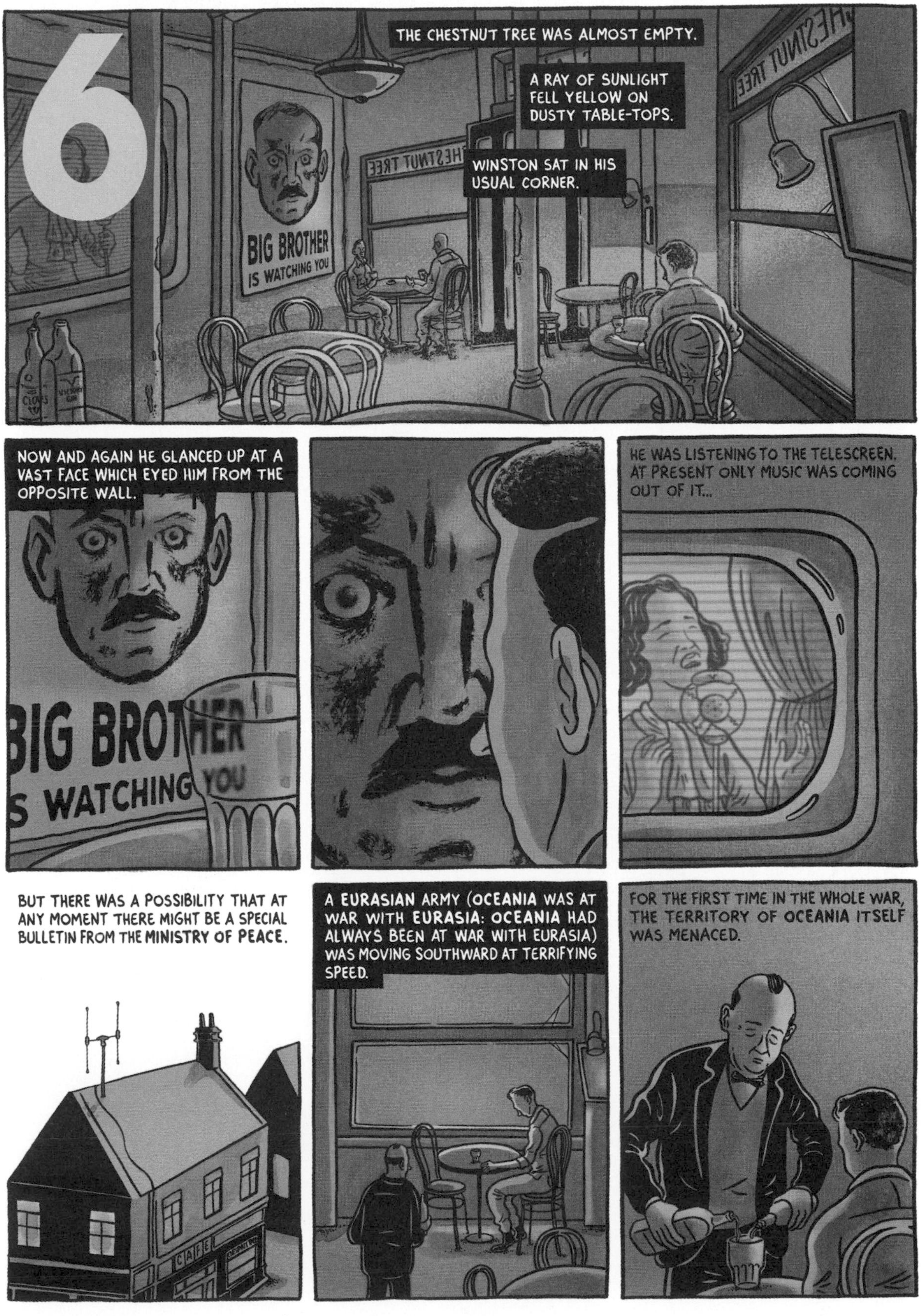
6
THE CHESTNUT TREE WAS ALMOST EMPTY.
A RAY OF SUNLIGHT FELL YELLOW ON DUSTY TABLE-TOPS.
WINSTON SAT IN HIS USUAL CORNER.
BIG BROTHER IS WATCHING YOU
CHESTNUT TREE
NOW AND AGAIN HE GLANCED UP AT A VAST FACE WHICH EYED HIM FROM THE OPPOSITE WALL.
BIG BROTHER IS WATCHING YOU
HE WAS LISTENING TO THE TELESCREEN. AT PRESENT ONLY MUSIC WAS COMING OUT OF IT...
BUT THERE WAS A POSSIBILITY THAT AT ANY MOMENT THERE MIGHT BE A SPECIAL BULLETIN FROM THE MINISTRY OF PEACE.
CAFE
A EURASIAN ARMY (OCEANIA WAS AT WAR WITH EURASIA: OCEANIA HAD ALWAYS BEEN AT WAR WITH EURASIA) WAS MOVING SOUTHWARD AT TERRIFYING SPEED.
FOR THE FIRST TIME IN THE WHOLE WAR, THE TERRITORY OF OCEANIA ITSELF WAS MENACED.

WINSTON STOPPED THINKING ABOUT THE WAR. IN THESE DAYS HE COULD NEVER FIX HIS MIND ON ANY ONE SUBJECT FOR MORE THAN A FEW MOMENTS AT A TIME.

AS ALWAYS, THE GIN MADE HIM SHUDDER AND EVEN RETCH SLIGHTLY.

THE SMELL OF GIN, WHICH DWELT WITH HIM NIGHT AND DAY, WAS INEXTRICABLY MIXED UP IN HIS MIND WITH THE SMELL OF THOSE...

HE NEVER NAMED THEM, EVEN IN HIS THOUGHTS, AND SO FAR AS IT WAS POSSIBLE HE NEVER VISUALISED THEM. THEY WERE SOMETHING THAT HE WAS HALF AWARE OF, HOVERING CLOSE TO HIS FACE, A SMELL THAT CLUNG TO HIS NOSTRILS.

HE NEVER EVEN BOTHERED TO COUNT HIS DRINKS. HE HAD ALWAYS PLENTY OF MONEY NOWADAYS.

VICTORY GIN

HE HAD BEEN APPOINTED TO A SUB-COMMITTEE OF A SUB-COMMITTEE WHICH HAD SPROUTED FROM ONE OF THE INNUMERABLE COMMITTEES DEALING WITH MINOR DIFFICULTIES THAT AROSE IN THE COMPILATION OF THE ELEVENTH EDITION OF THE NEWSPEAK DICTIONARY.

THEY WERE ENGAGED IN PRODUCING SOMETHING CALLED AN **INTERIM REPORT**. IT WAS SOMETHING TO DO WITH THE QUESTION OF WHETHER COMMAS SHOULD BE PLACED INSIDE BRACKETS, OR OUTSIDE.

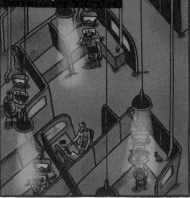

THERE WAS NO NEED TO GIVE ORDERS, THE WAITERS KNEW HIS HABITS. THE CHESSBOARD WAS ALWAYS WAITING FOR HIM, HIS CORNER TABLE WAS ALWAYS RESERVED.

ALWAYS, WITHOUT EXCEPTION, IT IS SO ARRANGED. IN NO CHESS PROBLEM SINCE THE BEGINNING OF THE WORLD HAS BLACK EVER WON.

DID IT NOT SYMBOLISE THE ETERNAL, UNVARYING TRIUMPH OF GOOD OVER EVIL?

BIG BROTHER IS WATCHING

WHITE ALWAYS MATES.

'THEY CAN'T GET INSIDE YOU,' JULIA HAD SAID...

BUT THEY COULD GET INSIDE YOU.

'WHAT HAPPENS TO YOU HERE IS FOR EVER,' O'BRIEN HAD SAID.

THAT WAS A TRUE WORD. THERE WERE THINGS, YOUR OWN ACTS, FROM WHICH YOU COULD NOT RECOVER.

SOMETHING WAS KILLED IN YOUR BREAST: BURNT OUT, CAUTERISED OUT.

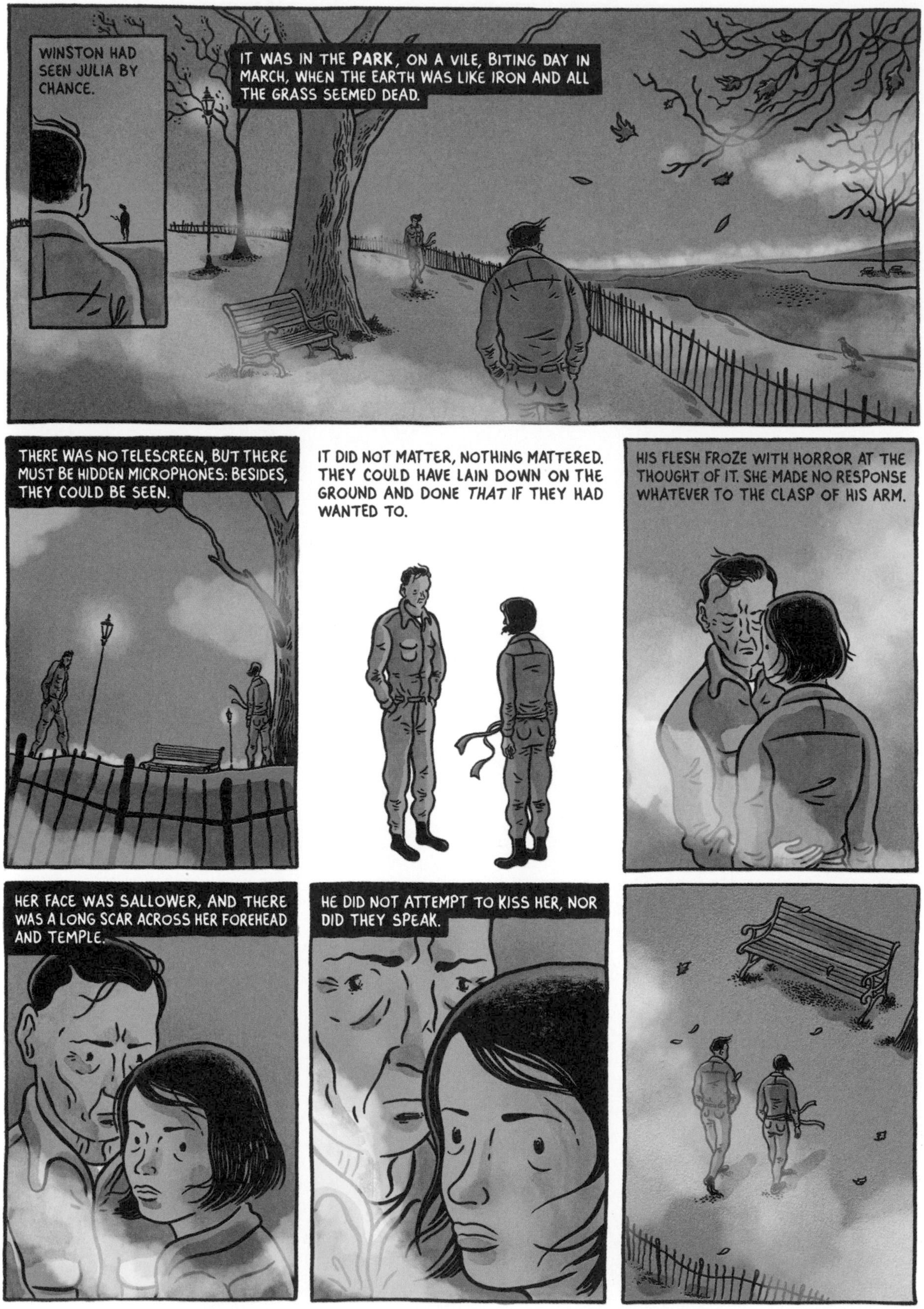
WINSTON HAD SEEN JULIA BY CHANCE.
IT WAS IN THE PARK, ON A VILE, BITING DAY IN MARCH, WHEN THE EARTH WAS LIKE IRON AND ALL THE GRASS SEEMED DEAD.
THERE WAS NO TELESCREEN, BUT THERE MUST BE HIDDEN MICROPHONES: BESIDES, THEY COULD BE SEEN.
IT DID NOT MATTER, NOTHING MATTERED. THEY COULD HAVE LAIN DOWN ON THE GROUND AND DONE THAT IF THEY HAD WANTED TO.
HIS FLESH FROZE WITH HORROR AT THE THOUGHT OF IT. SHE MADE NO RESPONSE WHATEVER TO THE CLASP OF HIS ARM.
HER FACE WAS SALLOWER, AND THERE WAS A LONG SCAR ACROSS HER FOREHEAD AND TEMPLE.
HE DID NOT ATTEMPT TO KISS HER, NOR DID THEY SPEAK.

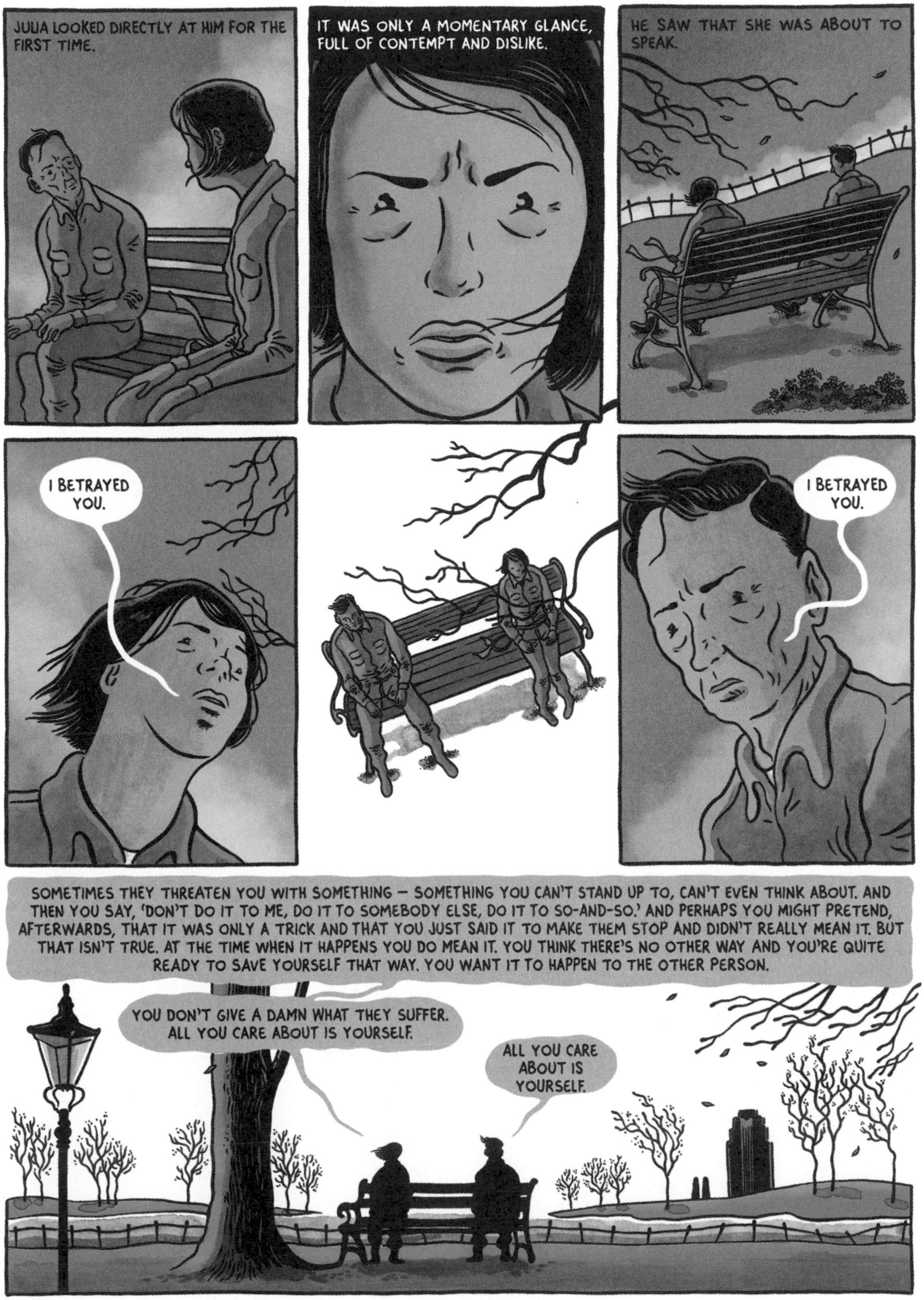
JULIA LOOKED DIRECTLY AT HIM FOR THE FIRST TIME.
IT WAS ONLY A MOMENTARY GLANCE, FULL OF CONTEMPT AND DISLIKE.
HE SAW THAT SHE WAS ABOUT TO SPEAK.
I BETRAYED YOU.
I BETRAYED YOU.
SOMETIMES THEY THREATEN YOU WITH SOMETHING – SOMETHING YOU CAN'T STAND UP TO, CAN'T EVEN THINK ABOUT. AND THEN YOU SAY, 'DON'T DO IT TO ME, DO IT TO SOMEBODY ELSE, DO IT TO SO-AND-SO.' AND PERHAPS YOU MIGHT PRETEND, AFTERWARDS, THAT IT WAS ONLY A TRICK AND THAT YOU JUST SAID IT TO MAKE THEM STOP AND DIDN'T REALLY MEAN IT. BUT THAT ISN'T TRUE. AT THE TIME WHEN IT HAPPENS YOU DO MEAN IT. YOU THINK THERE'S NO OTHER WAY AND YOU'RE QUITE READY TO SAVE YOURSELF THAT WAY. YOU WANT IT TO HAPPEN TO THE OTHER PERSON.
YOU DON'T GIVE A DAMN WHAT THEY SUFFER. ALL YOU CARE ABOUT IS YOURSELF.
ALL YOU CARE ABOUT IS YOURSELF.

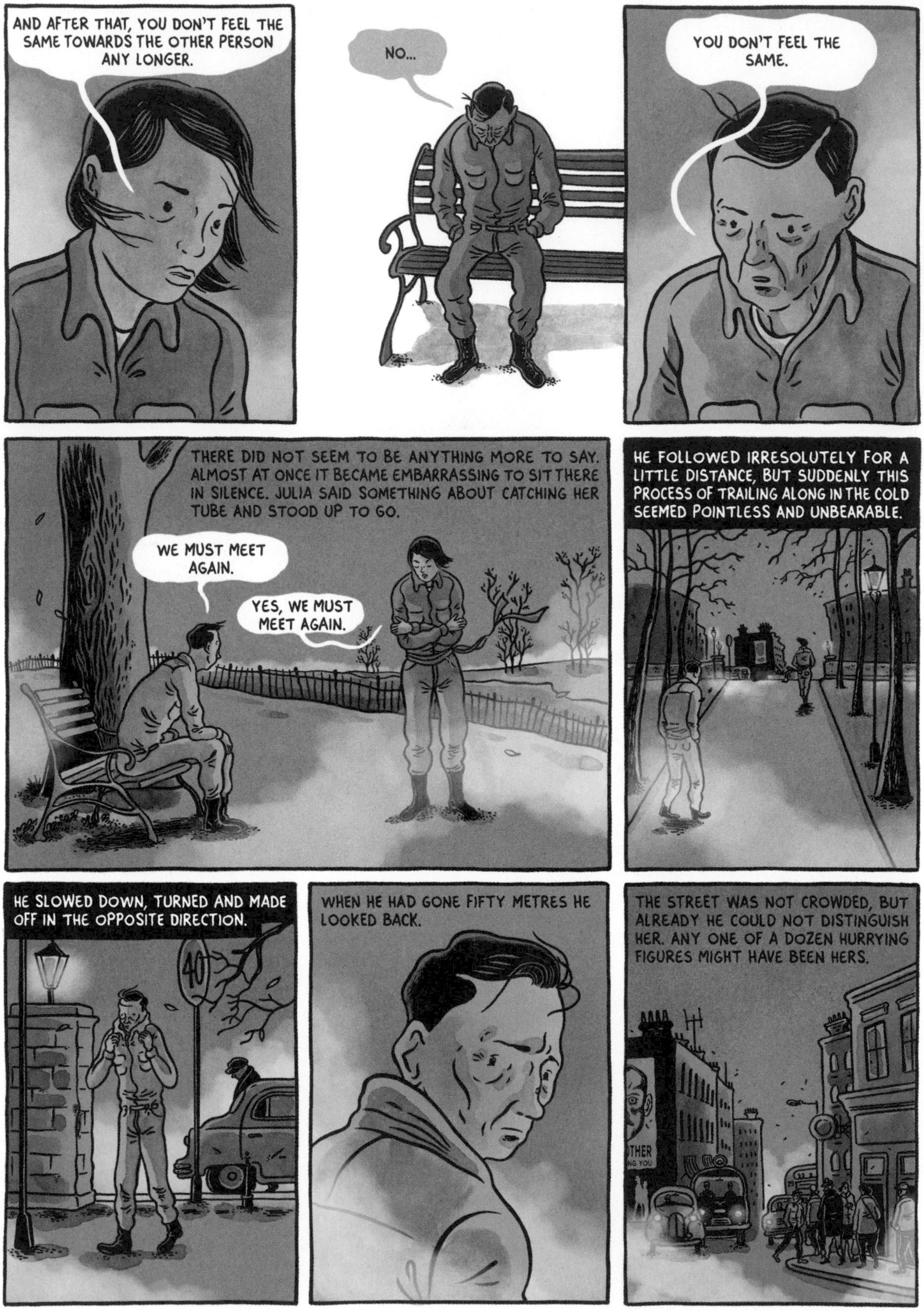
AND AFTER THAT, YOU DON'T FEEL THE SAME TOWARDS THE OTHER PERSON ANY LONGER.
NO...
YOU DON'T FEEL THE SAME.
THERE DID NOT SEEM TO BE ANYTHING MORE TO SAY. ALMOST AT ONCE IT BECAME EMBARRASSING TO SIT THERE IN SILENCE. JULIA SAID SOMETHING ABOUT CATCHING HER TUBE AND STOOD UP TO GO.
WE MUST MEET AGAIN.
YES, WE MUST MEET AGAIN.
HE FOLLOWED IRRESOLUTELY FOR A LITTLE DISTANCE, BUT SUDDENLY THIS PROCESS OF TRAILING ALONG IN THE COLD SEEMED POINTLESS AND UNBEARABLE.
HE SLOWED DOWN, TURNED AND MADE OFF IN THE OPPOSITE DIRECTION.
40
WHEN HE HAD GONE FIFTY METRES HE LOOKED BACK.
THE STREET WAS NOT CROWDED, BUT ALREADY HE COULD NOT DISTINGUISH HER. ANY ONE OF A DOZEN HURRYING FIGURES MIGHT HAVE BEEN HERS.
OTHER

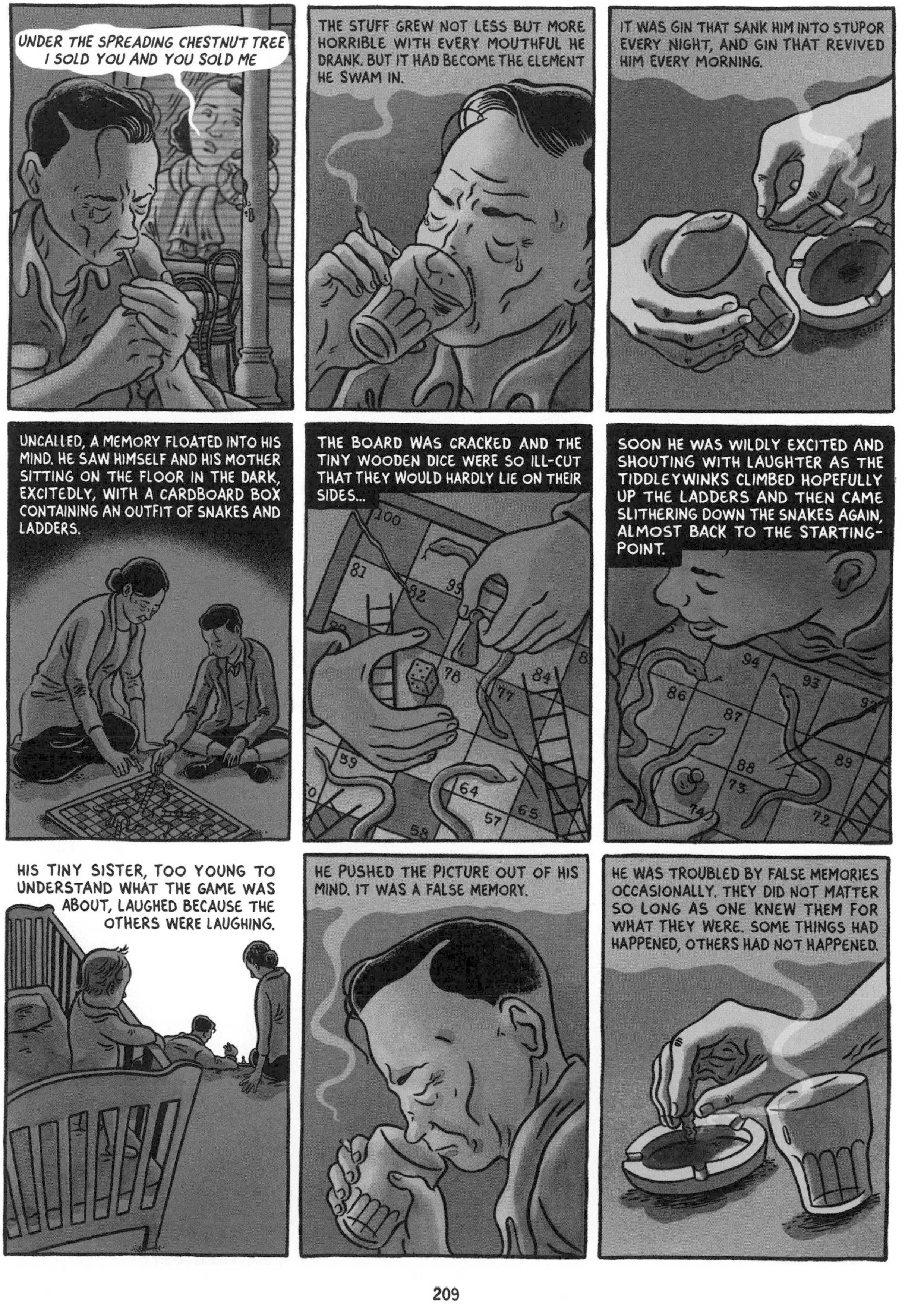
UNDER THE SPREADING CHESTNUT TREE I SOLD YOU AND YOU SOLD ME
THE STUFF GREW NOT LESS BUT MORE HORRIBLE WITH EVERY MOUTHFUL HE DRANK. BUT IT HAD BECOME THE ELEMENT HE SWAM IN.
IT WAS GIN THAT SANK HIM INTO STUPOR EVERY NIGHT, AND GIN THAT REVIVED HIM EVERY MORNING.
UNCALLED, A MEMORY FLOATED INTO HIS MIND. HE SAW HIMSELF AND HIS MOTHER SITTING ON THE FLOOR IN THE DARK, EXCITEDLY, WITH A CARDBOARD BOX CONTAINING AN OUTFIT OF SNAKES AND LADDERS.
THE BOARD WAS CRACKED AND THE TINY WOODEN DICE WERE SO ILL-CUT THAT THEY WOULD HARDLY LIE ON THEIR SIDES...
SOON HE WAS WILDLY EXCITED AND SHOUTING WITH LAUGHTER AS THE TIDDLEYWINKS CLIMBED HOPEFULLY UP THE LADDERS AND THEN CAME SLITHERING DOWN THE SNAKES AGAIN, ALMOST BACK TO THE STARTING-POINT.
HIS TINY SISTER, TOO YOUNG TO UNDERSTAND WHAT THE GAME WAS ABOUT, LAUGHED BECAUSE THE OTHERS WERE LAUGHING.
HE PUSHED THE PICTURE OUT OF HIS MIND. IT WAS A FALSE MEMORY.
HE WAS TROUBLED BY FALSE MEMORIES OCCASIONALLY. THEY DID NOT MATTER SO LONG AS ONE KNEW THEM FOR WHAT THEY WERE. SOME THINGS HAD HAPPENED, OTHERS HAD NOT HAPPENED.

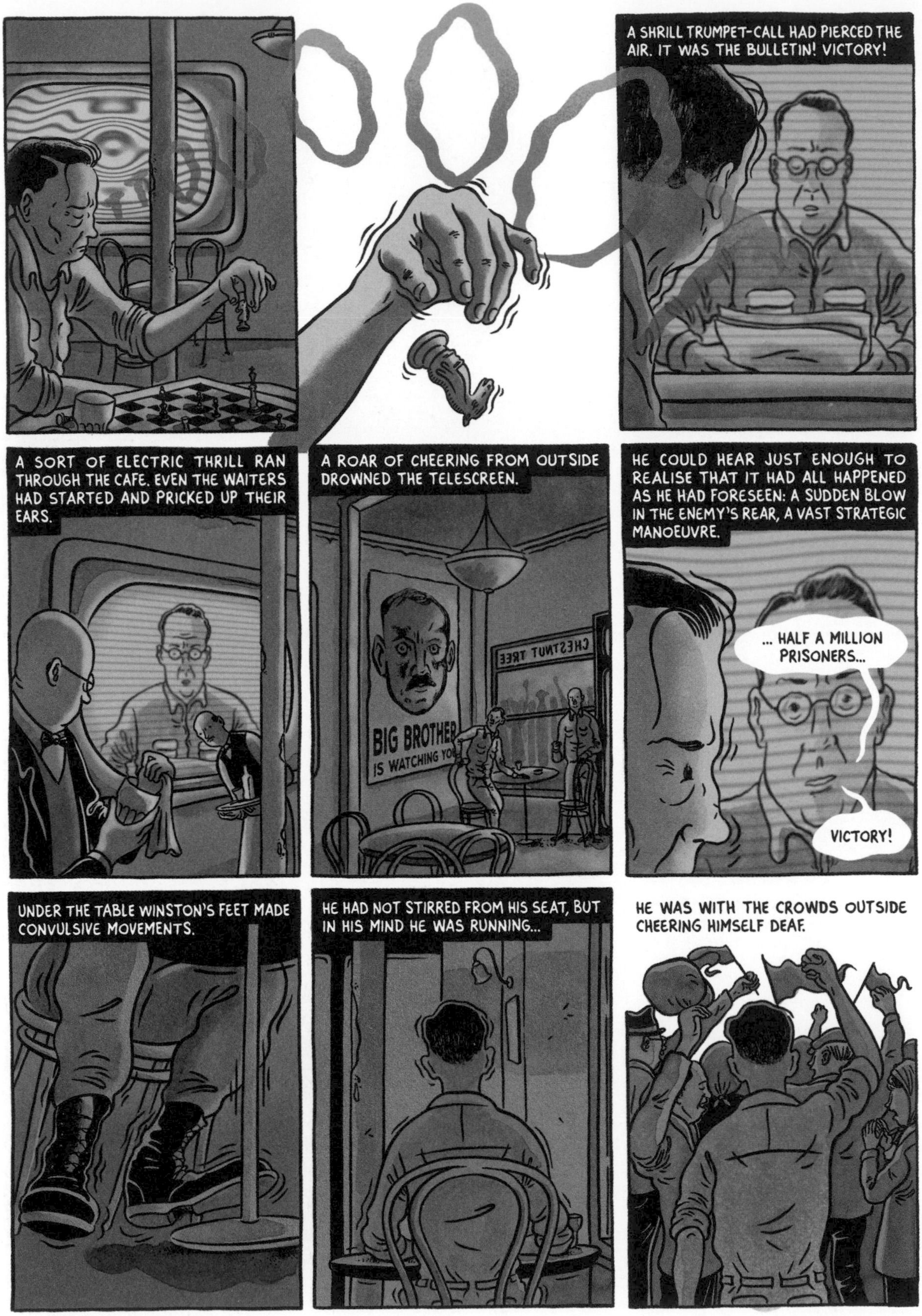
A SHRILL TRUMPET-CALL HAD PIERCED THE AIR. IT WAS THE BULLETIN! VICTORY!
A SORT OF ELECTRIC THRILL RAN THROUGH THE CAFE. EVEN THE WAITERS HAD STARTED AND PRICKED UP THEIR EARS.
A ROAR OF CHEERING FROM OUTSIDE DROWNED THE TELESCREEN.
BIG BROTHER IS WATCHING YOU
CHESTNUT TREE
HE COULD HEAR JUST ENOUGH TO REALISE THAT IT HAD ALL HAPPENED AS HE HAD FORESEEN: A SUDDEN BLOW IN THE ENEMY'S REAR, A VAST STRATEGIC MANOEUVRE.
... HALF A MILLION PRISONERS...
VICTORY!
UNDER THE TABLE WINSTON'S FEET MADE CONVULSIVE MOVEMENTS.
HE HAD NOT STIRRED FROM HIS SEAT, BUT IN HIS MIND HE WAS RUNNING...
HE WAS WITH THE CROWDS OUTSIDE CHEERING HIMSELF DEAF.

AH, IT WAS MORE THAN A EURASIAN ARMY THAT HAD PERISHED!...

MUCH HAD CHANGED IN HIM SINCE THAT FIRST DAY IN THE **MINISTRY OF LOVE**...

BUT THE FINAL, INDISPENSABLE, HEALING CHANGE HAD NEVER HAPPENED...

UNTIL THIS MOMENT.

HE WAS BACK IN THE **MINISTRY OF LOVE**, WITH EVERYTHING FORGIVEN, HIS SOUL WHITE AS SNOW...

HE WAS WALKING DOWN THE CORRIDOR, WITH THE FEELING OF WALKING IN SUNLIGHT, AND AN ARMED GUARD AT HIS BACK...

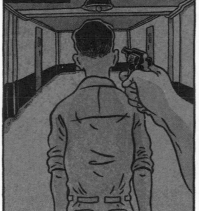

THE LONG-HOPED-FOR BULLET WAS ENTERING HIS BRAIN.

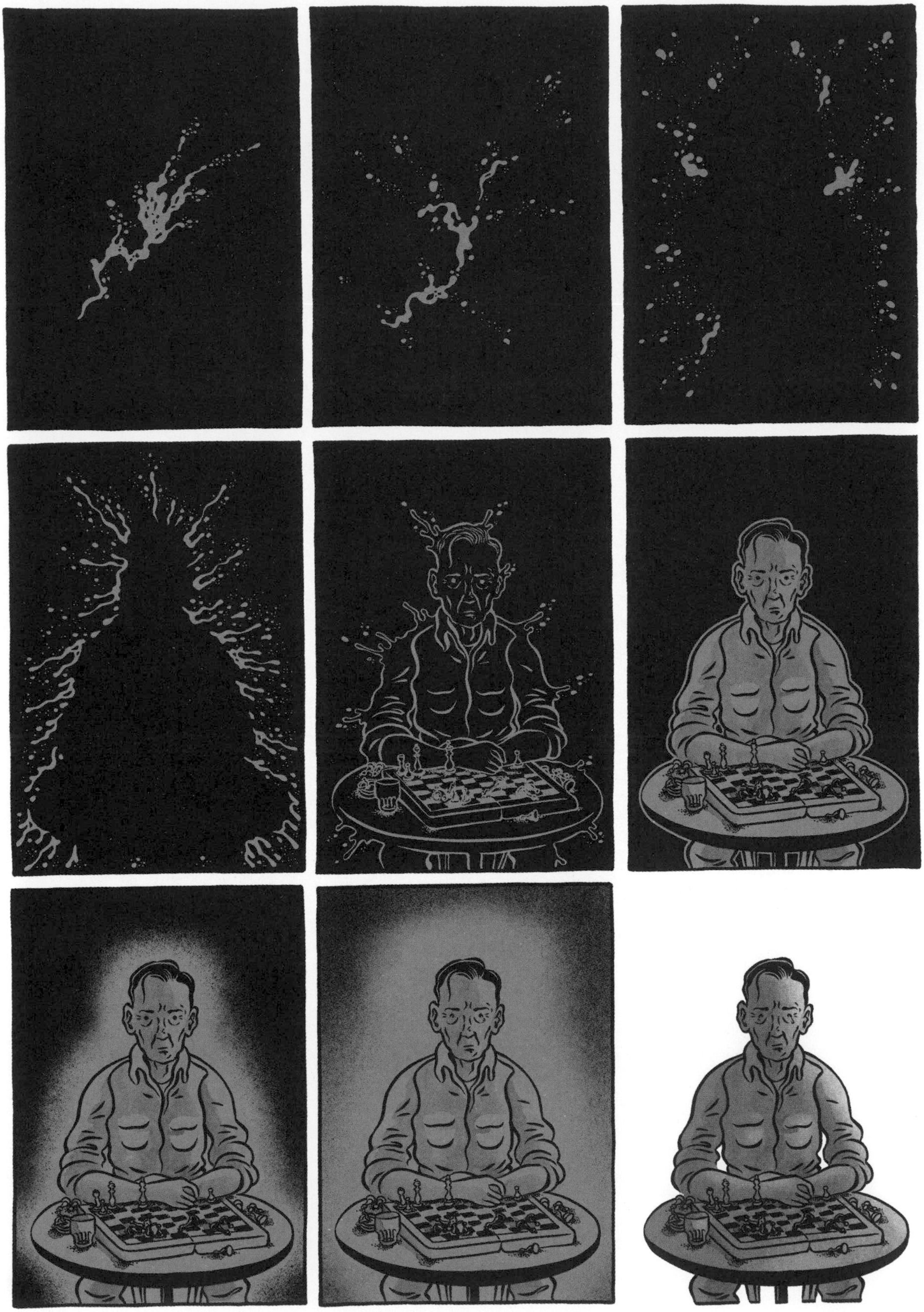

HE GAZED UP AT THE ENORMOUS FACE. FORTY YEARS IT HAD TAKEN HIM TO LEARN WHAT KIND OF SMILE WAS HIDDEN BENEATH THE DARK MOUSTACHE.
O CRUEL, NEEDLESS MISUNDERSTANDING! O STUBBORN, SELF-WILLED EXILE FROM THE LOVING BREAST!
BUT IT WAS ALL RIGHT, EVERYTHING WAS ALL RIGHT...
THE STRUGGLE WAS FINISHED...
BIG BROTHER
NG YOU

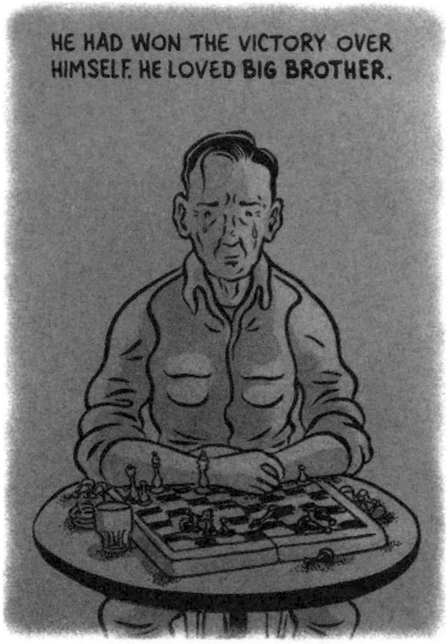
HE HAD WON THE VICTORY OVER
HIMSELF. HE LOVED BIG BROTHER.

THE END

Appendix

The Principles of Newspeak

Newspeak was the official language of Oceania and had been devised to meet the ideological needs of Ingsoc, or English Socialism. In the year 1984 there was not as yet anyone who used Newspeak as his sole means of communication, either in speech or writing. The leading articles in the *Times* were written in it but this was a *tour de force* which could only be carried out by a specialist. It was expected that Newspeak would have finally superseded Oldspeak (or Standard English, as we should call it) by about the year 2050. Meanwhile it gained ground steadily, all Party members tending to use Newspeak words and grammatical constructions more and more in their everyday speech. The version in use in 1984, and embodied in the Ninth and Tenth Editions of the Newspeak Dictionary, was a provisional one, and contained many superfluous words and archaic formations which were due to be suppressed later. It is with the final, perfected version, as embodied in the Eleventh Edition of the Dictionary, that we are concerned here.

The purpose of Newspeak was not only to provide a medium of expression for the world-view and mental habits proper to the devotees of Ingsoc, but to make all other modes of thought impossible. It was intended that when Newspeak had been adopted once and for all and Oldspeak forgotten, a heretical thought – that is, a thought diverging from the principles of Ingsoc – should be literally unthinkable, at least so far as thought is dependent on words. Its vocabulary was so constructed as to give exact and often very subtle expression to every meaning that a Party member could properly wish to express, while excluding all other meanings and also the possibility of arriving at them by indirect methods. This was done partly by the invention of new words, but chiefly by eliminating undesirable words and by stripping such words as remained of unorthodox meanings, and so far as possible of all secondary meanings whatever. To give a single example. The word *free* still existed in Newspeak, but it could only be used in such statements as 'This dog is free from lice' or 'This field is free from weeds'. It could not be used in its old sense of 'politically free' or 'intellectually free', since political and intellectual freedom no longer existed even as concepts, and were therefore of necessity nameless. Quite apart from the suppression of definitely heretical words, reduction of vocabulary was regarded as an end in itself, and no word that could be dispensed with was allowed to survive. Newspeak was designed not to extend but to *diminish* the range of thought, and this purpose was indirectly assisted by cutting the choice of words down to a minimum.

Newspeak was founded on the English language as we now know it, though many Newspeak sentences, even when not containing newly-created words, would be barely intelligible to an English-speaker of our own day. Newspeak words were divided into three distinct classes, known as the A vocabulary, the B vocabulary (also called compound words), and the C vocabulary. It will be simpler to discuss each class separately, but the grammatical peculiarities of the language can be dealt with in the section devoted to the A vocabulary, since the same rules held good for all three categories.

The A vocabulary. The A vocabulary consisted of the words needed for the business of everyday life – for such things as eating, drinking, working, putting on one's clothes, going up and down stairs, riding in vehicles, gardening, cooking, and the like. It was composed almost entirely of words that we already possess – words like *hit*, *run*, *dog*, *tree*, *sugar*, *house*, *field* – but in comparison with the present-day English vocabulary their number was extremely small, while their meanings were far more rigidly defined. All ambiguities and shades of meaning had been purged out of them. So far as it could be achieved, a Newspeak word of this class was simply a staccato sound expressing *one* clearly understood concept. It would have been quite impossible to use the A vocabulary for literary purposes or for political or philosophical discussion. It was intended only to express simple, purposive thoughts, usually involving concrete objects or physical actions.

The grammar of Newspeak had two outstanding peculiarities. The first of these was an almost complete interchangeability between different parts of speech. Any word in the language (in principle this applied even to very abstract words such as *if* or *when*) could be used either as verb, noun, adjective or adverb. Between the verb and the noun form, when they were of the same root, there was never any variation, this rule of itself involving the destruction of many archaic forms. The word *thought*, for example, did not exist in Newspeak. Its place was taken by *think*, which did duty for both noun and verb. No etymological principle was followed here: in some cases it was the original noun that was chosen for retention, in other cases the verb. Even where a noun and verb of kindred meaning were not etymologically connected, one or other of them was frequently suppressed. There was, for example, no such word as *cut*, its meaning being sufficiently covered by the noun-verb *knife*. Adjectives were formed by adding the suffix *-ful* to the noun-verb, and adverbs by adding *-wise*. Thus, for example, *speedful* meant 'rapid' and *speedwise* meant 'quickly'. Certain of our present-day adjectives, such as *good, strong, big, black, soft*, were retained, but their total number was very small. There was little need for them, since almost any adjectival meaning could be arrived at by adding *-ful* to a noun-verb. None of the now-existing adverbs was retained, except for a very few already ending in *-wise*: the *-wise* termination was invariable. The word *well*, for example, was replaced by *goodwise*.

In addition, any word – this again applied in principle to every word in the language – could be negatived by adding the affix *un-*, or could be strengthened by the affix *plus-*, or, for still greater emphasis, *doubleplus-*. Thus, for example, *uncold* meant 'warm', while *pluscold* and *doublepluscold* meant, respectively, 'very cold' and 'superlatively cold'. It was also possible, as in present-day English, to modify the meanings of almost any word by prepositional affixes such as *ante-, post-, up-, down-*, etc. By such methods it was found possible to bring about an enormous diminution of vocabulary. Given, for instance, the word *good*, there was no need for such a word as *bad*, since the required meaning was equally well – indeed, better – expressed by *ungood*. All that was necessary, in any case where two words formed a natural pair of opposites, was to decide which of them to suppress. *Dark*, for example, could be replaced by *unlight*, or *light* by *undark*, according to preference.

The second distinguishing mark of Newspeak grammar was its regularity. Subject to a few exceptions which are mentioned below, all inflections followed the same rules. Thus, in all verbs the preterite and the past participle were the same and ended in *-ed*. The preterite of *steal* was *stealed*, the preterite of *think* was *thinked*, and so on throughout the language, all such forms as *swam, gave, brought, spoke, taken*, etc., being abolished. All plurals were made by adding *-s* or *-es* as the case might be. The plurals of *man, ox, life*, were *mans, oxes, lifes*. Comparison of adjectives was invariably made by adding *-er, -est* (*good, gooder, goodest*), irregular forms and the *more, most* formation being suppressed.

The only classes of words that were still allowed to inflect irregularly were the pronouns, the relatives, the demonstrative adjectives and the auxiliary verbs. All of these followed their ancient usage, except that *whom* had been scrapped as unnecessary, and the *shall, should* tenses had been dropped, all their uses being covered by *will* and *would*. There were also certain irregularities in word-formation arising out of the need for rapid and easy speech. A word which was difficult to utter, or was liable to be incorrectly heard, was held to be *ipso facto* a bad word: occasionally therefore, for the sake of euphony, extra letters were inserted into a word or an archaic formation

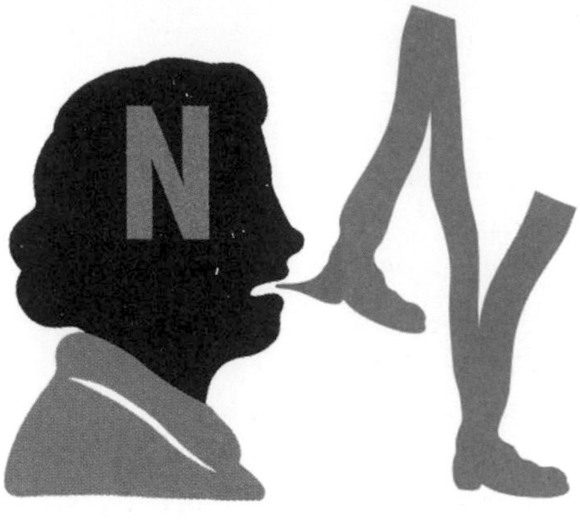
N

was retained. But this need made itself felt chiefly in connection with the B vocabulary. *Why* so great an importance was attached to ease of pronunciation will be made clear later in this essay.

The B vocabulary. The B vocabulary consisted of words which had been deliberately constructed for political purposes: words, that is to say, which not only had in every case a political implication, but were intended to impose a desirable mental attitude upon the person using them. Without a full understanding of the principles of Ingsoc it was difficult to use these words correctly. In some cases they could be translated into Oldspeak, or even into words taken from the A vocabulary, but this usually demanded a long paraphrase and always involved the loss of certain overtones. The B words were a sort of verbal shorthand, often packing whole ranges of ideas into a few syllables, and at the same time more accurate and forcible than ordinary language.

The B words were in all cases compound words.* They consisted of two or more words, or portions of words, welded together in an easily pronounceable form. The resulting amalgam was always a noun-verb, and inflected according to the ordinary rules. To take a single example: the word *goodthink*, meaning, very roughly, 'orthodoxy', or, if one chose to regard it as a verb, 'to think in an orthodox manner'. This inflected as follows: noun-verb, *goodthink;* past tense and past participle, *goodthinked*; present participle, *goodthinking;* adjective, *goodthinkful*; adverb, *goodthinkwise;* verbal noun, *goodthinker.*

The B words were not constructed on any etymological plan. The words of which they were made up could be any parts of speech, and could be placed in any order and mutilated in any way which made them easy to pronounce while indicating their derivation. In the word *crimethink* (thoughtcrime), for instance, the *think* came second, whereas in *thinkpol* (Thought Police) it came first, and in the latter word *police* had lost its second syllable. Because of the greater difficulty in securing euphony, irregular formations were commoner in the B vocabulary than in the A vocabulary. For example, the adjectival forms of *Minitrue*, *Minipax* and *Miniluv* were, respectively, *Minitruthful*, *Minipeaceful* and *Minilovely*, simply because *-trueful*, *-paxful* and *loveful* were slightly awkward to pronounce. In principle, however, all B words could inflect, and all inflected in exactly the same way.

Some of the B words had highly subtilised meanings, barely intelligible to anyone who had not mastered the language as a whole. Consider, for example, such a typical sentence from a *Times* leading article as *Oldthinkers unbellyfeel Ingsoc*. The shortest rendering that one could make of this in Oldspeak would be: 'Those whose ideas were formed before the Revolution cannot have a full emotional understanding of the principles of English Socialism.' But this is not an adequate translation. To begin with, in order to grasp the full meaning of the Newspeak sentence quoted above, one would have to have a clear idea of what is meant by *Ingsoc*. And in addition, only a person thoroughly grounded in Ingsoc could appreciate the full force of the word *bellyfeel*, which implied a blind, enthusiastic acceptance difficult to imagine today; or of the word *oldthink*, which was inextricably mixed up with the idea of wickedness and decadence. But the special function of certain Newspeak words, of which *oldthink* was one, was not so much to express meanings as to destroy them. These words, necessarily few in number, had had their meanings extended until they contained within themselves

* Compound words, such as *speakwrite*, were of course to be found in the A vocabulary, but these were merely convenient abbreviations and had no special ideological colour.

whole batteries of words which, as they were sufficiently covered by a single comprehensive term, could now be scrapped and forgotten. The greatest difficulty facing the compilers of the Newspeak Dictionary was not to invent new words, but, having invented them, to make sure what they meant: to make sure, that is to say, what ranges of words they cancelled by their existence.

As we have already seen in the case of the word *free*, words which had once borne a heretical meaning were sometimes retained for the sake of convenience, but only with the undesirable meanings purged out of them. Countless other words such as *honour*, *justice*, *morality*, *internationalism*, *democracy*, *science* and *religion* had simply ceased to exist. A few blanket words covered them, and, in covering them, abolished them. All words grouping themselves round the concepts of liberty and equality, for instance, were contained in the single word *crimethink*, while all words grouping themselves round the concepts of objectivity and rationalism were contained in the single word *oldthink*. Greater precision would have been dangerous. What was required in a Party member was an outlook similar to that of the ancient Hebrew who knew, without knowing much else, that all nations other than his own worshipped 'false gods'. He did not need to know that these gods were called Baal, Osiris, Moloch, Ashtaroth and the like: probably the less he knew about them the better for his orthodoxy. He knew Jehovah and the commandments of Jehovah: he knew, therefore, that all gods with other names or other attributes were false gods. In somewhat the same way, the Party member knew what constituted right conduct, and in exceedingly vague, generalised terms he knew what kinds of departure from it were possible. His sexual life, for example, was entirely regulated by the two Newspeak words *sexcrime* (sexual immorality) and *goodsex* (chastity). *Sexcrime* covered all sexual misdeeds whatever. It covered fornication, adultery, homosexuality and other perversions, and, in addition, normal intercourse practised for its own sake. There was no need to enumerate them separately, since they were all equally culpable, and, in principle, all punishable by death. In the C vocabulary, which consisted of scientific and technical words, it might be necessary to give specialised names to certain sexual aberrations, but the ordinary citizen had no need of them. He knew what was meant by *goodsex* –; that is to say, normal intercourse between man and wife, for the sole purpose of begetting children, and without physical pleasure on the part of the woman: all else was *sexcrime*. In Newspeak it was seldom possible to follow a heretical thought further than the perception that it *was* heretical: beyond that point the necessary words were non-existent.

No word in the B vocabulary was ideologically neutral. Λ great many were euphemisms. Such words, for instance, as *joycamp* (forced-labour camp) or *Minipax* (Ministry of Peace, i.e. Ministry of War) meant almost the exact opposite of what they appeared to mean. Some words, on the other hand, displayed a frank and contemptuous understanding of the real nature of Oceanic society. An example was *prolefeed*, meaning the rubbishy entertainment and spurious news which the Party handed out to the masses. Other words, again, were ambivalent, having the connotation 'good' when applied to the Party and 'bad' when applied to its enemies. But in addition there were great numbers of words which at first sight appeared to be mere abbreviations and which derived their ideological colour not from their meaning but from their structure.

So far as it could be contrived, everything that had or might have political significance of any kind was fitted into the B vocabulary. The name of every organisation, or body of people, or doctrine, or country, or institution, or public building, was invariably cut down into the familiar shape; that is, a single easily pronounced word with the smallest number of syllables that would preserve the original derivation. In the Ministry of Truth, for example, the Records Department, in which Winston Smith worked, was called *Recdep*, the Fiction Department was called *Ficdep*, the Teleprogrammes Department was called *Teledep*, and so on. This was not done solely with the object of saving time. Even in the early decades of the twentieth century, telescoped words and phrases had been one of the characteristic features of political language; and it had been noticed that the tendency to use abbreviations of this kind was most marked in totalitarian countries and totalitarian organisations. Examples were such words as *Nazi, Gestapo, Comintern, Inprecor, Agitprop.* In the beginning the practice had been adopted as it were instinctively, but in Newspeak it was used with a conscious purpose. It was perceived that in thus abbreviating a name one narrowed and subtly altered its meaning, by cutting out most of the associations that would otherwise cling to it. The words *Communist International*, for instance, call up a composite picture of universal human brotherhood, red flags, barricades, Karl Marx and the Paris Commune. The word *Comintern*, on the other hand, suggests merely a tightly-knit organisation and a well-defined body of doctrine. It refers to something almost as easily recognised, and as limited in purpose, as a chair or a table. *Comintern* is a word that can be uttered almost without taking thought, whereas *Communist International* is a phrase over which one is obliged to linger at least momentarily. In the same way, the associations called up by a word like *Minitrue* are fewer and more controllable than those called up by *Ministry of Truth*. This accounted not only for the habit of abbreviating whenever possible, but also for the almost exaggerated care that was taken to make every word easily pronounceable.

In Newspeak, euphony outweighed every consideration other than exactitude of meaning. Regularity of grammar was always sacrificed to it when it seemed necessary. And rightly so, since what was required, above all for political purposes, were short clipped words of unmistakable meaning which could be uttered rapidly and which roused the minimum of echoes in the speaker's mind. The words of the B vocabulary even gained in force from the fact that nearly all of them were very much alike. Almost invariably these words – *goodthink, Minipax, prolefeed, sexcrime, joycamp, Ingsoc, bellyfeel, thinkpol* and countless others – were words of two or three syllables, with the stress distributed equally between the first syllable and the last. The use of them encouraged a gabbling style of speech, at once staccato and monotonous. And this was exactly what was aimed at. The intention was to make speech, and especially speech on any subject not ideologically neutral, as nearly as possible independent of consciousness. For the purposes of everyday life it was no doubt necessary, or sometimes necessary, to reflect before speaking, but a Party member called upon to make a political or ethical judgment should be able to spray forth the correct opinions as automatically as a machine-gun spraying forth bullets. His training fitted him to do this, the language gave him an almost fool-proof instrument, and the texture of the words, with their harsh sound and a certain wilful ugliness which was in accord with the spirit of Ingsoc, assisted the process still further.

So did the fact of having very few words to choose from. Relative to our own, the Newspeak vocabulary was tiny, and new ways of reducing it were constantly being devised. Newspeak, indeed, differed from almost all other languages in that its vocabulary grew smaller instead of larger every year. Each reduction was a gain, since the smaller the area of choice, the smaller the temptation to take thought. Ultimately it was hoped to make articulate speech issue from the larynx without involving the higher brain centres at all. This aim was frankly admitted in the Newspeak word *duckspeak*, meaning 'to quack like a duck'. Like various other words in the B vocabulary, *duckspeak* was ambivalent in meaning. Provided that the opinions which were quacked out were orthodox ones, it implied nothing but praise, and when the *Times* referred to one of the orators of the Party as a *doubleplusgood duckspeaker* it was paying a warm and valued compliment.

The C vocabulary. The C vocabulary was supplementary to the others and consisted entirely of scientific and technical terms. These resembled the scientific terms in use today, and were constructed from the same roots, but the usual care was taken to define them rigidly and strip them of undesirable meanings. They followed the same grammatical rules as the words in the other two vocabularies. Very few of the C words had any currency either in everyday speech or in political speech. Any scientific worker or technician could find all the words he needed in the list devoted to his own speciality, but he seldom had more than a smattering of the words occurring in the other lists. Only a very few words were common to all lists, and there was no vocabulary expressing the function of Science as a habit of mind, or a method of thought, irrespective of its particular branches. There was, indeed, no word for 'Science', any meaning that it could possibly bear being already sufficiently covered by the word *Ingsoc*.

From the foregoing account it will be seen that in Newspeak the expression of unorthodox opinions, above a very low level, was well-nigh impossible. It was of course possible to utter heresies of a very crude kind, a species of blasphemy. It would have been possible, for example, to say *Big Brother is ungood*. But this statement, which to an orthodox ear merely conveyed a self-evident absurdity, could not have been sustained by reasoned argument, because the necessary words were not available. Ideas inimical to Ingsoc could only be entertained in a vague wordless form, and could only be named in very broad terms which lumped together and condemned whole groups of heresies without defining them in doing so. One could, in fact, only use Newspeak for unorthodox purposes by illegitimately translating some of the words back into Oldspeak. For example, *All mans are equal* was a possible Newspeak sentence, but only in the same sense in which *All men are redhaired* is a possible Oldspeak sentence. It did not contain a grammatical error, but it expressed a palpable untruth – i.e.

that all men are of equal size, weight or strength. The concept of political equality no longer existed, and this secondary meaning had accordingly been purged out of the word *equal*. In 1984, when Oldspeak was still the normal means of communication, the danger theoretically existed that in using Newspeak words one might remember their original meanings. In practice it was not difficult for any person well grounded in *doublethink* to avoid doing this, but within a couple of generations even the possibility of such a lapse would have vanished. A person growing up with Newspeak as his sole language would no more know that *equal* had once had the secondary meaning of 'politically equal', or that *free* had once meant 'intellectually free', than, for instance, a person who had never heard of chess would be aware of the secondary meanings attaching to *queen* and *rook*. There would be many crimes and errors which it would be beyond his power to commit, simply because they were nameless and therefore unimaginable. And it was to be foreseen that with the passage of time the distinguishing characteristics of Newspeak would become more and more pronounced – its words growing fewer and fewer, their meanings more and more rigid, and the chance of putting them to improper uses always diminishing.

When Oldspeak had been once and for all superseded, the last link with the past would have been severed. History had already been rewritten, but fragments of the literature of the past survived here and there, imperfectly censored, and so long as one retained one's knowledge of Oldspeak it was possible to read them. In the future such fragments, even if they chanced to survive, would be unintelligible and untranslatable. It was impossible to translate any passage of Oldspeak into Newspeak unless it either referred to some technical process or some very simple everyday action, or was already orthodox (*goodthinkful* would be the Newspeak expression) in tendency. In practice this meant that no book written before approximately 1960 could be translated as a whole. Pre-revolutionary literature could only be subjected to ideological translation – that is, alteration in sense as well as language. Take

for example the well-known passage from the Declaration of Independence:

> We hold these truths to be self-evident, that all men are created equal, that they are endowed by their Creator with certain unalienable Rights, that among these are Life, Liberty and the pursuit of Happiness. That to secure these rights, Governments are instituted among Men, deriving their just powers from the consent of the governed. That whenever any Form of Government becomes destructive of these ends, it is the Right of the People to alter or to abolish it, and to institute new Government . . .

It would have been quite impossible to render this into Newspeak while keeping to the sense of the original. The nearest one could come to doing so would be to swallow the whole passage up in the single word *crimethink*. A full translation could only be an ideological translation, whereby Jefferson's words would be changed into a panegyric on absolute government.

A good deal of the literature of the past was, indeed, already being transformed in this way. Considerations of prestige made it desirable to preserve the memory of certain historical figures, while at the same time bringing their achievements into line with the philosophy of Ingsoc. Various writers, such as Shakespeare, Milton, Swift, Byron, Dickens and some others were therefore in process of translation: when the task had been completed, their original writings, with all else that survived of the literature of the past, would be destroyed. These translations were a slow and difficult business, and it was not expected that they would be finished before the first or second decade of the twenty-first century. There were also large quantities of merely utilitarian literature – indispensable technical manuals, and the like – that had to be treated in the same way. It was chiefly in order to allow time for the preliminary work of translation that the final adoption of Newspeak had been fixed for so late a date as 2050.

GEORGE ORWELL was born in 1903 in Motihari, Bengal, India, the son of a British colonial civil servant. He was educated at Eton, and in 1922 joined the Indian Imperial Police in Burma, resigning in 1927 to become a writer. From 1933 to 1949 he published several novels and works of non-fiction. The tremendous success of his 'fairy story' *Animal Farm* (1945) was surpassed only with the publication, in 1949, of his masterpiece, *Nineteen Eighty-Four*. Orwell wrote the final pages of the novel in a remote house on the island of Jura, in the Scottish Hebrides, where he worked feverishly in between periods in hospital due to pulmonary tuberculosis. He died a few months after its publication, in January 1950.

FIDO NESTI was born in São Paulo in 1971, and has worked in illustration and comics for over thirty years. His drawings can be seen in the *Folha de S. Paulo* newspaper and in *New Yorker* magazine, as well as in various books and on covers. He has previously illustrated a comic strip adaptation of the Portuguese epic poem *The Lusiads* (*Os Lusíadas em Quadrinhos*, 2006) and a graphic novel (*A máquina de Goldberg*, 2012). *Nineteen Eighty-Four* had a great impact on him when he first read it in the year 1984, while at school, and he is still deeply impressed by the way the dystopian world created by Orwell is becoming ever more real. He lived in Airstrip One for a year, between 2000 and 2001.